AUTONOMOUS WEAI

The intense and polemical debate over the legality and morality of weapons systems to which human cognitive functions are delegated (up to and including the capacity to select targets and release weapons without further human intervention) addresses a phenomenon which does not yet exist but which is widely claimed to be emergent. This ground-breaking collection combines contributions from roboticists, legal scholars, philosophers and sociologists of science in order to recast the debate in a manner that clarifies key areas and articulates questions for future research. The contributors develop insights with direct policy relevance, including who bears responsibility for autonomous weapons systems, whether they would violate fundamental ethical and legal norms, and how to regulate their development. It is essential reading for those concerned about this emerging phenomenon and its consequences for the future of humanity.

NEHAL BHUTA is Professor of Public International Law at the European University Institute, Florence, and Co-Director of the EUI's Academy of European Law.

SUSANNE BECK is Professor of Criminal Law and Procedure, Comparative Criminal Law and the Philosophy of Law at Leibniz University Hanover.

ROBIN GEIß is Professor of International Law and Security at the University of Glasgow.

HIN-YAN LIU is Associate Professor at the Centre for International Law, Conflict and Crisis, Faculty of Law, University of Copenhagen.

CLAUS KREß is Professor of Criminal Law and Public International Law at the University of Cologne, where he is also Director of the Institute of International Peace and Security Law.

AUTONOMOUS WEAPONS SYSTEMS

SYSTEMS

Law, Ethics, Policy

Edited by

NEHAL BHUTA

SUSANNE BECK

ROBIN GEIß

HIN-YAN LIU

and

CLAUS KREß

CAMBRIDGE
UNIVERSITY PRESS

CAMBRIDGE
UNIVERSITY PRESS

University Printing House, Cambridge CB2 8BS, United Kingdom

Cambridge University Press is part of the University of Cambridge.

It furthers the University's mission by disseminating knowledge in the pursuit of education, learning and research at the highest international levels of excellence.

www.cambridge.org
Information on this title: www.cambridge.org/9781107153561

© Cambridge University Press 2016

First published 2016

Printed in the United States of America by Sheridan Books, Inc.

A catalogue record for this publication is available from the British Library

ISBN 978-1-107-15356-1 Hardback
ISBN 978-1-316-60765-7 Paperback

CONTENTS

CONTRIBUTORS

SUSANNE BECK Professor of Criminal Law and Procedure, Comparative Criminal Law and Philosophy of Law, Leibniz University of Hanover

EYAL BENVENISTI Anny and Paul Yanowicz Professor of Human Rights, Tel Aviv University Faculty of Law, Whewell Professor, Cambridge University Faculty of Law

NEHAL BHUTA Professor of Public International Law, European University Institute

DIETER BIRNBACHER Professor of Philosophy, University of Düsseldorf

GEOFFREY S. CORN Professor of Law and Presidential Research Professor, South Texas College of Law

ROBIN GEIß Professor of International Law and Security, University of Glasgow Law School

CHRISTOF HEYNS Professor of Human Rights Law, University of Pretoria, and United Nations Special Rapporteur on extrajudicial, summary or arbitrary executions

NEHA JAIN Associate Professor of Law, University of Minnesota Law School

PABLO KALMANOVITZ Associate Professor of Political Science, Universidad de Los Andes, Bogotá

SARAH KNUCKEY Faculty co-director of the Human Rights Institute, Lieff Cabraser Associate Clinical Professor of Law and Director of the Human Rights Clinic, Columbia Law School

CLAUS KREß Chair for German and International Criminal Law, Director of the Institute for International Peace and Security Law, University of Cologne

ELIAV LIEBLICH Assistant Professor, Radzyner Law School, Interdisciplinary Center (IDC)

HIN-YAN LIU Associate Professor, Faculty of Law, University of Copenhagen

ANDREA OMICINI Professor of Computer Engineering, Department of Computer Science and Engineering, University of Bologna

STAVROS-EVDOKIMOS PANTAZOPOULOS PhD Researcher, European University Institute

GIOVANNI SARTOR Professor of Legal Informatics and Legal Theory, European University Institute, and Professor in Legal Informatics, University of Bologna

DAN SAXON Assistant Professor and Tutor of International Humanitarian, Human Rights and Criminal Law, Leiden University College

NOEL SHARKEY Emeritus Professor of Artificial Intelligence and Robotics and Professor of Public Engagement, University of Sheffield, and Chairman of the International Committee for Robot Arms Control

LUCY SUCHMAN Professor of Anthropology of Science and Technology, Department of Sociology, University of Lancaster

GUGLIELMO TAMBURRINI Professor of Philosophy of Science and Logic, Department of Electrical Engineering and Information Technologies, University of Naples Federico II

JUTTA WEBER Professor of the Sociology of Media, Department of Media Studies, University of Paderborn

ACKNOWLEDGEMENTS

The editors gratefully acknowledge the financial support of the Thyssen Foundation, which provided core funding for the research workshop that culminated in this book. The workshop was convened on 24 and 25 April 2014, at the European University Institute in San Domenico di Fiesole, Tuscany, Italy. The project was also supported by the Academy of European Law of the European University Institute, the Global Governance Program of the European University Institute and through a grant from European University Institute's Research Council.

Anny Bremner, Joyce Davies and Valentina Spiga expertly managed the complex logistics of the project. Stacy Belden copy-edited the manuscript, and Anny Bremner greatly helped us in finalizing the text. Stavros Pantazopoulos corrected the text at the eleventh hour.

The editors also thank Elizabeth Spicer and Finola O'Sullivan of Cambridge University Press for their strong editorial support for this project from its inception. The cover art kindly provided by Dario Tironi is gratefully acknowledged.

PART I

Introduction

Autonomous weapons systems: living a dignified life and dying a dignified death

CHRISTOF HEYNS

Introduction

The ever-increasing power of computers is arguably one of the defining characteristics of our time. Computers affect almost all aspects of our lives and have become an integral part not only of our world but also of our very identity as human beings. They offer major advantages and pose serious threats. One of the main challenges of our era is how to respond to this development: to make sure computers enhance and do not undermine human objectives.[1]

The imposition of force by one individual against another has always been an intensely personal affair – a human being was physically present at the point of the release of force and took the decision that it would be done. It is inherently a highly controversial issue because of the intrusion on people's bodies and even lives. Ethical and legal norms have developed

---

This contribution overlaps with, and draws on, a number of earlier ones by the same author: a report to the Human Rights Council, Christof Heyns, Report of the Special Rapporteur on extrajudicial, summary or arbitrary executions, Doc. A/HRC/23/47, 9 April 2013; two presentations to the Convention on Prohibitions or Restrictions on the Use of Certain Conventional Weapons Which May Be Deemed to Be Excessively Injurious or to Have Indiscriminate Effects (CCW), 19 UNTS 1823 (1990), available at www.unog.ch/__80256e e600585943.nsf/(httpPages)/a038dea1da906f9dc1257dd90042e261?OpenDocument&Expa ndSection=1#_Section1 and www.unog.ch/80256EE600585943/(httpPages)/6CE049BE22E C75A2C1257C8D00513E26? and two forthcoming articles 'Autonomous weapons systems (AWS) and human rights law in the context of law enforcement' (*Human Rights Quarterly*, forthcoming 2016) and 'Autonomous weapons systems (AWS) and international law in the context of armed conflict'. I thank Thompson Chengeta and Petronell Kruger for their help with this contribution.

[1] See, e.g., E. Brynjolfsson and A. McAfee, *The Second Machine Age* (New York: Norton, 2014); N. Bostrom, *Superintellegence* (Oxford University Press, 2014). On the robotic weapons revolution, see P. Singer, *Wired for War: The Robotics Revolution and Conflict in the Twenty-First Century* (London: Penguin, 2009).

4

over the millennia to determine when one human may use force against another, in peace and in war, and have assigned responsibility for violations of these norms. Perhaps the most dramatic manifestation of the rise of computer power is to be found in the fact that we are on the brink of an era when decisions on the use of force against human beings – in the context of armed conflict as well as during law enforcement, lethal and non-lethal – could soon be taken by robots.

Unmanned or human-replacing weapons systems first took the form of armed drones and other remote-controlled devices, which allowed human beings to be physically absent from the battlefield. Decisions to release force, however, were still taken by human operatives, albeit from a distance. The increased autonomy in weapons release now points to an era where humans will be able to be not only physically absent from the battlefield but also psychologically absent, in the sense that computers will determine when and against whom force is released. The depersonalization of the use of force brought about by remote-controlled systems is thus taken to a next level through the introduction of the autonomous release of force.

Drones raise a host of questions, but what is asked in this chapter is how the international community should respond to the new development outlined above: autonomous weapons systems (AWS), which could soon have the power to inflict serious physical injury, or even death, on human beings? AWS may be defined as robotic weapons that, once activated, can select and engage targets without further human intervention.[2] They have sensors that provide them with a degree of situational awareness, computers that process the information, and effectors (weapons) that implement the 'decisions' taken by the computers.

It should be made clear that what is at stake here are decisions over critical functions – determinations about the release of force – and not decisions over other functions such as navigation and takeoff and landing. Moreover, the force at stake in this discussion is force that is used against human beings – not force used against objects such as incoming

[2] US Department of Defense (DoD) Directive 3000.09, 'Autonomy in weapon systems', 21 November 2012, Glossary part II, available at www.dtic.mil/whs/directives/corres/pdf/300009p.pdf; Human Rights Watch, *Losing Humanity: The Case against Killer Robots* (2012), 2, available at www.hrw.org/sites/default/files/reports/arms1112ForUpload_0_0.pdf; see also United Kingdom Ministry of Defence (MoD), 'The UK approach to unmanned aircraft systems', Joint Doctrine Note 2/11, 30 March 2011, paras. 202–3, available at www.gov.uk/government/publications/jdn-2-11-the-uk-approach-to-unmanned-aircraft-systems.

munitions or other robots, which does not raise the same considerations of intrusion on people's bodies and lives.[3] At the same time, the issue addressed is not confined to the use of lethal force; killing and injuring people raise largely the same questions of infringement of bodily security and are both under consideration here, although lethal force clearly constitutes the extreme case and, as such, receives the bulk of the attention.[4]

Increased levels of autonomy in the use of AWS in force delivery occur especially in the military context. A low level of machine autonomy, which is clearly subordinate to human autonomy, may in some cases be involved. An example would be the computer programs that suggest targets and angles of attack to drone operators.[5] On the other side of the spectrum, there are weapons whereby machines essentially take the targeting decisions out of human hands. One example would be the long-range anti-ship missile, a precision-guided anti-ship standoff missile with autonomous targeting capabilities that can detect and destroy specific targets within a group of numerous ships at sea.[6] Full machine autonomy has not yet been used against human targets, but the point has been reached where that possibility has become very real.

---

[3] See Jewish Virtual Library, available at www.jewishvirtuallibrary.org/jsource/Peace/Iron Dome.html; US Military, available at http://usmilitary.about.com/library/milinfo/navy facts/blphalanx.htm.

[4] Should the issue at stake in discussions about AWS be the use of lethal force by such weapons or any use of force against human beings? Since the debate on these new weapons started out as one on its military implications, it took a certain direction. What was discussed was the infliction of death in the context of armed conflict, where the use of force is regulated with reference to international humanitarian law and the use of deadly force against legitimate targets is the norm. Terminology such as 'lethal autonomous weapons' is used. See CCW Meeting on Lethal Autonomous Weapons Systems, available at http://bit.ly/1jSlCro. I used the term 'lethal autonomous robotics' in my report in 2013. Heyns, Doc. A/HRC/23/47. This terminology may suggest an approach in terms of which this was seen as an international humanitarian law issue, and the appropriate international fora for the discussion of AWS were considered to be disarmament bodies. With time, however, there was a realization that the underlying issue was the use of autonomous force against human beings in general, also during policing operations, when the use of graduated force is required and deadly force is the exception. The same issues of bodily integrity and human dignity arise, and, in many cases, it is impossible to foresee in advance whether force will be lethal or not. As such, the more inclusive term 'autonomous weapons systems' appears to be more appropriate.

[5] See P. Scharre, 'Autonomy: killer robots and human control in the use of force', part 2 (2014), available at http://justsecurity.org/12712/autonomy-killer-robots-human-control-force-part-ii.

[6] See Lockheed Martin, available at www.lockheedmartin.com/us/products/LRASM.html.

Most of the unmanned systems that are becoming available to those who engage in ordinary law enforcement are remote controlled.[7] However, some level of autonomy in force release is also becoming available for law enforcement purposes. For example, a fixed automatic tear gas system that can be fitted to police barriers during demonstrations is available. It releases doses of tear gas if a perpetrator ignores the warning and penetrates further into a restricted area.[8] Some automation is also present in so-called automated rifle scoping, where a computer decides when to release fire against a human-selected target. The computer increases the first shot success probability – and, thus, diminishes the chances of bystanders being hit – by releasing fire only when a trajectory has been found that compensates for the effect of gravity, wind and so on.[9]

AWS, whether used in armed conflict or law enforcement, are weapon platforms, and any weapon can in principle be fitted onto an AWS. Therefore, the important distinguishing feature between different kinds of AWS is not the weapons they use but, rather, how they take their decisions – their levels of autonomy. While some AWS operate at low levels of autonomy, under close human control, it is also clear that some AWS will be able to operate at high levels of independence. It has become customary to refer to those systems in which there is no meaningful human control over force release as 'fully autonomous' weapons systems.

There are a number of reasons why AWS are being developed. The primary rationale for the development of unmanned systems in general (remote-controlled weapons and AWS) is their ability to protect personnel who are kept out of harm's way. However, what motivates the additional move from remote control to autonomous weapons release? The main argument is that AWS may be quicker at engaging intended targets because they can process information faster.[10]

---

[7] E.g., police UAV drones, remote aerial platform tactical reconnaissance, available at www.policeuavdrones.com/.
[8] See Security Research Map, available at www.securityresearchmap.de/index.php?lang=en&contentpos=4046. See also Roto Concept, available at www.rotoconcept.com.
[9] See Motherboard, available at http://motherboard.vice.com/blog/long-shot-inside-the-scope-of-smart-weapons.
[10] T. K. Adams, 'Future warfare and the decline of human decision making', *Parameters: United States Army War College Quarterly*, 31(4) (2001), 57–8; G. E. Marchant *et al.*, 'International governance of autonomous military robots', *Columbia Science and Technology Law Review*, 12 (2011), 280; Heyns, Doc. A/HRC/23/47, 8.

Furthermore, it is also sometimes argued that the superior processing powers of AWS can prevent the wrong targets from being hit.[11] To the extent that this argument is correct, the increased depersonalization in the deployment of force brought about by AWS may thus lead to greater personalization in targeting outcomes and saving lives or preventing unwarranted injuries. For example, in an armed conflict, robots that are programmed to return fire may be able to engage in more incisive exploration as to whether a perceived threat is real before it uses force than its human counterpart can. Humans in such a situation may be inclined to shoot earlier out of fear and, in the process, kill civilians who are not engaged in hostilities.[12]

Increasingly autonomous weapons have been developed largely in the military context, but some of the same arguments in favour of AWS may also be used in the law enforcement context. Automation of force can arguably allow greater speed and accuracy in targeting or preventing the excessive use of force. This potential could be used, for example, in a hostage situation where all of the hostage takers need to be hit at the same time to protect the lives of the hostages. In both the military and policing contexts, robots can do the dull, dangerous and dirty work.

However, there are serious questions to be asked on the use of AWS. The ethical and legal considerations applicable to the use of force against human beings today are largely expressed through the use of human rights language. International law has formulated a number of explicit rules that determine when such force may be used, and there is broad ethical support for this approach. Human rights law stipulates as a general rule that one person may use force against another only where the interest protected outweighs the harm done (that is, the force used is proportionate) and there is no other way to prevent such harm (the force used must be necessary) and it may only be used against an imminent attack.

When lethal force is used by law enforcement officials – that is, the harm done is that someone is killed – the proportionality requirement can only be fulfilled if the interest that is protected is the life of another

---

[11] See, e.g., B. J. Strawser, *Killing by Remote Control: The Ethics of an Unmanned Military* (Oxford University Press, 2013), 17. See also M. Horowitz and P. Scharre, 'Do killer robots save lives?' available at www.politico.com/magazine/story/2014/11/killer-robots-save-lives-113010.html.

[12] R. C. Arkin, 'Lethal autonomous weapons systems and the plight of the non-combatant' (2014), 3, available at www.unog.ch/80256EDD006B8954/%28httpAssets%29/54B1B7 A616EA1D10C1257CCC00478A59/$file/Article_Arkin_LAWS.pdf.

person. This has been called the 'protect life' principle: as a general standard, a life may only be taken if it is absolutely necessary to protect another life.[13] The 'protect life' principle is the guiding star whenever lethal force is used. However, the exceptional circumstances that prevail during armed conflict – such as the difficulty of exercising control over the use of force over a long distance and the fog of war – make it, on a temporary basis, an impossible standard to enforce. During armed conflict, human rights law remains valid, but it is interpreted with reference to the rules of international humanitarian law (IHL).[14]

In essence, the rules of IHL are those of distinction (only legitimate targets may be attacked); proportionality (any incidental or collateral damage inflicted on civilians who are not directly participating in hostilities must not be excessive in relation to the military advantages obtained); and precaution (feasible precautions must be taken to protect civilians).[15] These are the explicit rules of international law. However, it could also be argued that it is an implicit assumption of international law and ethical codes that humans will be the ones taking the decision whether to use force, during law enforcement and in armed conflict. Since the use of force throughout history has been personal, there has never been a need to make this assumption explicit. The advent of AWS makes addressing this issue now a priority. I will briefly address the three main questions raised by AWS.

'Can they do it?'

Can AWS, as a practical matter, meet the explicit rules regarding the use of force, as set out earlier, in the context of law enforcement or armed conflict? The right to life may potentially be infringed by AWS in

---

[13] See Principle 9 of the Basic Principles on the use of Force and Firearms by Law Enforcement Officials, available at www.unrol.org/files/BASICP~3.PDF, adopted by the Eighth United Nations Congress on the Prevention of Crime and the Treatment of Offenders, Havana, Cuba, 27 August – 7 September 1990. It is a minimum standard, in that not all uses of deadly force in order to save life are justified. It may, for example, not be acceptable to kill innocent bystanders to save someone on the proverbial runaway trolley.

[14] *Legality of the Threat or Use of Nuclear Weapons*, Advisory Opinion, ICJ Reports (1996) 226, para. 25, available at www.refworld.org/docid/4b2913d62.html.

[15] For a discussion, see, e.g., S. Oeter, 'Methods and means of combat: I General rules' in D. Fleck (ed.), *The Handbook of International Humanitarian Law*, 2nd edn (Oxford University Press, 2008), 130, 134; J-M. Henckaerts and L. Doswald-Beck, *Customary International Humanitarian Law*, vol. 1: *Rules*, Rules 7, 14–24 (Cambridge University Press, 2005), 25–9, 46–76.

a number of ways if they are used in these contexts.[16] The most often cited instance is when the deployment of force through AWS results in the direct use of force against those who are not considered to be legitimate targets under the law.[17] The wrong people may be hit because computers may not be able to identify the correct targets. Clearly, autonomous technology can assist in simple cases, but more complicated decisions may specifically require human judgment.

In law enforcement situations, proper targeting may require an understanding of human intentions. The determination whether there is an imminent attack that warrants the use of force may simply not be made properly by computers, now or in the future. In the case of armed conflict, machines, for example, may not always be able to distinguish those who are wounded or in the process of surrendering from those who may legitimately be targeted. They also may not be able to differentiate between civilians who are directly participating in hostilities and those who are not.

Even if the force used is not misdirected, the level of the force used by AWS may still be excessive. In law enforcement, any force used must be the minimum required by the circumstances. During armed conflict, excessive force may manifest itself in unacceptably high levels of collateral or incidental casualties.[18] It is difficult to imagine that machines will ever be able to take such decisions in a reliable way. Again, the concern is that robots may not be able to make the essentially qualitative, often value-based, decisions that are required to ensure that such force is not excessive.

---

[16] According to Article 6(1) of the International Covenant on Civil and Political Rights 1966, 999 UNTS 171, '[e]very human being has the inherent right to life. This right shall be protected by law. No one shall be arbitrarily deprived of his life.'

[17] In terms of Article 48 of Protocol Additional to the Geneva Conventions of 12 August 1949, and Relating to the Protection of Victims of International Armed Conflicts to the Geneva Conventions (Additional Protocol I) 1977, 1125 UNTS 3, to 'ensure respect for and protection of the civilian population and civilian objects, the Parties to the conflict shall at all times distinguish between the civilian population and combatants and between civilian objects and military objectives and accordingly shall direct their operations only against military objectives'. At no time shall parties make civilians the object of attack.

[18] Article 51(5)(b) of Additional Protocol I to the Geneva Conventions: 'Among others, the following types of attacks are to be considered as indiscriminate: (b) an attack which may be expected to cause incidental loss of civilian life, injury to civilians, damage to civilian objects, or a combination thereof, which would be excessive in relation to the concrete and direct military advantage anticipated.' Excessive collateral damage may also occur where no force should have been used at all, because excessive incidental casualties are unavoidable.

'Should they do it?'

However, even if we were to assume that the answer to the first question is affirmative – if it is accepted that AWS can engage in reasonably accurate targeting – a further question presents itself: is it right for machines to have the power of life and death over humans or the ability to inflict serious injury? This question brings us back to the argument that there may be an implicit requirement in terms of international law and ethical codes that only human beings may take the decision to use force against other humans. The implication of this approach bears emphasis. If there is such a requirement, then even if the correct target is hit and the force used is not excessive – and, in that sense, the explicit requirements of international law are met in a formal way – it will remain inherently wrong for a machine to make the determination that such force be used against a human being.

Seen from this perspective, it could be an inherently arbitrary deprivation of the right to life if the decision to use deadly force is delegated to machines. Human life, it has been argued, can only be taken as part of a process that is potentially deliberative and involving human decision making.[19] While the infliction of deadly force, especially during armed conflict, is often not deliberative in practice, AWS, which implies a high degree of autonomy, decisively rules out that possibility.

I would like to advance a further consideration to support the above contention, namely the implications of fully autonomous AWS for the right to dignity. To allow such machines to determine whether force is to be deployed against a human being may be tantamount to treating that particular individual not as a human being but, rather, as an object eligible for mechanized targeting.[20] It should be recognized that the exact contents and interpretation of the right to dignity is contested, and some call it a conversation stopper.[21] What cannot be contested, however, is that the concept of dignity has played a central role and

---

[19] P. M. Asaro, 'On banning autonomous weapon systems: human rights, automation and the dehumanisation of lethal decision making', *International Review of the Red Cross*, 94 (886) (2012), 2, 8–17. See also P. M. Asaro, 'Robots and responsibility from a legal perspective', available at www.peterasaro.org/writing/ASARO%20Legal%20Perspective.pdf.

[20] R. Sparrow, 'Robotic weapons and the future of war' in J. Wolfendale and P. Tripodi (eds.), *New Wars and New Soldiers: Military Ethics in the Contemporary World* (Farnham: Ashgate, 2012), 11; A. M. Johnson, 'The morality of autonomous robots', *Journal of Military Ethics*, 134 (2013), 134; Heyns, Doc. A/HRC/23/47, 18, para. 95.

[21] D. Birnbacher, 'Ambiguities in the concept of *Menschenwürde*' in K. Bayertz (ed.), *Sanctity of Life and Human Dignity* (New York: Springer, 1996), 107.

served as a driving force in the development of both human rights law[22] and IHL.[23] It can be expected that it will and should continue to play a role in both of these branches of law when new challenges are confronted.

Dignity, at least in the Kantian tradition, advances the idea of the infinite or incommensurable value of each person.[24] It has been argued that to have the decision whether you live or die – or be maimed – taken by machines is the ultimate indignity.[25] Robots cannot be programmed to respond in an appropriate way to the infinite number of possible scenarios that real life – and real people – offers.[26] Death by algorithm means that people are treated simply as targets and not as complete and unique human beings, who may, by virtue of this status, deserve to meet a different fate.

A machine, which is bloodless and without morality or mortality, cannot do justice to the gravity of the decision whether to use force in a particular case, even if it may be more accurate than humans.[27] This decision is so far-reaching that each instance calling for its use requires that a human being should decide afresh whether to cross that threshold if it is not to become a mechanical – and inhuman – process. Moreover, the dignity of those in whose name fully autonomous AWS are used may also be implicated. When such AWS dispense force on their behalf, they may not be able to act as moral agents who take their own

---

[22] Dignity has been called the 'mother' of human rights. See B. Schlink, 'The concept of human dignity: current usages, future discourses' in C. McCrudden (ed.), *Understanding Human Dignity* (Oxford University Press, 2013), 632. See also P. Carozza, 'Human dignity and judicial interpretation of human rights: a reply', *European Journal of International Law* 19 (5) (2008), 931–44, available at http://ejil.oxfordjournals.org/content/19/5/931.full; Nils Petersen, 'Human dignity, international protection', available at http://opil.ouplaw.com/view/10.1093/law:epil/9780199231690/law-9780199231690-e809?print.

[23] See, e.g., the view of the International Committee of the Red Cross (ICRC) as expressed in www.icrc.org/eng/resources/documents/article/other/ihl-human-rights-article-011207.htm. See also Rule 90 of the ICRC's Customary Law Study in Henckaerts and Doswald-Beck, *Customary International Humanitarian Law*, vol. 1; Geneva Conventions, Common Article 3(1)(c); Additional Protocols I, Article 75(2) and preamble and Protocol Additional to the Geneva Conventions of 12 August 1949, and Relating to the Protection of Victims of Non-International Armed Conflicts 1978, 1125 UNTS 609, Article 4(2).

[24] R. J. Scott, '*Dignité/dignidade*: organising against threats to dignity in societies after slavery' in McCrudden, *Understanding Human Dignity*, 69.

[25] Major General R. H. Latiff and P. McCloskey, 'With drone warfare, America approaches the robo-rubicon', *Wall Street Journal* (14 March 2013).

[26] See Human Rights Watch, 'Shaking the foundations: the human rights implications of killer robots' (2014), 2, available at www.hrw.org/sites/default/files/reports/arms0514_ForUpload_0.pdf.

[27] See Asaro, 'On banning autonomous weapon systems', 695; see also 689, 694–700.

decisions; instead, they abdicate their moral responsibility to bloodless entities. They are unable to assume, and exercise, responsibility.

Issues of accountability

The modern concept of human rights entails that certain core values are protected, and, if they are violated, there is accountability. Accountability is part of the protection of a particular right. A lack of accountability for a violation of the right to life, for example, is in itself a violation of that right.[28] Accountability can take many forms, including criminal prosecution, civil damages, disciplinary steps or the offering of redress or compensation. In addition to individual responsibility, institutions, such as states or corporations, may be held accountable. To the extent that this approach is to be followed in the case of AWS, the depersonalized use of force will result in depersonalized forms of responsibility.

Accountability is traditionally premised on control. For example, under criminal responsibility, one cannot be held responsible for that which is outside your control. To the extent that AWS allow for, and are under, human control, humans will remain responsible. However, to the extent that AWS are outside human control, it appears that there may be an accountability vacuum. There is clearly no point in putting a robot in jail.

Even where humans as a collective do exercise significant control over AWS, there may be uncertainty about whether each – or any – individual should be held to account in a specific case. Some form of human control over AWS may be exercised on different levels in the wider loop – for example, through computer programming, through the decision that the military will use such weapons, through the commander who orders subordinates to do so, and so on. It is not clear how responsibility should be assigned in such cases and to what extent it may be appropriate to hold

---

[28] Human Rights Committee (HRC), General Comment no. 31: 'The nature of the general legal obligation imposed on states parties to the covenant', UN Doc. CCPR/C/21/Rev.1/Add.13 (2004) adopted on 29 March 2004, paras. 16 and 18; see also HRC, General Comment no. 6, UN Doc. HRI/GEN/1/Rev.1 at 6 (1994); 'Basic principles and guidelines on the right to a remedy and reparation for victims of gross violations of international human rights law and serious violations of international humanitarian law', Resolution 60/147 adopted by the General Assembly on 16 December 2005, A/60/509/Add.1 adopted and proclaimed by UN General Assembly Resolution 60/147 of 16 December 2005, para. 4; ECtHR, *McCann and others v. The United Kingdom*, Appl. no. 18984/91, judgment of 27 September 1995, para. 169.

some of those agents – for example, the programmers – accountable.[29] If everyone is responsible, then no one is. This uncertainty may widen the accountability vacuum, and, as indicated, a lack of accountability constitutes a violation of the rights in question, such as the right to life.

In focusing on the new technologies, one can easily get lost in the technical details and be overwhelmed by how quickly the technology develops and how difficult it is to predict its future development. In order to get a grip on the issues that are raised by AWS and to develop an international response, it is useful to ask oneself at the outset what it is that one wants to protect and develop one's approach around the answer. What is the main concern raised by AWS?

The main concern appears to be that machine autonomy will undermine human autonomy in an area of great significance – the use of force against the human person. As a result, there is an emerging view that, in order to distinguish acceptable from unacceptable autonomy in force deployment, the central question is whether AWS will allow 'meaningful human control' over the decision in a specific case to release force against human beings.[30] If there is such control, there are not any special objections to AWS; if there is not such control, there is a strong case to be made that such weapons and their use should be prohibited.

As is clear from the earlier discussion, if there is no meaningful human control, it is likely that some targeting decisions cannot be made properly (such as proportionality decisions in armed conflict and establishing whether an attacker is truly about to launch an attack in law enforcement); that the right to life and the right to dignity may be undermined and that there could be a responsibility vacuum. Thus, human autonomy is undermined by such systems. However, where meaningful human control is present, such technology can enhance human autonomy to the extent that it allows humans to make better decisions. In order to be acceptable, therefore, AWS must remain tools in the hands of humans.

Exactly what is meant by meaningful control is subject to debate. The relationship between human and machine autonomy in the use of

---

[29] See M. Sassóli, 'Autonomous weapons and international humanitarian law: advantages, open technical questions and legal issues to be clarified', *International Law Studies / Naval War College*, 90 (2014), 309.

[30] See, e.g., remarks by Thomas Nash, Director, Article 36, Informal Expert Meeting on Lethal Autonomous Weapon Systems, Convention on Certain Convention of Weapons, Geneva (2014), available at www.unog.ch/80256EDD006B8954/%28httpAssets%29/260 33D398111B4E8C1257CE000395BBB/$file/Article36_Legal+Aspects_IHL.pdf.

force can take a range of forms.[31] At one end of the spectrum, humans can have full control. They are fully in the loop. Moving up the scale towards greater machine autonomy, a range of scenarios can be envisaged. For example, AWS may suggest angles of attack or targets (as with armed drones) to human operators, who can follow the suggestion or leave it, and AWS may proceed to select and engage a target unless a human intervenes. At the other end of this spectrum, human intervention may be absent, and the machine makes the relevant determinations without further human intervention. Full autonomy exists where humans no longer exercise meaningful human control.

Under any foreseeable scenario, there will be some human involvement in targeting decisions. The crude distinction that is sometimes made between humans 'in the loop' and 'out of the loop' in the context of AWS is thus not necessarily helpful. Humans may be out of the immediate decision-making loop, but they are never completely out of the wider decision-making loop and influence the process through actions such as computer programming and by deciding where and when AWS are to be deployed or when an attack is to be aborted. Moreover, it is not foreseen that AWS will replace entirely human soldiers but, rather, that they will fight alongside each other.[32] However, how does one determine when humans have ceded too much control to machines and when humans no longer have meaningful control and the machines have full autonomy?

The requirement of 'meaningful human control' in design and use appears to be a proper starting point for developing a response to the emergence of AWS. Indeed, few will argue against the importance of the retention of such control. At the same time, it should be recognized that it is an open-ended concept, and much will depend on the contents that it is given. There will also be disagreement on whether new law is needed to address this issue and, if so, what the nature of such law should be.[33] Much work is still required to give the concept application in the real world.

Whether full machine autonomy is present depends not only on the design of the machine itself – seen in isolation, based purely on its technical specifications – but it also depends on the context of its use.

---

[31] See Scharre, 'Autonomy', 6–7.

[32] R. Arkin, 'Governing lethal behaviour: embedding ethics in a hybrid deliberative/reactive robot architecture', Technical Report GIT-GVU-07-11 (2011), 5, available at www.cc .gatech.edu/ai/robot-lab/online-publications/formalizationv35.pdf.

[33] K. Anderson and M. Waxman, 'Law and ethics for autonomous weapon systems: why a ban won't work and how the laws of war can', Jean Perkins Task Force on National Security and Law Essay Series (Hoover Institution and Stanford University, 2013), 2.

Are AWS deployed in an environment where they have to make far-reaching decisions on targeting and the level of force used or are those decisions in fact taken by a human operator who decides, for example, to deploy AWS against a target in an area where there are few or no other people who could be hit?[34] Assuming that some consensus can be reached about the elements of meaningful human control and that acceptable and unacceptable AWS can thus be distinguished from each other, I would like to conclude by first making some comments about those AWS that allow for meaningful human control and those that do not allow for such control.

Conclusion

In the case of AWS which retain meaningful human control, it is clear that the involvement of some level of autonomy cannot justify targeting outcomes that are worse than they would have been if humans acted on their own – more misdirected fire and more instances of the use of excessive force. However, is it sufficient that such technology merely leads to outcomes that match those that humans would have achieved on their own?[35] Although it will be difficult to assess in practice, I want to contend that if technology in general – including autonomy – is used in targeting decisions, it should at least lead to outcomes that match those of humans. But perhaps the bar should be lifted further, and it should lead to better, more accurate, outcomes than would have been the case if humans acted on their own. In other words, AWS should not merely be tools in the hands of humans, but they should also be good tools that enhance human autonomy.

Indeed, one of the key justifications for the use of unmanned systems in general, and AWS in particular, is that their 'surgical precision' can

---

[34] For a discussion of some of the considerations that should play as role in this regard, see United Nations Institute for Disarmament Research, 'The weaponisation of increasingly autonomous technologies: considering how meaningful human control might move the discussion forward' (2014), 5, available at www.unidir.org/files/publications/pdfs/consid ering-how-meaningful-human-control-might-move-the-discussion-forward-en-615 .pdf; Heyns, 'Autonomous weapons systems and international law in the context of armed conflict'.

[35] For the approach that robots merely need to match the performance of humans (and without setting the 'meaningful human control' requirement), see P. Lin et al., 'Robots in war: issues of risk and ethics' in R. Capurro and M. Nagenborg (eds.), Ethics and Robotics (Heidelberg: Akademische Verlagsgesellschaft, 2009), 50; Sassóli, 'Autonomous weapons and international humanitarian law', 320.

save lives.[36] Using AWS is akin to calling in the assistance of specialists, who are generally held to higher standards. If surgical precision in targeting is available, surgical standards should apply. The world's reaction to drones has also been telling – there is arguably much more attention and adverse reaction to killings by drones than in cases when manned systems are used. This reaction seems to suggest an emerging state and international practice that holds the use of advanced technology to a higher standard.

I made the point earlier that the 'protect life' principle applies to all uses of force by law enforcement officials, though temporary exceptions are made in the case of armed conflict. However, if the circumstances that justify such a more permissive approach no longer exist, it seems logical to accept that the 'protect life' principle demands a more rigorous approach. That is, if technology allows states more control over long-distance use of force and lifts the fog of war, it could be argued that states should be held to higher standards – there is less of a justification for the lower standards posed by IHL and more reason to resume the default position of human rights law. For example, where smart bombs, or other technology that allows for better targeting, are available there should be less tolerance for collateral damage.[37] Moreover, should technology be developed that makes capture, rather than kill, possible, it should be used. Those who use advanced technology should also expect to be held to higher standards as far as accountability and transparency are concerned – as is the call already from many human rights groups in the context of armed drones.[38]

Is there any room for the use of AWS with meaningful human control in law enforcement? It should be clear that the ethos of policing is in

---

[36] Arkin, 'Lethal autonomous weapons systems'.

[37] See J. D. Herbach, 'Into the caves of steel: precaution, cognition and robotic weapon systems under the international law of armed conflict', *Amsterdam Law Forum*, 4(3) (2012), 10.

[38] C. Heyns, Report of the Special Rapporteur on extrajudicial, summary or arbitrary executions, Doc. A/68/30532, 12 August 2013, 37, paras. 95–101; see also International Human Rights and Conflict Resolution Clinic at Stanford Law School and Global Justice Clinic at NYU School of Law, 'Living under drones: death, injury, and trauma to civilians from US drone practices in Pakistan' (2012), 122, available at www.livingunderdrones.org /wp-content/uploads/2013/10/Stanford-NYU-Living-Under-Drones.pdf; Human Rights Watch, 'A wedding that became a funeral: US drone attack on marriage procession in Yemen' (2014), 25 available at www.hrw.org/sites/default/files/reports/yemen0214_For Upload_0.pdf; Human Rights Watch, 'Between a drone and Al-Qaeda: the civilian cost of US targeted killings in Yemen' (2013), 89, available at www.hrw.org/sites/default/files/ reports/yemen1013_ForUpload.pdf.

many respects different from that of fighting a war. The rules about the use of force are much more restrictive as far as law enforcement is concerned – and closer to the 'protect life' principle. In determining who may be targeted, status or conduct is not sufficient in the law enforcement paradigm – force may be used only against an imminent threat. In order to determine whether someone is a legitimate target, reliance often has to be placed on the intention of the parties involved, which requires human interpretation.

Moreover, the police have an obligation to protect the rights of the population, which is quite different from that of soldiers during armed conflict, and this goal requires the physical presence of those who decide on the use of force.[39] Police officers, for example, may well be called upon to protect the right to life of those caught up in demonstrations. The use of unmanned systems during law enforcement in general may thus be problematic because policing is, and should be, a human affair. Moreover, the speed of encounters during law enforcement is generally much lower than during armed conflict. As a result, the case for the use of AWS during law enforcement is much weaker than during armed conflict.

It should also be pointed out that armed drones are often used in contexts where there is no international agreement that there is an armed conflict, but the more permissive rules of IHL on the use of force are invoked by the responsible states. This has been criticized by the international community, which demands that the stricter rules of human rights law be met.[40] The same criticism is likely to be levelled against the use of AWS under such circumstances.

As for AWS without meaningful human control, the argument is sometimes made that they can save lives on the battlefield.[41] If the right to life is the supreme right, so the argument goes, surely the potential of saving lives must trump any considerations about human dignity or other such concerns. It may be argued, for example, that if at some point it becomes

---

[39] The police have an obligation to protect the human rights of the population that they serve during law enforcement, which is not present to the same degree during armed conflict. General Comment no. 31, paras. 2 and 5.

[40] Heyns, Doc. A/68/30532, 21–5; B. Emmerson, Report of the Special Rapporteur on the promotion and protection of human rights and fundamental freedoms while countering terrorism, Doc. A/68/389, 18 September 2013, 18–20.

[41] R. C. Arkin, *Governing Lethal Behaviour in Autonomous Robots* (Boca Raton, FL: Chapman & Hall/CRC, 2009); R. C. Arkin, 'Lethal autonomous systems and the plight of the non-combatant', *Ethics and Armed Forces*, 1 (2014), 5; Anderson and Waxman, 'Law and ethics for autonomous weapon systems', 6, 8, 13.

clear that, measured over many years, an army with fully autonomous weapons makes fewer targeting mistakes and uses less excessive force, AWS should be allowed, even if they have full autonomy, at least in the context of armed conflict.

Of course, there is no evidence at present that this will ever be the case. But, for the sake of argument, even if it is assumed that such a situation could arise, there are still good reasons why fully autonomous AWS should be banned. One reason relates to the nature of the right to life. As stated earlier, a lack of accountability for violations of the right to life is in itself a violation of that right, and if AWS create an accountability vacuum where mistakes occur, then the right to life is infringed. Moreover, the lack of a deliberative process, or at least its possibility, could constitute an arbitrary deprivation of life.

Moreover, the contention that the right to life is the supreme right and that the preservation of life trumps all other considerations, such as the right to dignity, cannot be accepted without further reflection. The notion of the indivisibility and interdependence of all rights militates against the idea of an absolute hierarchy of rights, because it would mean that if there were a clash of rights – when it really matters – the one right would always trump the other. Dignity, if it is to assume its position as a meaningful right, must in some cases be able to trump other rights, including the right to life.[42] It could be argued, for example, that due to privacy considerations we put restraints on mass surveillance – or at least believe there should be such constraints – even if such surveillance would be likely to save lives.

Human rights, for their part, are trumps over considerations of long-term utility. As such, the argument that in the aggregate AWS can possibly save lives in the long run cannot serve to justify short-term and concrete violations of the right to life or the right to dignity. Likewise, in armed conflict, the requirements of IHL must be met in each attack.[43]

The depersonalization of the use of force through autonomous targeting thus presents opportunities as well as threats. A nuanced approach is called for in order to distinguish between those instances where it can

---

[42] See, e.g., the German Federal Constitutional Court case where legislation authorizing the shooting down of an aeroplane that is used in a terrorist attack was found to be unconstitutional inter alia because of its impact on the right to dignity. Bundesverfassungsgericht (BVerfG – Federal Constitutional Court), 59; *Neue Juristische Wochenschrift* (*NJW*) 751 (2006), 15 February 2006, 1 BvR 357/05.

[43] Sassóli, 'Autonomous weapons and international humanitarian law', 321.

enhance or undermine human autonomy. It is of great importance that this distinction be made, and the notion of meaningful human control provides a useful starting point. What is at stake is the preservation and cultivation of nothing less than the right to live a dignified life – and to die a dignified death.

PART II

Meanings of autonomy and human cognition
under automation

2

Staying in the loop: human supervisory control of weapons

NOEL SHARKEY

Introduction

There is an ongoing technological transformation in warfare with ever more control of weapons being delegated to computer systems. There is considerable international concern among states and civil society about where humans fit into the control loop. Rather than move to a point where computer programs control the weapons, it is proposed in this chapter that the right balance between the best of human abilities and the best of computer functionality will have significantly greater humanitarian impact. The psychological literature on human decision provides a foundation for the type of control required for weapons. A human control classification is provided that reframes autonomy/ semi-autonomy in terms of levels of supervisory control. This allows for greater transparency in command and control and the allocation of responsibility.

There is considerable, and increasing, international discussion and debate about whether or not we should allow the decision to kill a human to be delegated to autonomous weapons systems (AWS) – systems that, once activated, can track, identify and attack targets with violent force without further human intervention. The discussion has ranged from moral and legal implications,[1] to

Some portions of this chapter have previously appeared in N. Sharkey, 'Towards a principle for the human supervisory control of robot weapons', *Politica e Società*, 2 (2014), 305–24. The author would like to thank Maya Brehm (Article 36) for assistance with some of the ideas in this chapter.

[1] See P. Asaro, 'On banning autonomous weapon systems: human rights, automation and the dehumanisation of lethal decision-making', *International Review of the Red Cross*, 94 (2012), 687–709; C. Heyns, Report of the Special Rapporteur on extrajudicial summary or arbitrary executions, Doc. A/HRC/23/47, 9 April 2013. See also C. Heyns, 'Autonomous weapons systems: living a dignified life and dying a dignified death', Chapter 1 in this volume.

technical and operational concerns,[2] to issues about international security.[3]

It seems clear that for the foreseeable future,[4] we cannot guarantee that AWS will be able to fully comply with international humanitarian law (IHL), except perhaps in some very narrowly subscribed circumstances.[5] Apart from problems with the principles of distinction and proportionality in determining the legitimacy of targets, AWS are, by definition, less predictable than other weapons systems. This means that it is unclear as yet how we could guarantee the quality of Article 36 weapon reviews for both hi-tech and lo-tech nations.[6] In addition, the US Department of Defense has pointed out a number of computer problems for the use of AWS.[7]

Some argue that such weapons could be used legally in certain very limited circumstances, while others maintain that at some point in the future they may be able to comply with IHL. However, these arguments are about an IHL-compliant technology that no one yet knows how to create. There is nothing wrong with technological ambitions or a general research agenda in civilian domains, but there is less room for such conjecture when discussing autonomous technologies of violence. For example, robot soccer is seen as a great research challenge and a chance to test robotics technology within a real-world application. The ultimate aim is to develop a team of autonomous humanoid robots that will beat

---

[2] See N. Sharkey, 'The evitability of autonomous robot warfare', *International Review of the Red Cross*, 94 (2012), 787–99; and N. Sharkey, 'Saying "No!" to lethal autonomous targeting', *Journal of Military Ethics*, 4(9) (2010), 299–313.

[3] Concerns have been expressed that unknown combating algorithms controlling autonomous weapons would interact in unpredictable ways. This could make it impossible for weapons reviews to guarantee compliance with international humanitarian law (IHL). N. Sharkey, 'The automation and proliferation of military drones and the protection of civilians', *Journal of Law, Innovation and Technology*, 3(2) (2011), 229–40.

[4] In the context of this chapter, foreseeable future means that it follows from an analysis of the current state of the technology, the ongoing research projects and the current empirical evidence from the technology. Any departure from a foreseeable future analysis is dependent on speculation about the future without clear supporting evidence.

[5] For example, it would be possible to set the coordinates for an autonomous drone as a substitute for a cruise missile, or they may be used against military objects.

[6] Geneva Conventions, 12 August 1949, 1125 UNTS 3, Article 36.

[7] US Department of Defense (DoD) Directive 3000.09, 'Autonomy in weapon systems', 21 November 2012, 14, points to potential problems with autonomous weapons: human error, human–machine interaction failures, malfunctions, communications degradation, software coding errors, enemy cyber attacks, infiltration into the industrial supply chain, jamming, spoofing, decoys, other enemy countermeasures or actions and unanticipated situations on the battlefield.

human world champions by 2050. No one knows if this will work, but the challenge enables the development of new methods of robot control and sensing that can be applied elsewhere.[8] Thus, success in the ultimate aim is not vital in order to reap the technological benefits. If the enterprise fails, we may invent a different kind of sport for humans and robots to play together (and still keep the old sport specifically for humans) with new rules of engagement to give robots an equal chance of victory.[9]

In contrast, if our thinking, our strategies and our funding are directed towards developing AWS, and it turns out that making them IHL compliant is not as successful as was hoped for, what will we do with this weapons technology? What if we get involved in serious conflicts? We may then have to change what IHL compliance means and modify the rules of engagement to give the new weapon a place. This very scenario has happened in the past with aerial bombardment and submarine warfare.

The limitations of technology is partly why technologically capable states such as the United Kingdom and the United States have made it clear that there will be a human in the loop for lethality decisions. In the United Kingdom, the parliamentary under-secretary of state, Lord Astor of Hever, said: '[T]he MoD [Ministry of Defence] currently has no intention of developing systems that operate without human intervention ... let us be absolutely clear that the operation of weapons systems will always be under human control.'[10] When the US Department of Defense (DoD) issued the first policy document on autonomous weapons, they stated: 'Autonomous and semi-autonomous weapons systems shall be designed to allow commanders and operators to exercise appropriate levels of human judgment over the use of force.'[11] What has not been made absolutely clear in the United Kingdom, however, is exactly what type of human control will be employed. Nor has the US DoD made any attempt to define 'appropriate

---

[8] For a fuller discussion, see E. Datteri and G. Tamburrini, 'Robotic weapons and democratic decision-making' in E. Hilgendorf and J.-P. Guenther (eds.), *Robotik und Gesetzegebung* (Baden-Baden: Nomos, 2013), 211–29.

[9] Tamburrini futher extends his arguments in this volume to consider the cultural production of ignorance. G. Tamburrini, 'On banning autonomous weapons systems: from deontological to wide consequentialist reasons', Chapter 6 in this volume.

[10] 26 March 2013. Cf. http://bit.ly/1lZMQyW_14.

[11] See note 4 in this chapter. But see D. Saxon, 'A human touch: autonomous weapons, DoD Directive 3000.09 and the interpretation of "appropriate levels of human judgment over the use of force"', Chapter 9 in this volume, about problems and the vagueness of US Department of Defense Directive 3000.09.

levels of human judgment'. Without addressing these points – and they are not easy to address – there is no transparency in the operation of such computerized weapons.[12] To say that there is a human in the control loop does not clarify the degree of human involvement.[13] It could simply mean a human programming a weapons system for a mission or pressing a button to activate it, or it could (hopefully) mean exercising full human judgment about the legitimacy of a target before initiating an attack.

Moreover, the terms 'autonomous' and 'semi-autonomous' weapons do not help to clarify the control issue. For example, the US navy uses three levels of control, while the US army uses ten.[14] This could be very confusing for a military commander having to work with several systems at different levels. States have ended up having long technological discussions about what are the levels of semi-autonomy and what they mean in terms of computing and robotics. The US DoD Defense Science Board's task force agrees: 'The Task Force reviewed many of the DoD-funded studies on "levels of autonomy" and concluded that they are not particularly helpful to the autonomy design process.' They recommended that 'the DoD abandon the use of "levels of autonomy" [because] they focus too much attention on the computer rather than on the collaboration between the computer and its operator/supervisor to achieve the desired capabilities and effects'.[15]

An alternative approach to the classification of autonomy and semi-autonomy is to turn the discussion on its head and reframe autonomy in terms of the type and quality of human control afforded by the different types of computerized weapons systems. An examination of scientific research on human supervisory control allows us to develop a classification system consisting of five levels of control.[16] The following list shows the five levels for the human supervisory control of weapons. These levels

---

[12] See S. Knuckey, 'Autonomous weapons systems and transparency: towards an international dialogue', Chapter 8 in this volume, for a detailed discussion about transparency.

[13] See Saxon, 'A human touch', for an excellent take on the problems and the vagueness of the DoD's Directive 3000.09.

[14] For some discussion and references, see N. Sharkey, 'Cassandra or the false prophet of doom: AI robots and war', *IEEE Intelligent Systems*, 28(4) (2008), 14–17.

[15] DoD Defense Science Board, 'The role of autonomy in DoD systems', Task Force Report, July 2012, 48, available at www.fas.org/irp/agency/dod/dsb/autonomy.pdf.

[16] This is adapted from early work on general (non-military) supervised control with ten levels of human supervisory control. T. B. Sheridan and W. Verplank, *Human and Computer Control of Undersea Teleoperators* (Cambridge, MA: Man–Machine Systems Laboratory, Department of Mechanical Engineering, Massachusetts Institute of Technology, 1978).

should not be considered to be absolutes; they are a work in progress and should be seen as a discussion prompt and an initial effort towards the development of a common understanding for all stakeholders.

Classification system for levels of human supervisory control of weapons:

1. Human engages with and selects target and initiates any attack;
2. Program suggests alternative targets and human chooses which to attack;
3. Program selects target and human must approve before attack;
4. Program selects target and human has restricted time to veto; and
5. Program selects target and initiates attack without human involvement.

The control of weapons mediated by computer programs requires that the human and machine operate together in a way that should optimize the strengths of both.[17] Computers are better and more efficient at some tasks than humans, while humans are better at other tasks. Examples are provided in Table 2.1.

Table 2.1 *Examples of tasks computers and humans are better at*[18]

Computers	Humans
• Calculate numbers	• Deliberative reasoning
• Search large data sets	• Perceive novel patterns
• Respond quickly to control tasks	• Meta-cognition
• Perform repetitive routine tasks	• Reasoning inductively

The ideal partnership

We are embarking on a path where human control of weapons is being increasingly ceded to computer programs. It is vital that we take the opportunity to use the evolution of technology to ensure that the partnership between human and machine increases rather than diminishes the ability of humans to ensure the legitimacy of the targets of attack.[19]

---

[17] This resonates with G. Sartor and A. Omicini, 'The autonomy of technological systems and responsibilities for their use', Chapter 3 in this volume.

[18] See also M. L. Cummings, 'Automation bias in intelligent time critical decisions support systems', American Institute of Aeronautics and Astronautics Third Intelligent Systems Conference, Chicago, 2004.

[19] See also the concerns of L. Suchman and J. Weber, 'Human–machine autonomies', Chapter 4 in this volume, on the human–machine relation.

Rather than making more and more hi-tech weapons with the aim of more effective killing and destruction of targets, would it not be better to create hi-tech weapons with the aim of having greater humanitarian impact?

Some may argue that making more precise weapons with greater accuracy is in effect enabling less collateral damage. However, at best, this achievement would be a 'side effect' to the goal of more effective killing with less ammunition. It is proposed here that greater humanitarian impact should be the explicit goal of new technological weapons – with greater technology should come greater responsibility towards civilians, civilian infrastructure and those *hors de combat*. The ideal would be to reduce collateral damage to zero and facilitate better opportunities for combatants to surrender.[20]

The question then is what might such humanitarian impact look like? If the configuration of a human and machine partnership is done correctly, we would ideally expect a commander (or operator) to be able to perform in the following way:

1. have full contextual and situational awareness of the target area at the time of initiating a specific attack;
2. be able to perceive and react to any change or unanticipated situations that may have arisen since planning the attack, such as changes in the legitimacy of the targets;
3. have active cognitive participation in the attack;
4. have sufficient time for deliberation on the nature of targets, their significance in terms of the necessity and appropriateness of an attack and the likely incidental and possible accidental effects of the attack; and
5. have a means for the rapid suspension or abortion of the attack.

Paul Scharre has correctly suggested that this list could rule out a large number of conventional weapons currently in use.[21] But the point here is not to look back at 'old' weapons but, rather, to look forward to upgrade our sensibility to civilian harm as a result of technological developments. According to Scharre, the current operating procedure is that the

---

[20] See E. Lieblich and E. Benvenisti, 'The obligation to exercise discretion in warfare: why autonomous weapons systems are unlawful', Chapter 11 in this volume, for a fuller discussion of the issue of surrender and autonomous weapons systems.

[21] P. Scharre, 'Autonomy, "killer robots" and human control in the use of force', part 2, *Just security*, July 2014, available at http://justsecurity.org/12712/autonomy-killer-robots-human-control-force-part-ii/.

commander has sufficient situational awareness of the target area at the time of planning an attack rather than full contextual and situational awareness at the time of the attack, as stated in point 1 of the list. However, it is unclear what exactly sufficient means in this context.

If one of the reasons for using advanced technology to apply violent force is genuinely to reduce or eliminate harm to civilians, to others *hors de combat* and to civilian infrastructure, then striving for full contextual and situational awareness at the time of attack is a way forward. It does not necessarily require a change in the law of armed conflict. It requires a change in the acceptability and responsibility standards for compliance with the law. These statements run the risk of condoning the use of distance killing, such as drone (remotely piloted aerial vehicle) strikes. This is not the intention of this chapter, which should be clear from the outset. There have been dubious uses of drones, which are at best legally questionable.

What is being suggested is a perilous path fraught with dangers of misuse of the technology to expand the battlefield to areas outside official conflict zones with the excuse of more humanitarian killing. It would require a considerable tightening of the current legal regime to ensure greater accountability and compliance with existing laws. The stated aim should be to raise the bar on humanitarian standards in conflict rather than to make entering into conflicts easier.[22] If modern technology is employed for the supervisory control of weapons, it should be possible for commanders to have active participation during attacks rather than simply in planning them. Even with a cruise missile, it should be possible to use advanced camera systems to view targets and ensure that their legitimacy has not changed since the launch.[23] This means satisfying point 2 in the earlier list, providing that there is an inbuilt facility to rapidly suspend or abort the attack (point 5).

None of this is easy in the delicate human–computer balancing act. It is vital that we use human reasoning at its best when we consider targeting with violent force. When humans fail at human–computer tasks, it can simply mean that they are being asked to perform in a mode of operation

---

[22] We should also be very wary of attempts to take such technological developments into the civilian world without due consideration of the potential for violations of human rights, including the right to life, privacy and dignity and the right to peaceful protest.

[23] Note that there is no intention here to legitimate the use of armed drones in warfare. These have been deployed into conflict with insufficient foresight and regulation about how they might best be used. And the use by the intelligence services is, at best, legally questionable.

that is not well suited to human psychology. This understanding needs to be part of the equation to ensure the efficient and meaningful human supervisory control of weapons. If we get the balancing act right, military objectives could be met while IHL is complied with at the same time in a better and more predictable way. Getting it wrong could result in considerable humanitarian problems.

Getting reasoning right

As a starting point to mapping what sufficient human control of weapons is, we can look at one of the most well-established distinctions in human psychology between automatic and controlled processes. It follows from more than 100 years of research on dual processing (1890).[24] Automatic processing refers to fast responses that are always cued automatically, such as those required for playing tennis or riding a bicycle. Controlled refers to slower deliberative processes that we need in order to make a thoughtful decision, such as determining the winner of a competition or judging a murder trial. Daniel Kahneman, winner of the Nobel memorial prize for his work on reasoning, used the dual process theory as an explanation for human decision making.[25] The terms automatic and deliberative processes will be used in this chapter for consistency and clarity.

The deliberative processes always come into play after the automatic and are thus slower – Kahneman calls them 'lazy processes'. They will go along with the automatic processes unless there is something surprising or irregular and/or we are operating in novel circumstances or performing tasks that require vigilance and/or deliberation. A downside of deliberative processes is that they require attention and free memory space. If a distraction takes our attention away or requires memory resources, automatic processes dominate. In fact anything that impacts on memory capacity or attention, such as stress or being pressured to

---

[24] W. James, *The Principles of Psychology* (New York: Holt, 1890) vol. 1. There is debate in the psychological literature about the underlying brain mechanisms (e.g. W. Schneider and J. M. Chen, 'Controlled and automatic processing: behavior, theory and biological mechanisms', *Cognitive Science*, 27 (2003), 525–59) and whether it is possible to create a unified model of the dual processes (e.g. S. B. T. Evans and K. E. Stanovich, 'Dual-process theories of higher cognition: advancing the debate', *Perspectives on Psychological Science*, 8(3) (2013), 223–41.

[25] D. Kahneman, *Thinking, Fast and Slow* (London: Penguin, 2011). He refers to the two processes as System 1 and System 2, these are exactly the same as the terms automatic and deliberative used here for clarity and consistency.

make a quick decision, could incapacitate deliberative reasoning. The upside of automatic processes is that they do not require active control or attention. Normally, both systems operate seamlessly together, and we do not even notice their interplay. However, the distinction should become clear by working through the following example devised by Kahneman.[26]

Example of automatic versus deliberative processing:

Task 1. *Go down each column in turn and say out loud 'lower' or 'upper case' for each word.*

LEFT		upper	
	left	lower	
right			LOWER
RIGHT		upper	
	RIGHT	UPPER	
	left		lower
LEFT			LOWER
	RIGHT	upper	

Task 2. *Repeat the exercise but this time say whether each word is to the right or left of its column.*

LEFT		upper	
	left	lower	
right			LOWER
RIGHT		upper	
	RIGHT	UPPER	
	left		lower
LEFT			LOWER
	right	upper	

This example illustrates the distinction between automatic and deliberative processes by showing them in conflict with one another. The task requires deliberative reasoning because saying upper/lower or right/left is

26 *Ibid.*

unusual when reading columns of words. However, you will find that one column was significantly easier than the other, and the easy column was different for both tasks. This is because we cannot help but automatically read the actual words and this interferes with the deliberative processes.

The relevance to weapons control is that both types of reasoning have different advantages and disadvantages. The advantage of automatic decision processes is that they can be trained through repetition and practice on routine tasks. They are needed for fast reaction in sports and for riding a bicycle, driving a car or in military routines. In fact, auto-maticity is used any time routine decisions have to be made rapidly for predictable events (and the word 'predictable' is highly important here). For automatic processes to work well, it is vital to have an environment that contains useful cues that, via practice, have been (over-)rehearsed.

For the right tasks, automatic reasoning can be a better option than deliberative reasoning, and it is not inherently bad. When initiated by well-practised cues, it reduces much of the tedium in our lives and saves us from a life of indecision. Members of the armed forces rehearse and are over-trained for many routine tasks that require automatic action on order. Fast automatic response can be trained with well-practised cues. These can be useful in military contexts such as when someone shouts 'fire in the hole' – a warning that should prompt those hearing it to immediately take cover. The question to ask about automatic reasoning is: does a given domain afford enough regularity to be learnable as an automatic process? When it comes to human supervised targeting, the unpredictable and unanticipated circumstances in a dynamically chan-ging environment play to the weakness of automatic reasoning.

Four of the properties of automatic reasoning from Kahneman illus-trate how it would be problematic for the supervisory control of weapons. Automatic reasoning:

- **neglects ambiguity and suppresses doubt**. Automatic processes are all about jumping to conclusions. They are guided by experience. An unambiguous answer pops up immediately and does not allow doubt. Automatic reasoning does not search for alternative interpreta-tions and does not examine uncertainty. So if something looks like it might be a legitimate target in ambiguous circumstances, automatic reasoning will be certain that it is legitimate.
- **infers and invents causes and intentions**. Automatic reasoning is adept at finding a coherent causal story to link together fragments of available information. Events including people (or even inanimate

objects such as robots) are automatically attributed with intentions that fit the causal story. For example, if a human operator is seeking out patterns of behaviour to determine a lethal drone strike, then seeing people load bales of hay or shovels onto a truck could initiate a causal story that they were loading rifles for an attack. This relates to assimilation bias in the human supervisory control literature.[27]

- **is biased to believe and confirm.** The operation of automatic reasoning has been shown to favour the uncritical acceptance of suggestions and maintains a strong bias. Thus, if a computer system suggests a target to an operator, automatic reasoning alone would make it highly likely that it would be accepted. This is known as automation bias in the supervisory literature.[28] When people seek out information to confirm a prior belief, this is confirmation bias.[29]

- **focuses on existing evidence and ignores absent evidence.** Automatic reasoning builds a coherent explanatory story without considering any evidence or contextual information that might be missing. This is why Kahneman uses the term WYSIATI or 'what you see is all there is'. It facilitates the feeling of coherence that makes us confident to accept information as true, whether it is or not. This is a problem if a more detailed analysis of the context of a target showed that it was not in fact legitimate. For example, a man not in uniform firing a rifle in the vicinity of an army platoon may be deemed to be a hostile target with WYSIATI. However, some deliberation and a quick scan around might reveal that he had actually just killed a wolf that had taken one of his goats.

What these properties of automatic reasoning show is that in the context of supervised control of lethal targeting, things could go badly wrong. It may work well for many instances and seem okay, but it does not work well when there is contradictory information of target legitimacy. Contradictory evidence could remain unseen or be disbelieved.

---

[27] J. M. Carroll and M. B. Rosson, 'Paradox of the active user' in J. M. Carroll (ed.), *Interfacing Thought: Cognitive Aspects of Human–Computer Interaction* (Cambridge, MA: MIT Press, 1987), 80–111.

[28] K. L. Mosier and L. J. Skitka, 'Human decision makers and automated decision aids: made for each other?' in R. E. Parasuraman and M. E. Mouloua (eds.), *Automation and Human Performance: Theory and Applications* (Mahwah, NJ; Lawrence Erlbaum Associates, 1996), 201–20.

[29] C. G. Lord, L. Ross and M. Lepper, 'Biased assimilation and attitude polarization: the effects of prior theories on subsequently considered evidence', *Journal of Personality and Social Psychology*, 47 (1979), 1231–43.

Doubt and uncertainty will be suppressed as will any notion that there is more evidence that cannot be seen.

In normal operations, both automatic and deliberative processes operate smoothly together. The point here is that it is vitally important that deliberative reasoning is enabled in the design of supervisory control for weapons systems. Although this is also subject to error and flaws, it does as good a job as can be done with uncertainty and doubt. If a supervisory weapons operator is distracted by another task or if they are stressed, their attentional capacity may be low. Many experimental studies have demonstrated that a small amount of interference to our attention or memory can disable the deliberative system. For example, when people are asked to do a task, such as verifying the truth or falsity of a statement, and, at the same time, are asked to add numbers, they will believe anything they are told.

In such circumstances, weapon supervisors trying to decide on the necessity or legitimacy of an attack may not be reasoning at an acceptable level. This is one reason why, in what is known as on-the-loop control, having a single operator controlling multiple weapons systems, could be disastrous. They would not be able to use their deliberative reasoning and could simply catch the downsides of automatic reasoning if there were problems or irregularities.

Deliberative reasoning meets supervisory control of weapons

Having discussed some of the relevant processes of human reasoning, we return to consider how they relate to the human supervisory weapons control framework introduced in the introduction of this chapter.[30] It is understood that some of the requirements proposed here are difficult to carry out in a military context, but the fact that they are difficult should not stop them from being discussed or attempted as much as is conceivable. They represent ideals that should be genuinely aspired to.

Level 1: A human deliberates about the target before initiating any attack

While this is clearly difficult in many circumstances, it is critically important to move towards the ideal of adhering to the strict

---

[30] There is a potential subclass of defensive autonomous weapons that may lie outside of this framework. These are weapons that sense and react to military objects. See Sharkey, 'Towards a principle for the human supervisory control of robot weapons'.

requirements of deliberative human control as described in the previous section. A human commander (or operator) must have full contextual and situational awareness of the target area at the time of a specific attack and be able to perceive and react to any change or unanticipated situations that may have arisen since planning the attack. There must be active cognitive participation in the attack and sufficient time for deliberation on the nature of the target, its significance in terms of the necessity and appropriateness of attack and the likely incidental and possible accidental effects of the attack. There must also be a means for the rapid suspension or abortion of the attack.

Level 2: A computer program provides a list of targets and a human chooses which to attack

This type of control could be acceptable if it is shown to meet the requirement of deliberative human control. A human in control of the attack would have to be in a position to assess whether an attack is necessary and appropriate, whether all (or indeed any) of the suggested alternatives are permissible objects of attack, and which target may be expected to cause the least civilian harm. This decision requires deliberative reasoning. Without sufficient time or in a distracting environment, the illegitimacy of a target could be overlooked. A rank-ordered list of targets is particularly problematic as there would be a tendency to accept the top-ranked target unless sufficient time and attentional space are given for deliberative reasoning.

Level 3: A computer program selects the target and a human must approve it before the attack is acceptable

This type of control has been experimentally shown to create what is known as automation bias or complacency, in which human operators come to accept computer-generated solutions as correct and disregard, or do not search for, contradictory information. In 2004, Missy Cummings conducted a study on an interface designed for supervision and resource allocation of an in-flight GPS-guided Tomahawk missile.[31] The task for operators was to decide which candidate missile from a pool of 8–16 would be the correct one to redirect to a time-critical emergent

---

[31] Cummings, 'Automation bias'.

target. The impact on the speed and accuracy of decision making was tested for two different methods to redirect Tomahawks in real time:

- the computer provided the operator with ranked recommendations, including the most 'optimal' missile given the situation (this is Type 3 in the earlier classification) and
- the computer filtered all of those missiles that were not candidates because of physical restraints (not enough fuel and so on), and the operator had to decide which missile (this equates to Type 2 in the earlier classification).

Cummings also manipulated the computer recommendations so that half the time they were correct and half the time they were wrong. The result was that Type 3 operators made significantly faster decisions overall and their accuracy was equal to the slower Type 2 operators when the computer recommendations were correct. However, when the computer recommendations were wrong, the Type 3 operators had a significantly decreased accuracy. This is known as automation bias: operators are prepared to accept the computer recommendations without seeking any disconfirming evidence.

Level 4: A computer program selects the target and the human has restricted time to veto

This option is unacceptable because it does not promote target identification. Providing only a short time to veto would reinforce automation bias and leave no room for doubt or deliberation. As the attack will take place unless a human intervenes, this undermines well-established presumptions under international humanitarian law that promote civilian protection. The time pressure will result in operators falling foul of all four of the downsides of automatic reasoning described earlier: neglects ambiguity and suppresses doubt, infers and invents causes and intentions, is biased to believe and confirm, focuses on existing evidence and ignores absent evidence. An example of the errors caused by fast veto came in the 2004 war with Iraq when the US army's Patriot missile system engaged in fratricide, shooting down a British Tornado and an American F/A-18, killing three pilots.[32]

---

[32] M. L. Cummings, 'Automation and accountability in decision support system interface design', *Journal of Technology Studies*, 32 (2006), 23–31.

Level 5: A computer program selects the targets and initiates attacks without human involvement

As argued earlier, such weapons systems could not comply with international law except in very narrowly bounded circumstances, and they are thus entirely unacceptable. This classification of levels of human control is just a beginning. We need to map out exactly the role that the human commander/supervisor plays for each supervised weapons system. Research is urgently needed to ensure that human supervisory interfaces make provisions to get the best level of human reasoning needed to comply with the laws of war in all circumstances.

Conclusions

There has been general agreement on the inadequacy of autonomous weapons systems to fully comply with current international humanitarian law in the foreseeable future. While there seems to be a big push by some states to develop weapons that could be used autonomously, states such as the United States and the United Kingdom have made it clear that, at least for the time being, computerized weapons systems will always be under some form of human control. However, it has not been made clear what exactly is meant by human control and how meaningful it will be. Thus, one aim of this chapter has been to pull apart and examine some of the ideal conditions for the control of computerized weapons by humans.

Both humans and computer systems have their strengths and weaknesses, and the aim of designing effective supervisory systems for weapons control is to exploit the strengths of both. In this way, it should be possible not only to gain better legal compliance but also to ensure that the partnership between human and machine is more humanitarian than machines or humans operating alone. Rather than making more hi-tech weapons with the aim of more effective killing and destruction of targets, it would better serve humanity to create hi-tech weapons with the explicit aim of eliminating civilian casualties and enabling the surrender of combatants.

To do this, we must urgently begin to develop a principle for the human control of weapons that is founded on an understanding of the process of human reasoning. Reframing autonomy in terms of human control will eliminate some of the technical complexity of engineering jargon and make it clear who is in control, where and when. This will not only make the control of weapons transparent for state weapons reviews and make the control clear to commanders, but it could also clarify who is responsible for mishaps and potential crimes.

The strict requirement for Level 1 control of weapons as specified earlier in this chapter may seem overly idealistic to some. Clearly, it is still very difficult to implement. However, it could be achievable if there was a will to push technological developments in that direction. It is certainly more achievable than creating autonomous weapons that could comply with IHL. If states are set to continue fighting wars and initiating conflicts, the least they can do is aspire to the goal of creating weapons that will produce zero civilian casualties.

3

The autonomy of technological systems and responsibilities for their use

GIOVANNI SARTOR AND ANDREA OMICINI

Introduction

In the discussion on autonomous systems and their regulation, distinct concepts of autonomy are put forward. For instance, the US Military Defense Science Board provides the following definition: 'Autonomy is a capability (or a set of capabilities) that enables a particular action of a system to be automatic or, within programmed boundaries, "self-governing."'[1] In a similar spirit, George A. Bekey describes autonomy as 'the capacity to operate in the real-world environment without any form of external control, once the machine is activated, and at least in some areas of operation, for extended periods of time.'[2] According to both definitions, autonomy consists in the capacity for 'sustained independent action'. Thus, a system is autonomous to the extent that it can accomplish a task by itself, without external directions. Once the system starts its activity, there is no need for other human or artificial agents to monitor its behaviour and govern its functioning.

Stuart Russell and Peter Norvig adopt a different perspective, characterizing autonomy as 'an agent's capacity to learn what it can to compensate for partial or incorrect prior knowledge'.[3] According to this definition, the focus is on cognitive capacity and, in particular, on the capacity to obtain new knowledge, interacting with the environment. Thus, an agent is autonomous to the extent that it is able to appropriately

---

[1] Department of Defense: Defense Science Board, *The Role of Autonomy in DoD Systems* (July 2012), 1, available at http://fas.org/irp/agency/dod/dsb/autonomy.pdf.

[2] G. A. Bekey, 'Current trends in robotics: technology and ethics', in P. Lin, K. Abney and G. A. Bekey (eds.), *Robot Ethics: The Ethical and Social Implications of Robotics* (Cambridge, MA: MIT, 2012), 18.

[3] S. J. Russell and P. Norvig, *Artificial Intelligence: A Modern Approach* (Upper Saddle River, NJ: Prentice Hall, 2010), 39.

expand or revise its initial stock of knowledge, so as to face the challenges of its environment. There is no need for others to reprogram an autonomous system or to provide it with new directives when novel situations are met.

Cristiano Castelfranchi and Rino Falcone adopt yet another approach, by grounding the autonomy of a system on the fact that the system tends to certain specific results due to its internal constraints or representations; it perceives and interprets its environment, defines and selects what stimuli to take into consideration, has internal states, and its behaviour also depends on such internal states.[4] Here the focus is on the cognitive architecture of the system and on the way in which this architecture mediates external inputs and system behaviour. A system is autonomous to the extent that it does not merely react to external stimuli but, rather, integrates such stimuli into its cognitive structures, by modifying appropriately its internal states, according to its own standards and procedures, so as to determine its behaviour. We shall see that these aspects of autonomy are connected but do not necessarily coexist and converge. Thus, by disentangling these aspects, we may obtain a better understanding of the nature and preconditions of autonomy. We shall then consider how this analysis of the notion of autonomy can be brought to bear on weapons systems, focusing on the targeting process. Finally, we shall draw some tentative conclusions concerning the regulation of autonomous weapons and the need to maintain sufficient human control.

Dimensions of autonomy: independence

We say that a technological device is independent to the extent that it is supposed to accomplish on its own, without external interventions, a high-level task.[5] For this purpose, we need to consider that the deployment of technologies usually takes place in the context of what is usually called a socio-technical system, namely, an integrated combination of human, technological and organizational components.[6] This applies to

---

[4] C. Castelfranchi and R. Falcone, 'Founding autonomy: the dialectics between (social) environment and agent's architecture and powers' in M. Nickles, M. Rovatsos and G. Weiss (eds.), *Agents and Computational Autonomy: Potential, Risks, and Solutions* (New York: Springer, 2005), 40.

[5] This corresponds to the idea of t-autonomy, discussed by Guglielmo Tamburrini, 'On banning autonomous weapons systems: from deontological to wide consequentialist reasons', Chapter 6 in this volume.

[6] P. Vermaas et al., *A Philosophy of Technology: From Technical Artefacts to Sociotechnical Systems* (San Rafael, CA: Morgan and Claypool, 2011), ch. 5.

both civil and military domains, whenever a coordinate deployment of human and technological resources is required.

In order to exemplify the idea of a socio-technical system, let us consider military or civilian aviation systems, starting from the aeroplane and moving up to the manned aircraft and, finally, to an aviation system as a whole. A modern aeroplane is a technological system resulting from a complex set of integrated technological components, such as the fuselage and the wings (with various control surfaces, including the rudder, stabilizers, flaps and so on), the propeller, the cockpit (with all control, navigation and information devices, such as the autopilot and a collision avoidance system). Aeroplanes as well as their components are technical artefacts – that is, physical objects endowed 'with a technical function and use plan'.[7] Each technical artefact was designed and made by human beings, possibly supported by other technical artefacts, such as software for computer-aided design. Most technical artefacts result from the integration of components. These components – such as an aeroplane's wings and cockpit, in the above example – may recursively include further technical artefacts.

Manned aeroplanes are supposed to be driven by humans (pilots). Therefore, a flying aircraft is usually a hybrid socio-technical entity including human operators (pilots) and the aeroplane (with all of its technological components). The integration of human and technological components is performed according to the use plan for the aeroplane (the instructions for its use), as understood and applied by the pilots. An unmanned aircraft is also a hybrid entity, including the aeroplane, the remote cockpit and remote pilots; the aeroplane, however, can operate independently when communications break down. Finally, the manned aircraft today is not an isolated system (as it could have been at the beginning of aviation); it is rather a component of a larger socio-technical system – civil or military aviation, which includes airports, their management, air traffic control infrastructures (which include both sophisticated technical equipment and trained individuals), the global positioning system (with its satellites) and many other systems providing information and support to aircraft.

Each component of a complex and multi-layered socio-technical system, such as an aeroplane, has a partial function to play in the overall working of the system – this function being defined by the specific role of

[7] *Ibid.*, 7.

that component.[8] The role of a component is first determined by the designers of the component and then is specified by those who have integrated the component into the higher units and from these units into the whole system. Thus, on the one hand, the designers of a component of an aeroplane have provided the component with the capacity to exercise a certain set of abstract functions, and, on the other hand, the builders of the aeroplane have integrated the component into the aeroplane, by assigning it a more specific role. For instance, a central processing unit, while having the abstract capacity to execute any algorithms, may be embedded in an aeroplane collision avoidance system, with the specific and exclusive function of computing trajectories of incoming objects.

We may ask, with regard to each component of a system, be it human or technological, what its independence is in the context of that system. Independence cannot just concern a component's ability to perform its specific function (for instance, the altimeter capacity to signal height), since then any component would be independent in its specific function. Rather, it concerns the extent to which the component is supposed to accomplish on its own, without contributions from other components, a certain high-level task, pertaining to the system we are considering. Thus, while the sound component of a collision avoidance system is supposed to respond with a sound to a certain numerical message coming from the collision detection component of that system, it plays a very limited role in the task of alerting the pilot to possible collisions, a task that pertains to the collision avoidance system as a whole. Similarly, the collision avoidance system in a modern aircraft is fully independent with regard to the task of detecting potential collisions and giving resolution advisories to pilots, instructing them on how to avoid such collisions (by telling one aeroplane to go up and the other to go down), but it is not fully independent with regard to the higher-level task of avoiding conflicts, which concerns the aeroplane-pilot system as a whole. In fact, the final determination on whether to comply with resolution advisories is still up to the pilots, even though they have the obligation to comply with the advisories unless they have reason to believe that by complying they would be putting safety at risk. As this example shows, we may also consider the independence of sets of components, possibly integrated

---

[8] On the notion of a function, see also the references to the technical and philosophical literature, see W. Houkes and P. Vermaas, *Technical Functions: On the Use and Design of Artefacts* (New York: Springer, 2010).

into subsystems (such as a collision avoidance system), with regard to the performance of particular tasks or subtasks. From this perspective, the whole technological apparatus of a socio-technical system, i.e., the set of all the hardware and software components of the system, is independent to the extent to which it can perform systemic functions without human contributions (for instance, to the extent to which an unmanned aircraft can execute its mission without any human control).

In many cases the determination of a course of action is allocated to a technological apparatus, but operators may override the determinations of that apparatus. For instance, cars or aeroplanes guided by autopilots instantiate a hybrid decision-making process, in which technology has the task of determining the actions to be taken under normal conditions, and humans have the task of checking indicia of exceptional conditions – such as an imminent collision danger – and of overriding the system when such conditions are likely to obtain. Thus, the technology is not fully independent in the performance of the system's task, since its functioning can be overridden by humans, nor are humans, since they are supposed to interfere only when they have appropriate evidence and the capacity to do better.

A twist in the notion of independence is that an agent (either human or artificial) may also have the ability to choose to enter into dependencies with others – on the basis of communicative and social skills that enable it to interact with the others – in order to better achieve certain goals or to achieve goals that it cannot achieve on its own. In fact, in social and legal contexts, autonomy also includes one's capacity to bind oneself, for instance, through contracts and promises and, in this way, to establish exchanges and collaborations. For instance, compare two drones: the first one is exploring an area on its own, the second one is exploring a part of a larger area, after negotiating with other drones regarding which parts each is exploring and exchanging information with other drones on significant aspects of the explored areas. Similarly, compare a military drone that is performing a mission on its own and sending the results to its remote base and a drone that is able to interact with a remote pilot while performing the mission, asking for instructions when alternatives are available or when certain conditions are met (for example, an approaching threat) and performing further inquiries when requested to do so. While the first drone in these comparisons relies only on its own equipment for the performance of its mission, the second has a larger space for action and choice, namely on the basis of its capacities for communication and coordination with others.

Finally, we must also distinguish between what we may call capability-independence, namely the capacity of a system to accomplish a task, and organizational independence, which concerns the fact that the system is supposed to achieve that task within the socio-technical infrastructure as a whole – that is, it is supposed to exercise independence within that infrastructure. There may be a mismatch between the two independencies. On the one hand, a system having the capacity for independent action may have no concrete possibility to deploy this capacity in its socio-technical environment since the system only participates in work-flows where it is subject to external monitoring and direction. Consider, for instance, a drone that has the capacity for autonomous flight, but which is guided by its remote pilots during all of its missions. On the other hand, a system without the capacity to independently perform a task may still be required to accomplish that task without external guidance, which is likely to lead to systemic failure. Consider, for example, a drone that is unable to independently keep its flight under extreme wind conditions, which is left on its own by the remote pilot under such conditions, and consequently crashes.

Dimensions of autonomy: cognitive skills

Independence only provides a partial perspective on the autonomy of a technological component. For instance, a landmine is completely independent in performing the operation for which it is deployed, namely blasting when a human or vehicle passes over it. However, it possesses very limited cognitive skills: it simply discriminates between two states (a pressure that is inferior or not inferior to the threshold), and it invariably links a single action to each one of these states (doing nothing or blasting). We would not consider the exercise of this simple reactive capacity as full-fledged 'autonomous decision making'.

On the other hand, consider a collision avoidance system issuing resolution advisories to pilots or a targeting system following targets and calculating trajectories until an operator pushes the 'fire' button. Such systems are not independent with regard to avoiding the collision (it is up to the pilot to comply with the advisory) or hitting the target (it is up to the operator to push the button). However, they perform autonomously highly complex discriminative functions, distinguishing many possible input states, integrating many different features of such states to determine what circumstances are most probable to obtain, and proposing the action that is most likely to produce the desired outcome under the given circumstances.[9] Consider also a face recognition system used for identifying individuals who are requesting access to a military facility, while the decision as to how to handle the identified and non-identified individuals lies with the competent security officers. Such a system is not independent when it comes to deciding what action to adopt with regard to the identified individuals, but it performs autonomously a knowledge-intensive cognitive (discriminatory) task by matching sensory clues from the scene and the stored features of the faces of listed individuals.

As these examples show, a second dimension of autonomy concerns cognitive skills. The larger the cognitive task assigned to an artificial system, the more we can say that this system is autonomous under this second dimension. It is autonomous in the sense that it performs a significant cognitive task by using its own abilities, which means that the resulting knowledge is to a larger extent the outcome of the activity of the system itself (rather than being provided to it as an external input). We may distinguish the different activities that are involved in a task that culminates in a decision to be taken and an action to be performed: acquisition and classification of input data (for example, sensing the environment to extract patterns of pressure, light or heat); information analysis to extract from the available data further information (for example, weather forecasts; determination of locations of possible targets); decision and action selection – that is, the construction and adoption of plans of action (for example, flight routes and ballistic flight paths) and plan implementation, which involves the performing of the planned actions under the indicated conditions and monitoring the plan execution (for example, flying according to the established route).

In each of these different activities, automation can play a larger or a smaller role, absorbing more or less of the involved cognitive skills.[10] With regard to the acquisition of input data, the system may simply provide the operator with whatever rough input data it obtains through its sensors, or it can take a more active role, eliminating noise, integrating data from different sources and filtering out irrelevant aspects or highlighting relevant ones. With regard to information analysis, an

[9] On measuring the discriminative capacity of a system, see G. Tononi, 'Consciousness as integrated information: a provisional manifesto', The Biological Bulletin, 215 (2008), 216.

[10] See L. Save and B. Feuerberg, 'Designing human-automation interaction: a new level of automation taxonomy' in D. De Waard, K. Brookhuis, F. Dehais, C. Weikert, S. Röttger, D. Manzey, S. Biede, F. Reuzeau and P. Terrier (eds.), Human Factors: A View from an Integrative Perspective. Proceedings of the HFES Europe Chapter Conference, Toulouse (Groningen: HFES Europe, 2012), 43.

automated system may provide, either on its initiative or upon request, different analyses of the situation (for example, anticipating weather conditions on the expected flight trajectories or possible encounters) and take the initiative of alerting the operator of possible risks (for example, bad weather or approaching objects). With regard to decision and action selection, the automated component could (i) make suggestions to human operators, who are then free to decide otherwise if they opine differently; (ii) offer an exhaustive list of options, among which operators must choose; (iii) choose directly the option to be implemented, informing the operators (who may or may not have the possibility of interrupting the action); or (iv) choose an option without providing any information. Consider, for instance, the case of a collision avoidance system, which presents pilots with instructions, or of an autopilot, which decides on its own the aircraft route but which may be overridden by human pilots. Consider also the case of a robotic weapon system that responds directly to an attack, with or without the possibility of a human intervention to monitor and override the determinations of the system.

Finally, the share delegated to an automated component with regard to action execution may be less or more intensive. A human may start and monitor the execution, with the system providing support information (for example, on the evolution of the flight/trajectory, possibly highlighting variations from what was planned). Alternatively, the system itself may start execution, with the operator having (i) the possibility to intervene and override; (ii) just the possibility of interrupting execution under extreme conditions; or (iii) no possibility to monitor and intervene.

In conclusion, in all of these cognitive activities – information acquisition, information analysis, action decision and action implementation – we may say that the autonomy of a device increases as the device is delegated a larger share of the required cognitive tasks. This may lead to an increased independence of the device from human intervention or, rather, to an increased interaction/collaboration between the human and the artificial component. The fact that humans remain in the loop – contributing to the choice of options to be undertaken or having the power to override or interrupt the implementation of the machine-selected options – does not exclude the possibility of technological devices executing the larger share of the cognitive functions involved in the performance of the task. These functions may indeed be coupled with the ability to interact with human operators, receiving and transmitting information and negotiating with them the actions to be executed.

Human operators may anticipate certain features of the cognitive determinations that will be adopted by automated devices. However, anticipations will usually only concern abstract features of the working of the device; it would be impossible, or in any case impractical, for humans to repeat each single information processing operation performed by the device, upon every input item. Thus, the pilot, having delegated to the flight management system the task of maintaining the route to the destination, may assume that the system will make all of the adjustments needed for this purpose, without knowing what these adjustments will be (the pilot may be resting or may be engaged in other operations while the system manages the flight) and without reproducing the computational processes that the system will execute for this purpose. Rather, the pilot will anticipate certain aspects of behaviour of the system, on the basis of his awareness of the general function (keeping the route) of the system and of certain sub-functions needed for this purpose (keeping the height and balance of the aircraft, turning at the appropriate points, reacting in certain ways to incoming winds and so on). The pilot, in other terms, will adopt the strategy that Dennett calls the 'design stance': he will describe and anticipate the behaviour of the flight system on the assumption that the system will perform the functions for which it has been designed, as these functions are described in its use-plan.[11]

In certain cases, it may even be appropriate to approach a system by using what Daniel Dennett calls the 'intentional stance', i.e., making the assumption that the system has certain objectives and will make the choices that are best suited to achieve those objectives, given the information (the beliefs) that it has. Thus, in the case of an advanced flight management system, the pilot may anticipate the behaviour of the system by assuming that the system is pursuing a set of goals, such as maintaining the route, getting to its destination in time, economizing fuel and so on, and that the system will make whatever determinations are appropriate to this purpose, on the basis of the information available to it. When we adopt the design stance, or the intentional stance, our ability to foresee the behaviour of a system does not depend on our knowledge of the ways in which the system is built or on the knowledge of its internal mechanism. Rather, it depends on the assumption that the system has the capacity to determine itself to behave in ways that are appropriate to its goals. Thus, our ability to forecast the behaviour of a purposive system does not exclude, but, rather, presupposes, the system's autonomous capacity to achieve its goals.

[11] D. C. Dennett, *The Intentional Stance* (Cambridge, MA: MIT Press, 1989).

In general, when a human designer or operator delegates a cognitive function to a technological system, the following holds true:

- the delegator chooses to delegate choices instrumental to the execution of that function to the cognitive skills of the delegate system;
- the delegator does not know, and thus does not intentionally pre-select, what the delegated system will choose to do in future situations.

The fact that the operator has not fully anticipated the behaviour of the delegated system does not constitute a limitation or a failure in the use of that system, but, rather, it is the very reason why a cognitive system is used: to substitute human cognition when it is not required or not available.

While we need to distinguish the ideas of independence and cognition, there is a connection between the two, in the sense that the delegation of a cognitive activity may involve a degree of independent determination and decision making, according to the openness of the delegation at issue – that is, to the extent to which the delegator under-determines the object of the delegation and the ways of achieving that object.[12] For addressing openness by making appropriate determinations, corresponding cognitive skills may be needed. For example, the delegated artefact must possess the capacity to engage in means–end determinations, if its input instructions indicate the objective to be achieved, but do not specify the ways to achieve this objective.

Dimensions of autonomy: cognitive-behavioural architecture

The previous sections have focused on the independent performance of tasks delegated to a technological device and on the cognitive skills deployed in these tasks. Here we shall consider which kind of cognitive and behavioural architectures may support independence and cognition in an autonomous artificial agent. For this purpose, we shall distinguish adaptiveness and teleology, as architectural dimensions enabling the exercise of autonomy. Moreover, we shall address interaction architectures for the autonomy of multi-agent systems.

Adaptiveness

John Holland provides the following overarching definition of an adaptive agent,[13] which covers any kind of system (biological, ecological,

---

[12] See C. Castelfranchi and R. Falcone, 'Towards a theory of delegation for agent-based systems', *Robotics and Autonomous Systems*, 24 (1998), 141.

[13] J. Holland, *Signals and Boundaries Building Blocks for Complex Adaptive Systems* (Cambridge, MA: MIT Press, 2012), 24.

technological or social): 'Adaptive agents are defined by an enclosing boundary that accepts some signals and ignores others, a "program" inside the boundary for processing and sending signals, and mechanisms for changing (adapting) this program in response to the agent's accumulating experience.' We may also say that an artificial system is adaptive when its behaviour is auto-teleonomic – that is, when the system has the capacity to change its patterns of behaviour in order to better achieve its purposes, in the particular environment in which it operates (such purposes being selected by the system itself, provided by its user, or hardwired in its architecture).[14] Consequently, an adaptive system exhibits the following main features:

- it interacts with its environment, getting inputs and providing outputs;
- on the basis of environmental inputs, it changes the internal states on which its behaviour depends.

According to the above criteria, an autonomous system must have the capacity to modify itself in order to better align its behaviour to its intended purposes in the context in which it operates. Thus, an adaptive system needs to have a feedback or homeostatic mechanism, which keeps the system focused on its objective by changing its internal state as the environment changes, and so enabling the system to act as required by the changed environment. For instance, the automatic pilot in a drone needs to be able to react to changing environmental conditions, such as speed and direction of the wind, and adapt its flight parameters so as still to be able to reach its destination under the changed conditions. This capacity is sometimes called autonomicity.[15]

Obviously, highly intelligent systems fully qualify for adaptiveness, which would be the case, for instance, if a car was able to conduct itself in such a way as to discharge its purpose, overcoming various issues that may emerge along the way, such as encounters with other cars, signals, road blockages and being able to plan and replan its route. Similarly, a drone that is able to determine and modify its flight route and possibly even to recognize its targets under different environmental conditions would be classified as an adaptive artefact.

---

[14] C. Castelfranchi and R. Falcone, 'From automaticity to autonomy: the frontier of artificial agents' in H. Hexmoor, C. Castelfranchi and R. Falcone (eds.), *Agent Autonomy* (New York: Springer, 2003), 103.

[15] As the capacity to govern itself, see W. Truszkowski, L. Hallock, C. Rouff, J. Karlin, J. Rash, M. G. Hinchey and R. Sterritt, *Autonomous and Autonomic Systems* (New York: Springer, 2009).

However, a limited capacity for adaptive action can also be found in less advanced systems. For instance, even a remotely piloted aircraft system that is just capable of maintaining the route established by the remote pilot – by monitoring its position and modifying its flight plan to remedy deviations caused by external conditions, such as wind or pressure – would qualify for limited adaptiveness. Similarly, an intelligent bomb able to track its target and adjust its trajectory to the movement of the target would also meet the requirements for adaptiveness. Both systems would be able to interact with the environment and adjust their internal states and, consequently, their behaviour as needed to accomplish their tasks.

We exclude adaptiveness in automated entities that receive input from their environment but are merely reactive, since they provide a predetermined action for each such input. In such cases, the interaction with predetermined aspects of the environment triggers different responses of the system, but it does not change the internal state of the system and thus its behavioural patterns. As a simple example of a non-adaptive system, consider a homeostatic system that maintains a certain temperature by reacting in a predetermined way – for example, switching on or off a heater – to any possible misalignment from the target temperature.

On the other hand, adaptiveness should be attributed to artefacts that have the capability to learn, so as to increase their capacity to face similar circumstances in the future (increasing successes and diminishing failures). Consider, for instance, the case of a target-recognition system based on a neural network. Such a system would improve its performance through reinforcement learning by strengthening the neural connections that have enabled correct identifications of targets and by weakening the connections that have led to mistaken identifications. As a result of this learning process, the system would achieve arrangements of its network that were not anticipated when the system was put in place.

Adaptiveness is a precondition of cognitive autonomy, since it means that the behavioural patterns of the system are not pre-arranged at the design stage. The designers of an adaptive system only specify the behavioural patterns of the system at a meta-level, namely, by providing the system with a learning mechanism through which it can determine its behavioural patterns, on the basis of its experience. As Stuart Russell and Peter Norvig argue, there is no autonomy 'to the extent that an agent relies on prior knowledge of its designer rather than on its own percepts'.[16] An autonomous agent must be able to learn 'what it can to compensate for partial or incorrect prior knowledge'.

Teleology

A teleologic system is characterized by the fact that it has an explicit representation of its basic cognitive states such as:

- goals – as representational structures that specify objectives to be achieved by the system;
- beliefs – as representational structures that track aspects of the environment;
- plans – as representational structures that specify how to reach the goals, given the beliefs, through actions of the system.

A teleologic system includes the features that characterize the so-called belief-desire-intention (BDI) architecture for intelligent agents.[17] In order to realize its desires (goals), the teleologic system constructs plans of action on the basis of its model of the relevant facts (beliefs) and commits itself to act according to the chosen plans (intentions). Note that by using the terminology of beliefs, desires and intentions to denote cognitive structures of artificial systems, we are not assuming that such structures are similar to those existing in the human mind. The only assumption is that BDI systems share with the homonymous human mental states the functions that we associate with such mental states (indicating objectives, tracking the environment and directing future actions).

A teleologic system, according to this characterization, is necessarily adaptive, since it selects its plans exactly in order to achieve its goals, given its beliefs, which reflect its changing environment. Such a system performs both epistemic cognition and practical cognition. In its epistemic cognition, it adopts new beliefs on relevant aspects of the environment, given pre-existing inputs (perceptions) and beliefs. In its practical cognition, it adopts new sub-goals and plans, given its pre-existing goals and beliefs. A teleologic system, for instance, can be implemented in a drone having the goal of destroying a target. The achievement of this goal would require that the drone flies to the target zone, identifies the

---

[16] Russell and Norvig, *Artificial Intelligence*, 39.

[17] A. S. Rao and M. P. Georgeff, 'Modelling rational agents within a BDI architecture' in R. Fikes and E. Sandewall (eds.), *Proceedings of Knowledge Representation and Reasoning* (New York: Springer, 1991), 473.

target, and then selects and implements a way to eliminate it. Such a drone would have an internally stored representation of its goals, acquire inputs from the environment, process such inputs to determine the relevant environmental conditions, identify its target, develop and implement flight plans to reach the target and then select and carry out action plans to destroy it.

According to this characterization, teleologic systems are a strict subset of adaptive systems. For instance, a sensor system based on a neural network, which discriminates between different signals and learns to improve its outputs through a learning process, qualifies as an adaptive system while not being a teleologic one. In a non-teleologic, but adaptive, system, behavioural patterns are selected on the basis of the fact that they achieve the purpose of the system, but cognition is only implicitly represented in the internal states of the system. While the internal states that specify the system's behavioural patterns – for example, the arrangements of a neural network – are selected on the basis of environmental inputs and the system's goals, the system does not model explicitly the environment and its goals.

Not only individual artefacts, but also collectives of them, can have an adaptive non-teleologic behaviour. This is the case for collectives endowed with swarm intelligence. In fact, the purpose-oriented behaviour of such collectives emerges from the actions of the individuals, though this purpose is not present in the individuals themselves, which blindly reproduce simple patterns of action. In the military domain, this may apply to drones flying in a flock, where the persistence of the flight formation is only determined by the fact that each drone keeps a certain distance from the others. Similarly, a set of land vehicles involved in the elimination of landmines may cover all of the area to be cleaned since each of them follows certain simple rules concerning movements and distances from the others.[18]

The cognitive architecture of a teleological system may include additional components, which may enable higher levels of autonomy. For instance, John Pollock distinguishes values from desires, arguing that while desires (goals) prompt an intelligent system to develop plans of action, values enable it to assess the comparative merits of such plans.[19] Similarly, Cristiano Castelfranchi and Fabio Paglieri

---

[18] On the possibilities of achieving complex behaviour without a teleological architecture, see R. A. Brooks, *Cambrian Intelligence* (Cambridge, MA: MIT Press, 1999).

[19] J. L. Pollock, *Thinking about Acting: Logical Foundations for Rational Decision Making* (Oxford University Press, 2006).

argue for the need to distinguish different kinds of goals according to the role they play in guiding action.[20] Thus, an agent able to be guided not only by desires but also by values would gain an increased level of adaptiveness/teleology.

Another important extension for a teleological system would consist in the capacity to be guided by norms, operating as (possibly defeasible) constraints over the system's teleological reasoning.[21] Many interesting issues pertain to engineering the norm-following behaviour of autonomous systems.[22] Two techniques may be distinguished to constrain the behaviour of a robotic system:

- regimentation: it is impossible for the system to violate the norm – that is, the norm is modelled in the system's architecture as an overriding exception (as indefeasible constraints, pre-empting means–end reasoning);
- normative guidance: it is possible for the system to act against the norm, depending on the outcome of its deliberative process (the norm is just a defeasible constraint, to be followed unless there are overriding reasons against compliance).

It seems that only teleologic systems can be fully endowed with the capacity to be guided by norms, as elements that play a specific role in the deliberative process of such systems. At most, merely adaptive systems could be trained through reinforcement learning, so that they acquire the tendency to avoid undesired behaviour. Norm guidance raises a number of difficult issues pertaining to the application of norms to concrete situations. In particular, norm-governed artificial systems should be endowed with the motivation to respect the applicable norms, and should be able to recognize operative facts that trigger normative outcomes according to such norms. For example, a norm-guided weapon system should be able to recognize that a certain object is a civilian facility, which should not be targeted. Additional cognitive skills are required to combine norm- and value-based thinking in order to address the conflicts of norms and underlying goals.

---

[20] C. Castelfranchi and F. Paglieri, 'The role of beliefs in goal dynamics: prolegomena to a constructive theory of intention', *Synthese*, 155 (2007), 237.

[21] On norms in robots for the military, see R. Arkin, *Governing Lethal Behavior in Autonomous Robots* (Boca Raton, FL: CRC Press, 2009).

[22] For various considerations, see *ibid*. See also W. Wallach and C. Allen, *Moral Machines: Teaching Robots Right from Wrong* (Oxford University Press, 2008).

A further layer of architectural autonomy – available in artificial systems only to a very limited extent – would consist in a system being reflective, namely being able to access its cognitive states (beliefs, desires, intentions and values) and to question the merit of having such states on the basis of other cognitive states. A fully reflexive system would be able to ask itself whether it should have a certain belief, given the evidence it has, whether it should have a certain intention, given its objectives, whether it should endorse a certain norm, given the effects of complying with that norm, whether it should have certain objectives, given its values.

Multi-level autonomy

The mere duality system level / component level (or macro-level/micro-level) cannot fully express the articulation of complex artificial systems.[23] Intermediate notions – such as meso-level, subsystem and system of systems – are to be used in order to capture a complexity that approaches more and more the complexity of natural systems, and in particular the hierarchical organization of biological systems.[24] Accordingly, an account of architectures enabling autonomy requires developing a more articulated pattern than the mere system–component dichotomy, i.e., the pattern of multi-level autonomy.

A starting point is the observation that what a component is, what a system is, and what their mutual relationship is, is a matter of choice by either the observer (or the scientist's viewpoint) or the designer (the engineer's viewpoint). Whether a technical artefact is taken to be a component of a system or a system as a whole simply depends on the most suitable level of abstraction adopted in observing and designing the artefact. For instance, a cockpit can be viewed as either a component of an aeroplane or a multi-component system by itself. As a result, the dimensions of autonomy considered here – independence, cognitive skills and cognitive architecture – need to be applied along a whole hierarchy of system–subsystems relationships in order to fully exploit their modelling power. The need for this can be easily understood by observing well-known complex social systems, such as ant societies or urban traffic. In ant societies, for instance, ants can be seen to be the main independent components, whose behaviour can be roughly depicted as

---

[23] F. Zambonelli and A. Omicini, 'Challenges and research directions in agent-oriented software engineering', *Autonomous Agents and Multi-Agent Systems*, 9 (2004), 253.

[24] M. Grene, 'Hierarchies in biology', *American Scientist*, 75 (1987), 504.

being automatic. However, the system they belong to – the ant society – clearly exhibits a meaningful level of adaptiveness, which is not inherited from its components, coming instead from their way of interacting. The traffic management system of a modern city is also an easy example of teleologic components (human-driven vehicles) that compose a teleonomic, adaptive system (the city traffic as a whole) whose cognitive architecture is not directly entailed by the cognitive architecture of its components.

In software engineering, the notion of an agent is used both to model autonomy and to encapsulate autonomy in software architectures. When addressing the systemic issues of autonomous weapons systems (AWS), however, the more articulated notion of multi-agent systems (MAS) is required,[25] as an ensemble of autonomous agents, each one with its own individual goals, interacting (communicating, collaborating, cooperating and coordinating) towards the achievement of the overall designed systemic goal. Nowadays, most of the complex computational systems of interest can be conceived, modelled and engineered as MAS. As a result, discussing multi-level autonomy in the context of MAS makes it possible to understand the potential consequences of such a notion for artificial systems, in general, and for AWS, in particular.

A group of agents coordinating in order to achieve some (local, non-individual) goal is called an agent society. Coordination models are the cores around which agent societies can be built.[26] Coordination media are the computational abstractions working as the social components that encapsulate social (coordination) laws and gear an agent group towards the achievement of the social goal while (possibly) respecting the individual agent's autonomy.[27] For instance, norms represent one of the best-known coordination mechanisms, whereas computational institutions (which are also known as electronic institutions[28]) play the role of coordination abstractions provided by the middleware.

[25] W. van der Hoek and M. Wooldridge, 'Multi-agent systems' in F. van Harmelen, V. Lifschitz and B. Porter (eds.), *Handbook of Knowledge Representation* (Amsterdam: Elsevier, 2008), 887.

[26] D. Gelernter and N. Carriero, 'Coordination languages and their significance', *Communications of the ACM*, 35 (1992), 97.

[27] P. Ciancarini, 'Coordination models and languages as software integrators', *ACM Computing Surveys*, 28 (1996), 300.

[28] P. Noriega and C. Sierra, 'Electronic institutions: future trends and challenges' in M. Klusch, S. Ossowski and O. Shehory (eds.), *Cooperative Information Agents VI* (New York: Springer, 2002), 14.

From a software engineering viewpoint, agent societies may be seen as representing a layering mechanism,[29] where agents and societies, and the corresponding individual and social goals, can be used as abstraction tools. Each group of agents could be seen in principle as a single agent at a higher level of abstraction, and, vice versa, each agent could be modelled/built as an agent society at a deeper level of detail, with the global MAS level working as the uppermost layer. Accordingly, individual/social/global goals could in principle be layered in the same way. Thus, the notion of layering allows the complexity of system–subsystem relationships to be captured and modelled, potentially matching the complexity of natural systems.

As a result, an MAS could, in principle, be conceived, designed and built as an autonomous system made of autonomous components. Even more, each agent society could be handled in the same way. Thus, autonomy could be conceived as a multi-level property of computational systems designed as an MAS, a property that is associated with each agent, with the agent societies, and with the global MAS level as well. The key point is the fact that conceptually there is no direct dependence between the diverse levels of autonomy at the different levels of the MAS. In coordinated systems, the coordination media could embed (i) the reactive behaviour for an automatic coordinated behaviour, (ii) the implicit mechanisms for a teleonomic behaviour of the agent society or (iii) the operational plans for teleologic social behaviour.[30] All of these options are independent of the level of autonomy of the individual agents composing the agent society.

This is exactly what happens in the social systems used earlier as examples – that is, ant societies and urban traffic. For instance, according to both ethologists[31] and computer scientists,[32] coordination mechanisms (stigmergy, in particular) are what makes 'automatic' ants build up

---

[29] A. Molesini, A. Omicini, A. Ricci and E. Denti, 'Zooming multi-agent systems' in J. Müller and F. Zambonelli (eds.), *Agent-Oriented Software Engineering VI* (New York: Springer, 2006), 81.

[30] This could be achieved, for instance, by adopting ReSpecT tuple centres as coordination media, see A. Omicini and E. Denti, 'From tuple spaces to tuple centres', *Science of Computer Programming*, 41 (2001), 277.

[31] P.-P. Grassé, 'La reconstruction du nid et les coordinations interindividuelles chez Bellicositermes natalensis et Cubitermes sp. La théorie de la stigmergie: essai d'interprétation du comportement des termites constructeurs', *Insectes Sociaux*, 6 (1959), 41.

[32] H. V. D. Parunak, '"Go to the ant": engineering principles from natural multi-agent systems', *Annals of Operations Research*, 75 (1997), 69.

robustly adaptive ant societies. In urban traffic systems, cognitive stigmergy coordination makes teleologic components build up a complex
adaptive system.[33]

A more articulated reference model for MAS, such as the A&A (Agents
and Artefacts) meta-model,[34] could make the picture even more intri-
cate. In fact, an MAS is basically composed by agents and artefacts, where
artefacts (as the tools that agents use to achieve their own goals) are
typically automatic deterministic entities. However, by extending the
layering to include artefacts as well, any level of an MAS, in theory,
could feature any sort of automatic/autonomic/autonomous behaviour,
independently of any other individual/social/global property. Thus,
determining to what extent, and at what levels, a complex MAS (or, in
general, any complex artificial system) is automatic, adaptive, or teleologic generally requires an in-depth analysis. The picture could be made
simpler by assuming that the global level of autonomy of an MAS is the
only relevant system feature. However, issues such as responsibility and
liability cannot be *a priori* reduced to the simple observation of the main
level of an MAS. For instance, an individual agent may participate at the
same time in more than one MAS, possibly expressing different levels of
independence, cognitive skills or cognitive architecture in diverse contexts. Moreover, a single component of more than one system could in
principle work as an element of inter-system interference, possibly unde-
tected, which could make issues such as responsibility and liability much
more complex.

This holds true, for instance, when dealing with non-determinism,
such as stochastic behaviour in nature-inspired models. In fact, upper-
level behaviour could appear by emergence without any linear connection with the lower-level components – as in the case of swarm systems,
cited earlier. When coordination artefacts are used to encapsulate local
interactions leading to self-organizing behaviours, teleonomic components that self-organize around deterministic-automatic coordination
media could give rise to totally unpredictable system behaviour.
However, such behaviour may be classified as being adaptive since it
tends to autonomously preserve some essential system properties when
the environment changes. The system's behaviour can even (possibly) be

[33] A. Ricci, A. Omicini, M. Viroli, L. Gardelli and E. Oliva, 'Cognitive stigmergy: towards
a framework based on agents and artifacts' in D. Weyns, H. V. D. Parunak and M. Fabien
(eds.), *Environments for Multi-Agent Systems III* (Springer, 2007), 124.
[34] A. Omicini, A. Ricci and M. Viroli, 'Artifacts in the A&A meta-model', *Autonomous
Agents and Multi-Agent Systems*, 17 (2008), 532.

classified as being teleologic when coordination artefacts contain the local policies explicitly designed to produce the overall self-organizing behaviour.[35]

Autonomy in weapons systems

The three dimensions of autonomy we have described – independence, cognitive skills and cognitive architecture – are not always jointly present. First of all, independence in the performance of a task does not entail high-level cognitive capacities, not even those that would be needed to appropriately perform the task, nor does it require a developed cognitive architecture. For instance, a landmine is fully independent in its operation, but has little discriminative capacity and no adaptive or teleological architecture. On the other hand, possessing and deploying high-level cognitive skills does not entail independence in the exercise of delegated tasks, as such tasks may be accomplished collaboratively through interaction and communication with other artificial or human agents. Consider, for instance, an intelligence flight system on a military drone, which provides information and suggestions to the remote pilot and receives requests and commands from the latter.

Cognitive performance also does not necessarily require adaptiveness since pre-programmed capacities may be sufficient for the tasks at stake. Consider, for instance, a weapon such as a torpedo or a missile, which directs itself to a source of noise or heat. In such cases, the weapon may not even need to store the position of the source; it may be sufficient that when sensing the noise or heat emitted by the source, the weapon changes its direction in such a way as to approach its target. In this example the environment itself, as perceived through the device sensor, is the source of the needed information, without being modelled inside the device.[36] The capacity to pursue goals through contextualized planning (teleology) also may not be needed since the contribution of the system may be limited to the collection and analysis of information. Consider, for instance, the component of a targeting or security system that deals with the recognition of movements and faces.

---

[35] A. Omicini, A. Ricci, M. Viroli, C. Castelfranchi and L. Tummolini, 'Coordination artifacts: environment-based coordination for intelligent agents' in *Proceedings of the Third International Joint Conference on Autonomous Agents and Multiagent Systems* (Washington, DC: IEEE, 2004), 286.

[36] On relying on environmental inputs for intelligent behaviour, see Brooks, *Cambrian Intelligence*, ch. 3.

However, there is a connection between these three dimensions. Cognitive features (skills and architecture) may increase the scope for autonomy as independence – in particular, independence pertaining to the accomplishment of actions requiring cognition such as learning and decision making. Such features may, on the other hand, also increase the system's capacity to interact with others and possibly to undertake commitments with them, recognize their authority and comply with their requests.

The three dimensions of autonomy are present, to different degrees, in a number of systems that are deployed in the military domain. This chapter will focus on those tasks that support the use of force – that is, target selection and engagement. The crucial phase is represented by target selection, which involves 'the determination that an individual target or a specific group of targets is to be engaged' – as specified in the US 2012 Directive on Autonomy in Weapons Systems.[37]

This directive distinguishes autonomous and semi-autonomous weapons depending on their role in targeting. Autonomous weapons are those that 'once activated, can select and engage targets without further intervention by a human operator', while semi-autonomous weapons systems are 'intended to only engage individual targets or specific target groups that have been selected by a human operator'. The directive sets restrictions on the use of autonomous weapons, which should only be used to apply non-lethal, non-kinetic force. Under human supervision, however, autonomous systems may engage non-human targets for the defence of manned installations or platforms. Semi-autonomous weapons systems, on the other hand, may be deployed for any purpose, including the exercise of lethal force against humans, subject only to certification.

As observed by Mark Gubrud, the distinction between autonomous and semi-autonomous weapons is questionable and possibly misleading since semi-autonomous weapons also contribute to selecting targets to be hit.[38] In fact, we can often distinguish two phases in the targeting process involving semi-autonomous weapons: first humans delimit the domain of the targets to be selected (the objects within a certain area or having certain properties) and then the machine selects what particular objects to engage within that domain. This applies to all weapons that exercise an ability to actively engage targets, i.e., to all 'projectiles, bombs, missiles,

---

[37] US Department of Defense (DoD) Directive 3000.09, 'Autonomy in weapon systems', 21 November 2012, available at www.dtic.mil/whs/directives/corres/pdf/300009p.pdf.

[38] M. Gubrud, 'Semiautonomous and on their own: killer robots in Plato's Cave', *Bulletin of the Atomic Scientists Online* (April 2015).

torpedoes and other weapons that can actively correct for initial-aiming or subsequent errors by homing on their targets or aim-points after being fired, released, or launched'.

In fact, these self-guided munitions can be divided into two categories, according to Paul Scharre and Michael Horowitz:[39] projectiles designed to hit a particular target based on its signature (go-onto-target) and projectiles designed to hit a particular geographic location where the target is located (go-onto-location-in-space). When launching such a projectile, the human operator gives it a generic description of its target, on the basis of the target features (the signature) or location. Then, it is up to the munitions to instantiate this generic description to a specific object, locking on to that object. Thus, the engagement of the target is the outcome of a double choice: the human choice to deploy the weapon, giving it a specific signature or location – a choice that restricts the possible targets of the weapon – and the weapon choice to select and engage a particular object. As observed by Gubrud, there is no reason for denying the decisional quality of this second choice, which may involve discrimination under conditions of uncertainty.[40] Consider, for instance, a missile launched to target battleships in a certain area, which has to determine whether to engage a particular ship depending on whether it is an innocent cruiser or an enemy vessel. Such a determination involves autonomy at least in two of the senses we have described, namely as independence (in selecting the target to engage within the assigned area) and as cognitive skill (in determining whether any particular ship encountered falls into the target description).

A semi-autonomous weapon may also rely on a cognitive architecture of the type described earlier (the teleological ability to develop plans on how to detect and engage the target, given the available information). As an example of such weapons, Gubrud discusses the long-range anti-ship missile that was released by Lockheed-Martin, which can 'reroute around unexpected threats, search for an enemy fleet, identify the one ship it will attack among others in the vicinity, and plan its final approach to defeat antimissile systems – all out of contact with any human decision maker (but possibly in contact with other missiles, which can work together as a team)'.[41]

---

[39] P. Scharre and M. C. Horowitz, 'An introduction to autonomy in weapon systems', CNAS Working Paper (February 2015).
[40] Gubrud, 'Semiautonomous and on their own'.   [41] *Ibid.*

Even when a human has the task of 'pushing the button', ordering a specifically identified target to be engaged, important aspects of the decisional process that leads to selection and engagement may be delegated to an automated system. In fact, the targeting process includes all aspects of decision making that we have described earlier, and all of them can be automated partially or totally: the acquisition and classification of input data about the potential targets, available resources and environmental conditions (through various kinds of sensors); information analysis to assess the aspects, features and locations of targets (through pattern recognition and computations); decision and action selection for determining how to engage the target (identifying and selecting a strategy); implementation of the chosen strategy (by directing the payload to the destination and possibly monitoring and adjusting trajectories). A distinction of the different ways in which humans may be involved in targeting is provided by Noel Sharkey, who distinguishes the following options, on a scale that is characterized by an increasing delegation of the targeting decision to the machine: 1. human deliberates about a target before initiating any attack; 2. machine provides a list of targets and human chooses which to attack; 3. machine selects target and human must approve before attack; 4. machine selects target and human has restricted time to veto; 5. machine selects target and initiates attack without human involvement.[42] According to Sharkey, only the first two levels are consistent with sufficient human control over the targeting process.

Since the integration of human and machine components in decision making does not exclude the fact that the machine exercises autonomy, we should not assume that the mere fact of keeping humans in the loop is sufficient to overcome the worries pertaining to the deployment of machine intelligence in targeting. Nor does human contribution and machine autonomy always provide a zero sum so that increasing the one entails a corresponding diminution of the other. Much depends on whether the machine autonomy is being deployed in order to restrict the need for human deliberation and situational awareness, or rather to expand it, by providing better knowledge and a larger set of reasons on which an appropriate action can be based.

---

[42] N. Sharkey, 'Towards a principle for the human supervisory control of robot weapons', *Politica e Società*, 3 (2014), 305.

Kinds of responsibilities

Let us now consider how the distinct dimensions of autonomy, and their convergence or mismatch, can affect the responsibilities related to the deployment of the artefacts instantiating such dimensions.[43]

The first notion of responsibility concerning technological components is functional responsibility, which joins functional failure with causality: the harm would not have resulted had the responsible component correctly exercised the function attributed to it. Indeed, any component and subcomponent of a socio-technical system may fail to exercise its function as expected. As a consequence, the system as a whole may fail, with harmful consequences, for which the malfunctioning component may be said to be responsible. For example, assume that a failure in the fuel gauge system causes an aeroplane to leave with insufficient fuel and thus to crash. In such a case, even though the interruption of the functioning of the propeller was the immediate cause of the fall of the aeroplane, we can say that the propeller was not functionally responsible for the crash, since it worked properly according to its use plan – responsibility is to be allocated to the fuel gauge system.

The second notion of responsibility concerns what we may call blameworthiness and consists of the fact that the failure that caused the harm involves a fault, namely a substandard behaviour in a moral agent. This kind of responsibility is hardly applicable to automated devices, even when they are autonomous, but it may concern their designers and integrators. Faulty design may result in the device's inability to exercise the abstract function attributed to it; faulty integration may result in the device's inability to implement its specific role in the system since this role does not match the device's abstract function. As an example of the first kind of fault, consider a computer supporting an automatic pilot in a drone or a targeting system. Should the computer circuits burn out due to a design failure, and should an accident result, then the fault is to be allocated to the developers of the computer. On the other hand, should the speed of the computer, as indicated by the producer, be insufficient for the timely performance of the needed computations, then the fault should be allocated to those who chose to include that component in the system.

---

[43] On responsibility in general, see H. L. A. Hart, *Punishment and Responsibility* (Oxford University Press, [1967] 2008), 210. See also M. Bovens, *The Quest for Responsibility: Accountability and Citizenship in Complex Organisations* (Cambridge University Press, 1998).

In general, the humans who design an automated device will be blameworthy for the harm caused by the device, when they negligently or intentionally contribute to delivering a device that either (a) would not achieve the intended function, or (b) would achieve the intended function, but this function necessarily entails unacceptable consequences. Similarly, the humans deploying a well-functioning automated device may be blameworthy for the harm caused by the device, when either (a) the device is used outside the circumstances where it should have been deployed, or (b) the device is used for its designed function, but this function necessarily involves unacceptable consequences.[44] Consider, for instance, landmines, which are devices that are highly independent in their operation but have insufficient capacities for discrimination and proportionate response. Blame for the damage resulting from landmines can be put both on the producer of the landmines, who has intentionally delivered a product that could only be used in violation of the laws of war, as well as upon those who decided to deploy landmines, knowing of their likely impacts on civilians. Alternatively, consider a flight management software program that stops working due to a programming mistake and causes an accident. Blame could be put on the developers of the software if due care could have prevented the mistake as well as on its integrators, if they installed the software on the aeroplane, knowing that it was unsafe or omitting sufficient controls.

In order to independently exercise its tasks, a system must possess different capacities: behavioural competence (the capacity to perform all of the actions that are needed to implement the tasks), epistemic competence (the ability to get all of the knowledge that is needed to act effectively and proportionately in the given context), practical reasoning skills (the ability to design and select a plan of actions that may achieve the purpose), even moral skills/attitudes (the ability to comply with the applicable norms and respect the relevant values). Should a system fail to possess all of these capacities, and should damage result from the lack of them, those who designed and deployed the system may be blameworthy and even criminally liable. Consider, for instance, the case of an autonomous missile used in naval warfare, which hits an innocent cruiser, exchanging it for an enemy battleship. Responsibility may be put both on the decision makers and designers who equipped the ship with missiles

---

[44] The responsibility of human users (commanders) for choice to deploy an autonomous system is addressed in the contribution by Pablo Kalmanovitz, 'Judgment, liability, and the risks of riskless warfare', Chapter 7 in this volume.

that did not possess the discriminating capacity required for their intended task, and on the commander who chose to deploy the missile.

Though blame for damage caused by an autonomous system can, at the state of the art, be properly attributed only to humans, there is a derived sense in which we may speak of blameworthiness also with regard to an artificial system. This may be the case when an autonomous system was supposed to comply with norms and take care of certain interests but has failed to meet such commitments. Blameworthiness of an autonomous system seems to presuppose that the system has a teleologic architecture and, moreover, that it can 'experience' blame, having emotions or some functional equivalent to emotions.[45] No system, at least among those commercially available, seems yet to fully possess such features. Science fiction writers, however, have addressed this possibility. For instance, Ian M. Banks describes an artificial intelligence that commits suicide since it is unable to overcome its sense of guilt after having participated in a disruptive war.[46]

Finally, a third notion of responsibility concerns legal liabilities for harm, which in tort law can extend well beyond the area where moral blameworthiness applies. In fact, tortious liability may be related to the mere causality of harm (strict liability), to the ownership or custody of the object that caused the harm (liability of owners or guardians), to being the principal to the agent who caused the harm (vicarious liability), to malfunctions resulting from faulty design or manufacturing (product liability), to failures in embedding the device into a larger system (again, design liability) and to failures in maintaining or deploying a device (negligence, vicarious liability and organizational liability). In the criminal domain, on the contrary, *mens rea* is generally required in modern legal systems so liability must be accompanied by blameworthiness.[47]

---

[45] On emotions and affective computing, see R. W. Picard, *Affective Computing* (Cambridge, MA: MIT Press, 2000); M. Minsky, *The Emotion Machine* (New York: Simon & Schuster, 2006).

[46] I. Banks, *Look to Windward* (London: Orbit, 2000).

[47] There is a huge literature on law and robots. Among the recent publications having a general scope, see, for instance, Y.-H. Weng, C.-H. Chen and C.-T. Sun, 'Toward the human–robot co-existence society: on safety intelligence for next generation robots', *International Journal of Social Robotics*, 1 (2009), 267; S. Chopra and L. F. White, *A Legal Theory for Autonomous Artificial Agents* (University of Michigan Press, 2011); C. Boscarato, 'Who is responsible for a robot's actions?' in B. van der Berg and L. Klaming (eds.), *Technologies on the Stand: Legal and Ethical Questions in Neuroscience and Robotics* (Oisterwijk: Wolf, 2011) 383; B. Calo, 'Robotics and the lessons of cyberlaw', *California Law Review*, 103 (2015), 101.

The considerations so far developed also apply to systems that consist of multi-layered structures of more or less autonomous components, as observed earlier in this chapter. We argue that with regard to such systems, a recursive approach to the identification of functional responsibilities, blameworthiness and legal liability is required. We need to identify how dysfunctions at one level might emerge at another level and how such failures may be linked to inappropriate design and deployment choices pertaining to single components or to the arrangement of their integration. For instance, a team of robots could be composed of perfectly working individuals, which altogether – as a robot system – may nonetheless cause havoc just because the patterns for their interaction were not appropriately defined. Alternatively, the test suite for a distributed robot system might point out no issues thanks to a fault-tolerant definition of the coordination patterns, possibly hiding flaws in the design of individual robots, which could emerge later at execution time.

Compliance with the laws of war

Let us now focus on whether a technological system may possess, to the required degree, the capacities required for the independent exercise of harmful and particularly lethal force. Military necessity – namely, the fact that an action contributes to relevant military objectives – provides no exemption from the respect of the imperative laws of war.[48] Among such imperative laws, there is the principle of distinction, requiring that 'the Parties to the conflict shall at all times distinguish between the civilian population and combatants and between civilian objects and military objectives and accordingly shall direct their operations only against military objectives'.[49] The corollaries of distinction include the prohibition to attack civilians, the prohibition to launch indiscriminate attacks and the obligation to take precautions to minimize civilian damage. The principle of proportionality, as related to distinction, addresses side-effects affecting civilians and entails the prohibition to cause damage to civilians that would be excessive with regard to the 'concrete and direct

---

[48] See M. N. Schmitt, 'Military necessity and humanity in international humanitarian law: preserving the delicate balance', *Virginia Journal of International Law*, 50 (2010), 795. For a broader discussion, see M. Walzer, *Just and Unjust Wars* (New York: Basic Books, [1977] 2006).

[49] Protocol Additional to the Geneva Conventions of 12 August 1949, and Relating to the Protection of Victims of International Armed Conflicts (Additional Protocol I) 1977, 1125 UNTS 3, Art. 52.

military advantage anticipated', as specified in Article 57(2) of Additional Protocol I.[50] Thus, proportionality not only requires harmful force to be necessary to achieve a war aim, but it also requires that civilian harm be limited as much as possible and that civilian losses, even when they are side-effects of military actions, are not disproportionate with regard to the expected military benefit.

When assessing the legality of the independent deployment of autonomous weapons for the delivery of lethal force, the crucial legal issue to be addressed concerns whether such systems are able to comply with the principle of the laws of war, and in particular with distinction and proportionality.

Two different positions have emerged concerning this issue.

On the one hand, it has been claimed that we cannot exclude that autonomous weapons may be as good as humans in implementing the laws of war, or even better than them.[51] In fact, machines excel in a number of cognitive skills that are relevant for avoiding indiscriminate and disproportionate damage: calculating positions and trajectories, identifying objects and individuals at a distance, recognizing relevant patterns in large data sets, applying numerous and complex but clear rules to a given situation. Moreover, they are able to face contexts of risk and danger without being overwhelmed by those emotions and attitudes that so often lead humans to commit atrocities: fear, revenge, panic, genocidal hatred and so on.

On the other hand, it has been observed that no machine can today proficiently replicate certain human cognitive skills that are needed in many contexts to use force consistently with the principles of distinction and proportionality, such as the capacity of understanding language, 'reading' other peoples' intentions and attitudes and anticipating their behaviour, reacting creatively to unexpected circumstances, figuring out when we should deviate from established rules to face exceptional situations and assessing the significance of gains and losses for the human interests involved.[52]

It seems to us that the opposition of machine skills vs human skills should be overcome. The legal issue to be addressed with regard to the use of technologies in war scenarios is not whether machines are better than humans or vice versa, it rather concerns what kind of systemic

[50] Ibid.
[51] As argued in particular by Arkin, Governing Lethal Behavior in Autonomous Robots.
[52] N. Sharkey, 'Grounds for discrimination: autonomous robot weapons', RUSI Defense Systems, 11 (2008), 86.

arrangement would better prevent indiscriminate or disproportionate uses of lethal force.

It appears that in many domains – the transport system, robotic healthcare, online trading, nuclear power plants and other critical systems – the best performance today can be obtained neither by humans alone, nor by machines alone, but rather through the integration of humans and machines. In such domains, optimal performance can be obtained only by combining humans and technologies in so-called hybrid systems or joint cognitive systems, through co-agency and interaction.[53] Thus, we should not aim at substituting humans with machines. We should but rather aim at a 'symbiotic partnership' between humans and machines, which, not only 'will perform intellectual operations much more effectively than man alone can perform them',[54] but will also perform such operations better than machines alone.

We would argue that also with regard to the deployment of lethal force there are many scenarios where only the integration of humans and machines would, at the current state of technology, implement at best the principles of distinction and proportionality, preventing unjustified damage. When a party has indeed the technical capacities for achieving such integration, any different arrangements would entail a violation of such principles. Thus, the rejection of machine autonomy as independence in the use of lethal force does not entail the rejection of machine cognition in war scenarios. Technologies that are able to perform complex cognitive tasks as well as technologies that are able to learn from their mistakes (adaptiveness), to model their environment, pursue goals, apply norms and engage in communication (teleology) may contribute not only to the war aims of the parties but also to the objective of preventing unjustified damage. We need to consider what may be the best integration between human and machine intelligence, taking into account the risks that may be related to the use of adaptive and goal-oriented intelligence, namely, the fact that the behaviour of the autonomous artificial agents may develop in unexpected directions.

One way to address the matter may be to distinguish epistemic and practical aspects in cognitive processes, the first being directed at

---

[53] For this idea, see E. Hollnagel and D. D. Woods, *Joint Cognitive Systems* (New York: Basic Books, 2005). For a broader perspective on the constitution of agency, see the contribution by L. Suchman and J. Weber, 'Human–machine autonomies', Chapter 4 in this volume.

[54] J. C. R. Licklider, 'Man–computer symbiosis', *IRE Transactions on Human Factors in Electronics*, HFE-1 (1960), 4.

extracting and analysing information on the relevant contextual conditions, and to determine the effects of possible initiatives, while the latter concerns the choice of the actions to be taken and the ways to implement them. Automated intelligence could be used without any limitation for the first kind of cognitive process as long as it provides a useful input, which also contributes to human situational awareness. With regard to the second kind of process, the best and safest option might consist in limiting machine intelligence – when the use of harmful, and, in particular, lethal, force is at issue – to the following main roles: (i) an exploratory role, consisting of identifying a non-exhaustive list of possible choices of action and (ii) a constraining role, consisting of highlighting options that, according to the machine assessment, are likely to be unacceptable since they are ineffective, illegal or immoral. Limiting the decisional role of the machine to an exploratory and constraining function would have the advantage of ensuring not only that humans remain in the loop but also that they maintain a substantive role in decision making, a role which is not limited to the ratification of machine choices.

The idea that lethal force should not be applied without meaningful human control seems to limit, in particular, arrangements in which the determination of the target to be engaged results from the combination of two selections: a human preliminary determination identifying a range of possible targets (according to their nature or location), and a machine determination selecting a specific target within that range. Such arrangements should only be permitted under specific circumstances, as in missile and artillery interception systems that are defending human-inhabited vehicles or locations.[55]

Responsibility and liability gaps

A frequent criticism against the deployment of autonomous systems points to the fact that the use of such systems could determine responsibility and liability gaps, namely the impossibility of attributing moral responsibilities (blameworthiness) and legal liabilities to anyone for certain harms caused by the systems' autonomous operation. In fact, neither the designers nor the users would be at fault with regard to harm that could not be anticipated and remedied at the design stage (given the existing technological knowledge) and could not be addressed at the

---

[55] M. Gubrud and J. Altmann, 'Compliance measures for an autonomous weapons convention', ICRAC Working Paper (2013), 2.

deployment stage.[56] Consider, for instance, how a usually reliable collision avoidance system may under particular conditions issue a wrong advisory, which the pilot follows, having no indication that the advisory is wrong. Similarly, a military system that is usually highly precise in computing missile trajectories may under exceptional environmental conditions fail to work appropriately, causing unjustified harm to civilians. In both of these examples, as nobody is at fault, nobody is blameworthy – and, thus, nobody, it seems, should be criminally liable. This conclusion, however, appears to clash with our instinctive idea that whenever something goes wrong there should be someone to blame and punish for it.

We shall argue that in analysing responsibility and liability gaps resulting from the deployment of autonomous systems, we need to distinguish the civilian domain from the use of force in the military domain. While in the civilian domains appropriate remedies can easily be found, this is not the case in the military domain.

Liability gaps should not prevent the civilian deployment of a socially useful technology. Consider, for instance, the case of autonomous cars. Assume that such cars would radically reduce road accidents and injuries to humans but that they would also cause a few accidents for which nobody could be blamed or convicted, as such accidents could not be anticipated and prevented through a better design or through reasonable care. Under such conditions it would be unreasonable to prohibit the use of autonomous cars. We should be concerned with the overall reduction of harm and with the possibility of compensating victims, rather than with the worry of finding somebody to blame and punish for every harmful event. This conclusion is supported by the consideration that in the civilian domain (1) general legal principles restrict the use of technological systems for harmful activities (2) the deployment of dangerous technologies can be limited when their social costs exceed their benefits, and (3) the damaged party can in many cases obtain compensation also when nobody is at fault.

First, the deployment of a system with the intent to cause damage to the life, physical integrity or property of other people, or with the awareness that this is likely to happen, would represent a legal offence under both criminal and private law.

---

[56] See A. Matthias, 'The responsibility gap: ascribing responsibility for the actions of learning automata', *Ethics and Information Technology*, 6 (2004), 175; more recently, see D. G. Johnson, 'Technology with no human responsibility?', *Journal of Business Ethics*, 127 (2015), 708, 709.

Second, dangerous technologies are usually regulated so as to ensure that their use is socially beneficial. Thus, authorization to deploy autonomous technologies usually requires some evidence that they provide for a level of risk to third parties that is inferior – or at least not superior – to the level that would exist without such technologies. For instance, even though autonomous cars may lead to some accidents that would not have happened had autonomous cars not been introduced, the greater number of accidents allegedly prevented through this technology justifies its permissibility and even the active support for its deployment.

Third, the worry that a blameworthiness gap could deprive victims of reparations can be overcome through legal mechanisms based on strict liability and compulsory insurance, possibly limited by caps and exceptions. In fact, various forms of strict and semi-strict liability already apply to a large extent to the development and deployment of technological tools involving risks for users and third parties.

Unfortunately, these considerations on the limited significance of liability gaps in the civilian domain do not apply to the military domain, where liability gaps appear to be a much more serious issue.

First, military necessity justifies, in general, intentionally harming and killing the adversary in order to achieve military objectives. Even acting with the awareness of causing harm to civilians may be justified in a war scenario, if the proportionality test is satisfied. In particular, military necessity justifies the deployment of intelligent weapons as they can deliver advantages to the party using them, such as force multiplication, expansion of the battle space, extension of the war fighter's reach and casualty reduction.[57]

Second, while states have an interest in prohibiting or limiting the civilian use of technologies whose social costs exceed their social benefits, in the military domain they have no interest in unilaterally renouncing destructive technologies. The fact that autonomous weapons have an augmented potential for warfare may lead instead to an increased arms race, as each party has an incentive to acquire destructive technologies, unless limitations can be agreed with the potential adversaries, and their implementation can be effectively enforced.

Third, in the military domain, there is little scope for civil liability to cover harm falling outside the criminal domain. Thus, no remedy would be available to the parties damaged by the behaviour of autonomous

---

[57] See G. E. Marchant *et al.*, 'International governance of autonomous military robots', *Columbia Science and Technology Law Review*, 12 (2011), 272.

weapons in violation of the laws of war, whenever no human appears to be criminally responsible for such violations. Moreover, as long as only criminal liability is at stake, the stringent criteria for the evaluation of evidence in criminal cases would prevent in many cases the determination of individual responsibilities for damage caused by autonomous weapons, providing impunity even for humans who have culpably contributed, as programmers, designers or deployers, to make such weapons engage in illegal harmful behaviour.[58] Expanding the notion of command responsibility may make it possible to extend the scope for individual responsibilities of deployers of autonomous systems, but this concept resists being enlarged too much, as criminal liability presupposes the proof of wrongdoing by individuals.[59]

In conclusion it seems highly probable that autonomous weapons would engage in actions such that (a) they would represent material violations of criminal laws of war (b) they would not lead to any proven responsibility of human individuals and (3) they would cause damage for which victims could not receive any remedy. The impunity enjoyed by autonomous weapons may even increase the chance that such weapons engage in actions prohibited by the laws of war, in the pursuit of the objectives assigned to them. Autonomous weapons could even be maliciously deployed in actions involving potential collateral damage, in consideration of their impunity and of the difficulty of proving responsibilities of specific individuals. Only the design of systems such that the pursuit of their operational task is always overridden by ethical-legal requirements, properly understood and applied, could alleviate these concerns.[60]

In this volume, responsibility gaps consequent to the use of autonomous systems are addressed by Hin-Yan Liu, who argues that the gaps should be remedied through a direct criminalization of the use of such systems, in analogy with the prohibition against the use of child

---

[58] In this volume, the use of civil law principles for damage caused by autonomous weapons has been advocated in Neha Jain's contribution in this volume, but it remains to be established how civil remedies would apply in the context of armed conflict. See N. Jain, 'Autonomous weapons systems: new frameworks for individual responsibility', Chapter 13 in this volume.

[59] See P. Kalmanovitz, 'Judgment, liability and the risks of riskless warfare', Chapter 7 in this volume.

[60] R. C. Arkin, P. Ulam and A. Wagner, 'Moral decision-making in autonomous systems: enforcement, moral emotions, dignity, trust and deception', *Proceedings of the IEEE*, 100 (2011), 571.

soldiers.[61] It seems to us that we need to distinguish two main rationales for the prohibition against using child soldiers. The first, and more important rationale concerns protecting children from being used as child soldiers. This reason obviously does not apply to autonomous weapons. The second rationale pertains to the need to prevent violations of the laws of war by child soldiers, under the assumption that child soldiers would commit such violations more often than adult soldiers, due to their still limited cognitive skills and capacity for self-control. This rationale would fall within the considerations that we developed in the previous section, namely, it would pertain to the fact that autonomous weapons do not possess the cognitive skills that are required for using lethal force in compliance with the laws of war, so that their deployment may ground a responsibility in their user/commander, at least for recklessness.

A different set of arguments against the use of irresponsible systems for delivering lethal force may be based on a deontological-dignitarian perspective, which views allowing machines to target humans as dignitary harm in itself, both to victims being targeted and to the commanders of such machines.[62] From this perspective, while we may accept that humans may be killed by other humans or that humans may order other humans to perform tasks involving killing humans, we cannot accept killer machines or commanders directing a machine to tasks that involve killing humans. Making humans' life or death dependent upon the judgment of a machine would involve degrading humanity and human agency. The necessary immunity of the mechanical authors of atrocities from moral blame and legal punishment – as these cannot apply to existing autonomous systems – would make even more unacceptable the use of machines for delivering lethal force. Immunity for wrongful killings would express even greater disregard for human dignity. These arguments, however, presuppose an ethical-deontological perspective that goes beyond the approach that is adopted in this chapter, which focuses on the differential amount of harm, and of violations of humanitarian law, resulting from the deployment of autonomous weapons rather than of human soldiers.

---

[61] H.-Y. Liu, 'Refining responsibility: differentiating two types of responsibility issues raised by autonomous weapons systems', Chapter 14 in this volume.

[62] P. Asaro, 'On banning autonomous weapon systems: human rights, automation, and the de-humanization of lethal decision-making', International Review of the Red Cross, 94 (2012), 887. See also Tamburrini, 'On banning autonomous weapons systems'.

Conclusion

Autonomous artefacts will soon become commonplace, both in civil and in military domains. To correctly deploy them, and regulate their usage, it is important to understand the scope and the limits of their autonomy. We have distinguished three orthogonal aspects of autonomy:

- independence, which concerns a system's capacity to achieve a task on its own (capacity independence) and its being entrusted with such an independent achievement (organizational independence);
- cognitive skills, which concern a system's ability to perform complex discriminative functions pertaining to information acquisition, analysis, decision adoption and implementation;
- cognitive architecture, which consists of a system's possession of teleonomy (direction to a purpose), adaptiveness (the capacity to get inputs from the environment and change internal states in such a way as to better respond to challenges) and teleology (the capacity to have representations of the environment and goals to achieve and to identify appropriate means).

As we have observed, there is a link between these aspects since an adaptive and teleological architecture may enable the integration of multiple knowledge-intensive skills, and thus increase the capacity for independent action. However, the three aspects must be distinguished, since they are not always jointly present and their mismatch can give rise to malfunctions and liabilities. In particular, we have argued that the independence of technological systems is questionable whenever better performance could be obtained by combining technologies and humans into hybrid or joined cognitive systems – that is, by integrating mechanical and human skills.

This does not rule out the use of devices, and even weapons, endowed with cognitive skills and cognitive architectures, as long as the interaction and coordination between humans and such systems is engineered in such a way as to limit unnecessary and disproportionate harm and is consistent with the applicable laws. For this purpose, however, it seems that humans should remain in the loop, having a meaningful control over the exercise of force against human beings. This conclusion is also supported by the fact that using autonomous systems to deliver lethal force without human control could extend the scope of liability gaps, namely, instances of harmful behaviour for which nobody can be considered criminally responsible, and for which damaged individuals have little chance of getting any remedy.

Our analysis has focused on a particular set of legal considerations pertaining to the use of autonomous weapons, namely, on whether their use may lead to violations of humanitarian laws. We have not addressed the broader political arguments that could support initiatives for an international treaty to prohibit the independent deployment of autonomous weapons, or to establish a moratorium. In fact, it may be argued that it is in the interest of the international community to avoid a new arms race, leading to high-risk scenarios. The future of humanity would be at risk as a consequence of the proliferation of more and more intelligent weapons, having superhuman capacities to communicate, store and retrieve information and capable of independently delivering lethal force against humans.

4

Human–machine autonomies

LUCY SUCHMAN AND JUTTA WEBER

> We are responsible for the world of which we are a part, not because it is an arbitrary construction of our choosing but because reality is sedimented out of particular practices that we have a role in shaping and through which we are shaped.
>
> Karen Barad, *Meeting the Universe Halfway*[1]

> [R]esearch and development in automation are advancing from a state of automatic systems requiring human control toward a state of autonomous systems able to make decisions and react without human interaction. DoD will continue to carefully consider the implications of these advancements.
>
> US Department of Defense, *Unmanned Systems Integrated Roadmap*[2]

This chapter takes up the question of how we might think about the increasing automation of military systems not as an inevitable 'advancement' of which we are the interested observers, but rather as an effect of particular world-making practices in which we need urgently to intervene. We begin from the premise that the foundation of the legality of killing in situations of war is the possibility of discrimination between combatants and non-combatants. At a time when this defining form of situational awareness seems increasingly problematic,[3] military investments in the automation of weapon systems are growing. The trajectory of these

---

[1] K. Barad, *Meeting the Universe Halfway* (Durham, NC: Duke University Press, 2007), 390.

[2] US Department of Defense (DoD), *Unmanned Systems Integrated Roadmap FY2013–2038* (Washington, DC: DoD, 2013), 15.

[3] Christiane Wilke observes that the figures of civilian and combatant are not only gendered and aged (women and children being the canonical instances of the first category) but also raced. Both, moreover, are increasingly problematic, as 'the rise of the figure of the "unlawful combatant" ... is accompanied by a corresponding rise of the figure of the illegitimate, non-innocent, suspicious civilian'. C. Wilke, 'Civilians, combatants and histories of international law', 28 July 2014, available at http://criticallegalthinking.com/2014/07/28/civilians-combatants-histories-international-law/. See also D. Gregory, 'Keeping up with the drones', 20 November 2014, available at http://geographicalimaginations.com/2014/11/20/keeping-up-with-the-drones/.

investments, moreover, is towards the development and deployment of lethal autonomous weapons – that is, weapon systems in which the identification of targets and the initiation of fire is automated in ways that preclude deliberative human intervention. Challenges to these developments underscore the immorality and illegality of delegating responsibility for the use of force against human targets to machines, and the requirements of international humanitarian law that there be (human) accountability for acts of killing. In these debates, the articulation of differences between humans and machines is key.

The aim of this chapter is to strengthen arguments against the increasing automation of weapon systems, by expanding the frame or unit of analysis that informs these debates. We begin by tracing the genealogy of concepts of autonomy within the philosophical traditions that animate artificial intelligence, with a focus on the history of early cybernetics and contemporary approaches to machine learning in behaviour-based robotics. We argue that while cybernetics and behaviour-based robotics challenge the premises of individual agency, cognition, communication and action that comprise the Enlightenment tradition, they also reiterate aspects of that tradition in the design of putatively intelligent, autonomous machines. This argument is made more concrete through a reading of the US Department of Defense's (DoD) *Unmanned Systems Integrated Roadmap: FY2013–2038*, particularly with respect to plans for future autonomous weapons systems (AWS). With that reading in mind, we turn to resources for refiguring agency and autonomy provided by recent scholarship in science and technology studies informed by feminist theory. This work suggests a shift in conceptions of agency and autonomy, from attributes inherent in entities to effects of discourses and material practices that either conjoin humans and machines or delineate differences between them. This shift leads in turn to a reconceptualization of autonomy and responsibility as always enacted within, rather than as being separable from, particular human–machine configurations. We close by considering the implications of these reconceptualizations for questions of responsibility in relation to automated/autonomous weapons systems. Taking as a model feminist projects of deconstructing categorical distinctions while also recognizing those distinctions' cultural-historical effects, we argue for simultaneous attention to the inseparability of human–machine agencies in contemporary war fighting and to the necessity of delineating human agency and responsibility within political, legal and ethical/moral regimes of accountability.

In proposing a reconceptualization of autonomy in the context of this chapter, we wish to be clear that our discussion is in no way meant to diminish the importance, or the possibility, of taking an operational approach to defining what have been categorized as lethal autonomous weapons. Mark Gubrud proposes[4] that we begin with the definition offered by the US DoD, which states that an AWS is 'a weapon system that, once activated, can select and engage targets without further intervention by a human operator. This includes human-supervised AWS that are designed to allow human operators to override the operation of the weapon system but that can select and engage targets without further human input after activation.'[5] Taking up the key phrase 'select and engage', Gubrud observes that 'selection' or targeting is complicated by the fact that 'the status of an object as the target of a weapon is an attribute of the weapon system or persons controlling and commanding it, not of the object itself ... an object harmed without having been selected is called "collateral damage", be it a house, a garden, or a person'.[6] Target selection, Gubrud argues, is where the crucial questions and indeterminacies lie, and the operator, 'the final human in the so-called "kill chain" or "loop"',[7] should be the final decision point. Gubrud concludes that insofar as any weapon system involves the delegation of responsibility for target selection and engagement from operator to machine (whatever the precursors to that delegation in terms of intelligence reports, target lists and the like), that system is in violation of the principle of human control.

It is as a way of addressing these questions that those campaigning for a ban on lethal autonomous weapons have insisted on the need to preserve 'meaningful human control' over target selection and engagement.[8] The word 'meaningful' here is meant to anticipate and reject the proposition that any form of oversight over automated target identification constitutes 'human control'. Noel Sharkey offers a list of progressively greater levels of human control:

---

[4] M. Gubrud, 'Autonomy without mystery: where do you draw the line?', 9 May 2014, available at http://gubrud.net/?p=272.

[5] US Department of Defense (DoD) Directive 3000.09, 'Autonomy in weapon systems', 21 November 2012, available at www.dtic.mil/whs/directives/corres/pdf/300009p.pdf.

[6] Gubrud, 'Autonomy without mystery'.   [7] *Ibid.*

[8] Article 36: 'Key areas for debate on autonomous weapon systems: memorandum for delegates at the Convention on Certain Conventional Weapons', paper presented at the Meeting of Experts on Lethal Autonomous Weapons Systems, Geneva, 13–16 May 2014, available at www.article36.org/wp-content/uploads/2014/05/A36-CCW-May-2014.pdf.

1. human engages with and selects target and initiates any attack;
2. program suggests alternative targets and human chooses which to attack;
3. program selects target and human must approve before attack;
4. program selects target and human has restricted time to veto;
5. program selects target and initiates attack without human involvement.[9]

On Sharkey's analysis, while Levels 1 and possibly 2 provide for what he identifies as 'the minimum necessary conditions for the notion of meaningful control',[10] the rest do not.[11]

In this chapter, we develop the argument, implicit in these discussions, that the adjudication of questions of autonomy and responsibility requires as its unit of analysis specific configurations of humans and machines. As we elaborate below, contemporary social theory has effectively challenged the premise that autonomy can be adequately understood as being an intrinsic capacity of an entity, whether human or machine, shifting the focus instead to the capacities for action that arise out of particular socio-technical systems. The concept of 'configuration' further orients us to relevant assumptions regarding humans, machines and the relations between them and to the practical consequences of particular human–machine assemblages.[12] Thus, to understand the agencies or capacities of either people or technologies requires an analysis of the dynamics of the socio-technical relations through which they are conjoined. Different configurations effect different distributions of agency between persons and technologies, making different capacities for action possible. In thinking about life-critical technical systems, it is the question of what conditions of

---

[9] See N. Sharkey, 'Staying in the loop: human supervisory control of weapons', Chapter 2 in this volume.

[10] N. Sharkey, 'Towards a principle for the human supervisory control of robot weapons', *Politica e Società*, 2 (2014), 305–24.

[11] Sharkey in this volume cites the US DoD Science Board Task Force's review of many DoD-funded studies regarding 'levels of autonomy', which concluded that such designations are not particularly helpful in as much as 'they focus too much attention on the computer rather than on the collaboration between the computer and its operator/ supervisor to achieve the desired capabilities and effects'. DoD, Directive 3000.09, 48. We return to the question of agency in human–machine configurations below.

[12] See L. Suchman, *Human–Machine Reconfigurations: Plans and Situated Actions* (New York: Cambridge University Press, 2007); L. Suchman, 'Configuration' in C. Lury and N. Wakeford (eds.), *Inventive Methods* (London: Routledge, 2012), 48.

possibility a particular configuration affords for human responsibility and accountability that is key.[13]

Autonomy: from Enlightenment reason to cybernetics

As background to this argument, we turn next to a brief review of shifting conceptualizations of autonomy as they have developed within the fields of cybernetics, artificial intelligence and robotics since the mid twentieth century. Within the context of the modern episteme, one function of the concept of autonomy has been to posit an essential difference between humans and machines. Introduced by Enlightenment thinkers, autonomy was grounded in the idea of the individual self-determination[14] of the liberal subject. In Immanuel Kant's conception, the compliance of the human subject with moral law is the basis for human dignity.[15] And though autonomy of communities was a well-known concept in ancient Greece, autonomy now signified for the first time the idea of the right of self-determination of individual subjects. While nineteenth-century natural sciences debated the mechanistic, versus the vitalistic, nature of the living – life's deterministic or dynamic nature – the then dominant discourse of the humanities promoted the idea of the singularity of the human, and made it a widely accepted idea in liberal political discourse.

The reconfiguration of this concept of autonomy took its start in the 1920s and 1930s with the 'new sciences' of system theory and cybernetics. The biologist Ludwig von Bertalanffy, in his general systems theory,[16]

---

[13] For further discussion regarding responsibility and liability for autonomous weapons systems (AWS), see G. S. Corn, 'Autonomous weapons systems: managing the inevitability of "taking the man out of the loop"', Chapter 10 in this volume; N. Jain, 'Autonomous weapons systems: new frameworks for individual responsibility', Chapter 13 in this volume; H.-Y. Liu, 'Refining responsibility: differentiating two types of responsibility issues raised by autonomous weapons systems', Chapter 14 in this volume.

[14] *Self-determination* or *self-government* are the English terms for the German concept *Selbstbestimmung*. The term self-government already includes a cybernetic notion as governor, which is the translation of the Greek word *cybernetes*.

[15] 'Autonomy of the will is the property of the will through which it is a law to itself (independently of all properties of the objects of volition). The principle of autonomy is thus: "Not to choose otherwise than so that the maxims of one's choice are at the same time comprehended with it in the same volition as universal law".' I. Kant, *Groundwork for the Metaphysics of Morals* (New Haven: Yale University Press, [1785] 2002), 58.

[16] L. von Bertalanffy, 'Der Organismus als Physikalisches System Betrachtet', *Die Naturwissenschaften*, 33 (1940), 521; see also H. Penzlin, 'Die theoretische und institutionelle Situation in der Biologie an der Wende vom 19. zum 20. Jh.' in I. Jahn, R. Löther and K. Senglaub (eds.), *Geschichte der Biologie: Theorien, Methoden, Institutionen, Kurzbiographien*, 3rd edn (Heidelberg and Berlin: Spektrum, 2000), 431.

conceptualized all living organisms as systems based on homeostatic balance. In this new logic, all organisms were regarded as being able to maintain steady states as well as their structure and identity in interaction with their environment and to regenerate and reproduce themselves.[17] This system of logic was ascribed not only to single organisms but also to collectives, whether they were biological, technical, economic or social.[18] This idea enables, in turn, the translation of organic and non-organic entities – of the material and non-material – into objects of communication and control.

The important transformation was to background defining features and intrinsic properties of organisms (including humans), which had been the main focus of concern prior to this, and to focus instead on goal-oriented behaviour. This combination of a powerful systems analogy and the concept of self-regulation, as well as the shift from essence to behaviour, increasingly blurred the boundary between humans and machines.[19] Systems theory along with cybernetics shifted the paradigm of science from energy towards information and from intrinsic properties of entities towards their behaviour. The cyberneticians' interest in the behaviour of a system was driven by their involvement in military research, which occurred during the Second World War as Norbert Wiener worked on an anti-aircraft predictor. The calculation of aircraft trajectories was made possible only by neglecting the intrinsic features of the pilot and his machine and conceptualizing them as one entity – as a system – while concentrating on their behaviour.[20] Though Wiener did not succeed in building the predictor during the Second World War, cybernetics nonetheless successfully articulated the belief 'that machines and organisms were behaviourally and in information terms "the same"'.[21]

---

[17] K. Gloy, *Das Verständnis der Natur*, vol. I: *Die Geschichte des wissenschaftlichen Denkens* (Munich: Beck, 1995).

[18] G. Leps, 'Ökologie und Ökosystemforschung' in I. Jahn, R. Löther and K. Senglaub (eds.), *Geschichte der Biologie: Theorien, Methoden, Institutionen, Kurzbiographien*, 3rd edn (Heidelberg and Berlin: Spektrum, 2000), 601.

[19] N. K. Hayles, 'Computing the human' in J. Weber and C. Bath (eds.), *Turbulente Körper, soziale Maschinen: feministische Studien zur Wissenschaftskultur* (Opladen: Leske & Budrich, 2003), 99.

[20] P. Galison, 'The ontology of the enemy: Norbert Wiener and the cybernetic vision', *Critical Inquiry*, 1 (1994), 228; P. Edwards, *The Closed World: Computers and the Politics of Discourse in Cold War America* (Cambridge, MA: MIT Press, 1996).

[21] G. Bowker, 'How to be universal: some cybernetic strategies, 1943–70', *Social Studies of Science*, 23 (1993), 107.

Cybernetics can be interpreted as an early technoscience, which aimed at constructing (anti-)systems with teleological behaviour. Cybernetics blackboxed not only machines but also any entities, including non-human and human organisms. In his book *The Human Use of Human Beings*,[22] Wiener claims that instead of materiality it is the organization or form of an entity that guarantees its identity in its ongoing transformation processes.[23] In principle, he sees no difference between the transport of matter or messages.[24] And it is not only specific materiality that is regarded as being irrelevant. Wiener as well as Claude Shannon introduced a new and purely formal concept of information, which sidestepped the context and meaning of information to ensure its computability. Both interpret information to be 'a principle of statistical quantification whose universal scope is equalled only by its indifference towards the specific nature of signals (physical, biological, technical or human)'.[25] While Shannon prioritized linearity in the famous sender–receiver model,[26] the concept of circular causation was central to Wiener's idea of communication.[27] Organisms and machines feed back certain information from specific parts of the system into the whole, which now has become an information network; this information is then supposed to help to regulate and thereby enhance the performance of the whole network.

The strong focus on information and feedback, and on the interaction of systems, is an identifying development of cybernetics,[28] which gave up

---

[22] N. Wiener, *The Human Use of Human Beings: Cybernetics and Society* (Boston: Riverside Press, 1950); see also J. Weber, 'Blackboxing organisms, exploiting the unpredictable: control paradigms in human–machine translation' in M. Carrier and A. Nordmann (eds.), *Science in the Context of Application* (New York: Springer, 2011), 409.

[23] In the history of philosophy – from Aristotle to contemporary approaches in philosophy of mind – we find a polarization of substance and form, matter and information. See T. Adorno, *Negative Dialektik* (Frankfurt a.M.: Suhrkamp, [1966] 1982); J. Weber, *Umkämpfte Bedeutungen: Naturkonzepte im Zeitalter der Technoscience* (New York: Campus, 2003). These approaches take for granted that matter is passive and the form is imprinted on matter – it gets 'informed'. This approach has been extensively criticized by Marxists, phenomenologists, feminist philosophers, discourse theoreticians and post-colonial theory scholars.

[24] Wiener, *The Human Use of Human Beings*; see also Weber, *Umkämpfte Bedeutungen*.

[25] C. Lafontaine, 'The cybernetix matrix of French theory', *Theory, Culture and Society*, 24 (2007), 27, 31.

[26] C. Shannon and W. Weaver, *The Mathematical Theory of Communication* (Urbana: University of Illinois Press, 1949).

[27] Lafontaine, 'The cybernetix matrix of French theory'.

[28] K. Hayles, *How We Became Posthuman: Virtual Bodies in Cybernetics, Literature, and Informatics* (University of Chicago Press, 1999).

on analysing intrinsic features of organisms, materiality or nature in favour of the frame of a functionalist logic. However, in the seminal paper 'Behavior, purpose and teleology', Norbert Wiener, Arturo Rosenblueth and Julian Bigelow claim that active purposeful behaviour is primarily based on negative feedback, 'signals from the goal [that] are necessary at some time to direct the behavior'.[29] Against the idea of functional relationships, Rosenblueth, Wiener and Bigelow claim a dependant, inter-objective relation between a system and its goal, which is not intentional but also non-random. They interpret purpose as 'the awareness of voluntary activity'.[30] In this way, cybernetics endows every single actor – whether human or machine – with a certain autonomy and 'elbow-room', by conceptualizing a systems' behaviour as at least partially teleological and adaptive:

> Perhaps the most fundamental contribution of cybernetics is its explanation of purposiveness, or goal-directed behaviour, an essential characteristic of mind and life, in terms of control and information. Negative feedback control loops which try to achieve and maintain goal states were seen as basic models for the autonomy characteristic of organisms: their behaviour, while purposeful, is not strictly determined by either environmental influences or internal dynamical processes. *They are in some sense 'independent actors' with a 'free will'.*[31]

On this basis, one could argue that the idea of autonomous systems begins with the cybernetician's claim of purposeful and goal-oriented behaviour as an attribute of any system. But what does this mean? And why do Francis Heylighen and Cliff Joslyn use quotation marks in their reference to the free will of the machine?

While the Enlightenment concept of autonomy is grounded in the idea of a free and self-aware subject, one which can self-determinedly and consciously choose its maxims,[32] the cyberneticians explain purposeful behaviour not in rational-cognitivist terms, but rather as a pragmatic physiological mechanism that can be automated: 'A torpedo with a target-seeking mechanism is an example. The term servo-mechanisms

---

[29] A. Rosenblueth, N. Wiener and J. Bigelow, 'Behavior, purpose and teleology', *Philosophy of Science*, 10 (1943), 18, 19.

[30] *Ibid.*, 18.

[31] F. Heylighen and C. Joslyn, 'Cybernetics and second-order cybernetics' in R. Meyers (ed.), *Encyclopedia of Physical Science and Technology*, 3rd edn (New York: Academic Press, 2001), 3 (emphasis added).

[32] Which need to be generalizable to be ethical according to Kant. See Kant, *Groundwork for the Metaphysics of Morals*.

has been coined precisely to designate machines with intrinsic purposeful behaviour.'[33] In this respect, cybernetics does not rely on assumptions of representation, symbol processing or pre-programmed plans to execute behaviour, but rather on a pragmatic idea of a system's performance in interaction with its goal. The rhetoric of purpose and self-determination primarily rests on the fact that the system 'self-decides' again and again how to adjust its behaviour to achieve its goal. While the course of the machine towards the goal is not pre-programmed – in the case of the target-seeking torpedo, for example – the goal is pre-given. At the same time, the machine is at least partially flexible in seeking how to achieve its goal. In the logic of the cyberneticians, voluntary action (the philosopher's 'free will') and dynamic goal-oriented behaviour are more or less synonymous.

The dynamic relation between the servo-mechanism and the target – between the system and its goal – becomes possible through a tight coupling of system and environment. System and environment are regarded as separate, but closely interacting, entities. Wiener and his colleagues were interested in feedback – purposeful 'non-extrapolative, non-predictive' behaviour,[34] which could only be realized on the basis of the intimate interaction between different objects in a dynamic system–environment relation. In order to integrate the non-predictive into their calculations, they understood that the control of dynamic systems cannot be static or (too) centralized. Cybernetics is not so much about the exact calculation of behaviour, but rather about its probabilistic estimate,[35] which is also the reason why the cyberneticians were interested in probability and game theory. And though concepts such as purpose, behaviour and teleology were stigmatized in late nineteenth- and early twentieth-century biology as vitalistic and non-scientific, cybernetics now managed to reformulate them as grounding concepts of a new, flexible technoscience of communication and control.[36]

The systems analogy, as well as the understanding of systems as goal-directed and purposeful, is a central precondition for the idea of the

[33] Rosenblueth, Wiener and Bigelow, 'Behavior, purpose and teleology', 19.   [34] *Ibid.*
[35] For the differences in the epistemological approaches of Wiener and von Neumann, see J. Lenhard, 'Computer simulation: the cooperation between experimenting and modeling', *Philosophy of Science*, 74 (2007), 176.
[36] M. Osietzki, 'Das "Unbestimmte" des Lebendigen als Ressource wissenschaftlich-technischer Innovationen: Menschen und Maschinen in den epistemologischen Debatten der Jahrhundertwende' in J. Weber and C. Bath (eds.), *Turbulente Körper, soziale Maschinen: feministische Studien zur Wissenschaftskultur* (Opladen: Leske & Budrich, 2003), 137.

'autonomy' of so-called smart and intelligent (war) machines. As developed by Ludwig von Bertalanffy, and further elaborated by the cyberneticians, the systems analogy made it possible to shift the analysis of the information sciences from the intrinsic properties of entities towards their behaviour. The concept of behaviour was redefined as purposeful, moreover, insofar as any system's performance was directed through its interactions with its stipulated goal. The meaning of autonomy thereby shifted from the philosophical idea of the capacity of a self-aware and self-determined subject conforming to a (generalizable) moral law towards the technoscientific idea of autonomy as the operations of a pragmatic, physiological servo-mechanism.

Symbol-processing artificial intelligence

For manifold reasons, cybernetics did not dominate the field of artificial intelligence in the long run.[37] Already in the late 1960s, the symbol-processing approach of artificial intelligence, which was oriented towards mathematics and logic, won over the more biologically oriented approaches of cybernetics and early connectionism. Traditional, symbolic artificial intelligence is dominated by the paradigm of information processing in which intelligence, the brain and the calculation of symbols are equated. Intelligence is seen less as a property than as a capability to think – which is understood as the processing of symbols and, correspondingly, as the computing of algorithms. This research paradigm also abstracts from the physical and concentrates on the representation of knowledge – that is, the adequate modelling of the world via symbols and logical inference as the decisive features of intelligence. Intelligence and the human brain are regarded as fundamentally computational in structure and function. Input is given, then it is processed, and finally output is generated. This procedure of input processing output was translated into the sense-think-act cycle of humans (and machines). The system receives input from the outside world via sensors (sense), interprets the sensory data via symbol processing and develops a plan (think). As output, the system executes an action according to the plan (act). Accordingly, symbolic artificial intelligence repeats traditional, rational-cognitive conceptions of human intelligence in terms of planning. It does not promote the idea of autonomy of technical systems in the sense of the randomly

[37] J. P. Dupuy, *The Mechanization of Mind* (Princeton University Press, 2000); Weber, 'Blackboxing organisms'.

based, self-learning behaviour of so-called new artificial intelligence.[38] The symbolic approach worked very well in strongly rule-based environments such as chess playing or factory manufacturing but ran into severe problems when applied to mobile robots in dynamic, real-world environments.

Definitions of what a robot comprises share the common requirement that a machine can engage in a sequence of 'sense, think and act' or perception, reasoning and action. The question of what counts as sensing or perception is key here, however. Does 'sense, think and act' refer to an assembly line robot that performs an action 'at a certain location in a coordinate system representing real space'[39] or through machine 'vision' in a highly controlled environment where the consequences of failure are acceptable? Or does it invoke sensing and perception as dynamic, and contingent, capacities in open-ended fields of (inter)action with potentially lethal consequences? This leads as well to the question of what any instruction or plan presupposes about the capabilities required to carry it out. In the 1970s and 1980s, US researchers working in the field of artificial intelligence adopted the premise that plans, understood as a precondition for rational action, could be implemented as a device for structuring cognition and action in computational machines.

In *Plans and Situated Actions*,[40] the first author challenged this approach, proposing that rather than thinking of plans as cognitive control structures that precede and determine actions, they are better understood as cultural devices produced and used within specific sites of human activity. One entailment of this proposition is that planning is itself a form of situated activity that results in projections that bear consequential, but irremediably indeterminate, relation to the actions that they anticipate. Most importantly (and problematically) for the project of designing autonomous machines, plans and any other form of prescriptive specification presuppose competencies and *in situ* forms of interaction that they can never fully specify. The corollary of this is that the efficacy of plans relies upon the ability of those who 'execute' or 'implement' them to find the relation of the conditions and actions specified to some actual, particular occasion. And how to do that is not, and cannot be, fully specified. Prescriptive specifications such as plans,

---

[38] We return to new artificial intelligence in the following section.
[39] S. M. Riza, *Killing without Heart: Limits on Robotic Warfare in an Age of Persistent Conflict* (Dilles, VA: Potomac Books, 2013), 14.
[40] Suchman, *Human–Machine Reconfigurations*. Suchman, 'Configuration'.

instructions and the like, in other words, presuppose an open horizon of capabilities that irremediably exceed their representational grasp.

Behaviour-based robotics

In the mid 1980s, a new, behaviour-based artificial intelligence and robotics developed that reinvented many insights of traditional cybernetics as it tried to avoid representations of the world and stressed the importance of (real-world) experience, negative feedback, situatedness, autonomy of the system and a tight coupling of system and environment.[41] Behaviour-based, or situated, robotics is inspired by first-order cybernetics but also by the theory of dynamic systems. The interest in materiality and embodiment that this approach promoted is now regarded by many as a necessary condition for real intelligence.[42] Roboticist Rodney Brooks adopted an idea of situated action as part of his campaign against representationalism in artificial intelligence and within a broader argument for an evolutionarily inspired model of intelligence.[43] For Brooks, 'situated' means that creatures reflect in their design an adaptation to particular environments. At the same time, the forms of adaptation to date are primarily focused on navigation, and the environment is delineated principally in terms of physical topographies. Brooks' situatedness is one that is largely emptied of sociality, and the creature's 'interactions' with the environment comprise variations of conditioned response, however tightly coupled the mechanisms or emergent the effects.

Nevertheless, cybernetics as well as behaviour-based artificial intelligence aims at overcoming the static and mechanistic paradigm of the 'traditional' sciences[44] in order to encompass dynamic and complex

---

[41] R. Brooks, 'A robust layered control system for a mobile robot', *IEEE Journal of Robotics and Automation* (1986), 14; L. Steels, 'Towards a theory of emergent functionality' in *From Animals to Animats: Proceedings of the First International Conference on Simulation of Adaptive Behavior* (Cambridge, MA: MIT Press, 1990), 451.

[42] K. Dautenhahn and T. Christaller, 'Remembering, rehearsal and empathy: towards a social and embodied cognitive psychology for artifacts', available at ftp://ftp.gmd.de/GMD/ai-research/Publications/1996/Dautenhahn.96.RRE.pdf; R. Pfeifer and C. Scheier, *Understanding Intelligence* (Cambridge, MA: MIT Press, 1999); S. Nolfi and D. Floreano, *Evolutionary Robotics: The Biology, Intelligence, and Technology of Self-Organizing Machines. Intelligent Robots and Autonomous Agents* (Cambridge, MA: MIT Press, 2000).

[43] R. Brooks, *Cambrian Intelligence: The Early History of the New Artificial Intelligence* (Cambridge MA: MIT Press, 1999); R. Brooks, *Flesh and Machines: How Robots Will Change Us* (New York: Pantheon, 2002).

[44] A. Pickering, 'Cybernetics and the mangle: Ashby, Beer and Pask', *Social Studies of Science*, 32 (2002), 413.

behaviours of organic and technical systems. In new artificial intelligence/behaviour-based robotics, the idea of autonomous systems gains momentum. Definitions of autonomy range – depending on the context and task of the system – from autonomy of energy supply or mobility to autonomy through adaptivity, embodied intelligence and learning behaviour (realized as computable, technical processes). While projects in autonomous energy supply or mobility aim to go beyond automation, they are mostly regarded as middle-range steps towards the achievement of full autonomy in the sense of the capability to operate 'in the real world without any form of external control'.[45] More ambitious approaches in robotics aim at adaptive learning behaviour intended to make the machine independent from human supervision and intervention.[46]

New robotics takes on the cybernetic idea of goal-oriented, 'purposeful' behaviour and tight system–environment coupling but reaches beyond it. Adaptive and biologically inspired robotics wants to include random behaviour as well.[47] There is a new interest in unpredictability and the unknown, as an integral factor of control and the systematization and exploitation of processes of trial and error.[48] While traditional artificial intelligence worked with pre-given rules for the robot's sensing and acting behaviours, behaviour-based robotics claims to build robots that can handle unpredictable situations in real-world environments. Therefore, biologically inspired concepts such as adaptation, imitation and experience-based learning[49] are the centre of attention.

Robots are posited to learn either through imitation (supervised learning) or through autonomous self-exploration. In the latter case, they should deduce the implicit general rules of a specific experience and adapt them in future situations. Learning is conceptualized as permanently acquiring new behaviours through autonomous self-exploration and through interaction

[45] G. Bekey, *Autonomous Robots: From Biological Inspiration to Implementation and Control* (Cambridge, MA: MIT Press, 2005).

[46] J. Beer, A. Fisk and W. Rogers, 'Towards a psychological framework for level of robot autonomy in human–robot interaction' (Technical Report HFA-TR-1204. Atlanta, GA: Georgia Institute of Technology, School of Psychology, 2012); T. Fong et al., 'A survey of socially interactive robots', *Robotics and Autonomous Systems*, 42 (2003), 143–66.

[47] E.g. R. Pfeifer, 'On the role of embodiment in the emergence of cognition and emotion', January 2000, available at www.ifi.unizh.ch/groups/ailab/publications/2000.html; Nolfi and Floreano, *Evolutionary Robotics*.

[48] Weber, 'Blackboxing organisms'.

[49] A. Billard, S. Calinon and R. Dillmann, *Learning from Human Demonstration. Handbook of Robotics* (Cambridge, MA: MIT Press, 2013). Fong et al., 'A survey of socially interactive robots'; O. Sigaud and J. Peters, 'From motor learning to interaction learning in robots', *Studies in Computational Intelligence*, 264 (2010), 1.

with the environment via trial and error. The improved performance of the system is built on structural changes of the system (a kind of permanent self-reorganization). The basis of the autonomous learning process is unsupervised learning algorithms (as in value-based or reinforcement learning), which are supposed to enable agents to develop new categories and thereby adapt to the environment, though the new 'relevant configurations have to be selected using a value system'.[50] So while, on the one hand, the physical – and not the computational – structure of the agent and the 'tight coupling of embodiment, self-organization and learning'[51] are regarded as highly relevant to machine learning, on the other hand, the performance of the machine depends upon a pre-given value system in which the behavioural goals of the agent are inscribed. The value systems then 'evaluate consequences of behaviour'.[52]

Behaviour-based robotic agents seem to have more autonomy – understood as self-guided behaviour – in comparison to traditional agents of symbolic artificial intelligence and even of cybernetics. The agenda of continuous self-exploration on the basis of self-learning algorithms makes so-called emergent[53] or unpredictable behaviour at least partially possible. The behaviour is not pre-programmed, but rather the outcome of a kind of systematized tinkering and situated experimenting of the system with its environment. However, this exploration is guided by pre-given value systems to make an 'assessment' of the experiences of the system possible. New experiences must be 'evaluated' through these pre-given values and categories. It seems that the robot behaviour shifts to another level: it is no longer totally pre-programmed but, instead, more flexible. The behaviour is mediated by random effects of the system's architecture[54] or learning algorithms, which can result in interesting, so-called emergent effects of the robot's behaviour, which are then exploited via post-processing.[55] The systems are regarded as being

---

[50] Pfeifer and Scheier, *Understanding Intelligence*, 500.
[51] R. Pfeifer, M. Lungarella and F. Iida, 'Self-organization, embodiment, and biologically inspired robotics', *Science*, 318 (2007), 1088, 1090.
[52] Pfeifer and Scheier, *Understanding Intelligence*, 498–9.
[53] Emergence is understood in this context as the development of something qualitatively new on a higher and more complex level – a process that cannot be explained on a causal basis as a linear evolution or growth of complexity. See Hayles, *How We Became Posthuman*, 225.
[54] Brooks, 'A robust layered control system'; for a critique, see, Weber, 'Blackboxing organisms'.
[55] Specifically, reading the log files of the robot and trying to deduce how a new behaviour pattern of the robot was generated.

autonomous because of their sometimes unforeseen and even more rare (random) problem-solving behaviour. To address these machines as partners,[56] however, means to ignore the extent to which today's behaviour-based robots also rely on traditional symbolic artificial intelligence approaches, including huge amounts of pre-given systems structures (that is, the system architecture) and variables (such as the value system), as well as pre-programmed, determining software programs.

In their enthusiasm for the new, but nevertheless quite limited, capacities of behaviour-based agents, some roboticists' claims for real autonomous systems are greatly exaggerated. The claims are also grounded in a profound semantic shift in the meaning of autonomy, which is primarily defined as the capability to explore random real-world environments, by which sometimes unforeseen and useful behaviour might emerge. If the behaviour of these robots appears much more flexible than that of traditional robots, it is only because of the extremely static, non-dynamic behaviour of agents built in the tradition of symbolic artificial intelligence. The so-called autonomy of the behaviour-based agent is ontologically quite different from the original understanding of autonomy as self-determination, the ability to choose one's own (ethical) maxims of acting, or at least to comply with the dominant moral law.

As a result of the not exactly calculable behaviour of the agents of new artificial intelligence, and the invisibility of the underlying variables, categories and value systems in the robots' architecture, many people are intrigued by the more dynamic ontology of the bio-cybernetic sciences. In science communication, roboticists even enforce these impressions by dubious promises of agents that will soon be intelligent, develop human-like capabilities and (possibly if not inevitably) overtake humans in their moral and creative capabilities.[57] The ever-increasing competition between human and machinic autonomy seems to have

---

[56] Brooks, 'A robust layered control system'; T. Christaller *et al.*, *Robotik: Perspektiven für menschliches Handeln in der zukünftigen Gesellschaft* (Berlin: Springer, 2001).

[57] Think, e.g., of the prediction of roboticists that a robot soccer team will defeat the human world champion soccer team in 2050 or that there will be reliable software for moral decision making for lethal weapon systems in the foreseeable future. For the soccer example, see H. Kitano and M. Asada, 'The RoboCup Humanoid challenge as the millennium challenge for advanced robotics', *Advanced Robotics*, 13 (2000), 723. For a moral decision-making software, see R. Arkin, P. Ulam and A. Wagner, 'Moral decision-making in autonomous systems: enforcement, moral emotions, dignity, trust and deception', *Proceedings of the IEEE*, 100 (2012), 3. For a critique of the latter claim, see P. Asaro, 'How just could a robot war be?' in P. Brey, A. Briggle and K. Waelbers (eds.), *Current Issues in Computing and Philosophy* (Amsterdam: IOS Press, 2000), 50.

reached its point of culmination in the contemporary discussion of the right of 'autonomous' weapons to decide the life and death of human beings. In the debate on AWS, it becomes even more obvious how autonomy is configured as self-sufficient, adaptive and self-determined performance, on the one hand, and pre-programmed, fully automated execution under perfect human control, on the other. These two imaginaries are profoundly intermingled, with questionable rhetorical and practical effects.

Figuring the future of machine autonomy in military robotics

To see how the traces of these histories are co-mingled in contemporary rhetorics of AWS, we turn to a reading of the US DoD's *Unmanned Systems Integrated Roadmap: FY2013–2038 (USRM)*. In a grammatical construction that posits a future knowable in the present (along with a characteristic elision of the difference between description and aspiration), the *USRM* informs us that '[t]he future of autonomous systems is characterized as a movement beyond autonomous mission *execution* to autonomous mission *performance*'.[58] 'Execution' and 'performance' are differentiated within the text by the former's reliance on a pre-programmed plan, while the latter involves the realization of goals that may change dynamically over a mission's course. Implicitly positing the existence of a future system capable of engaging in autonomous performance, pre-programming in this imaginary 'goes beyond system operation into laws and strategies that allow the system to self-decide how to operate itself'.[59] With that said, the document's authors are quick to restore the human to the loop. On the one hand, goals are directed by humans, while, on the other hand, 'automation is only as good as the software writer and developer because the control algorithms are created and tested by teams of humans':

> In these algorithms, the 'patterns of life' are critical to automation and must be observed and captured properly to ensure accuracy and correctness of a decision-making process within the software. Ensuring accuracy and correctness requires a continual process in which the observe – orient – decide – act (OODA) loops in the software are continually updated via manual analysis, training, and operator understanding of algorithm inputs and outputs. The human brain can function in dynamic environments and adapt to changes as well as predict what will happen next. In simplistic terms, the algorithms must act as the human brain does.[60]

[58] US DoD, *Unmanned Systems Integrated Roadmap*, 66 (emphasis in the original).
[59] *Ibid.*, 66.   [60] *Ibid.*, 67.

This passage is problematic, on our analysis, on several grounds. First, it presupposes that relevant circumstances can be rendered algorithmically, and still adequately, as 'patterns of life', a form of profiling that has been effectively critiqued in assessments of the use of related techniques in campaigns of targeted killing.[61] Second, the reference to 'a decision-making process within the software' elides the difference between algorithmic and judgmental 'decision', again presuming the possibility of the latter's translation into the former. Finally, while insisting on the continued necessity of human oversight in the form of 'updating', the passage concludes by invoking a brain-based figure of human cognition and reasserting the possibility of its algorithmic replication.

Having set out the requirements for machine intelligence, the *USRM* goes on to provide a three-part account of the future of research and development in autonomous systems, beginning with:

> 4.6.1 Today's state (2013–2017)
>
> In general, research and development in automation is advancing from a state of automatic systems requiring human control toward a state of autonomous systems able to make decisions and react without human interaction.[62]

While framing this section of the report as the current state of the art, the opening statement again conflates the descriptive with the promissory. The 'in general' implies not only a trend or tendency but also a kind of inevitability.[63] The document goes on to acknowledge that at present

---

[61] International Human Rights and Conflict Resolution Clinic (Palo Alto, CA: Stanford Law School) and Global Justice Clinic (New York: NYU School of Law), *Living under Drones: Death, Injury and Trauma to Civilians from US Drone Practices in Pakistan*, September 2012, available at http://chrgj.org/wp-content/uploads/2012/10/Living-Under-Drones.pdf; C. C. Heyns, 'Targeting by drones: protecting the right to life', paper presented at the European University Institute and Global Governance Programme on Targeted Killing, Unmanned Aerial Vehicles and EU Policy, European University Institute in Florence, 22 February 2013.

[62] US DoD, *Unmanned Systems Integrated Roadmap*, 68.

[63] For a critique, see N. Sharkey, 'The evitability of autonomous robot warfare', *International Review of the Red Cross*, 94 (2012), 787–99; N. Sharkey and L. Suchman, 'Wishful mnemonics and autonomous killing machines', *AISBQ Quarterly, Newsletter of the Society for the Study of Artificial Intelligence and the Simulation of Behaviour*, 136 (2013), 14. In his chapter in this volume, Dan Saxon posits that increasing speed and concomitant arguments of military necessity and advantage will further undermine the Directive's already too vaguely specified standard of 'appropriate levels of human judgment over the use of force'. D. Saxon, 'A human touch: autonomous weapons, DoD Directive 3000.09 and the interpretation of "appropriate levels of human judgment over the use of force"', Chapter 9 in this volume.

'systems that are autonomous require highly structured and predictable environments'[64] but with the implication that this is just a temporary phase, rather than a characterization of the results of the past fifty years or more of research and development in machine intelligence and robotics. The discussion of 'today's state' and the 'near term' of the next four years includes a figure[65] that sets out '[t]he Army's Vision for 5 Problem Domains' in research and development in robotics, in which the domains are anthropomorphized as 'Think–Look–Move–Talk–Work'. Figure 24 of this text (reproduced below as Table 4.1) warrants a closer reading.

Reproduced from the *Robotic Collaborative Technology Alliance (RCTA) FY2012 Annual Program Plan,* the figure sets out the US Army's vision in the familiar form of a matrix, a representational device designed to ensure systematic and comprehensive consideration of orthogonal relations between two sets of categories, while at the same time asserting the systematicity of the analysis that it represents. The columns set out the five 'barriers to achieving our vision'. These name familiar problem areas that have vexed the project of artificial intelligence since its inception. For example, the premise that the army's vision requires its autonomous devices to have a world model adopts a conventional symbolic-processing approach to artificial intelligence, based in the encoding of a representation of the 'world' in which the device is to act, as a precondition for its effective and appropriate operation. However, while the characterization of existing models as 'simplistic and shallow' suggests that the challenge is to develop models that are more complex and deep, the wider premise that autonomous agency relies upon, and can be achieved through, the encoding of a model of the world as an *a priori* for action has, as we have discussed earlier, come under widespread critique, both within the field of artificial intelligence and among its philosophical and cultural critics.

While there is no question that human actors are continually engaged in rendering the world intelligible, it does not follow that this is done through a process of mapping between some cognitive model 'inside' the head of the individual and a world 'out there'. Rather, 'the world' is a very general gloss for an open horizon of potentially relevant circumstances. How a circumstance is articulated as such and made relevant, moreover, is not given in advance, but rather the recognition and/or articulation of something as a relevant circumstance is part of the ongoing, generative practices through which actions are rendered sensible and accountable.

---

[64] US DoD, *Unmanned Systems Integrated Roadmap,* 68.   [65] *Ibid.,* 70, figure 24.

Table 4.1 *Army's vision for five problem domains (think – look – move – talk – work) (US DoD, Unmanned Systems Integrated Roadmap, figure 24)*

Barriers to achieving our vision →	Simplistic and shallow world model	Mobility-focused perception	Tele-operated or (at best) scripted planning	No shared understanding of missions and roles	Missing or shallow learning capabilities
	World model is either at only a metric level precluding reasoning, or at only a cognitive level without physical grounding	Objects in the world are perceived primarily only as mobility regions not as discrete objects of semantic and cognitive importance	Bots are almost always tele-operated or at best only perform scripted behaviors – and scripting all needed behaviors is not tractable	Bots are opaque and distributed, and cannot explain what they are doing – primarily because they don't know	Bots must be explicitly programmed to do tasks, so it is intractable to predict the needed scope of behavior. Any learning capability is shallow and lacks generalization
'Think' Adaptive tactical reasoning Understand tasks, missions (METT-TC [Mission, Enemy, Terrain, Troops – Time, Civilian Consideration])	World model needs to represent concepts such as missions, tasks, and generally METT-TC.		Robots need to generate behaviors pertinent to achieving the mission, adapt to changing situation.	Robots need to be able to follow instructions given at a semantic or cognitive level, not just "go to (x,y)."	

Table 4.1 (*cont.*)

Barriers to achieving our vision →	Simplistic and shallow world model	Mobility-focused perception	Tele-operated or (at best) scripted planning	No shared understanding of missions and roles	Missing or shallow learning capabilities
Follow semantic instructions					
Generate behaviors to achieve mission, adapting to changing situation					
Understand teammates and what they need to know					
'Look' Focused situational awareness					
Maintain SA relevant to current task/ mission	World model needs to represent, maintain, monitor, and correct all info needed for SA.	Robot needs to contribute to the general SA of the unit, noting salient observations.		Robot needs to report on salient observations as needed to other elements of its unit.	Robot should learn by comparing its observations and actions to those of its human counterparts.
Contribute to general SA of unit					
Look for salient unforeseen events					

Task / Activity	World model	Robot perception	Robot movement	Robot cognitive interaction	Robot learning
Observe and report on salient activity					
'Move' **Safe, secure and adaptive movement** Move cognitively in reaction to safest route in the world (as people do) with GPS or other metric crutches Move in tactically and continually relevant manner Adjust to mobility challenges such as terrain, weather, barriers	World model needs to store and operate upon all entities needed to relate movement to tactical constraints.	Robot must perceive all entities in its environment relevant to safe, secure, and adaptive movement.	Robots must move in a tactically correct manner and react to changes in mission or circumstances.		Robot needs to learn from its movement experience whether from mobility challenges or tactical behavior.
'Talk' **Efficient interactive communication** Receive and acknowledge semantic instructions	World model needs to have shared mental models as a basis for	Robot needs to send and receive information relevant based on a shared perception		Robot needs to receive and acknowledge cognitive-level instructions	Robot needs to be able to learn through cognitive-level interaction with human teammates.

Table 4.1 (cont.)

Barriers to achieving our vision →	Simplistic and shallow world model	Mobility-focused perception	Tele-operated or (at best) scripted planning	No shared understanding of missions and roles	Missing or shallow learning capabilities
Explain own behavior Report information relevant to mission Seek guidance as needed	human–robot interaction.	(common ground).		and similarly explain its own behavior.	
'Work' Interaction with physical world Inspect and manipulate objects Transport objects as needed Open doors, windows, hoods, trunks, etc. Use tools as needed	World model needs to represent wide variety of objects to be manipulated.	Robot needs to perceive well enough to interact effectively with objects in a 3D world.	Robot needs to figure out how and when to manipulate or transport objects as needed.		Robot needs to learn from interaction with the physical world, e.g. when door is locked.

This helps to account, in turn, for the remaining problems, or rather characteristics, of the state of the art: machine 'perception' narrowly construed as obstacle avoidance; reliance on remote operation or pre-scripted behaviours and the irremediable incompleteness of the latter; inability to comprehend the situation of one's action and the lack of anything beyond the most technical sense of 'learning' from experience in ways that can inform future actions. The column headings of the figure indicate, in sum, troubles in the conception of machine autonomy at work in the *USRM*, insofar as it presupposes the possibility of specifying relevant conditions of combat and appropriate responses within the range of capacities for sensing that are built into the system.

So what of the other axis of the matrix, the 'five problem domains' labelled 'Think–Look–Move–Talk–Work'? Treated as separable 'domains', each of these prescribes a corresponding requirement for the 'world model', reiterating the premise that the model provides the basis for effective action. The remainder of the cells are filled with general characterizations of those capabilities that the robot 'must' or 'needs to' have – for example, 'understand teammates and what they need to know' or 'contribute to general S[ituational] A[wareness] of the unit' or 'seek guidance as needed'. However, these are precisely those abilities that the *x*-axis of the matrix has identified as being resistant to all of the efforts to achieve them to date. One way to read this figure, then, is as a demon-stration of the limits of an approach to autonomy based on modelling and planning and of the decomposition of human action into multiple, separate domains. The persuasive intent of the matrix is not, however, to call the project of model-based robotics into question, but rather to urge that efforts be redoubled.

While this figure makes clear the significant and substantial unsolved problems that face attempts to create autonomous, intelligent robots, there is no indication of the timeframe for their solution. Nonetheless, section 4.6.2 of the *USRM* assures us that '[t]he middle-term future state in the 2017–2022 time frame will consist largely of a further maturation of near-term capabilities ... and move the capability further along the scale from automation to autonomous behavior', while section 4.6.3 on the 'Long-term future state (beyond 2022)' asserts again that '[t]he long-term state for unmanned systems will bring further maturation of the middle-term capabilities. It will also bring higher levels of automation'.[66] Both of these sections then go on to sketch out the imagined or desired

---

[66] US DoD, *Unmanned Systems Integrated Roadmap*, 71.

next configurations of automated/autonomous systems for each of the armed services, but without having addressed the fundamental problems that continue to resist technological solution.

Refiguring autonomous agency

Our starting observation, set out in this chapter's opening section, is that the project of machine intelligence is built upon, and reiterates, traditional notions of agency as an inherent attribute and autonomy as a property of individual actors. This conception of agency has been profoundly challenged, however, within contemporary science and technology studies. While focused on relations of subjects (scientists, technologists) and objects (natural kinds, artefacts) within the technosciences, these studies are a rich resource for a broader reconceptualization of autonomous agency.

In the field of science studies, Andrew Pickering develops the metaphor of the 'mangle' to argue that what he names 'material agency' is always temporally emergent in practice[67] rather than fixed in either subjects or objects. Karin Knorr-Cetina adopts a trope of 'epistemic cultures' to think about laboratories as mutually shaping arrangements of scientists, instruments, objects and practices aimed at the production of observably stabilized instantiations of 'reality effects'.[68] The notion of 'reconfiguration' is central to her analysis, as the process through which subject/object relations are reworked.[69] Charles Goodwin's analyses of what he names 'professional vision'[70] demonstrate in detail how the acquisition of professional competency comprises processes through which practitioners learn to 'see' the objects of their profession, at the same time that those objects are reflexively constituted through the same practices by which they become intelligible.[71] Taken together, these analyses support an understanding of agencies as always relational and give us, in turn, a different way of conceptualizing the problem of attributions of knowledge and agency to machines. The problem is less

---

[67] Pickering, 'Cybernetics and the mangle'.

[68] K. Knorr-Cetina, *Epistemic Cultures: How the Sciences Make Knowledge* (Cambridge, MA: Harvard University Press, 1999), 26–33.

[69] Suchman, *Human–Machine Reconfigurations*.

[70] C. Goodwin, 'Professional vision', *American Anthropologist*, 96 (1994), 606; C. Goodwin, 'Seeing in depth', *Social Studies of Science*, 25 (1995), 237.

[71] R. Prentice, 'The anatomy of a surgical simulation: the mutual articulation of bodies in and through the machine', *Social Studies of Science*, 35 (2005), 837; M. Myers, 'Molecular embodiments and the body-work of modeling in protein crystallography', *Social Studies of Science*, 38 (2008), 163.

that we attribute agency to computational artefacts than that our language for talking about agency, whether for persons or artefacts, presupposes a field of discrete, self-standing entities. Latour takes us closer to the domain of the weapon system, with his reflections on the gun:

> You are different with a gun in your hand; the gun is different with you holding it. You are another subject because you hold the gun; the gun is another object because it has entered into a relationship with you. The gun is no longer the gun-in-the-armory or the gun-in-the-drawer or the gun-in-the-pocket, but the gun-in-your-hand ... If we study the gun and the citizen [together] ... we realize that neither subject nor object ... is fixed. When the [two] are articulated ... they become 'someone/something' else.[72]

These inquiries re-specify agency from a capacity intrinsic to singular actors (human or artefactual) to an effect of subject/object relations that are distributed and always contingently enacted. In the words of feminist theorist Karen Barad, 'agency is not an attribute but the ongoing reconfigurings of the world'.[73] Methodologically, this view of the nature of socio-material agencies has two broad implications. First, it demands attention to the question of frames, of the boundary work through which a given entity is delineated as such. Beginning with the premise that discrete units of analysis are not given but made, we need to ask how any object of analysis – human or machine or a combination of the two – is called out as being separate from the more extended networks of which it is part. This work of cutting the network is a foundational move in the creation of socio-technical assemblages as objects of analysis or intervention.[74] In the case of the robot, or autonomous machine more generally (as in the case of the individual human as well), this work takes the form of modes of representation that systematically foreground certain sites, bodies and agencies while placing others offstage. Our task as analysts is then to expand the frame to a wider field of view that acknowledges the effects created through a particular framing, while also explicating the hidden labours and unruly contingencies that inevitably exceed its bounds.

---

[72] B. Latour, *Pandora's Hope: Essays on the Reality of Science Studies* (Cambridge, MA: Harvard University Press, 1999), 179–80.

[73] Barad, *Meeting the Universe Halfway*, 141.

[74] M. Strathern, 'Cutting the network', *Journal of the Royal Anthropological Institute*, 2 (1996), 517.

Implications for the debate over AWS

Applied to the case of weapon systems, these methodological shifts have profound political and moral consequences. With respect to automation and autonomy, an understanding of agency not as an attribute of either humans or machines, but rather as an effect of particular human–machine configurations opens the possibility of explicating the systematic erasures of connection and contingency through which discourses of autonomous agency operate. And it opens as well the question of how to configure socio-technical assemblages in such a way that humans can interact responsibly in and through them.[75] At the same time, we face a certain tension in thinking about responsibility and the human in these terms. Cybernetics and new artificial intelligence abandon the idea of intrinsic properties of humans or non-humans and stress the interaction of systems and their environments. And as we have discussed, contemporary science and technology studies – particularly those that have been informed by feminist theory – effectively dissolve the problematic idea of human autonomy in favour of attention to the human/non-human relations through which what we call human agency is produced as one effect. However, in engaging discourses of autonomous weaponry, it seems crucial to articulate the particular agencies and responsibilities of the human war fighter and their resistance to translation into executable code. This is not so much a contradiction to be resolved, we would argue, but a trouble with which we need to stay. As well as recognizing the epistemic situatedness of our concept of autonomy, we need to explore the ways in which our agencies are entangled with, and dependent upon, the technological world today and to analyse our particular agencies within the assemblages that we configure and that configure us.[76]

In the opening pages of *Killing without Heart*,[77] Air Force Colonel M. Shane Riza reflects on the shifting agencies and responsibilities of the 'human in/on the loop' and the 'string of events [that] we technological warriors facetiously call the "consecutive miracles" that comprise the effective functioning of technologically advanced weapon systems'.[78] He points to the ways in which pilots and engineers in the

---

[75] This task is made more difficult by the lack of transparency that characterizes initiatives in AWS development. See S. Knuckey, 'Autonomous weapons systems and transparency: towards an international dialogue', Chapter 8 in this volume.

[76] See P. Kalmanovitz, 'Judgment, liability and the risks of riskless warfare', Chapter 7 in this volume.

[77] Riza, *Killing without Heart*.   [78] Ibid., 4.

field are called upon to mitigate shortcomings of weapons development contracts in their failure to fully address the contingencies of use. At the same time, he emphasizes that the issue for him is not the dependency of the fighter on the technology: 'I am comfortable in the knowledge that my mastery, such as it was, of the technology at my fingertips successfully took me into battle and brought me back.'[79] Rather, what he is concerned about is the decision (not) to kill, which he defines as the red line between automation and robotic autonomy. Riza makes a strong distinction between automated weaponry and 'autonomous killers'[80] and proposes that meaningful discussion of developments in weapons systems requires that we 'come to grips with the clear distinction between automation and autonomy and navigate the all-too-unclear realm of the latter's spectrum'.[81] He includes landmines and machine guns among automated weaponry, while autonomy is exemplified by 'a small tracked robot carrying a shotgun or assault rifle with the ability to select and fire on targets of its own choosing'.[82] This categorization is challenged, however, by the analogy between landmines and 'killer robots' made by campaigners such as Article 36's Matthew Bolton,[83] who observes that the campaign to ban landmines was based precisely on their 'autonomy', albeit a self-firing triggered not by 'decision', but rather by the simple trip wire of a proximate body. And Riza agrees with this further on, when he notes that:

> [a]ntipersonnel mines of the kind that kill hundreds of innocent people every year are indiscriminate by their very nature, and indiscriminate killing had been against the law of war in written form for a hundred years before the [Ottawa Accord of 1997] – and against the norms of behavior for a millenium before that. We should have known better than to field them.[84]

It is the question of discrimination, specifically between combatants and non-combatants, that becomes crucial, and recourse to the human, whether 'in' or 'on the loop', is complicated by the nexus of intensifying speed and increasing automation that characterizes modern weapon systems. Citing the 'friendly fire' incidents of the 2003 invasion of Iraq, when Patriot missiles shot down two allied aircraft killing their crews, Riza concludes that '[t]he decisions to fire in these instances were made

---

[79] Ibid., 6.   [80] Ibid., 12.   [81] Ibid., 13.   [82] Ibid., 12.
[83] Article 36, 'Ban autonomous armed robots', 5 March 2012, available at www.article36 .org/statements/ban-autonomous-armed-robots/.
[84] Riza, Killing without Heart, 29.

by humans, but their decisions were radically influenced – perhaps to the point of abdication – by basic artificial intelligence'.[85] This incident troubles the clarity of the line between automation and autonomy, along with the questions of agency and responsibility that the human in/on the loop is imagined to resolve.[86]

The interrelated dangers of increasing automation in weapons systems and the shift towards weapons autonomy pose two critical challenges. On the one hand, we need to understand the ways in which automation establishes its own circular logics of necessity, as the shortened time frames that result become, in turn, the justification for further automation. Following Riza, we can understand that the 'loop' in which humans and machines are conjoined in contemporary weapons systems, whether the humans are figured as 'in' or 'on' that loop, diminishes the possibility of judgments not to kill. In this logic of no time for communication or consideration, machine autonomy becomes the necessary extension to automation. At the same time that we identify the connecting logics of automation and autonomy, however, we need as well to articulate their differences. More specifically, if our concern is to interrupt the vicious cycle of automation in war fighting, and the political and economic investment in a future of autonomous weapons that it justifies, one strategy is to make the discontinuity between automation and autonomy more evident.[87] To do that, we need a critical examination of the assumptions that underwrite conceptions of autonomy, whether human or machine, in the fields of artificial intelligence and robotics. We also need to develop a concept of autonomy that comprises fully the socio-political dimensions of human–machine interaction. Applied to weapons systems, this means that the question is less about automation versus autonomy than it is about what new forms of agency are enabled by contemporary configurations of war fighting and with what political, ethical, moral and legal consequences.

---

[85] *Ibid.*, 20.

[86] See also C. Heyns, 'Autonomous weapons systems: living a dignified life and dying a dignified death', Chapter 1 in this volume.

[87] This is the basis for the 'Campaign to Stop Killer Robots', a coalition of non-governmental organizations dedicated to the development of an arms control ban on lethal autonomous weapons. See www.stopkillerrobots.org.

PART III

Autonomous weapons systems and human
dignity

5

Are autonomous weapons systems a threat to human dignity?

DIETER BIRNBACHER

Introduction: human dignity – an integrative and open concept

'Human dignity' has become one of the most important integrative formulas in international politics. Since 1948, when it was introduced into Article 1 of the United Nations Universal Declaration of Human Rights, it has successfully functioned as an umbrella concept that bridges seemingly insurmountable ideological gulfs and provides a basis for consensus and compromise.[1] Similarly to other political guiding concepts such as justice, liberty, peace or, more recently, sustainability, human dignity is an essentially open concept that leaves room for varying interpretations and contextualizations and thereby allows even the otherwise fiercest adversaries to speak with one voice.

Another reason why human dignity has been increasingly introduced into constitutions and international treaties since 1948 is the wish for an absolute – a foundational principle that overarches, as it were, all constitutional and other political principles, a common reference point that is beyond controversy and conflict and plays the role, in Kantian terms, of an *a priori* to which all other political ideas are subject. Human dignity is predestined for this role because of two characteristic factors: the openness of its content and its independence of any particular metaphysical background theory. The extent to which the concept is semantically open is documented by its function as a heuristic tool in the process of gradually extending the canon of basic human rights. Although it is generally agreed that there is a stable connection between the idea of human dignity and the idea of basic human rights, the number and identity of the rights associated with the idea of human dignity is not static but, rather, dynamic. What human dignity implies – its content and

---

[1] Universal Declaration of Human Rights, UN GA Res. 217 (III) A, 10 December 1948.

consequences – has no fixed magnitude but is open to interpretations that extend its range and content into new directions, though in continuity with its established content. Extensions usually respond to new threats posed, for example, by new and unexpected political constellations, natural phenomena or technological developments. That human dignity shares this dynamic character with human basic rights supports the widely held assumption that the notions of human dignity and basic human rights are closely linked to each other.

The essential openness of human dignity has two consequences: first, that its content cannot be identified with any exhaustive list of basic human rights. There can be no such thing as a timeless canon of human rights, which somehow represents what human dignity is. This would be incompatible with the fact that human dignity is a productive concept that has not only generated new human rights not recognized before but also new kinds of human rights, such as, for example, social rights and rights to participation, and that can be expected to generate new human rights in the future. An example from recent history is the right to informational autonomy, which the German Constitutional Court defined as a basic right on the background of the concept of human dignity and which was added to the rights conventionally recognized on a constitutional level. The canon was extended because it was felt that the right to privacy can be violated not only by intrusions into the private sphere in a physical sense but also by intrusion into the private sphere in an informational sense – that is, into information (of all kinds, including visual information) that people do not wish to reveal about themselves or do not wish to see made public.

The second consequence of the productive nature of the concept of human dignity is that its content could not even be hypothetically exhausted by a list of basic human rights because it has, besides its deontic component implying certain rights and duties, an evaluative component that ascribes to human beings a specific and exclusive value and on which the exceptional normative status of human beings is assumed to depend. The basic rights ascribed to humans are assumed to flow from this specific value, with human dignity as the justificatory basis of these rights.[2] The evaluative component of the concept is made explicit in some historically crucial formulations of the concept, notably

---

[2] See D. Jaber, *Über den mehrfachen Sinn von Menschenwürde-Garantien* (Frankfurt am Main: Ontos, 2003), 96ff; D. P. Sulmany, 'Human dignity and human worth' in J. Malpas and N. Lickiss (eds.), *Perspectives on Human Dignity: A Conversation* (Dordrecht: Springer, 2007), 9.

in the Universal Declaration of Human Rights, which juxtaposes the dignity and the worth of the human person in the fifth sentence of the preamble.

The same formula has been recapitulated in some of the manifestos against the development of autonomous weapons systems (AWS). For example, the recent Human Rights Watch manifesto on what it calls 'killer robots' quotes the Vienna Declaration of the 1993 World Conference on Human Rights as affirming that 'all human rights derive from the dignity and worth inherent in the human person'[3] and asserts that 'fully autonomous weapons could undermine the principle of dignity, which implies that everyone has a worth deserving of respect'.[4] Though it is controversial whether the evaluative content of the concept of human dignity – the ascription of a specific and supreme worth to human beings – is suited to fully justifying its deontic content – the ascription of an open list of basic rights[5] – this evaluative content is the best candidate for explaining the factual productivity of the concept. Even if there is no strictly deductive relation between the possession of value (or worth) and the possession of rights, the ascription of value might well continue to motivate the ascription of rights.

The second feature that makes human dignity particularly suited for the role of an integrative and overarching concept is that it is compatible with a great variety of metaphysical frameworks in which it can be embedded and from which it has drawn additional motivation and support and continues to do so. Human dignity, for example, can be embedded in a Stoic, Kantian, Christian or otherwise mono- or polytheistic metaphysics, provided this assigns the human being a special position that elevates it over the rest of nature. The fact that human dignity can be embedded in these diverse metaphysical frameworks means that it is not by itself bound to any of these frameworks in particular. As an 'uninterpreted thesis', as the first German Federal President Theodor Heuss called it, one can subscribe to it even without subscribing to any of these more ambitious metaphysics.

---

[3] Human Rights Watch and International Human Rights Clinic, *Shaking the Foundations: The Human Rights Implications of Killer Robots* (New York: Human Rights Watch, 2014), 23, available at www.hrw.org/reports/2014/05/12/shaking-foundations. Vienna Declaration, 32 ILM 1661 (1993).
[4] *Ibid.*, 3.
[5] Cf. D. Birnbacher, 'Kann die Menschenwürde die Menschenrechte begründen?' in B. Gesang and J. Schälike (eds.), *Die großen Kontroversen der Rechtsphilosophie* (Paderborn: Mentis, 2011), 77.

Inflationary tendencies and their inherent danger

The concept of human dignity is a concept with particularly strong moral force. Saying that a certain action or practice is contrary to human dignity means uttering a particularly strong moral reproach. Violations of human dignity are not only morally problematic, but they are to be morally condemned and, as a rule, punished by law. The reason behind this is that human dignity and the basic human rights flowing from it protect fundamental human interests. Acting contrary to these interests tends to deprive people of most or all of the other interests and goods that are important to them and prevents them from leading a satisfactory life or makes it excessively difficult for them.

The moral gravity of any violation of human dignity confers on the concept a distinctive emphasis and pathos that goes further than the emphasis accompanying most other moral concepts. This emphasis is easily exploited by inflationary usages that stretch it beyond recognition, by applying it to objects beyond its established scope or by using it in a purely expressive manner. As far as I can see, there are three tendencies that should be seen as inflationary in so far as they have the inevitable consequence of weakening the normative force of the concept to a point where it is no longer able to fulfil its distinctive function in moral, political and legal discourse.

The first tendency is to apply the concept not only to human individuals but also to the human species as a whole – for example, in the context of the prohibition of human cloning and of the production of man–animal hybrids. There are good reasons to prohibit both of these practices, but it can be doubted that they constitute, as is very often alleged, violations of human dignity. Human dignity, in its established use, is applicable, as a matter of principle, only to individuals. Otherwise, the link would be broken with basic rights. Basic rights are universal rights held by individuals. The right to freedom, to life, to bodily integrity, let alone the right to paid holidays, do not even seem to make sense outside the context of individual right holders. It is questionable, however, whether the infringement of human dignity involved in cloning or in the production of man–animal hybrids can be understood as an infringement of the human dignity of individuals. In the first place, it is not clear whose dignity is violated by these practices. In the case of cloning, it might be the 'original' on which the clone is copied or the cloned individual; in the case of the man–animal hybrid, it may be the individual whose genetic material has combined with that of an animal or the individual resulting from the process. In all of these cases, it is unclear whether any of these individuals can be said to be infringed in his or her basic rights to an extent that justifies the heavy reproach of an infringement of human dignity. In the hypothetical case of human cloning, neither the 'original' nor the clone will, as a rule, be prevented from leading a satisfactory life by the process, and the same may be true of the hybrid being, unless it should prove impossible to protect what might be something like the 'elephant man' in David Lynch's movie from public mobbing in ways other than by permanent exclusion from human contact.

There seems to be no other way out of the dilemma, in these cases, than to apply the concept of human dignity to the human species as a whole and to condemn the relevant actions or practices as violations against – what? – the purity, identity or specificity of humanity as a whole? I doubt whether such a notion really makes sense. At the same time, I cannot but realize that a large number of authors are tempted to say something that amounts to the assertion of a specific dignity of the species over and above the dignity of any of its members. One is not surprised to find something of the kind also in the literature on AWS. In this case, the fact that it is not human agents but, rather, robots who decide to pull the trigger with the intention of taking human life is sometimes taken to amount, by itself, to a 'dehumanization', suggesting that it is somehow against the dignity of humanity as a species. Thus, in his 2013 report to the United Nations General Assembly the special rapporteur on extrajudicial, summary or arbitrary executions, Christof Heyns, writes:

> Delegating this process [of deciding on targets] dehumanizes armed conflict even further and precludes a moment of deliberation in those cases where it may be feasible. Machines lack morality and mortality, and should as a result not have life and death powers over humans.[6]

Evidently, in a descriptive sense, the process of delegating the selection of targets and hitting the chosen targets in fact 'dehumanizes' warfare – the process is no longer (only) in the hands of human agents. However, at the same time, the word 'dehumanizes' carries evaluative overtones. It condemns the practice as transcending the threshold between what is compatible and what is incompatible with human dignity. This dignity, however, can only be the dignity of mankind – the dignity of the human

---

[6] C. Heyns, Report of the Special Rapporteur on extrajudicial, summary or arbitrary executions, UN Doc. A/HRC/23/47, 9 April 2013, 17.

species as such. Since the robot is not itself a person, it cannot be its individual dignity that is infringed by its actions.

There is no reason to doubt that judgments of this kind are the authentic expression of a genuine intuition. However, this does not exempt it from conceptual and normative scrutiny. In this case, 'dehumanizing' seems problematic on both counts. It is doubtful whether the concept of dignity can be explicated in a way that makes it applicable to abstractions such as the human species, and it is doubtful whether the normative judgment about the delegation of the selection of targets to robots can be upheld. A strong reason against the transference of the concept of human dignity to abstract objects is the implausibility of regarding violations of this hypothetical dignity with the same gravity as violations of individual dignity. If this were so it would be hard to explain why the penal sanctions for violations of the hypothetical species' dignity are so much milder than for violations of individual dignity. In Germany, for example, the sanctions for attempts at human cloning and for the production of man–animal hybrids are significantly lower than they are for paradigmatic cases of violations of individual human dignity such as torture or taking children as hostages for the sake of money – practices by which human beings are treated as a 'mere means' for self-serving interests. What is lost, in these extended uses, is the fact that human dignity is closely connected with subjectivity and with the possession of moral rights. Even if these moral rights are the basis of corresponding legal rights, these legal rights must have a basis in moral rights. They cannot, for example, be the legal rights of purely legal persons such as companies, associations or states.

The second problematic extension of the use of the concept of human dignity is the tendency to weaken the distinctively strong force of the concept by identifying human dignity with the whole of morality. This kind of inflation has become common especially in 'moral cultures' such as the German-speaking world where the heritage of Immanuel Kant's moral philosophy has been influential, or where it has, as it has in Germany, served as a central inspiration of constitutional norms. Kant's moral philosophy is anything other than a coherent and unitary conception. However, among the many different strands of thought that have gone into it, there is at least one according to which acting against morality is, as such, acting against human dignity or, to be more exact, against the agent's own human dignity. In acting immorally, a human being is violating its own dignity as a being endowed with practical reason. It fails to respect its own sovereignty as a being and is in the cosmically exceptional position to be at the same time the master and the slave of practical reason.

This use of human dignity as an equivalent of morality as a whole is widespread in modern moral discussion, both popular and academic. It is not surprising to find it also in the literature on AWS. Thus, one finds Peter Asaro writing in an article on AWS: 'As a matter of the preservation of human morality, dignity, justice, and law we cannot accept an auto-mated system making the decision to take a human life.'[7] Here, 'dignity' seems to be used in an unspecific way of reaffirming, and giving further emphasis to, a moral judgment. This use is problematic, however, for at least three reasons. The first is that it makes the concept lose its specificity and power. Every immoral act, even that of lesser significance, would be against human dignity. The second is that it fails to account for the fact that human dignity is a specifically defensive or protective notion.

The possession of human dignity implies rights (against others) but no duties against others, whereas morality comprises both rights and duties. The fact that a human individual possesses human dignity confers a number of basic rights on him but no basic duties. The notion of human dignity that has become a central part and premise of political thought, international treaties and national constitutions is no longer the Kantian one, according to which it is possible to act against one's own human dignity. Human dignity in its modern sense is always related to the other. What makes one easily overlook this essential restriction in the concept are some of the other uses of the concept of dignity, which are firmly established in our moral vocabulary, such as the concepts of personal dignity or status dignity. Both personal dignity and status dignity (the dignity of the 'dignitarian') differ from human dignity in crucial respects. They are not universal, they are highly culture-relative and they do not have the same distinctive normative status as human dignity. What is most relevant in our context, however, is that these forms of dignity are, in contrast to human dignity, associated with duties besides rights – the privileges of the dignitarian go together with duties, against oneself and others, and so do the various ego-ideals usually subsumed under the concept of personal dignity.

Still another reason why the use of a concept of human dignity in this extended sense can be called inflationary is that it tends to produce the

---

[7] P. Asaro, 'On banning autonomous weapon systems: human rights, automation, and the dehumanization of lethal decision-making', *International Review of the Red Cross*, 94 (2012), 687, 708.

illusion that affirming that an action is against human dignity adds anything substantial to the judgment that it is morally wrong. It tends to give the wrong impression of justifying the judgment of immorality, whereas it only reaffirms it. A critic of the inflationary use of the concept of human dignity in the German-speaking world, Norbert Hoerster, has succinctly exemplified this kind of illusory argument by quoting the pseudo-reasons given in the catechism of the Catholic Church for condemning sexual intercourse between unmarried people: that it is 'a grave violation of the dignity of these people'.[8] The appearance of substantial argument is given to what amounts, at best, to a tautology.

The third indistinctive use of the notion of human dignity cumulates, in non-academic discourse, in the merely expressive use of the concept, which is devoid of any descriptive content whatsoever. If used in this way, it becomes, as far as its content is concerned, an empty formula – a *Leerformel* – which functions as the expression of an emotional reaction, comparable to an inarticulate utterance of disgust – of what has become known as the 'yuk factor'. Although the kind of revulsion expressed by such invocations of human dignity is sometimes stylized as a genuine moral reaction,[9] it is far from clear if the rejection of innovative practices such as human cloning or surrogate motherhood – two practices that are very often rejected as violations of human dignity by conservative lawyers and politicians, Church officials and the media – is motivated by, or can be explained as, an expression of genuine moral principles. Its role is rather that of a purely rhetorical device, designed to stop discussion short, so as if to keep off bad demons by what anthropologists call 'apotropaic gestures'. Appeals to human dignity are suited to this function for many reasons. Like the concept of God, they are accompanied by a lot of emotions but are semantically vague and open to interpretation; they are efficient as 'conversation stoppers' and as devices for protecting taboos and they claim authority though it is unclear where exactly this authority derives from.

I do not want to assert that any of the uses made of the concept of human dignity in the literature on AWS answer to this description. It cannot be overlooked that references to human dignity function very frequently as formulae that give appeals to established human rights

---

[8] N. Hoerster, 'Zur Bedeutung des Prinzips der Menschenwürde', *Juristische Schulung*, 82 (1983), 93.

[9] Cf. Leon Kass' dictum that 'repugnance is the emotional expression of deep wisdom, beyond reason's power fully to articulate it'. L. Kass, 'The wisdom of repugnance', *The New Republic*, 2 (1997), 17, 20.

more emphasis, without adding to this appeal any independent content.[10]

Automatic weapons systems and human dignity: whose dignity?

The mentioned uses of the concept of human dignity deserve to be called inflationary uses in so far as they overstretch the concept by interpreting it either as a concept applicable to abstract objects such as humanity (in the sense of being human or the human species taken as a whole), a concept that is identical to that of morality in its entirety, including positive duties, or as a purely expressive concept devoid of descriptive content, comparable to concepts such as 'good' or 'awful'. Against these inflationary uses, the proper and established use has been defended, according to which the concept of human dignity is (i) applicable only to human individuals; (ii) a moral concept of particular normative force implying certain human rights without implying human duties; and (iii) a 'thick' concept with considerable expressive content whose content, however, is not exhausted by the expression of revulsion or horror but, instead, refers to a number of defined basic rights.

Taking these conditions as starting points, three questions have to be answered: (i) if AWS are against human dignity, whose dignity is at stake; (ii) what constitutes the violation of human dignity in the case of AWS; and (iii) what is specific about AWS that justifies the particularly strong rejection of these weapons (and only of these weapons) as being contrary to human dignity? Regarding the first question, there is, I believe, only one serious candidate: the civilians threatened by attacks from AWS either as direct targets or as incidental losses in attacks directly aimed at military targets such as combatants or non-human objects. Civilians are victimized by military attacks in a special sense. Soldiers are part of the game, as it were, whereas civilians are not. Soldiers engage in acts of war – they are the active players. Therefore, they are also passive players. They usually know what they have to expect in both roles, and they often have a chance to opt out. Civilians, as a rule, are much less concerned about the rules of war. They often do not know what they have to expect and opting out, by taking refuge in more peaceful regions or countries, is often impossible or extremely burdensome. It is civilians who can be

---

[10] See, e.g., B. Docherty, 'The human implications of "killer robots"', 10 June 2014, available at www.hrw.org/news/2014/06/10/human-rights-implications-killer-robots.

expected to experience the highest degree of threat if such warfare involves the deployment of AWS.

Regarding the second question about what exactly constitutes the violation of human dignity, the answer evidently depends on the catalogue of components of human dignity or basic human rights presupposed. On this, there is a great measure of consensus. Differences concern the margins rather than the 'hard core'. Some years ago, I tentatively submitted the following list of basic human rights implied by human dignity:

1. the right not to be severely humiliated and made the object of public contempt;
2. the right to a minimum of freedom of action and decision;
3. the right to receive support in situations of severe need;
4. the right to a minimum of quality of life and relief of suffering;
5. the right not to be treated merely as a means to other people's ends, i.e. without consent and with severe harm or risk of harm.[11]

I now would add the right to privacy as a further right and, at the same time, emphasize that in each case, only a minimum of the respective right is covered by human dignity. This is necessary to forestall an excess of conflicts between these rights and, thus, within the concept of human dignity.

Of these rights, there is only one, as far as I can see, that is explicitly protected by the legal documents on warfare, the first right on severe humiliation. Articles 8 and 21 of the Rome Statute of the International Criminal Court prohibit and make punishable, in conformity with the Geneva Conventions, 'committing outrages upon personal dignity, in particular humiliating and degrading treatment'.[12] This exclusiveness is in surprising conformity with much of the philosophical discussion on human dignity in the last two decennia. At least a significant fraction of European writers on human dignity – as well as the Israeli philosopher Avishai Margalit – have defended the priority of the protection of human persons from humiliation as the 'core content' of human dignity.[13] For example, a Swiss group of authors wrote in 1998: 'Whenever we ascribe

---

[11] Birnbacher, 'Kann die Menschenwürde die Menschenrechte begründen?', 254ff.
[12] Rome Statute of the International Criminal Court, UN Doc A/CONF.183/9, 1 July 2002. Geneva Conventions, 12 August 1949, 1125 UNTS 3.
[13] A. Margalit, *The Decent Society* (Cambridge, MA: Harvard University Press, 1996). See also E. Hilgendorf (ed.), *Menschenwürde und Demütigung: Die Menschenwürdekonzeption Avishai Margalits* (Baden-Baden: Nomos, 2013).

dignity to a person, we ascribe to him or her the moral right not to be demeaned.'[14]

In the context of the discussion on AWS, the same right is sometimes invoked as a, or even as the, crucial argument against the moral and legal legitimacy of AWS. At the Conference on Autonomous Weapons, which took place in Florence in April 2014, the UN special rapporteur on extrajudicial, summary or arbitrary executions, Christof Heyns, declared in his opening address that 'giving machines greater power to take life and death decisions is demeaning' and that AWS should therefore be taken to violate the 'right to dignity'.[15]

However, can it really be said that AWS humiliate those who are chosen by them as targets or taken in the bargain as incidental victims? And can the kind of threat to which civilians are exposed in the case of attacks by AWS really be taken to be included in the kind of war atrocities that Articles 8 and 21 of the Rome Statute are intended to prohibit? To me, this seems doubtful. Obviously, Articles 8 and 21 aim at the protection of the personal dignity of persons involved in war. Such acts, as a rule, are done in situations where the victims are face to face with those who torture, demean, mob, lynch or expose them to public derision. These paradigm cases of infringements of personal dignity are far removed from attacks by unmanned missiles or drones that select their personal targets with the help of programmed algorithms. I even doubt that it is conceptually possible to seriously talk of humiliating or demeaning behaviour in this context.

However, even if we were to concede that AWS can be said to demean those who are threatened by them, it is far from certain that the right to non-humiliation has a legitimate claim to primacy within the list of rights implied by human dignity. The most that can be said about this right is that it incorporates most directly the kind of derogation of the inherent worth of every and any human being that lies at the root of the basic rights included in human dignity. This does not imply that it deserves a special status. Letting a human being wilfully die from hunger or to

[14] P. Balzer, K. P. Rippe and P. Schaber, *Menschenwürde vs. Würde der Kreatur: Begriffsbestimmung, Gentechnik, Ethikkommissionen* (Freiburg and Munich: Alber, 1998), 31.

[15] C. Heyns, 'The challenge of autonomous weapons systems to legal regulation', paper presented at the Conference on Autonomous Weapons Systems – Law, Ethics, Policy, Academy of European Law, European University Institute, 24–25 April 2014. See C. Heyns, 'Autonomous weapons systems: living a dignified life and dying a dignified death', Chapter 1 in this volume.

imprison him or her without due process are no less violations of human dignity than torture and humiliation.

How AWS threaten human dignity

As I see it, the threat to human dignity that AWS constitute lies in their inherent risk of violating the fourth and fifth rights in the earlier list. The risk that their deployment involves is essentially that they pose threats to civilians that are incompatible with even a minimal quality of life and that they risk making civilians the mere means of aims that are in no way their own aims, with risks of serious harm to life and physical and mental integrity. AWS have a number of features that are likely to cause severe dread, especially in civilians.

The first feature is the asymmetry of forces if AWS are used only on one side. Morally, symmetry and asymmetry are crucial moral variables, and they are deeply influenced by the use of robots.[16] If the fighting occurs among AWS on both or all sides of an armed conflict, there would be much less of a moral problem and fewer issues with human dignity. The fight would have the character of a competition between machines vicariously standing for the technical skills of the combatants. The combatants delegate, as it were, their fighting power to their products – not unlike fights between chess computers of different origin or fights between the teams of soccer robots manufactured and programmed by the engineering faculties of different universities.

Warfare with AWS would be a variant of cyber-warfare. In certain respects, the autonomous weapons already now in use – for example, ballistic missiles for automatically fighting enemy missile attacks – can be looked upon as a variant of such games. They are directed at enemy missiles, not at human beings – combatants or civilians – and find and strike at their targets autonomously. Of course, they are not fully autonomous. There is always someone who decides about their installation and program. However, this program serves only to enable the robot missile to start on its mission on its own, given certain conditions. In most cases, however, the deployment of AWS will be characterized by a significant asymmetry between the weapon and its potential targets. AWS are highly invulnerable by being free from fear, with their deployers carrying, as

---

[16] See E. Datteri and G. Tamburrini, 'Robotic weapons and democratic decision-making' in E. Hilgendorf and G. Philipp (eds.), *Robotik und Gesetzgebung* (Baden-Baden: Nomos, 2013), 211, 214.

Christof Heyns rightly says in his report to the UN, 'no cost except the economic'.[17]

Another feature that is driven to its extreme by AWS is the unpredictability of attacks. Given that AWS are truly autonomous, they decide themselves who is to be made the object of attack, by using their inbuilt intelligence and without any direct control by a human control unit. This capability makes attacks highly unpredictable and exacerbates the threat issuing from these weapons for civilians. The program according to which these robots function may be more inscrutable than the decisions of soldiers or commanders. Differently from the behaviour of human fighters, they are not only beyond the comprehension by commonsense standards and experience but also beyond the powers of even the most sophisticated psychology. It might be said, therefore, that attacks by AWS have an element of the treacherous and, in this way, resemble landmines whose destructive power is likewise characterized by a high degree of unpredictability. It is primarily because of the complete lack of control over the destructive effects of these weapons that they have been prohibited by the Ottawa accord of 1997. In fact, landmines are in many respects an analogue of AWS. They, too, are programmed to detonate autonomously, with the only difference being that they are activated by contact rather than by something as sophisticated as a quasi-decision of their own. It is interesting to note, in this context, that treacherous attacks, among others, are prohibited as war crimes in Article 8 of the Rome Statute.

Another problem AWS pose is their limited capacity to discriminate between combatants and non-combatants and to observe the rules of proportionality. It is clear that such a capacity must be built into autonomous weapons if they are to be in conformity with the laws of war. However, even if weapons of this kind are deployed in areas where there is no certainty about the absence of civilians, the question remains whether the risks of non-discrimination can be sufficiently reduced and robots be entrusted with the task of judging proportionality. Even if targeted against, among others, military machinery manned by soldiers, it has to be questioned whether robots can be expected to master the fine-tuning of aggression that is required by the rules of war. Can a robot, for example, recognize surrender with sufficient reliability? Can a robot be entrusted to know how many victims it has produced and whether the rule of proportionality has been observed? There remains a serious risk

---

[17] Heyns, Report of the Special Rapporteur, 12.

that even the most technically accomplished systems malfunction, leaving behind them a hecatomb of innocent victims. There is already now some experience from the use of drones in Afghanistan to support what has been rightly called the 'illusion of accuracy'.[18] This risk is the more serious the more probable it is that a certain measure of over-confidence in machinery will distort the judgments of commanders in the future, in the same way it has done in the past.

There are, then, a number of reasons why the mental pain produced by being threatened by attacks by AWS might, under certain circumstances, become so intense that their deployment must be judged to be contrary to the human dignity of their actual and potential victims. It is important to see that this judgment is not dependent on objective, but, rather, on subjective parameters. The intensity of threat felt by human subjects, is, as we know, strongly dependent on the apparent source of the threat. Natural threats produce much less fear and anguish than anthropogenic ones, and intentional threats such as those triggered by warfare produce more fear and anguish than accidental ones. The most fear is produced by arbitrary and unpredictable attacks such as those deliberately initiated by terror groups. Deliberately producing fear by threats of this kind is a well-known method of pressurizing, blackmailing and torture. By producing unrelieved mental pain, by severely restricting freedom and by possibly making the victim a mere means to an end that has nothing to do with him or her, they may be held to be sufficiently close to 'classical' violations of human dignity such as torture or brain-washing to be regarded as such.

It should be noted that this argument implies that it is only certain uses of AWS that constitute violations of human dignity and not these weapons themselves – in contrast to arguments for a ban or a moratorium of the development of these systems, according to which these weapons are by their very nature incompatible with human dignity. I do not think that arguments of this categorical kind can be formulated in a coherent and plausible way. What is contrary to human dignity is not these weapons themselves but, rather, the uses to which they might be put. My argument is, consequently, unspecific. It applies to certain uses of certain weapons, no matter whether they involve AWS, remote-controlled long-distance missiles, drones, air strikes or conventional ballistic weapons.

---

[18] N. Sharkey, 'Automating warfare: lessons learned from the drone', *Journal of Law, Information and Science*, 21 (2012), available at www.austlii.edu.au/au/journals/JlLawInfoSci/2012/8.html.

Are AWS intrinsically incompatible with human dignity?

The fact that the reasons for judging AWS to be incompatible with the principles of human dignity are unspecific has two implications: first, that the morally problematic features of AWS are not restricted to this particular weapons system and, second, that these features are extrinsic rather than intrinsic and depend essentially on the probability that these systems tend more than others to be used in ways contrary to human dignity. The first implication is supported by the fact that any single morally problematic feature of AWS is shared by other weapons systems and that some of them sometimes exemplify all of these features conjointly. A high degree of invulnerability is characteristic also of tanks, missiles and stealth bombers. A complete absence of fear is characteristic of long-range weapons such as remote-controlled missiles and drones that do their fatal work without risk to the commanders. Discrimination of combatants and non-combatants and judgments of proportionality are no less difficult in air strikes and long-range attacks than they are with AWS. These may even be more accurate in their targeting and more considerate in their fighting habits than manned systems, not least because of the absence of emotions such as anger, hate and vengefulness, which are the main motivations of war crimes. Even the report by Christof Heyns to the UN concedes as much in stating that 'humans are not necessarily superior to machines in their ability to distinguish'.[19] Above all, robots might be less susceptible to errors by miscalculation, prejudice and other forms of emotional distortions of judgment in the turmoil of war. At least in theory, all of the features that make AWS appear to be problematic from the viewpoint of human dignity might be present in conventional acts of war. Just imagine a scenario in which fighting robots were replaced with hypothetical humans who have the same aggressiveness, intelligence, Achilles-like invulnerability and Siegfried-like absence of fear.

The reasons put forward to show that AWS are intrinsically incompatible with human dignity invariably fail to convince: that, as machines, AWS cannot comprehend the value of human life; that, as machines, AWS cannot take responsibility; and that, differently from human actors, a machine cannot act mercifully or compassionately. The argument that machines cannot comprehend the value of human life is given great credit – for example, in the 2014 Human Rights Watch report on killer robots:

---

[19] Heyns, 'Report of the Special Rapporteur', 13.

> Fully autonomous weapons could undermine the principle of dignity, which implies that everyone has a worth deserving of respect. As inanimate machines, fully autonomous weapons could truly comprehend neither the value of individual life nor the significance of its loss. Allowing them to make determinations to take life away would thus conflict with the principle of dignity.[20]

This is spurious. Of course, machines cannot comprehend the value of human life. But why should this make a difference to their victims if, alternatively, they are threatened with being wounded or killed by manned weapons such as bombers? For the victims whose dignity is at stake, it is a matter of indifference whether the threat they are exposed to comes from manned or unmanned weapons, provided all other parameters of the situation are equal. As I have argued, if their subjective condition – and nothing else – is crucial for determining whether their human dignity is violated or not, the exact source of their subjective condition cannot be relevant, except that it has an anthropogenic and not merely natural origin.

The argument that machines cannot take responsibility has, again, an air of triviality. Nevertheless, this argument plays a role in much of the polemical literature. Peter Asaro, for example, writes:

> I would submit that, when viewed from the perspective of engineering and design ethics, intentionally designing systems that lack responsible and accountable agents is in and of itself unethical, irresponsible, and immoral.[21]

Against this, one is inclined to say that, of course, machines are unable to take responsibility for their decisions, however autonomous they may be, but why should this make a difference to their dignity-infringing effects. The variables that are decisive for their dignity-infringing effects may indeed be more frequent in warfare involving AWS than in conventional warfare. However, that does not show that AWS are intrinsically opposed to respecting the human dignity of their victims. Furthermore, even if the system is autonomous, it is not autonomous to the extent that it is completely independent of human authorship. It is programmed, started and deployed by human beings. The responsibility for its operations lies unconditionally with them.

Does the necessary absence of mercy and compassion on the part of robots make a difference to the threat to human dignity coming from

---

[20] Human Rights Watch, *Shaking the Foundations*, 3.
[21] Asaro, 'On banning autonomous weapon systems', 695.

AWS? Again, Christof Heyns has suggested this in his keynote address statement to the Florence conference:

> The most offensive part is probably not the fact of being killed by a machine, but rather the deprivation of hope for some kind of mercy or reprieve that this technology brings. Since there is no deliberative process, there is no possibility of a higher appeal, no prospect of human empathy.[22]

This is no doubt an interesting thought. However, again, we should remind ourselves that it is only what people experience, in fact, that can be relevant to the extent to which what they suffer is so grave that it should count as a violation of human dignity. Therefore, mere potentialities can count only if the thought of them is a crucial variable in their mental life. It is doubtful, however, whether the mere potentiality of a human commander's mercy or compassion should make a difference if, in fact, this potentiality does not materialize. It must be asked: is an attack by a terror bomber less cruel only because the commander of the aeroplane might in principle be merciful whereas an autonomous system would not – if, in fact, the hope that this happens is as futile in the one case as in the other?

We should beware of idealizations of human warfare. Historical experience provides plenty of examples of war practices that, in terms of the concept of human dignity as it is understood at present, have not only been clear cases of war crimes but, even worse, also violations of the dignity of their victims. The introduction of AWS does not mean the introduction of an altogether new quality of warfare. It introduces, however, new dangers and risks that should make us take precautions against potentially unethical uses of these weapons.

---

[22] Heyns, 'Challenge of autonomous weapons systems', 13.

6

On banning autonomous weapons systems: from deontological to wide consequentialist reasons

GUGLIELMO TAMBURRINI

Introduction

This chapter examines the ethical reasons supporting a moratorium and, more stringently, a pre-emptive ban on autonomous weapons systems (AWS). Discussions of AWS presuppose a relatively clear idea of what it is that makes those systems autonomous. In this technological context, the relevant type of autonomy is task autonomy, as opposed to personal autonomy, which usually pervades ethical discourse. Accordingly, a weapons system is regarded here as autonomous if it is capable of carrying out the task of selecting and engaging military targets without any human intervention.

Since robotic and artificial intelligence technologies are crucially needed to achieve the required task autonomy in most battlefield scenarios, AWS are identified here with some sort of robotic systems. Thus, ethical issues about AWS are strictly related to technical and epistemological assessments of robotic technologies and systems, at least insofar as the operation of AWS must comply with discrimination and proportionality requirements of international humanitarian law (IHL). A variety of environmental and internal control factors are advanced here as major impediments that prevent both present and foreseeable robotic technologies from meeting IHL discrimination and proportionality demands. These impediments provide overwhelming support for an AWS moratorium – that is, for

The author is most grateful to Jürgen Altmann, Noel Sharkey, Leen Spruit, Giuseppe Trautteur and the editors of this volume for their stimulating and helpful comments on a draft of this chapter. The research leading to these results has been partially funded by the Robotics Coordination Action for Europe programme, which has received funding from the European Community Seventh Framework Programme (FP7/2007–2013) under Grant Agreement ICT-611247. The author is solely responsible for its content. It does not represent the opinion of the European Community, and the Community is not responsible for any use that might be made of the information contained therein.

a suspension of AWS development, production and deployment at least until the technology becomes sufficiently mature with respect to IHL. Discrimination and proportionality requirements, which are usually motivated on deontological grounds by appealing to the fundamental rights of the potential victims,[1] also entail certain moral duties on the part of the battlefield actors. Hence, a moratorium on AWS is additionally supported by a reflection on the proper exercise of these duties – military commanders ought to refuse AWS deployment until the risk of violating IHL is sufficiently low.

Public statements about AWS have often failed to take into account the technical and epistemological assessments of state-of-the-art robotics, which provide support for an AWS moratorium. Notably, some experts of military affairs have failed to convey in their public statements the crucial distinction between the expected short-term outcomes of research programmes on AWS and their more ambitious and distant goals. Ordinary citizens, therefore, are likely to misidentify these public statements as well-founded expert opinions and to develop, as a result, unwarranted beliefs about the technological advancements and unrealistic expectations about IHL-compliant AWS. Thus, in addition to the forms of consequential ignorance induced by the usual secrecy and reticence surrounding military technologies, the inadvertent or intentional failure to distinguish clearly between the long-term visionary goals of AWS research and its short-term outcomes hampers public debate about a moratorium and the related democratic deliberations on AWS.

Technical and epistemological assessments of AWS compliance with IHL play a central role in arguments for a moratorium, but they generally recede into the background of arguments for a pre-emptive ban on AWS. Notably, Peter Asaro advanced an argument for banning AWS,[2] which is independent of current and foreseeable failures to comply with IHL discrimination and proportionality requirements. Asaro's argument is distinctively based on the defence of human rights and dignity from a deontological standpoint.

Additional reasons for a pre-emptive ban on AWS are defended here from a consequentialist – rather than a deontological – standpoint in normative ethics. These reasons deserve special attention as they

---

[1] C. Heyns, Report of the Special Rapporteur on extrajudicial, summary or arbitrary execution, UN Doc. A/HRC/23/47, 9 April 2013.

[2] P. Asaro, 'On banning autonomous weapon systems: human rights, automation, and the de-humanization of lethal decision-making', *International Review of the Red Cross*, 94 (2012), 687.

effectively countervail reasons for the future deployment of AWS that are equally advanced on consequentialist grounds in ethics. Consequentialist reasons for the future deployment of AWS are typically based on the expectation of IHL-compliant AWS that will bring down the number of fatalities among combatants, innocent casualties and collateral damage, as a result of their targeting and engagement capabilities that surpass those of emotionally frail and cognitively more limited human soldiers.[3] However, one should carefully note that these reasons flow from a fairly narrow appraisal of the expected consequences of AWS deployment. From a wider consequentialist perspective, the risk of a new arms race and global destabilization – up to and including nuclear destabilization – prevails over the allegedly good consequences of AWS deployment.[4] Accordingly, the consequentialist arguments in normative ethics are found to provide strong support for a pre-emptive ban on AWS, and they converge with deontological arguments that are based on the defence of human dignity and rights.

On the definition of AWS

Taking for granted the customary description of a weapons system as a set of devices and tools that are used for offensive or defensive fighting, the distinctive problem concerning AWS is circumscribing the class of weapons that deserve to be called autonomous. Philosophical definitions of what one may aptly call *personal* autonomy (or *p*-autonomy) are hardly useful in this circumstance, insofar as only conscious individuals, who are additionally assumed to be free and capable of acting on their genuine intentions, are *p*-autonomous. Therefore, no machine that one can make an educated guess about – that is, on the basis of current scientific and technological knowledge – satisfies the requirements for *p*-autonomy.[5]

More pertinent and informative for the purpose of defining and identifying AWS is the idea of *task* autonomy (*t*-autonomy), which is

---

[3] R. C. Arkin, *Governing Lethal Behavior in Autonomous Robots* (Boca Raton, FL: CRC Press, 2009); R. C. Arkin, 'Lethal autonomous systems and the plight of the non-combatant', *AISB Quarterly*, 137 (2013), 1.

[4] J. Altmann, 'Arms control for armed uninhabited vehicles: an ethical issue', *Ethics and Information Technology*, 15 (2013), 137.

[5] The notion of *p*-autonomy, which plays pivotal roles in moral philosophy and law, will turn out to be useful in the ensuing discussion of moral responsibilities of human beings who are in charge of activating an autonomous weapons system (AWS).

construed here as a three-place relationship between a system S, a task t, and another system S'. Roughly speaking, a system S is said to be autonomous at some task t from another system S' (S is t-autonomous from S') if S accomplishes t regularly without any external assistance or intervention by S'. At the age of 10 months, babies usually fail to be autonomous at walking, insofar as they need parental support to do so, whereas most toddlers past the age of 15 months are autonomous from human beings or from any other supporting system at performing this task. Robots that one meets on factory floors are autonomous from human workers at a variety of assembling, painting and payload transportation tasks. Clearly, a system that is autonomous at a task t may fail to be autonomous at many other tasks: car factory robots and toddlers are usually unable to prepare good strawberry ice cream without significant external support. Moreover, a system that is autonomous at t from a system S' may fail to be autonomous at the same task t from another system S''. For example, a driverless car is autonomous from humans at the task of driving but may depend on a GPS system to carry it out correctly.[6]

The US Department of Defense (DoD) proposed a definition of AWS that relies on t-autonomy, insofar as it involves a weapons system S, the complex task t of selecting and engaging military targets and human beings as the systems S' from which S must be autonomous. According to this definition, any weapons system is autonomous 'that, once activated, can select and engage targets without further intervention by a human operator'.[7] The complex task of selecting and engaging targets can be divided into a variety of subtasks: sensory data must be acquired and processed in order to identify, track, select and prioritize targets before one can decide, on the basis of a given set of engagement rules, whether to apply force against them. Therefore, the design and implementation of all but the most rudimentary types of AWS must rely on artificial intelligence and robotic technologies for artificial perception and situational awareness, action planning and reactive behaviour. Thus, most AWS satisfying the DoD's definition are sensibly regarded as some sort of robotic system.

---

[6] The notion of t-autonomy discussed here is closely related to the idea of independence for technological devices examined in the contribution by G. Sartor and A. Omicini, 'The autonomy of technological systems and responsibilities for their use', Chapter 3 in this volume.

[7] US Department of Defense (DoD) Directive 3000.09, 'Autonomy in weapon systems', 21 November 2012, 13–14, available at www.dtic.mil/whs/directives/corres/pdf/300009p .pdf.

Assuming the DoD's definition in the ensuing discussion, let us now turn to consider some specific robotic systems that are autonomous according to this definition. A relatively simple case in point is the Samsung system SGR-A1 – a robotic stationary platform designed to replace or to assist South Korean sentinels in the surveillance of the demilitarized zone between North and South Korea.[8] The SGR-A1 can be operated in either unsupervised or supervised modes. In the unsupervised mode, the SGR-A1 identifies and tracks intruders in the demilitarized zone, eventually firing at them without any further intervention by human operators. In the supervised mode, firing actions are contingent on the judgment and the 'go' command of military officers. Thus, the SGR-A1 counts as an AWS according to the DoD's definition if it operates in the unsupervised mode, and it does not count as such if it operates otherwise. In the latter case, it is better viewed as a combination of a decision-support system with a remote-controlled firing device.

The supervised SGR-A1 preserves almost every t-autonomy required of an AWS, insofar as it performs regularly, and without any human intervention, the perceptual and cognitive tasks of target identification and tracking in its intended operational environment. Accordingly, this robotic sentinel affords a vivid and straightforward illustration of the fact that a simple on/off operational mode switch can make the difference between an AWS and a non-autonomous weapon system. The risk of the SGR-A1 performing poorly at targeting and engagement tasks is reduced in either one of its operational modes by a crucial environmental factor. The Korean demilitarized zone is severely constrained. Human access to areas monitored by the SGR-A1 is categorically prohibited; any human being detected there is classified as a target and perceptual models enabling one to discriminate between human targets and non-targets are available. The Korean robotic sentinel is unable to deal proficiently with more challenging perceptual discrimination and decision-making problems, such as those arising in more cluttered and highly dynamic warfare scenarios, where AWS are required to distinguish belligerents from non-belligerents and friends from foes. Accordingly, attributions of t-autonomies, which enable a weapon system to qualify as autonomous are inherently context dependent, insofar as suitable boundary and initial conditions must be in place for a system S to perform t correctly without any external intervention by human beings. This observation suggests

---

[8] A. Krishnan, *Killer Robots: Legality and Ethicality of Autonomous Weapons* (Aldershot: Ashgate, 2009).

that t-autonomy should be more accurately construed as a relationship between four elements: a system S, a task t, a system S' from which S does not depend to accomplish t and an environment where t must be performed.

Since an AWS can be correctly described as being autonomous in some environments and as non-autonomous in other environments, the problem arises as to whether and how one gets to know that a particular operating environment is included in the class of environments in which a weapons system counts as an AWS. This problem must be duly taken into account by AWS producers, insofar as they have to state the boundary conditions for the intended use of their products, and by military commanders too, insofar as they have to evaluate whether the operational scenario they are dealing with belongs to the class of environments in which the AWS can correctly perform the target selection and engagement task for which it was designed. Major scientific and technological hurdles have to be solved in order to put the prospective AWS producers and users in the right position to adequately address this problem. To illustrate, let us examine an analogous epistemic problem arising in the context of t-autonomies that is of interest to industrial and service robotics.

How does one know that AWS will behave as it is intended?

Environmental conditions contribute to how robotic behaviours are shaped in ways that one can hardly overrate. The tortuous paths that insect-like robots trace on a beach result from the application of a fairly uniform gait on uneven and unsteady walking surfaces. Variable illumination conditions may hinder the visual recognition of obstacles on the trajectory of both outdoor and indoor robots. The water just spilled on the kitchen floor, the Persian carpet recently placed in the living room and many other causal factors changing frictional coefficients may perturb the trajectory of mobile robots negotiating the floors of our homes. Accordingly, good models of robot interactions with the environment must be available to predict, identify and reduce external sources of perturbations that the robot's control system cannot adequately deal with.

Adapting environments to the perceptual, cognitive and action capabilities of robotic systems is a heuristic strategy enabling one to rule out a wide variety of causal factors that jeopardize robotic compliance with task assignment. This strategy is extensively pursued in industrial robotics. For example, one may limit the dynamic behaviour and the sort of items allowed in the industrial robot workspace so that only items that the robot can properly recognize, manipulate or avoid contact with are permitted there. In particular, since human workers are a major source of change, which is both dynamic and difficult to predict, one must strictly regiment human–robotic interactions or fully segregate robots from the workspaces that are assigned to factory workers.

Human–robot segregation policies are no longer available when one moves away from assembly lines and other orderly industrial task environments towards the current frontiers of service and social robotics, where diverse human–robot interactions are often an integral part of the task requirements. To illustrate, consider the prospective use of autonomous mobile robots as assistants or caregivers to people in their homes, especially to elderly or disabled people. A carrier robot must be able to safely take a human being from, say, a bed to an armchair and back again, and a servant robot must be able to grasp cups and glasses and use them properly to serve beverages. In order to be granted permission to sell such robots, prospective manufacturers must supply proper evidence that the autonomous personal care and assistance robots they intend to commercialize are able to perform safely the required *t*-autonomies in normal operating conditions.

Accordingly, the International Organization for Standardization (ISO) 13482 (ISO 2014) demands that each autonomous care robot must be tested carefully for a 'sufficiently low' level of risk to users, and it points to the option of 'constraining the operational scenarios' as a suitable strategy for achieving this goal.[9] However, one cannot pursue this strategy to the point of transforming human dwellings into robotized factory floors or into the likes of the selfish giant's garden in Oscar Wilde's tale, where children are not admitted to play lest they interfere with the proper working of some personal care and assistant robot. In the end, one can only hope to lower drastically the interaction risk by improving the robot control system, by limiting human–robot interaction to a minimum and by warning users about the chief environmental conditions that are likely to disrupt robotic behaviours.

Warfare scenarios resemble neither the orderly factory floors inhabited by industrial robots nor the relatively uneventful homes in which one

---

[9] Organization for International Standardization, *International Standard 13482: Robots and Robotic Devices: Safety Requirements for Personal Care Robots* (Geneva: Organization for International Standardization, 2014), 33.

usually lives. Each fighting side strives to generate unexpected events that defy the opponent's predictions. And the interaction of partially known causal factors in warfare scenarios produces events that are unpredictable on the basis of past experience, knowledge of the battlefield situation and available models of warfare operations. It is in these unstructured and surprise-seeking conditions that AWS must operate. Here, one can neither resort to the ISO's recommendation of 'constraining operational scenarios', for one does not know and control all of the involved forces, nor confidently believe that the more important 'abnormal' situations perturbing the desired AWS behaviours have been properly taken care of.

From AWS epistemology to moral reasons for a moratorium

The epistemic predicament concerning unstructured warfare scenarios is enhanced by an appraisal of the state-of-the-art technologies for robotic perception. Consider the problem of recognizing *hors de combat* people – one has to be able to tell bystanders from foes and hostile opponents from surrendering, unconscious or otherwise inoffensive opponents. Identifying behaviours that conventionally or inconventionally carry surrender messages involves the viewpoint-independent classification of bodily postures and gestures in variable illumination conditions, in addition to an understanding of emotional expressions and real-time reasoning about deceptive intentions and actions in unstructured warfare scenarios. Thus, engineers who wish to endow an AWS with IHL-compliant competences face a distinctive challenge from the fact that adequate sets of rules for perceptual classification are difficult to isolate and state precisely.

Instead of attempting to furnish robots with an exhaustive set of rules for perceptual classification, one may opt instead to give them the capability of learning these rules from experience. The learning robot must identify classification rules on the basis of some finite set of training data, usually containing instances of correct and incorrect classifications. Once this learning phase is concluded, the reliability of the rule that has been learned can be assessed by theoretical or empirical methods.[10] In either case, however, the results that are obtained are contingent on a variety of background assumptions.[11] Thus, for example, the outcomes of

---

[10] T. M. Mitchell, *Machine Learning* (New York: McGraw Hill, 1997).

[11] M. Santoro, D. Marino and G. Tamburrini, 'Robots interacting with humans: from epistemic risk to responsibility', *AI and Society*, 22 (2008), 301.

empirical testing on learned rule reliability depend on the assumption
that the training and testing data are significant representatives of the
perceptual classification problems that the robot must solve. Similarly,
probabilistic bounds on error frequency that one establishes within the
more abstract mathematical framework of statistical learning theory are
contingent on the assumption that the training data were independently
drawn from some fixed probability distribution.[12] Assumptions of both
kinds are crucial in addressing the ethical and legal problems that concern learning robots,[13] but they are difficult to buttress in the case of
human–robot interactions envisaged in service and social robotics and,
a fortiori, in surprise-seeking, erratic and unstructured warfare scenarios.

Scientists in the field of robotics have frequently emphasized the
formidable scientific and technological challenges that have to be met
before one can realistically envisage IHL-compliant AWS. Thus, Noel
Sharkey has stated that '[c]urrently and for the foreseeable future no
autonomous robots or artificial intelligence systems have the necessary
properties to enable discrimination between combatants and civilians or
to make proportionality decisions'.[14] And Ronald Arkin has advanced an
argument for a moratorium that hinges on the current and foreseeable
limitations of robotics systems: '[T]he use and deployment of ethical
autonomous robotic systems is not a short-term goal ... There are
profound technological challenges to be resolved, such as effective
in situ target discrimination and recognition of the status of those
otherwise hors de combat.' For this reason, he claims, 'I support the call
for a moratorium to ensure that such technology meets international
standards before being considered for deployment.'[15]

[12] V. Vapnik, The Nature of Statistical Learning Theory, 2nd edn (New York: Springer, 2000).
[13] D. Marino and G. Tamburrini, 'Learning robots and human responsibility', International Review of Information Ethics, 6 (2006), 46.
[14] N. Sharkey, 'Saying "no!" to lethal autonomous targeting', Journal of Military Ethics, 9 (2010), 369, 378.
[15] As a suitable benchmark to verify international standards, Arkin proposes the capability of a robot to behave as well as, or better than, our soldiers with respect to adherence to the existing international humanitarian law (IHL). Let us note in passing that the successful implementation of an ethical inference engine conforming, e.g., to the ethical governor architecture outlined in Arkin's scholarship, would be largely insufficient to enable an AWS to comply with IHL. Indeed, the moral arguments licensing any such conclusion must include among their premises perceptually corroborated statements concerning, e.g., the presence or absence of hostile combatants and non-belligerents, thereby presupposing an adequate solution to the perceptual classification problems mentioned above. R. C. Arkin, 'Governing lethal behavior: embedding ethics in a hybrid deliberative/reactive robot

Arkin's argument espouses a broad consequentialist framework for ethical theorizing about an AWS moratorium insofar as the moral permission to deploy them is contingent on discrimination and proportionality principles, in addition to the casualty reduction benefits that one may obtain from AWS that behave according to very conservative firing decisions that human soldiers cannot afford to apply in view of their legitimate self-preservation concerns. Within this consequentialist ethical framework, the epistemological reflections on state-of-the-art and foreseeable developments in robotics and artificial intelligence overwhelmingly support the moral obligation of suspending AWS development, production and deployment at least until compliance with IHL principles and other envisaged benefits has been convincingly demonstrated. One can adduce additional moral reasons for an AWS moratorium from a deontological standpoint in ethical theorizing.

As Pablo Kalmanovitz emphasizes in his contribution to this volume,[16] the deployment of an AWS is not an automated action but, rather, the deliberate decision of some military commander. In their deliberations, commanders are morally responsible for taking all reasonable steps to ensure that their orders comply with IHL proportionality and distinction requirements. Thus, in particular, commanders are morally responsible for activating an AWS only if their knowledge licences the judgment that the risk of running counter to IHL requirements is acceptably low. This moral requirement entails that commanders must be given in advance adequate information, based on extensive modelling and testing activities, about IHL-compliant activations of AWS and their boundary conditions. However, the epistemic uncertainties mentioned above vividly demonstrate that this information is presently unavailable. Therefore, commanders ought to refuse systematically to deploy AWS, given that they are not in a position to assert that the risk of running counter to IHL requirements is acceptably low. By the same token, the respect that is due to military commanders – *qua* agents who have to make real moral choices – demands that AWS should not be supplied as equipment for possible use in combat at least while the present epistemic uncertainties persist.

The latter conclusion about respect for the commander's moral agency is reinforced by considering the notion of dignity – in the sense of

architecture', Technical Report GIT-GVU-07-11 (2007); R. C. Arkin, *Governing Lethal Behavior in Autonomous Robots*.
[16] P. Kalmanovitz, 'Judgment, liability and the risks of riskless warfare', Chapter 7 in this volume.

personal and rank dignity, which is discussed by Dieter Birnbacher in his contribution to this volume.[17] Unlike human dignity, which is exclusively associated with human rights, Birnbacher points out that both personal and rank dignity are also associated with duties. Thus, in particular, the rank attributed to military commanders comes with the moral duty to assess the risk of violating IHL requirements and to set out their orders accordingly. Moreover, the commander's personal dignity is derivatively involved as well, insofar as the commanders' prerogatives and duties are an integral part of their culturally determined personal dignity.

To sum up, convincing arguments for an AWS moratorium have been advanced from both a deontological and a consequentialist standpoint in ethical theorizing. Arguments of both kinds involve as a crucial premise educated guesses about the current and foreseeable developments in robotics and artificial intelligence. Surprisingly enough, some public statements about AWS happen to neglect entirely these technological assessments and related epistemic predicaments, thus jeopardizing the correct development of democratic debates and giving rise to unjustified biases in decision-making processes about an AWS moratorium.

Democratic decision making in the fog of AWS agnotology

'A lot of people fear artificial intelligence', John Arquilla was quoted as claiming in a *New York Times* article of 28 November 2010, but 'I will stand my artificial intelligence against your human any day of the week and tell you that my A.I. will pay more attention to the rules of engagement and create fewer ethical lapses than a human force.'[18] This claim by the executive director of the Information Operations Center of the US Naval Postgraduate School echoes an earlier statement issued by Gordon Johnson of the Joint Forces Command at the Pentagon, who asserted that robotic soldiers 'don't get hungry, they're not afraid. They don't forget their orders. They don't care if the guy next to them has just been shot. Will they do a better job than humans? Yes.'[19]

---

[17] D. Birnbacher, 'Are autonomous weapons systems a threat to human dignity?', Chapter 5 in this volume.
[18] 'War machines: recruiting robots for combat', *New York Times* (28 November 2010), available at www.nytimes.com/2010/11/28/science/28robot.html?_r=0.
[19] 'New model army soldier rolls closer to battle', *New York Times* (16 February 2005), available at www.nytimes.com/2005/02/16/technology/new-model-army-soldierrolls-closer-to-battle.html.

There is an evident tension between these statements and the assessment of the current and foreseeable capabilities of robotic systems by
scientists working in artificial intelligence and robotics.[20] One should
carefully note that these statements, issued by experts in military affairs,
are addressed to a wide audience of people who are generally unfamiliar
with both weapons systems and the state of the art in artificial intelligence
and robotic technologies. Tagged as well-founded expert opinions, these
statements are likely to elicit or reinforce unrealistic beliefs and expectations in public opinion about robotic weapons in general and about AWS
in particular. Since democratic decision making in technologically afflu-
ent societies is bound to rely on information that is supplied by experts,
these unrealistic beliefs and expectations may unduly influence the formation of public opinion and democratic deliberations about AWS by
ordinary citizens and their political representatives.

It is useful to distinguish the mechanism that gives rise to this form of
consequential ignorance from other mechanisms and forms of ignorance
production about AWS. Robert Proctor coined the word 'agnotology' to
designate the study of the cultural production of ignorance and its effects
on both individual and collective decision-making processes.[21] He identified various mechanisms of ignorance production, including both
ignorance as an active construct and ignorance as selective choice.
A blatant example of the former mechanism is the tobacco industry's
policy of inducing doubts about the dangers of smoking. A more subtle
example of the latter mechanism is any process of selecting research
themes, which usually involves pruning alternative research themes.

Public debates and democratic deliberations concerning the prospective uses of AWS are hampered by ignorance as an active construct,
insofar as secrecy and reticence often surround the development and
deployment of military technologies. Moreover they are hampered by
selective choice, to the extent that AWS research projects are preferred
over research projects that more clearly prize the ethical, political and
military advantages flowing from the meaningful human control on
robotic weapons that Noel Sharkey examines in his contribution to this

---

[20] R. C. Arkin, 'Lethal autonomous systems'; N. Sharkey, 'Cassandra or the false prophet of
doom: AI robots and war', *IEEE Intelligent Systems*, 23 (2008), 14; N. Sharkey, 'Grounds
for discrimination: autonomous robot', *RUSI Defence Systems*, 11 (2008), 86; Sharkey,
'Saying "no!" to lethal autonomous targeting'.

[21] R. Proctor, 'A missing term to describe the cultural production of ignorance (and its
study)' in R. Proctor and L. Schiebinger (eds.), *Agnotology: The Making and Unmaking of
Ignorance* (Stanford University Press, 2008), 1.

volume. And they are also hampered by what one may aptly call the *temporal framing* mechanism of ignorance production. This mechanism induces false beliefs about the time scales of envisaged technological advancements from a failure to convey clearly the distinction between the long-term (and often admittedly visionary) goals of ambitious technological research programs, on the one hand, and their expected short-term outcomes, on the other hand.[22]

The distinction between long-term and short-term goals is crucial to understand what actually goes on in many research programmes in robotics. Long-term visions of research programmes in home service robotics envisage robots that are endowed with the versatile competences of human butlers, tutors and assistants. These long-term visions are useful insofar as they play regulative and inspirational roles in inquiry. They should be clearly distinguished, however, from the short-term goals driving daily research activities on home robots. These technological short-term goals, unlike the underlying long-term visions, are expected to be feasible on the basis of state-of-the-art technologies and to feed the pipeline between technological inquiry and industry.[23] Thus, short-term goals of research on home robots are not concerned with the development of ideal butlers but, rather, with robots that selectively perform vacuum-cleaning jobs, tele-presence and medication-taking reminder services, assistance in emergency calls, and so on.

RoboCup affords another vivid illustration of the interactions between, and the respective roles of, the long-term and short-term goals of technological inquiry. RoboCup, which is familiar to the general public for its robotic soccer tournaments, cultivates the ambition of putting together a robotic soccer team that will beat the human world champion team. Fulfilling this long-term goal presupposes so many far-reaching advances

---

[22] Similarly asynchronous goal-pursuing processes are postulated in two-process models of scientific inquiry (Godfrey-Smith), which notably include Lakatos' scientific research programs and Laudan's research traditions. See P. Godfrey-Smith, *Theory and Reality: An Introduction to the Philosophy of Science* (University of Chicago Press, 2003); I. Lakatos, 'Falsification and the methodology of scientific research programmes' in J. Worrall and G. Currie (eds.), *Philosophical Papers*, vol. 1: *The Methodology of Scientific Research Programmes* (Cambridge University Press, 1978), 8; L. Laudan, *Progress and Its Problems: Toward a Theory of Scientific Growth* (University of California Press, 1977). See also E. Datteri and G. Tamburrini, 'Robotic weapons and democratic decision-making' in E. Hilgendorf and J.-P. Guenther (eds.), *Robotik und Gesetzegebung* (Baden-Baden: Nomos, 2013), 211; G. Tamburrini, 'On the ethical framing of research programs in robotics', *AI and Society* (forthcoming).

[23] Tamburrini, 'On the ethical framing of research programs'.

in sensorimotor and cognitive skills of multi-agent robotic systems that one may sensibly doubt whether the research efforts of a few generations of committed scientists will suffice to bridge the gap between vision and reality. Beating the best human soccer team, the RoboCup manifesto acknowledges, 'will take decades of efforts, if not centuries. It is not feasible, with the current technologies, to accomplish this goal in any near term.' However, the RoboCup's elusive long-term goal has a significant role to play in the context of RoboCup research activities, insofar as it enables one to shape a fruitful research agenda by suggesting 'a series of well-directed subgoals', which are both feasible and technologically rewarding.[24] In particular, periodic RoboCup tournaments enable scientists to improve continually on the playing capabilities of robotic soccer teams and to identify, on the basis of the playing performances of the winning teams, the benchmarks that the robotic teams participating in the next tournaments will be confronted with.

Having an AWS achieve human-like capabilities in the way of IHL discrimination and proportionality requirements is comparable to the RoboCup's long-term, visionary goal of beating the human world champion soccer team with a team of robots. Both are formidable and possibly unattainable technological challenges. However, the RoboCup's long-term goal is prized for its role in shaping fruitful research agendas towards sub-goals that are feasible, technologically rewarding and morally permissible per se. In contrast, the long-term goal of AWS research may only result in the short term with a weapon system that fails to comply with IHL and that is not morally permitted on both deontological and consequentialist grounds.

Experts speaking to restricted circles of peers may abstain from signalling whether they are speaking from the long-term or short-term perspective of a research programme. Indeed, shared background knowledge enables each member of the audience to identify which perspective the speaker is talking from. In public statements about their work, however, experts can no longer count on the shared background of tacit knowledge that shapes communication styles within communities of experts. Accordingly, experts wishing to provide correct and accessible public information must give adequate information about the expected

[24] See RoboCup, available at www.robocup.org/about-robocup/objective/. The full quotation is: 'Needless to say, the accomplishment of the ultimate goal will take decades of efforts, if not centuries. It is not feasible, with the current technologies, to accomplish this goal in any near term. However, this goal can easily create a series of well-directed subgoals. Such an approach is common in any ambitious, or overly ambitious, project.'

temporal frame for the various goals of the research programmes they talk about. Temporal framing mechanisms of ignorance production are activated by inadvertent or intentional failures to meet this challenge. And, clearly, the resulting agnotological effects are likely to be further amplified at the hands of both sensationalist media reporting and individual psychological responses.[25]

Moral responsibilities in democratic deliberation about AWS and other novel technologies are distributed in accordance with a sensible division of epistemic labour.[26] Citizens have the moral responsibility of reducing their consequential ignorance about scientific and technological matters, which threatens their moral values and aspirations. Experts carry the moral responsibility of supplying what is, to their best knowledge, correct and adequate scientific and technological information for democratic decision making. In many circumstances, however, citizens fail to collect the relevant background information, eventually choosing alternatives that conflict with their own interests and moral values. And experts exacerbate states of consequential ignorance by intentionally or inadvertently supplying inaccurate or incorrect information for social and political deliberation. It is worth contrasting, from this perspective of temporal framing ignorance production and its moral implications, the public statements by military experts quoted at the beginning of this section with the following statement about AWS attributed to Ronald Arkin in an *International Herald Tribune* article, dated 26 November 2008: 'My research hypothesis is that intelligent robots can behave more ethically in the battlefield than humans currently can.'[27] Arkin is careful to emphasize that he is advancing a research hypothesis, thereby implying that his educated guess may be refuted like any other research hypothesis, remain unfulfilled for a long time to come or even be relinquished in the long run for persistent lack of substantial rewards. Elsewhere, he states that '[i]t is too early to tell whether this venture will be successful', emphasizing that there are 'daunting problems' of a technical nature that remain to be solved.[28] No trace of similar temporal

---

[25] For some pertinent psychological models explaining psychological responses overestimating or devaluing the expected outcomes of technological research, see F. Scalzone and G. Tamburrini, 'Human–robot interaction and psychoanalysis', *AI and Society*, 28 (2013), 297.

[26] P. Kitcher, *Science in a Democratic Society* (Amherst, NY: Prometheus Books, 2011).

[27] 'Robot may be more "humane" soldier', *International Herald Tribune* (26 November 2008).

[28] Arkin, *Governing Lethal Behavior in Autonomous Robots*.

and epistemic qualifications is found in the public statements by Arquilla and Johnson quoted at the beginning of this section.

In conclusion, temporal frame mechanisms of ignorance production give rise to screening-off effects and biases that unduly affect democratic debates and decision making about AWS. Communication ethics demands that all stakeholders in these debates carefully check their statements for these effects. Once temporal frames are correctly conveyed, one has to come to terms with the fact that developing perceptual, reasoning and action capabilities that may enable an AWS to surpass a human soldier in the way of IHL compliance is a formidable and possibly unattainable technological challenge – no less formidable than the RoboCup's regulative idea of beating the human world champion soccer team with a team of robots. Thus, a proper understanding of the involved temporal scales enables one to endorse a major premise of the arguments that, from both a deontological and consequentialist viewpoint in normative ethics, converge on the need for an AWS moratorium.

Wide consequentialist reasons for banning AWS

Let us finally turn to a consideration of the arguments for a ban on AWS. The epistemic predicaments that loom so large on arguments for a moratorium play only a minor role. Indeed, the upshot of the ethical arguments for banning AWS is to show that, no matter how well AWS will come to perform their targeting and engagement tasks, there are overriding moral reasons to forbid their use. Asaro's argument for banning AWS, which is supposed to apply to any conceivable AWS, no matter whether or how well it complies with IHL, is advanced from a distinctively deontological standpoint in normative ethics.[29] According to Asaro, human beings have the right of not being deprived of their life arbitrarily – that is, without the respect that other human beings owe to them as potential victims of lethal force. For killing decisions to count as non-arbitrary, Asaro argues, they must be taken on the basis of a responsible exercise of human judgment and compassion. Since AWS fail to meet these requirements, their use must be absolutely prohibited. In particular, Asaro remarks: 'The decision to kill a human can only be legitimate if it is non-arbitrary, and there is no way to guarantee that the use of force is not arbitrary without human control, supervision and responsibility. It is thus immoral to kill without the

[29] Asaro, 'On banning autonomous weapon systems'.

involvement of human reason, judgement and compassion, and it should be illegal.' And he goes on to claim that '[a]s a matter of the preservation of human morality, dignity, justice and law, we cannot accept an automated system making the decision to take a human life. And we should respect this by prohibiting autonomous weapon systems. When it comes to killing, each instance is deserving of human attention and consideration in light of the moral weight that is inherent in the active taking of a human life.'[30]

It was suggested that a ban on AWS can be supported exclusively if one endorses a similar deontological standpoint in normative ethics and shares with Asaro the view that potential victims of lethal force in warfare have certain inalienable rights: 'The moral support for a ban on the deployment of any autonomous robotic weapon depends entirely on whether it is decided that there is a human right not to be the target of a robotic weapon.'[31] However, this claim overlooks the fact that significant arguments for a ban on AWS have been advanced neither on the basis of a deontological framework in normative ethics nor by appealing to fundamental human rights but, rather, by adopting a purely consequentialist standpoint. Any consequentialist argument for or against a ban on AWS is presently bound to focus on the expected, rather than the actual, consequences of their deployment since these weapon systems have not yet been deployed. Building on a distinction between narrow and wide consequentialist reasons, it is argued here that by sufficiently enlarging the temporal and spatial horizon of the expected consequences,

---

[30] See *ibid.*, 708. It is worth noting that Asaro's appeal to human dignity can be construed in terms of both a Kantian conception of human dignity and the recently revived conception of human dignity as rank, already mentioned above, and according to which a high-ranking status must be extended to every human being. See J. Waldron, *Dignity, Rank and Rights* (Oxford University Press, 2013). This generalization of status affords the same kind of protection from degrading treatment offered by the familiar Kantian construals of dignity. According to Asaro, delegating to AWS life or death decisions results in inhumane and degrading treatment of potential victims. Christof Heyns examines Asaro's argument in the context of a call for an AWS moratorium (see Heyns, Report of the Special Rapporteur on extrajudicial, summary or arbitrary execution). Lieblich and Benvenisti, in their contribution to this volume, extend Asaro's motives for protecting potential victims of AWS attacks; and Birnbacher, in his contribution to this volume, critically examines Asaro's use of the notion of human dignity. E. Lieblich and E. Benvenisti, 'The obligation to exercise discretion in warfare: why autonomous weapons systems are unlawful', Chapter 11 and D. Birnbacher, 'Are autonomous weapons systems a threat to human dignity?', Chapter 5 in this volume.

[31] J. P. Sullins, 'An ethical analysis of the case for robotic weapons arms control' in K. Podins, J. Stinissen and M. Maybaum (eds.), *Proceedings of the Fifth International Conference on Cyber Conflict* (Tallinn: NATO CCD COE Publications, 2013), 487, 497.

the consequentialist reasons offered for a ban largely outweigh those offered for future AWS deployment.

To begin with, let us recall that the consequentialist reasons for the future deployment of AWS include reduced casualties not only in one's own and the opponents' camp but also among non-belligerents as a result of more accurate targeting and a more conservative decision to fire, which are free from human self-preservation concerns.[32] These reasons for the future deployment of AWS concern only expected battlefield performances and some of their outcomes. Consequences that one may expect on a more global scale are neglected, therefore revealing a narrow consequentialist perspective on AWS' future deployment. Instead, a broad consequentialist standpoint takes into account the expected effects on peace stability, on incentives to start wars by the newly introduced conventional armament, on the likelihood of escalation from conventional to nuclear warfare and on the disruption of extant nuclear deterrence factors. Sharkey takes a broad consequentialist standpoint when he points out that 'having robots to reduce the "body-bag count" could mean fewer disincentives to start wars', thereby suggesting that a reduction of one's own casualties in the short term cannot compensate for the higher numbers of casualties and destruction caused by increased numbers of conflicts that AWS may facilitate in the long term.[33] On more general grounds, Jürgen Altmann suggests that the list of issues that are usually addressed be extended if one wants to provide a balanced aggregate assessment of the expected costs and benefits flowing from future AWS deployment:

> If new classes of conventional weapons are emerging, as is the case with armed uninhabited vehicles, they should be assessed with respect to questions such as do they make war more likely and do they raise other dangers. Envisioned short-term military advantages should be weighed against the probable long-term consequences for national, and, in particular, international, security.[34]

---

[32] Arkin, *Governing Lethal Behavior in Autonomous Robots*.

[33] Sharkey, 'Cassandra or the false prophet of doom', 16; see also F. Sauer and N. Schörnig, 'Killer drones: the silver bullet of democratic warfare?', *Security Dialogue*, 34 (2012), 363, 365.

[34] See also J. Altmann, 'Preventive arms control for uninhabited military vehicles' in R. Capurro and M. Nagenborg (eds.), *Ethics and Robotics* (Amsterdam: IOS Press, 2009), 69, 80–1: 'Seen from a narrow standpoint of national military strength, these developments will provide better possibilities to fight wars and to prevail in them. However, if one looks at the international system with its interactions, the judgment will be different, in particular concerning armed robots/uninhabited systems. Destabilization and proliferation could make war more probable, including between great/nuclear powers.'

AWS are potentially more threatening to global security than many other conventional weapons. In particular, swarms of aerial AWS that are capable of initiating coordinated attacks on great numbers of civilian infrastructures and military objectives raise serious concerns in connection with a new arms race and its expected impact on global destabilization. This observation shows the implausibility of the *ceteris paribus* assumption that the deployment of AWS on the battlefield will not have an ethically significant impact on causal factors and strategic reasons underlying the decision to start or escalate armed conflicts. However, this is exactly the implicit assumption on which the force of narrow consequentialist arguments for the future deployment of AWS entirely depends.

The threat of destabilization raised by swarms of AWS may be a sufficiently serious incentive for a conventional war. However, one should be careful to note that AWS, more than many other conventional arms, have the potential to deliver destructive attacks on strategic nuclear objectives. Swarms of AWS might be capable of delivering a powerful first strike against the opponent's nuclear arsenals, to the extent that they may thwart the opponent's second-strike capability of responding with nuclear retaliation. In this scenario, traditional nuclear deterrence based on mutually assured destruction would no longer be appealing and first-strike strategies would be prized instead.

Let us now try and assess from a wide consequentialist standpoint the aggregate of expected benefits and costs flowing from AWS deployment. By permitting the future deployment of AWS, one might expect reduced casualties among belligerents and non-belligerents in some battlefield scenarios. At the same time, however, one would significantly raise the risk of a new arms race and global destabilization, by providing incentives for the commencement of wars and by weakening traditional nuclear deterrence factors based on mutually assured destruction. As far as the latter kind of risk is concerned, one can hardly think of a more critical danger to humankind than the danger of setting off a nuclear conflict, and one can hardly think of a more desirable state for humankind than the state of nuclear peace preservation. Since the expected costs of an arms race and destabilization outweigh the sum of the expected benefits flowing from AWS future deployment, opting for a pre-emptive ban on AWS is tantamount to choosing the collective rule of behaviour that is expected to produce the most preferable set of consequences in a global geopolitical context.

In conclusion, there is a strong confluence on an international pre-emptive ban on AWS from both a deontological and a broad consequentialist standpoint in normative ethics. The introduction of a ban on AWS will raise the problem of enforcing international interdictions on the development, production and deployment of AWS. Runaway development of AWS under a ban will be facilitated by adaptations of cutting-edge robotic technologies that were originally intended for civilian applications. For example, European Union (EU) programmes supporting research in robotics have excluded the funding of scientific and technological research for military applications. However, the outcomes of EU projects for, say, swarming robot technologies can be used straightforwardly to develop swarms of AWS, such as the swarms of autonomous robot boats already developed by the US Navy.[35] Artificial intelligence scientist Stuart Russell goes as far as suggesting that 'the technology already demonstrated for self-driving cars, together with the human-like tactical control learned by DeepMind's DQN system, could support urban search-and-destroy missions'.[36] Accordingly, in a comprehensive system of compliance for a pre-emptive ban on AWS measures,[37] one will have to include the careful assessment of advances in robotics that are made possible by non-military research programmes so as to adequately benefit monitoring and early-warning procedures.

[35] For European Union-funded projects on swarming robots, see Horizon 2020, 'The way of the future: "swarming" robots', 6 February 2014, available at http://ec.europa.eu/programmes/horizon2020/en/news/way-future-%E2%80%98swarming%E2%80%99-robots; for more information on navy swarm boats, see 'US navy could "swarm" foes with robot boats', CNN (13 October 2014), available at http://edition.cnn.com/2014/10/06/tech/innovation/navy-swarm-boats/.

[36] S. Russell, 'Take a stand on AI weapons', Nature, 521 (2015), 415, 415.

[37] M. Gubrud and J. Altmann, 'Compliance measures for an autonomous weapons convention', ICRAC Working Papers, 2 (2013), available at http://icrac.net/resources/.

PART IV

Risk, transparency and legal compliance in the regulation of autonomous weapons systems

7

Judgment, liability and the risks of riskless warfare

PABLO KALMANOVITZ

Critics of autonomous weapons systems (AWS) claim that they are both inherently unethical and unlawful under current international humanitarian law (IHL). They are unethical, it is said, because they necessarily preclude making any agent fairly accountable for the wrongful effects of AWS, and because allowing machines to make life or death decisions seriously undermines human dignity: only moral beings should make such decisions and only after careful moral deliberation, for which they could be held accountable. AWS are inherently unlawful, critics say, because they cannot possibly comply with the core IHL principles of discrimination and proportionality.

Contrary to these critics, I argue in this chapter that AWS can conceivably be developed and deployed in ways that are compatible with IHL and do not preclude the fair attribution of responsibility, even criminal liability, in human agents. While IHL may significantly limit the ways in which AWS can be permissibly used, IHL is flexible and conventional enough to allow for the development and deployment of AWS in some suitably accountable form. Having indicated how AWS may be compatible with IHL and fair accountability, I turn to a serious worry that has been largely neglected in the normative literature on AWS. The development of AWS would deepen the already ongoing and very troubling dynamics of asymmetrical and so-called riskless warfare. While IHL-compatible AWS could be developed, in principle, and agents in charge of designing, testing and deploying AWS could be held accountable for wrongful harms, there are troublingly few incentives to duly control and minimize the risks to foreign civilians in the contexts of asymmetrical warfare. The most

For helpful comments and suggestions, I am grateful to the volume editors and to audiences at the European University Institute in Florence, in particular, Or Bassok, Nehal Bhuta, Claus Kreß and Martin Scheinin.

troubling aspects of AWS, I suggest, are not matters of deep ethical or legal principle but, rather, the lack of incentives for implementing effective regulations and accountability.

The main goal of this chapter is to articulate this distinct worry and emphasize how serious it is. Once this is appreciated, it will be clear that more attention needs to be paid to determining what conditions would allow for the effective oversight of AWS development, testing and eventual use. Such oversight may be accomplished partly by defining liability criteria for agents working within the industrial and organizational complex behind AWS design, production and use. Ultimately, however, public scrutiny may be the only available effective push for IHL compliance and accountability. Secrecy under the guise of national security undermines the clearest incentive for effective regulation, namely naming and shaming before public opinion.

The first section of the chapter argues that it is conceivable that AWS could be designed and deployed in keeping with the IHL principles of proportionality and distinction. These principles limit permissible deployment to narrowly circumscribed conditions in time and space but do not altogether preclude their use. The second section argues that AWS deployment need not undermine the basis for fairly attributing responsibility to human agents; neither fair criminal liability nor lesser forms of liability are inherently incompatible with the autonomy of so-called killer robots. The third section turns to the lack of incentives to adequately test and assess the compliance of AWS with IHL. In asymmetrical warfare, which is a very likely context of AWS deployment, the proper incentives for risk control are lacking. The fourth section briefly concludes.

Practical reasons versus algorithmic calculations

The defining mark of AWS is that, once activated, they can 'select and engage targets without further intervention by a human operator'.[1] The ultimate decision to kill rests on a machine, not on a human operator. Anti-personnel mines count as AWS according to this definition, but the unprecedented and most troubling issues raised by AWS follow from the use of cutting-edge technology to design far more sophisticated autonomous decision-making processes.

---

[1] United States Department of Defense (DoD) Directive 3000.09, 'Autonomy in weapon systems', 21 November 2012, 13, available at www.dtic.mil/whs/directives/corres/pdf/300009p.pdf.

Military technology has been moving in the direction of automation for decades. The deployment of weapons with limited autonomy is foreseeable in the near future. Already the US Navy Phalanx system can autonomously search, detect and engage targets, but it has not yet been launched without direct human oversight and control.[2] Britain's 'fire-and-forget' Brimstone missiles can distinguish among tanks, cars and buses without human assistance and can hunt targets autonomously in pre-designated areas. A swarm of Brimstones was deployed in Libya in 2011 against a group of tanks, which were destroyed in a coordinated way that, according to a *New York Times* report, would have been impossible for human operators.[3] Israel's Harpy anti-radar missile system can detect and autonomously destroy enemy radars when they are turned on, and its Guardium sentry robot has been designed to autonomously patrol and identify 'suspicious elements' on the border with Gaza. It may eventually be allowed to use force autonomously. South Korea's SGR-A1 system similarly identifies and tracks intruders autonomously in the demilitarized border with North Korea and can be set to fire without human intervention.[4]

Given that weapon technology already performs a wide range of functions autonomously, it may seem that the automation of the actual use of force would only be another step in an ongoing trend. Critics have argued to the contrary. According to Peter Asaro, deploying AWS amounts to crossing a 'principled boundary' on a technological slippery slope, namely the principle that 'a human being needs to be meaningfully involved in making the decision of whether or not lethal force will actually be used in each case'.[5] Crossing this boundary amounts to giving up human responsibility and judgment in the use of lethal force, which is inherently wrong. Similarly, Mary Ellen O'Connell holds that it is a bedrock principle of law and morality that 'a human being who has training and a conscience and who may be held accountable should always make the awesome, ultimate decision to kill'.[6] It is a basic principle of morality, these critics submit, that

---

[2] G. Marchant *et al.*, 'International governance of autonomous weapons systems', *Columbia Science and Technology Law Review*, 12 (2011), 272, 276–7.

[3] J. Markoff, 'Fearing bombs that can pick whom to kill', *New York Times* (12 November 2014), A1.

[4] A. Krishnan, *Killer Robots: Legality and Ethicality of Autonomous Weapons* (Aldershot: Ashgate, 2009), 71–3.

[5] P. Asaro, 'On banning autonomous weapon systems: human rights, automation, and the dehumanization of lethal decision-making', *International Review of the Red Cross*, 94 (2012), 687, 707.

[6] M. E. O'Connell, 'Banning autonomous killing' in M. Evangelista and H. Shue (eds.), *The American Way of Bombing* (Ithaca, NY: Cornell University Press, 2014), 224, 232.

human life can only be taken upon serious moral reflection and that only a human being can so reflect and be accountable for the decision.

There are two distinct worries and one implicit assumption in this challenge. The assumption, which Asaro makes explicitly, is that the type of judgments often required by IHL is not amenable to computer modelling and cannot be machine learned.[7] The worries are, first, that automating the decision to use lethal force would necessarily make it unaccountable and, second, that by automating lethal decisions too much control would be lost to technologies that we should distrust in principle. Human 'sovereignty' over human life, writes O'Connell, must always be retained.[8] Nearly thirty years ago, the International Committee of the Red Cross (ICRC) *Commentary on the Additional Protocols* already warned that the progressive 'automation of the battlefield' could lead to a situation in which, 'if man does not master technology, but allows it to master him, he will be destroyed by technology'.[9]

This consequentialist worry is indeed troubling given the potential of AWS to act unforeseeably. Utmost caution is always called for when designing and deploying new types of lethal weaponry. However, as is often the case with consequentialist objections, there are consequentialist rejoinders. Some authors think that AWS technology bears the promise of improving decision making and making targeting 'more precise and less harmful for civilians caught near it'.[10] As Michael Schmitt and Jeffrey Thurnher note, human judgment can be less reliable than electronic sensors and computerized processing in the heat of battle. A 'human in the loop', they argue, is by no means reassuring, for there are situations in which acting consistently with IHL proves beyond the emotional and cognitive capacities of human beings.[11] Ronald Arkin argues that since AWS are not constrained by the instinct of self-preservation, they have the 'ability to act conservatively'. They can be programmed to avoid mistakes by holding fire and potentially sacrificing themselves before establishing accurately the lawfulness of their intended target.[12]

---

[7] Asaro, 'On banning autonomous weapon systems', 700.

[8] O'Connell, 'Banning autonomous killing', 236.

[9] C. Pilloud *et al.*, *Commentary on the Additional Protocols of 8 June 1977 to the Geneva Conventions of 12 August 1949* (The Hague: Martinus Nijhoff, 1987), 427–8.

[10] K. Anderson and M. Waxman, 'Law and ethics for autonomous weapons systems', American University Washington College of Law, Research Paper no. 2013–11 (2013), 1.

[11] M. Schmitt and J. Thurnher, '"Out of the loop": autonomous weapon systems and the law of armed conflict', *Harvard National Security Journal*, 4 (2013), 231, 248–9.

[12] R. Arkin, *Governing Lethal Behavior in Autonomous Robots* (Aldershot: Ashgate, 2009), 29–36.

It does not seem possible to settle this dispute at a high level of abstraction. Each specific design of AWS would have to be examined for its potential impact, but at the current stage of technological development, sufficiently specific analysis appears impossible. A more promising line of critique is based not on the conjectural consequences of AWS deployment but, rather, on the nature of the decision to use force in keeping with the norms and principles of IHL. Core IHL principles require highly complex forms of human judgment, which, it has been said, machines inherently do not have.[13]

Consider first the principle of proportionality. As stated in Article 57 of Additional Protocol I, proportionality mandates that 'those who plan or decide upon an attack shall refrain from deciding to launch any attack which may be expected to cause incidental loss of civilian life, injury to civilians, damage to civilian objects, or a combination thereof, which would be excessive in relation to the concrete and direct military advantage anticipated'.[14] As the ICRC *Commentary* notes, the proportionality rule is in reality an open-ended principle that calls for an 'equitable balance between the necessities of war and humanitarian requirements'.[15] Leaving aside the serious worry that this balancing act is somewhat like comparing apples and oranges,[16] the clear instances offered in the *Commentary* may be cited for illustration. Thus, a single missing soldier cannot justify the obliteration of a whole village, or 'if the destruction of a bridge is of paramount importance for the occupation or non-occupation of a strategic zone, it is understood that some houses may be hit, but not that a whole urban area be leveled'.[17] However, very often – perhaps in most cases – judgments of proportionality will involve hard, indeed incalculable, choices over which people can reasonably disagree.

---

[13] Asaro, 'On banning autonomous weapon systems'; Human Rights Watch, *Losing Humanity: The Case against Killer Robots* (Cambridge, MA: Human Rights Program, Harvard Law School, 2012); O'Connell, 'Banning autonomous killing'; N. Sharkey, 'Saying "no!" to lethal autonomous targeting', *Journal of Military Ethics*, 9 (2010), 369; N. Sharkey, 'The evitability of autonomous robot warfare', *International Review of the Red Cross*, 94 (2012), 787.

[14] Protocol Additional to the Geneva Conventions of 12 August 1949, and Relating to the Protection of Victims of International Armed Conflicts (Additional Protocol I) 1977, 1125 UNTS 3.

[15] Pilloud *et al.*, *Commentary on the Additional Protocols*, 683.

[16] T. Hurka, 'Proportionality in the morality of war', *Philosophy and Public Affairs*, 33 (2005), 34.

[17] Pilloud *et al.*, *Commentary on the Additional Protocols*, 683.

One side of the proportionality balance has the incidental loss of civilian life, for which there may be standardized algorithmic estimation methods. According to Schmitt and Thurnher, the 'collateral damage estimate methodology' in the United States quantifies potential damage on the basis of factors such as the precision of a weapon, blast effect, attack tactics and the probability of civilian presence near targets.[18] This procedure could potentially be automated in a machine with enough data on terrain, civilian presence, weaponry and so on. However, as Schmitt and Thurnher further explain, this estimation method is used only to determine the level of command at which an attack that is likely to harm civilians must be authorized: the greater the risk, the more authority required for clearance. The rationale of this protocol is that the assessment of the expected military advantage, which is on the other side of the proportionality balance, is for a commander to make. The more potential harm there is to protected persons and goods, the more judgment and experience the commander must have when deciding if such harm would be 'in excess' of the military advantage.

Could this balancing estimation be automated? Possibly yes, but only within narrow settings.[19] Schmitt and Thurnher argue plausibly that AWS could be programmed with collateral damage thresholds under certain limited conditions. They give as an example setting 'a base maximum collateral damage level of X for [destroying an enemy] tank'.[20] Conceivably, in cases such as this one, a level of maximum allowable damage could be assigned *ex ante*. Sufficient knowledge would be required about the area where the tank is located and the contribution of its destruction to the war effort. For missions narrowly defined in time and space, threshold values could be set and updated in real time as the operations unfold.

To appreciate how wide this window of permissibility is, the nature of IHL proportionality must be correctly understood. Proportionality judgments must be both context specific and holistic. They are context specific because both civilian risk and military advantage are highly

---

[18] Schmitt and Thurnher, "'Out of the loop'", 255.

[19] Most critics deny that AWS could perform the required balancing estimation, but this flat denial is unwarranted. Compare Asaro, 'On banning autonomous weapon systems'; Human Rights Watch, *Losing Humanity*; O'Connell, 'Banning autonomous killing'; Sharkey, 'Saying "no!" to lethal autonomous targeting'; Sharkey, 'The evitability of autonomous robot warfare'; and also, if from a different legal angle, the contribution by E. Leiblich and E. Benvenisti, 'The obligation to exercise discretion in warfare: why autonomous weapons systems are unlawful', Chapter 11 in this volume.

[20] Schmitt and Thurnher, "'Out of the loop'", 256.

situational, uncertain, complex and dynamic,[21] and they are holistic because the military advantage of tactical actions has to be assessed relative to broader strategic considerations. As the ICRC Commentary puts it, 'an attack carried out in a concerted manner in numerous places can only be judged in its entirety'.[22] The tactical value of destroying one particular tank, and, hence, the admissibility of collateral damage, can vary depending on what is happening elsewhere in the war at the time.

The twofold requirement of contextual and holistic determination indicates how inescapable human decision making is in proportionality estimations. Tactical advantage is connected to strategy, which is ultimately connected to political goals. It is simply absurd to think that AWS could make proportionality judgments beyond narrow circumstances, as it amounts to expecting that they could decide on strategic and, ultimately, political goals. The prospects of a machine creatively engaging in discussions of strategy and political goals are remote, certainly not within the foreseeable future of technological development.[23] AWS estimates necessarily belong to narrow tactical actions.

Furthermore, setting threshold values for proportionality assessments in narrow settings would by no means make human judgments superfluous. On the contrary, judgment remains indispensable. Machines themselves cannot make the type of judgment that proportionality requires, but they could be programmed to proceed on the basis of human-made algorithms and choices of threshold values. Machines may perhaps be capable of attacking with 'surgical precision' but not of balancing reasonably the two sides of the proportionality rule. This impossibility is not technological but conceptual. In the context of AWS, the test of proportionality would apply to the human decision to deploy AWS in a certain way and to assign particular parameters of operation. To use the language of the ICRC *Commentary*, the human operator who deploys AWS would have to assess 'in good faith' and according to 'common sense' whether the interests of protected persons are duly taken into account, given the AWS algorithm and action parameters and the specific conditions of its deployment.[24]

The notion that algorithmic calculations could substitute for reasonableness rests on a misunderstanding of the nature of IHL proportionality.

---

[21] Human Rights Watch, *Losing Humanity*, 32–4.

[22] Pilloud *et al.*, *Commentary on the Additional Protocols*, 685.

[23] But cf. Krishnan, *Killer Robots*, 53–5.

[24] Pilloud *et al.*, *Commentary on the Additional Protocols*, 683–4; cf. Schmitt and Thurnher, '"Out of the loop"', 265–8.

The concept of reasonableness is broad and slippery, but it minimally refers to an expectation of due care in balancing conflicting values and legitimate interests in complex circumstances. According to Neil MacCormick, the common element in the various legal uses of the reasonableness criterion 'lies in the *style of deliberation* a person would ideally engage in, and the impartial attention he would give to competing values and evidences in the given concrete setting'.[25] Typical legal procedures involving standards of reasonableness consist of allegations and counter-allegations regarding the agent's weighing of conflicting relevant reasons, which the law itself does not attempt to settle *ex ante*. The issue to be decided when invoking a reasonableness test is whether sufficient reasons exist to act in ways that undermine certain legitimate interests or values. Correspondingly, unreasonableness refers to failures in human judgment, notably gross distortions in relative valuations, neglect of relevant interests, or the plain failure to bring in relevant reasons.[26] The clearest form of unreasonableness in IHL proportionality is to neglect fundamental civilian interests for the sake of negligible tactical advantage.

For present purposes, the relevant point is that reasonableness in practical deliberation can only take place among agents endowed with practical reason – that is, moral agents with the capacity to judge on alternative courses of action. AWS are certainly not the type of agent that could engage in this practice. By contrast, the human agents who design and operate AWS can, and indeed must, be held accountable in contexts of practical deliberation. The key question is what reasons *they* had to conclude that, given the AWS's algorithm and specifications, it would not harm the protected interests in excess of what would be gained by its use. IHL applies at least at the decision levels of programming, assigning parameters and deploying AWS. The law does set limits in each of these, but it need not proscribe AWS use.

Reasonableness and practical deliberation are also invoked in the IHL principle of distinction in ways pertinent for AWS use. Article 57 of Additional Protocol I mandates that 'those who plan or decide upon an attack shall do everything feasible to verify that the objectives to be attacked are neither civilians nor civilian objects'. As the ICRC *Commentary* notes,

---

[25] N. MacCormick, 'Reasonableness and objectivity', *Notre Dame Law Review*, 74 (1999), 1575, 1581 (emphasis added).

[26] *Ibid.* See further S. Besson, *The Morality of Conflict: Reasonable Disagreement and the Law* (Oxford: Hart, 2005); O. Corten, 'The notion of "reasonable" in international law: legal discourse, reason and contradictions', *International and Comparative Law Quarterly*, 48 (1999), 613.

the 'everything feasible' clause is open-ended and indicative of a margin of judgment; it can be interpreted as mandating decision makers to take all reasonable steps to identify and avoid harm to protected persons and objects.[27] What counts as being feasible or reasonable will vary with the situation and available technology; a balance must be made between the protection of civilians and the advancement of military objectives.

Schmitt and Thurnher emphasize the epistemic dimension of the 'everything feasible' clause and propose the test of a 'reasonable attacker' for autonomous weaponry. When estimating whether a potential target is legitimate, they argue, it should be considered what a reasonable human attacker would do if he had all of the information available via AWS sensors – if the human attacker would fire, it is legitimate for the AWS to fire.[28] This test is misplaced in two ways that illustrate the practical force of the reasonableness criterion when applied to AWS. First, the cognitive capacities of a human attacker need not be the baseline for the potentially far superior processing capacity of machines. Moreover, as the defenders of AWS are keen to emphasize, machines can be programmed to take higher risks in order to acquire more information to accurately identify targets before using force. The risk of self-destruction should weigh very differently in humans and machines. Second, the relevant question for a test of reasonableness is not what the machine should do but rather what the human beings 'who plan or decide upon an attack' should do before deploying AWS. Among other things, it must be considered whether they have taken all technologically feasible measures to minimize harm to civilians. The relevant consideration is not what a human being would do if he or she were in the AWS's place, but rather how human operators must proceed when fielding the AWS.

Whether AWS could be fittingly programmed for permissible deployment would have to be argued case by case. Sensors that are perfectly capable of detecting certain weapons could be presented as a reasonable basis for distinction under some circumstances but not in others. It seems unlikely that in counter-insurgency scenarios algorithms could perform autonomously and in keeping with the ICRC criteria of 'direct participation in hostilities'.[29] Such environments may be too complex to allow for automated force. It may well be that compliance with IHL will confine

---

[27] Pilloud et al., Commentary on the Additional Protocols, 678–83.
[28] Schmitt and Thurnher, '"Out of the loop"', 262–5.
[29] N. Melzer, 'Interpretive guidance on the notion of direct participation in hostilities under international humanitarian law', International Review of the Red Cross, 90 (2008), 991.

AWS to battle spaces with low or null civilian density, for example submarine warfare, missile shields or swarm technology.[30]

Accountability for AWS deployment

As noted above, critics of AWS have argued that they should be banned because they inherently preclude the fair attribution of responsibility. Since, by definition, AWS autonomously make the decision of which targets to engage, it would be unfair to hold commanders or anyone liable for a robot's decision. Fair criminal liability presupposes that commanders can foresee and intend the outcome of their actions. Both conditions are necessarily excluded by the autonomy of 'killer robots'.[31] Along these lines, Human Rights Watch concludes that, 'since there is no fair and effective way to assign legal responsibility for unlawful acts committed by fully autonomous weapons, granting them complete control over targeting decisions would undermine yet another tool for promoting civilian protection'.[32]

This objection to AWS presupposes, first, that machine autonomy necessarily makes the outcome of deployment completely unknown and, second, that accountability is fair only when an agent expressly intended to commit a wrongful deed. Both premises are overly strong and unwarranted. Different types and degrees of epistemic uncertainty may be distinguished in AWS, and forms of fair accountability exist that do not require a wrongful intention. Uncertainty and accountability are in fact connected in an intuitively obvious way: deploying a lethal AWS under complete uncertainty would be clearly wrong, comparable to releasing a toxic substance in an inhabited environment. Even if the person did not specifically intend to harm anyone, the very harmfulness of the released agent is enough for criminal liability – either criminal negligence or recklessness.

Of course, critics are rightly concerned about giving lethal decision-making powers to robots whose autonomous performance in complex environments would be uncertain. The 'computer revolution of warfare', which includes the extensive use of computerized sensors and complex

---

[30] N. Melzer, *Human Rights Implications of the Usage of Drones and Unmanned Robots in Warfare* (Brussels: European Parliament, 2013); Schmitt and Thurnher, "'Out of the loop'", 240.
[31] Asaro, 'On banning autonomous weapon systems'; O'Connell, 'Banning autonomous killing'; R. Sparrow, 'Killer robots', *Journal of Applied Philosophy*, 24 (2007), 62.
[32] Human Rights Watch, *Losing Humanity*, 42.

data analysis, and the prospective use of artificial intelligence for pattern recognition and other tasks, elicit fears that machines will eventually be created that 'can develop behaviours we did not anticipate and that we might not even fully understand'.[33]

Three levels of machine autonomy can be distinguished in increasing order of epistemic uncertainty, as Krishnan points out. *Pre-programmed* autonomous machines can perform functions autonomously but according to predetermined scripts – for instance, 'fire-and-forget' missile systems in which precise targets are identified in advance but pursued autonomously by machines. *Supervised* machines follow more open-ended scripts – for instance, 'locate all tanks in this area and prompt for targeting'. Machines of this type are already operational; they are overseen by human operators but in the near future may be left to decide autonomously on targeting. *Completely autonomous* machines, on the other hand, would be able to learn and adapt their behaviour to changing environments in pursuit of open-ended tasks. The ultimate goal of completely autonomous military robotics is to produce autonomous robot soldiers that could be deployed in battlefields and directed simply to neutralize enemy threats.[34]

Pre-programmed and supervised machines exist today, but completely autonomous machines do not. It is far from clear that the hurdles to complete autonomy will ever be overcome. As Guglielmo Tamburrini's contribution in this volume argues, autonomous cars and personal care robots – for example, robots assisting elderly people in retirement homes – already pose great challenges of risk control and public safety.[35] It may well be that the highly complex and strategically changing scenarios of battle will never allow for the development of fully autonomous robots performing within reasonable margins of risk. For AWS, there are risks of tactical failure (not accomplishing missions and thus being a waste of time and resources) and the humanitarian risk of excessively harming protected persons and goods.

Risk control in robotics depends on systematic testing under controlled conditions. Just as personal care robots and autonomous cars are subject to product liabilities and would have to be approved by public safety agencies before commercial use, AWS would have to be tested by equivalent military and humanitarian agencies. For a military commander to be

---

[33] Krishnan, *Killer Robots*, 58.   [34] *Ibid.*, 44–5, 70–3.
[35] G. Tamburrini, 'On banning autonomous weapons systems: from deontological to wide consequentialist reasons', Chapter 6 in this volume.

confident that he has taken all reasonable steps to avoid creating excessive risks to civilians, which he has a legal duty to do, he would have to trust that sufficient testing has been done on the AWS.

At a minimum, sufficient testing should provide the basis for defining a probability distribution over the set of outcomes in a deployment scenario; for each possible outcome, commanders should be able to estimate the expected impact on civilians. While AWS are non-deterministic and non-scripted to various degrees, in all cases their range of action should be bounded and probabilistically estimated. Deploying them under second-level uncertainty – uncertainty about the probabilistic range of action – would create inestimable risks on a civilian population, and would consequently be illegal. It is the legal duty of commanders to detect non-negligible dangers when using lethal force; if there is second-level uncertainty, they must abstain from deployment. Put otherwise, commanders must (legally) have well-grounded epistemic confidence regarding the range of action of AWS.

It is unclear whether there will be a time in which military commanders will have to make such judgments for a completely autonomous robot, but for pre-programmed and supervised machines this possibility is neither unlikely nor distant. Whatever technological progress is made, it is of fundamental importance for accountability that the deployment of AWS itself is not an automated action but, instead, the deliberate decision of a human commander. When there is uncertainty, the relevant practical question to ask is what steps have been taken to sufficiently determine and limit the risks created by the AWS. If the range of action and corresponding risk could not be anticipated with sufficient epistemic confidence, then it would be wrong to field the weapon, possibly a case of criminal negligence. The greater the uncertainty, the less reasonable it would be to believe that the risks are negligible.[36]

It is clear, then, that even if the effects of AWS cannot be exactly determined *ex ante*, it need not be unfair to hold some suitably defined agents liable for them. Currently under international criminal law, superiors

---

[36] Negligence in this sense must be distinguished from strict liability. If harm resulted from the malfunction of AWS, then commanders would have a defence in criminal proceedings, and it may be unfair to hold them liable. A commander's risk assessment could be sound on the basis of an AWS's past performance and due care in testing, but things could nonetheless go unexpectedly wrong. Like any machine, an AWS could malfunction. Liability must be made on the basis of the normal operation of AWS – that is, 'the outcome of a complex calculation of (or algorithm based upon) the relative weights of the battlefield factors the robot was programmed to consider'. Sparrow, 'Killer robots', n. 29.

who fail to avoid non-negligible risks to protected persons and goods can be liable for negligence or recklessness.[37] This form of liability could be extended naturally to the use of AWS, as Neha Jain's and Geoffrey Corn's contributions in this volume argue.[38] The liability in question derives from what H. L. A. Hart calls 'role responsibility' – that is, from the fact that a military commander or civilian superior 'occupies a distinctive place or office in a social organization, to which specific duties are attached to provide for the welfare of others or to advance in some specific way the aims or purposes of the organization'.[39] On this basis, officers can be made responsible for failing to do what is necessary to fulfil their duties.[40]

Criminal sanctions against commanders for creating non-negligible risks when deploying AWS is the most extreme form of liability, but other forms in other agents are conceivable as well.[41] A large and complex command structure is implicated in the operation of new weapon technologies. Those who actually field AWS would have to assume that their superiors and legal experts had duly overseen that the designers, programmers and testers had done their jobs competently. Arguably 'procurement officials' – that is, those charged with overseeing the design and testing of AWS – should share in criminal liability (according to Corn's contribution in this volume, they should bear most of the liability burden). But criminal liability aside, the consequences of excessive harm to protected persons and goods would have to be felt through the complex structure of the deploying state's armed forces, possibly in relatively milder forms of liability such as disciplinary

---

[37] K. Ambos, 'Superior responsibility' in A. Cassese, P. Gaeta and J. Jones (eds.), *The Rome Statute of the International Criminal Court: A Commentary* (Oxford University Press, 2002), 805.

[38] N. Jain, 'Autonomous weapons systems: new frameworks for individual responsibility', Chapter 13, and G. S. Corn, 'Autonomous weapons systems: managing the inevitability of "taking the man out of the loop"', Chapter 10 in this volume.

[39] H. L. A. Hart and J. Gardner, *Punishment and Responsibility: Essays in the Philosophy of Law*, 2nd edn (Oxford University Press, 2008), 212.

[40] While there is an obligation under IHL of due diligence in selecting targets and in preventing excessive harm to protected persons and goods, AWS nonetheless raise novel complex issues that may require the further elaboration of existing legal frameworks. IHL standards are currently addressed to the moment of selection of targets, not to the deployment of lethal weapons that undertake a relatively open-ended selection. Similarly, the doctrine of command responsibility, which underlies liability for criminal negligence, refers to the relationship between commanders and subordinates, not between commanders and machines. In this sense, my argument indicates how legal standards should be extended, and as such refers to norms *de lege ferenda* not *de lege lata*. I am grateful to Claus Kreß and Martin Scheinin for discussion of this point.

[41] M. Schulze, 'Autonomous weapons and distributed responsibility', *Philosophy and Technology*, 26 (2013), 203.

measures, professional disqualification and civil remedies. While developers, engineers, lawyers and technicians may be far from battlefields and, as such, not directly responsible for AWS fielding, they could lose their job or licence and be liable to pay remedies for their failure to anticipate foreseeable shortcomings or to duly test for risks.

In sum, for all these agents some form of liability is conceivable that would not be unfair. The most troubling issue is not fairness but, rather, the fact that the complex organizational structure behind AWS deployment can diffuse responsibility among many relevant agents to a vanishing point. This diffusion can be counter-balanced only by a positive role-based regime of liabilities. As the next section will argue, however, the incentives to create and enforce such a regime do not currently exist. Whether and how they could be created is a most pressing and neglected practical question.

Incentives for IHL compliance

I have argued that, in principle, it is mandatory to test and determine the risks generated by AWS and that superiors may be held fairly accountable for wrongful harms caused by fielding. A fundamental objection to AWS has thus proven to be unfounded. However, my discussion so far has taken place at an idealized level. While a regime of due care in testing and risk control, with suitable rules of liability, is in principle conceivable, the question whether such a regime is likely to be implemented, and whether states developing AWS would have enough incentives to fund and implement demanding risk-control programmes, and make their own officers, lawyers and contractors accountable for failures in weapon review or mishandling is an altogether different and very troubling matter.

AWS will add to the already stark asymmetries of so-called riskless warfare, in which risks are increasingly shifted to foreign civilians.[42] The aversion of states to endure casualties among their own forces and their reluctance to deploy 'boots on the ground', together with the imperative to maximize 'manpower efficiencies', feed the development of means of force that generate and externalize virtually all risks to enemy combatants and civilians. High-altitude bombings in Kosovo and

---

[42] P. Kahn, 'The paradox of riskless warfare', *Philosophy and Public Policy Quarterly*, 22 (2002), 2; D. Luban, 'Risk taking and force protection' in Y. Benbaji and N. Sussman (eds.), *Reading Walzer* (London: Routledge, 2014), 277–301.

elsewhere have already illustrated this trend, but drone technologies have deepened it, and AWS would do so even further. It is to be expected that the few states capable of developing and deploying AWS will further shift risks to foreign civilians, and it is by no means clear how this increased endangerment could be effectively reversed or constrained. On the contrary, the demanding challenges of risk control for weapon autonomy are likely to create ever-larger dangers to civilians.

Let us suppose, with Michael Walzer, Avishai Margalit and David Luban, that when determining the appropriate distribution of risk between military forces and civilians, discrimination should never be made on the basis of the endangered civilians' nationality. Whatever controls would have to be taken to minimize risks to civilian co-nationals in the course of military action, they are also due to foreign civilians.[43] This suggests a valuable heuristic baseline of risk distribution in the context of AWS: risks should be controlled as if those threatened by AWS deployment were civilians of the deploying side. The baseline may be purely hypothetical since AWS will probably be deployed only in enemy territory without endangering co-national civilians. Nonetheless, two types of pressures deviating from this baseline may be highlighted: the high demands of risk-control procedures and the elasticity of applicable standards.

There is currently no international agency that is authorized to test weapons and control for risks that could stand effectively for the worldwide protection of civilian interests. In contrast to the consumer protection agencies that set standards and require risk evaluations for autonomous robots for non-military uses, there are no international agencies designated to protect civilians against the risks generated by autonomous weapons. Article 36 of Additional Protocol I mandates that new weapons be duly tested for compatibility with IHL, but it does not institutionalize this duty at the international level. States parties explicitly declined to set up international bodies to oversee the review process.[44] Each AWS-developing state is in charge of testing, which raises several concerns.

First, states are of course interested parties in the review process, as one of the stronger motivations for designing and deploying AWS is precisely to minimize risks to their own armed forces. Foreign civilians have no

---

[43] *Ibid.* A. Margalit and M. Walzer, 'Israel: civilians and combatants', *New York Review of Books*, 14 May 2009.
[44] Pilloud *et al.*, *Commentary on the Additional Protocols*, 421–8.

voice or representatives in the review process. Furthermore, foreign civilians may either be too remote or held too much in suspicion to elicit sympathy among the deploying states' politicians or citizenry, or any potential sympathy may be obstructed by official secrecy and obfuscation.

Second, the testing and evaluation of any new weaponry is time consuming and expensive, both of which run against the budgetary constraints, tactical interests, and sense of urgency of deploying states. In times of shrinking defence budgets, it will be very tempting to opt for expediency. A recent commentary on AWS testing lays down the relevant trade-off clearly, but, revealingly, it does not rule out deployment when testing is manifestly insufficient: '[I]f a high statistical assurance is deemed necessary for civilian safety while budgetary constraints preclude the corresponding necessary development testing, then appropriate limits should be implemented regarding the approved applications for that weapon until field experience provides appropriate reliability confidence.'[45] The risks of such a 'test-as-we-go' approach are obvious, as the point of testing is precisely to determine the probabilistic ranges of action, without which no appropriate limits can be defined *ex ante* for further testing. Not only would each AWS have to be tested before fielding, but whole new testing methods may have to be created. According to a recent report on AWS by the US Defense Science Board, performance benchmarks in testing and evaluation are usually pre-scripted and deterministic, while AWS may require a 'systems engineering approach' with yet undefined probabilistic criteria.[46]

With respect to the elasticity of the applicable standards, references to reasonableness in the principles of distinction and proportionality make human judgment indispensable in AWS deployment, as was argued above. The flip side of this is that the applicable standards are vague and open ended, and accountability hard to enforce. References to reasonableness in law often have the function of concealing diverging interpretations and unresolved political tensions. Historically this was certainly the case with regard to IHL proportionality, as states opted for an open-ended rule after disagreeing on more exact formulations of the proper balancing of civilian protections and military necessity. As Olivier Corten has argued, such disagreements in international law may often be solved not by the normative force of the most appropriate considerations

---

[45] A. Backstrom and I. Henderson, 'New capabilities in warfare', *International Review of the Red Cross*, 94 (2012), 483, 509.
[46] US Defense Science Board, *The Role of Autonomy in DoD Systems* (Washington, DC: US Department of Defense, 2012), 62–4.

but, rather, by the sheer power of the parties: '[E]ach State maintains its own conception of what is reasonable, and will exercise its powers according to that conception.'[47] Sheer power, rather than argument, carries the day, which means that the interest of the stronger will prevail against the interests of foreign civilians who lack political voice or power.

In the context of asymmetrical warfare, the stronger party will have AWS capabilities, and so the open-ended reasonableness criterion is likely to incorporate its preference for shifting risks away from its own forces and economizing in testing. Whether or not a given level of AWS testing and risk control would exhaust 'all feasible precautions', and thus contribute to avoiding or minimizing the 'incidental loss of civilian life', will depend on some particular understanding of the proper balance of risks between enemy civilians and friendly forces. Walzer and Margalit's baseline is probably not the one that AWS developers will want to impose on themselves. Tactical gains may prove to be too alluring when testing is very expensive and time consuming, and humanitarian failure has no tangible costs. Furthermore, as is always the case with standards of reasonableness, actual practice will to some extent set the norm. IHL is structurally unequipped to stop the gradual and progressive shifting of risk towards enemy civilians. It may end up sanctioning the very eschewed distribution of risk favoured by the most powerful parties.

This is not to say that states equipped with AWS will be completely unconstrained. They may be motivated by the legitimacy costs of perceived disproportionate harm to civilians. Public opinion and the political consequences of naming and shaming may be a very real concern to decision makers, and, to this extent, states have an interest in being perceived as law compliant, however elastic the legal criteria may be. The use of easily accessible technologies to record the impact of AWS and to broadcast it in social media may have a real disciplining effect. There is also the imperative to minimize risks to friendly forces, which may require considerable amounts of testing and safety reviews, as well as the distinct ethos of the military profession, which may set limits on the range of actions military men are willing to undertake with AWS. These are all relevant and potentially effective constraints.

However, for a long time the most effective motivation for IHL compliance has been reciprocity – that is, the willingness to impose limits on one's own military means and actions out of the expectation that one's

---

[47] Corten, 'The notion of "reasonable" in international law', 618–20.

enemies may resort to similar means and actions. Such limitations are a matter of common interest.[48] It is unclear that the expectation of reciprocity could have any limiting role in AWS development, testing and deployment. Only states have the wherewithal to develop such technologies, and, for decades now, inter-state wars have become increasingly rare. This could change in the future, and AWS technology could spread. The prospect of an AWS arms race is often treated as a matter of great concern, and, surely, in many ways it is, but one potential positive effect is that it could trigger the type of incentives that have sustained IHL compliance for most of its history. If it were common knowledge for belligerents A and B that they could deploy AWS against each other or their allies, they would have strong incentives to agree on limitations and effective risk controls. As long as AWS technology remains in the possession of a few players who are unlikely to use it against each other, public opinion and the dynamics of naming and shaming may be the strongest driving force behind IHL compliance. Secrecy and obfuscation of AWS programmes may consequently be the most serious obstacle towards an effective control regime.

Conclusion

It has been argued that AWS are neither inherently wrong nor unlawful, and do not preclude in principle the fair attribution of liability to responsible agents. Principled critiques of AWS have failed to appreciate how flexible and strategically adaptable IHL principles are, and how long and mediated the distance between decision makers and the act of killing has already become in contemporary warfare.[49] Absent a treaty explicitly banning AWS, which appears unlikely to materialize, the main locus of normative action will have to take place within and through the language of IHL.

Consequently, when it comes to confronting and containing the serious risks created by the development of AWS, the claim that IHL flatly proscribes them seems to be a non-starter. More attention needs to be paid to the type of procedures that should be mandatory to control risks; they must be probabilistic and mindful of the dynamics of very complex organizational systems. The distribution of liability within the complex web of relevant decision makers deserves more careful attention.

[48] J. Morrow, 'The laws of war, common conjectures, and legal systems in international politics', *Journal of Legal Studies*, 31 (2002), 41; J. Morrow, 'When do states follow the laws of war?', *American Political Science Review*, 101 (2007), 559.
[49] D. Kennedy, *Of War and Law* (Princeton University Press, 2006).

Commanders are the most obvious responsible agents, but clearly they are not the only relevant ones. AWS do not altogether preclude liability, but they do raise challenging questions regarding who should be liable and in what ways, and also, as I have emphasized in this chapter, who will have the means and incentives to define and enforce such liabilities.

8

Autonomous weapons systems and transparency: towards an international dialogue

SARAH KNUCKEY

Introduction

The international debate around autonomous weapons systems (AWS) has addressed the potential ethical, legal and strategic implications of advancing autonomy, and analysis has offered myriad potential concerns and conceivable benefits. Many consider autonomy in selecting and engaging targets to be potentially revolutionary, yet AWS developments are nascent, and the debates are, in many respects and necessarily, heavily circumscribed by the uncertainty of future developments. In particular, legal assessments as to whether AWS might be used in compliance with the conduct of hostilities rules in international humanitarian law (IHL) are at present largely predicated upon a forecast of future facts, including about the sophistication of weapon technologies, likely capacities and circumstances of use, as well as the projected effectiveness of state control over any use.

To conclusively assess legal compliance, detailed information about the AWS as developed or used would be required. However, to date, only minimal attention has been paid to transparency in the AWS context. What kinds of AWS information (if any) should governments share, with whom and on what basis? How will the international community know if autonomy is developed in critical functions and, if AWS are deployed, if they are used in compliance with international law? How might autonomy developments be monitored to enable fact-based legal analysis? Or, if autonomous targeting is prohibited or specifically regulated, how might compliance best be assured? Will existing institutions, norms or requirements for transparency be adequate? These crucial questions have not yet been debated.

This chapter explores the challenge of fact-based legal assessments for autonomous systems, and proposes that the international community begin to focus directly and systematically on transparency around AWS development and use. As a step towards deepening an international AWS transparency dialogue, this chapter offers a broad framework for disentangling distinct categories of transparency information, relationships and rationales. Given the lack of an existing well-defined transparency architecture for weapons development and the use of lethal force, transparency discussions should not wait until AWS substantive debates further mature or for the international community to settle on a response to the substantive concerns raised. Rather, transparency should be analysed alongside ongoing legal, ethical and strategic debates. Without attending to transparency, states risk developing autonomy in an environment that lacks information-sharing norms designed to advance lawful weapon use and development, democratic legitimacy and states' strategic and security interests.

The challenge of fact-based legal assessments for autonomous systems

A rapidly expanding field of AWS scholarly literature, policy analysis, inter-governmental dialogue and academic and civil society research has explored the general contours of AWS development and deployment implications. Across the ideological spectrum and fields of expertise – including robotics, military and defence, philosophy, law, human rights and arms control – many analysts argue that a shift to autonomous lethal targeting raises new, complex and significant issues,[1] with some referring

---

[1] See, e.g., International Committee of the Red Cross (ICRC), *Autonomous Weapons: States Must Address Major Humanitarian, Ethical Challenges*, 2 September 2013, available at http://reliefweb.int/report/world/autonomous-weapons-states-must-address-major-humanitarian-ethical-challenges (describing the use of AWS as a 'profound change in the way war is waged'); N. Melzer for European Parliament, Directorate-General for External Policies, *Human Rights Implications of the Usage of Drones and Unmanned Robots in Warfare* (2013), 14 (autonomous developments 'may well entail a more fundamental revolution in warfare than the advent and integration of air warfare a century ago or of the internet in the past two decades'); United Nations (UN) Secretary-General Ban Ki-moon, message to the Conferences of the High Contracting Parties to the Convention on Certain Conventional Weapons and its Protocols, 14 November 2013; P. Asaro, 'On banning autonomous weapon systems: human rights, automation, and the dehumanization of lethal decision-making', *International Review of the Red Cross*, 94 (2012), 687; J. Thurnher, 'Examining autonomous weapon systems from a law of armed conflict perspective' in H. Nasu and R. McLaughlin (eds.), *New Technologies and the Law of Armed Conflict* (New York: Springer, 2014), 213; K. Anderson and M. Waxman, 'Law and ethics for autonomous weapon systems: why a ban won't work and how the laws of war can' Jean Perkins Task Force on National Security and Law Essay Series (Hoover Institution and

to autonomous lethal targeting as a potential 'paradigm' or 'qualitative' shift.[2] Within this broader debate, the question of whether autonomous systems will necessarily, or likely, violate IHL has emerged as a key point of contention.[3]

A basic definition of AWS as a system that can select and engage targets without human intervention is currently in wide use,[4] although

Stanford University, 2013), 2; Ambassador Jean-Hugues Simon-Michel, Permanent Representative of France to the Conference on Disarmament, statement to the Sixty-Eighth Session of the United Nations General Assembly First Committee: General Debate, 8 October 2013 ('*Nous devons regarder de l'avant et relever les défis de l'avenir. Un débat important a emergé depuis quelques mois sur la question des robots létaux pleinement autonomes. C'est un débat important car il pose la question fondamentale de la place de l'Homme dans la décision d'engager la force létale*'); Amnesty International, statement to the Convention on Conventional Weapons (CCW) Informal Meeting of Experts on Lethal Autonomous Weapons Systems, 15 April 2015; ICRC, closing statement to the CCW Meeting of Experts on Lethal Autonomous Weapons Systems, 17 April 2015 (autonomy 'raises fundamental questions about human control over the use of force').

[2] See, e.g., J. Kellenberger, keynote address: 'International humanitarian law and new weapon technologies', Thirty-Fourth Round Table on Current Issues of International Law, 8–10 September 2011.

[3] The majority of the legal debate has thus far focused on whether AWS would violate the conduct of hostilities rules of IHL – that is, whether AWS could be used in compliance with the fundamental rules (proportionality, distinction) governing the use of force in armed conflict. Much of the legal analysis, and particularly the analysis arguing against a ban on AWS, assumes that IHL would be the applicable legal framework and does not address the relevance of human rights law. For an analysis of AWS in light of human rights law, see Human Rights Watch (HRW) and the Harvard International Human Rights Clinic, *Shaking the Foundations: The Human Rights Implications of Killer Robots* (New York: Human Rights Watch, 2014) (arguing that AWS threaten the right to life, the right to a remedy and the principle of human dignity); Amnesty International, *Autonomous Weapons Systems: Five Key Human Rights Issues for Consideration* (London: Amnesty International, 2015). See also presentations by Christof Heyns and Bonnie Docherty at the CCW Meeting of Experts on Lethal Autonomous Weapons Systems, 16 April 2015.

[4] Other terms currently used to describe a similar concept include 'fully autonomous lethal robots' (in French, *les robots létaux pleinement autonomes* has been used), 'autonomous weapons' (in German, *autonome Waffen* has been used), 'lethal autonomous robots', 'lethal autonomous weapons systems', 'lethal autonomous systems', 'killer robots' and so on. At this stage of the debate, there is not much to be made of the variation in names, with the exception of 'killer robots', which is taken by some to be insufficiently neutral. For general descriptions of autonomous systems, see, e.g., US Department of Defense (DoD) Directive 3000.09, 'Autonomy in weapon systems', 21 November 2012, 13 (defining AWS as 'a weapon system that, once activated, can select and engage targets without further intervention by a human operator'); J. Klein, 'The problematic nexus: where unmanned combat air vehicles and the law of armed conflict meet', *Air and Space Power Chronicles* (22 July 2003) (defining autonomous operations as those where 'the aircraft can detect, identify, and engage enemy targets using its onboard weapons systems, without the direct intervention of personnel'); M. Schmitt and J. Thurnher, '"Out of the Loop": autonomous

AWS discourse is undergoing a complicated process of securing agreement about the meaning and scope of key elements of the definition, and there is ambiguity about the precise objects of analysis and contestation about how best to understand autonomy and human control.[5] Yet while definitions are evolving and AWS developments are only at an early stage, analysts have explored many factors relevant to assessing possible legal, ethical and strategic AWS implications.[6]

weapons systems and the law of armed conflict', *Harvard National Security Journal*, 4 (2013), 213, 235 ('The crux of full autonomy, therefore, is the capability to identify, target, and attack a person or object without human interface'); M. Wagner, 'Autonomy in the battlespace: independently operating weapon systems and the law of armed conflict' in D. Saxon (ed.), *International Humanitarian Law and the Changing Technology of War* (Leiden: Martinus Nijhoff, 2013), 99, 100–6; W. Boothby, 'How far will the law allow unmanned targeting to go?' in Saxon, *International Humanitarian Law*, 45, 48; Asaro, 'On banning autonomous weapon systems', 690–4; S. Killmister, 'Remote weaponry: the ethical implications', *Journal of Applied Philosophy*, 25 (2008), 121 ('progress is rapidly being made towards autonomous weaponry capable of selecting, pursuing, and destroying targets without the necessity for human instruction'); ICRC, statement to the 2013 meeting of the High Contracting Parties to the Convention on Certain Conventional Weapons, 13 November 2013 ('Fully autonomous weapon systems would be designed to operate with little or no human control and to search for, identify and target an individual with lethal force'); S. Knuckey, 'UN Secretary-General calls for more transparency about drone use', *Just Security* (5 December 2013), available at http://justsecurity.org/2013/12/05/secretary-general-report-transparency-drones/ (the Secretary-General defined AWS as a system that 'once activated, can select and engage targets and operate in dynamic and changing environments without further human intervention'). See also the statements of experts and states at the 2014 and 2015 CCW Meetings of Experts on Lethal Autonomous Weapons Systems.

5 See, e.g., M. W. Meier, US Delegation, statement to the 2013 meeting of the High Contracting Parties to the Convention on Certain Conventional Weapons, 14 November 2013 (noting that discussing AWS is not easy at the moment 'given the many different ways and words that people use to describe autonomy'); S. Townley, US Delegation, statement to the 2014 CCW Meeting of Experts on Lethal Autonomous Weapons Systems, 13 May 2014 (noting 'widely divergent' definitions); United Nations Institute for Disarmament Research (UNIDIR), *Framing Discussions on the Weaponization of Increasingly Autonomous Technologies* (UNIDIR, 2014), 2–5 (discussing various understandings). For additional discussion of autonomy, see presentations at the 2014 CCW Meeting of Experts (in particular, by Younwoon Park, Quentin Ladetto, Raja Chatila, Paul Scharre, Ronald Arkin, Noel Sharkey and Nils Melzer) and presentations at the 2015 CCW Meeting of Experts on Lethal Autonomous Weapons Systems (including by Stuart Russell, Maya Brehm, Paul Scharre, Neil Davison and Marcel Dickow).

6 For a brief summary of these factors, see S. Knuckey, 'Scientists from 37 countries call for ban on autonomous lethal targeting', *Just Security* (16 October 2013), available at http://justsecurity.org/2097/scientists-ban-autonomous-weapons-systems/. The diversity of factors under consideration at the international level are most evident in the agendas and statements of experts and states to the 2014 and 2015 CCW Meetings of Experts on Lethal Autonomous Weapons Systems. Those meetings have intentionally adopted a broad perspective, included views from many disciplines, avoided a narrow technical focus,

The legal literature has addressed whether AWS would be necessarily illegal or, if not, the circumstances in which AWS might raise legal concerns or conceivably satisfy legal requirements. Normatively, legal analysis has also focused on what, if any, new limits (such as a moratorium or treaty ban, or a requirement for weapons to be under meaningful human control) should be placed on the development and use of AWS. Many of the legal assessments are based upon varying degrees of pessimistic or optimistic assumptions or predictions about the likely trajectory of technological development. AWS prohibitionists argue that AWS would not be able to comply with IHL and advocate a new treaty clearly banning AWS. On the other end of the spectrum, AWS supporters, arguing against calls for a ban, put forward possible circumstances, developments or policies that they argue would structure the legal use of AWS. Between these positions, many analysts are undecided about the future of AWS and about what forms of new regulation might be an appropriate response to concerns raised. Anti-/pro-AWS views and pro-/anti-ban views do not necessarily map onto each other – other views expressed include the view that AWS would most likely violate the law but that no ban is needed because IHL could sufficiently regulate or prohibit AWS, or that legal compliance is possible but a ban is necessary for other reasons (for example, ethical, political or strategic concerns about AWS).

The international focus on AWS legality was significantly driven by a large consortium of disarmament, humanitarian and human rights non-governmental organizations (NGOs), working together with robotics and computer experts and others from a range of disciplines. The international campaign to ban AWS launched by those groups included among its core arguments the argument that AWS use would, or would be very likely to, violate fundamental IHL norms.[7] These

---

and encouraged debate about long-term and ethical issues. For a summary of the 2015 meeting, see M. Wareham, Campaign to Stop Killer Robots, 'Report on activities: Convention on Conventional Weapons second informal meeting of experts on lethal autonomous weapons systems', 4 June 2015, available at www.stopkillerrobots.org/wp-content/uploads/2013/03/KRC_CCWx2015_Report_4June2015_uploaded.pdf.

[7] See, e.g., S. Goose, HRW, statement to the 2013 Meeting of the High Contracting Parties to the Convention on Certain Conventional Weapons, 14 November 2013 (stating that one of the groups' central concerns is that AWS 'are likely to run afoul of international humanitarian law'); Pax Christi, statement to the 2013 Meeting of the High Contracting Parties to the Convention on Certain Conventional Weapons, 14 November 2013 ('we doubt these weapons can comply with the IHL principles of distinction and proportionality'); M. Wareham, Campaign to Stop Killer Robots, statement to the 2013

groups – as well as others expressing concern but not advocating prohibition[8] – pushed for international debate, and, during the ensuing intergovernmental meetings, some states adopted similar views.[9]

Arguments of necessary or very likely AWS non-compliance with IHL generally focus on the complexity of the rules for the legal use of force, the difficulty of translating those complex and context-dependent rules into computer programming, the many technical and legal obstacles to an AWS being able to (for example) effectively distinguish between protected individuals and permissible targets, and the highly context-specific nature of use of force assessments.[10] These arguments are often compelling on the extreme difficulty, perhaps impossibility, of programming

Meeting of the High Contracting Parties to the Convention on Certain Conventional Weapons, 14 November 2013; M. Bolton, International Committee for Robot Arms Control, ICRAC closing statement to the CCW Meeting of Experts, 17 April 2015. Non-governmental organization (NGO) pushback against AWS was predicted over a decade ago. Lt Col. Lazarski, 'Legal implications of the unmanned combat aerial vehicle', *Aerospace Power Journal*, 16 (3) (2002), 79 ('A lethal and, as of yet, unproven UCAV with autonomous or fully adaptive controls poses significant accountability problems and is sure to be challenged by groups such as Amnesty International').

[8] See, e.g., ICRC, statement to the 2013 Meeting of the High Contracting Parties to the Convention on Certain Conventional Weapons, 13 November 2013 ('Research in the area of autonomous weapons is advancing at a rapid pace. This should be a cause for concern, as it is far from clear whether autonomous weapons could ever be capable of being used in accordance with international humanitarian law. The ICRC has urged States, for several years, to fully consider the legal, ethical and societal issues related to the use of autonomous weapons well before such systems are developed').

[9] States that have called for a ban on AWS include Ecuador, Egypt, Cuba and Pakistan. Numerous other states have expressed serious concerns about the ability of AWS to comply with international law or have put forward a requirement for meaningful human control (e.g. Germany, the Netherlands). See further S. Knuckey, 'Start of first inter-governmental expert meeting on autonomous weapons', *Just Security* (13 May 2014), available at http://justsecurity.org/10422/start-inter-governmental-expert-meeting-autonomous-weapons/.

[10] See, e.g., N. Sharkey, 'The automation and proliferation of military drones and the protection of civilians', *Law, Innovation and Technology*, 3 (2011), 229, 236–7; Wagner, 'Autonomy in the battlespace', 122; HRW and International Human Rights Clinic (Human Rights Program at Harvard Law School), *Losing Humanity: The Case against Killer Robots* (New York: Human Rights Watch, 2012); Knuckey, 'Scientists from 37 countries'; M. Bishop, chair of the Society for the Study of Artificial Intelligence and the Simulation of Behaviour, quoted in S. Makin, 'Why we need to stop military killer robots now', *New Scientist* (21 May 2013), available at www.newscientist.com/article/mg21829170.300-why-we-need-to-stop-military-killer-robots-now.html#.UcnzDU9So_8; R. Sparrow, 'Lethal autonomous robots must be stopped in their tracks', *The Conversation* (4 June 2013), available at http://theconversation.com/lethal-autonomous-robots-must-be-stopped-in-their-tracks-14843; Flight Lieutenant Gulam and Captain Lee, 'Uninhabited combat aerial vehicles and the law of armed conflict', *Australian Army Journal*, 3 (2006), 123, 132.

systems with the sophistication necessary to autonomously operate and kill lawfully in unstructured and complex environments. Such concerns are especially salient when considering the use of AWS in counter-insurgency and counter-terrorism contexts, where distinguishing civilians from fighters is a core challenge, and where the countries most likely to invest in developing AWS have been recently and most involved in the use of lethal force.

However, and often in direct response to the use of AWS legal violation arguments to advance international efforts towards a pre-emptive AWS ban, ban opponents have challenged the assumptions, fact scenarios and projected future circumstances underlying the position that AWS would be illegal. These legal arguments, in their strongest versions, can be grouped into two general categories, which are here referred to as the 'structure and control' and 'technological development' arguments.

First, the operating context or use of force parameters for AWS could potentially be structured or controlled by a human so that operational complexity was reduced and human control and the likelihood of IHL compliance thereby improved. For example, Michael Schmitt and Jeffrey Thurnher argue that AWS would not necessarily violate the rule against indiscriminate attacks because 'even' an AWS that is completely unable to distinguish civilian from military targets 'can be used lawfully in certain environments' – such as one without any civilians.[11] And they predict that 'for the foreseeable future, autonomous weapons systems will only attack targets meeting predetermined criteria and will function within an area of operations set by human operators'.[12] Common examples offered to restrict AWS to improve legal compliance include limiting the weapons to certain geographic areas where the likelihood of any civilian presence is low (for example, limiting AWS to the high seas or undersea operations or to territory predetermined to be occupied by fighters), restricting permissible force to certain categories of more readily identifiable targets or limiting AWS to certain categories of force (for example, defensive only or territory patrol).[13] With respect to

---

[11] Schmitt and Thurnher, '"Out of the loop"', 246.   [12] Ibid., 241.

[13] See, e.g., J. Klein, 'The problematic nexus: where unmanned combat air vehicles and the law of armed conflict meet', Air and Space Power Chronicles (22 July 2003) (suggesting authorizing AWS to target within a human-defined 'kill box' or to attack targets preselected by humans); Schmitt and Thurnher, '"Out of the Loop"', 246 (referring to attacks in the desert and the high seas); Thurnher, 'The law that applies to autonomous weapon systems', American Society of International Law Insights 17(4) (2013), available at www.asil.org/insights/volume/17/issue/4/law-applies-autonomous-weapon-systems. ('There may be situations in which an autonomous weapon systems could satisfy this rule with a considerably low level ability to distinguish'); Anderson and Waxman, 'Law and

compliance with the principle of proportionality, some have additionally suggested that humans could continually update the AWS with a 'sliding scale' of a target's military advantage or build in strict rules of engagement, thereby making any use of force permissible only in bounds much narrower than what IHL itself would permit.[14] In this area, some disputes about potential AWS legality in part reflect differences over what commentators intend to connote by 'AWS'. Some of the heavily 'structured' systems argued to be viably IHL compliant are very different from the

ethics for autonomous weapon systems', 6 (arguing that early AWS will likely be used for machine-on-machine attacks and in areas where civilian presence is unlikely, such as an attack on a submarine); Boothby, 'How far will the law allow unmanned targeting to go?', 57 (suggesting human programmed parameters around 'timing, location, objective, and means of any unmanned autonomous attack'); D. Akerson, 'The illegality of offensive lethal autonomy' in Saxon, *International Humanitarian Law*, 65, 73–5 (arguing that fully autonomous offensive weapons are inherently illegal, while explicitly permitting those that are 'defensive in design', but conceding the difficulty of articulating a clear offensive-defensive line); A. Johnson and S. Axinn, 'The morality of autonomous robots', *Journal of Military Ethics*, 12 (2013), 129, 137–8 (arguing that fully autonomous weapons are inherently immoral, but making an exception for defensive weapons, which the authors see as 'extensions of electric fences'); B. N. Kastan, 'Autonomous weapons systems: a coming legal "singularity"?', *Journal of Law, Technology and Policy*, 1 (2013), 45, 57, 61–2 (suggesting a number of ways to increase AWS IHL compliance, including if AWS were used by the United States for deliberate (pre-planned) targeting, the AWS would fill the role of existing drone pilots and the 'designation of the target and the approval to attack it would remain with the commander', which could be used in areas without civilians or in which humans make proportionality assessments): R. Sparrow, 'Building a better warbot: ethical issues in the design of unmanned systems for military applications', *Science and Engineering Ethics*, 15 (2009), 169, 177 (suggesting the possibility of armed sentry robots patrolling marked off perimeters); R. Arkin, 'How not to build a terminator', presentation at Humanoids 2013: IEEE-RAS International Conference on Humanoid Robots, 15–17 October 2013, slide 34 (listing various circumstances for AWS use, including: room clearing, counter-sniper operations, and perimeter protection); United Nations Institute for Disarmament Research UNIDIR, *Framing Discussions on the Weaponization of Increasingly Autonomous Technologies* (Geneva: UNIDIR, 2014), 5 (discussing uses in the sea environment).

[14] Thurnher, 'The law that applies to autonomous weapon systems'; M. Schmitt, 'Autonomous weapon systems and international humanitarian law: a reply to the critics', *Harvard National Security Journal Features*, (2013), 1, 20–1 (raising the possibility of pre-programmed conservative thresholds); Anderson and Waxman, 'Law and ethics for autonomous weapon systems', 13 (raising conservative targeting thresholds). See also Boothby, 'How far will the law allow unmanned targeting to go?', 56–8 (arguing that there is 'currently no known software capable of mechanizing qualitative decision-making' for proportionality assessments but contending that autonomous attacks may be lawful where heavily constrained in advance, occurring, e.g., in 'remote, unpopulated or sparsely populated' areas); Schmitt and Thurnher, '"Out of the loop"', 23 (similarly arguing, with respect to the rule that where there is doubt as to civilian status, the individual must be presumed to be a civilian, that 'doubt values' could be pre-set and adjusted by humans).

'fully' autonomous systems envisaged by those in favour of a legal ban on AWS. The more operational constraints or limitations are proposed for a hypothetical AWS, the more theoretically predictable its use of force would be and the closer it may be to 'automated' rather than 'fully autonomous'. Relatedly, the later a human leaves the loop, or the more human-limited the operational context is, the more systems may be argued to be under effective human control. Thus far, however, in-depth public, expert or intergovernmental discussion about specifically what kinds of autonomous use of force parameter limitations might be technically and operationally feasible, ethically desirable and legally appropriate has not taken place.

Second, AWS agnostics and supporters challenge the technological assessments and predictions of those asserting AWS illegality. The technological development argument has three main variants: (i) the current assessments of existing technological capacities put forward by AWS prohibitionists are overly pessimistic;[15] (ii) future developments are likely to improve AWS functioning;[16] or (iii) technological

---

[15] See, e.g., Schmitt and Thurnher, '"Out of the loop"', 247 (noting advances in military technology, including of sensors); Thurnher, 'Examining autonomous weapon systems' (arguing that AWS 'should undoubtedly be able to conduct' a collateral civilian damage assessment, but acknowledging that weighing that against any military advantage would 'present challenges for AWS'); Schmitt, 'Autonomous weapon systems', 20 (similarly arguing that there is 'no question' an AWS could be programmed to 'determine the likelihood of harm to civilians in the target area', using an analysis similar to the collateral damage estimate methodology (CDEM) procedure, because the CDEM is already 'heavily reliant on scientific algorithms').

[16] Schmitt and Thurnher, e.g., express a more optimistic view of the projected technical capacity of AWS. Schmitt and Thurnher, '"Out of the loop"', 247 (stating that software to enable 'visual identification of individuals' for autonomous personality strikes 'is likely to be developed'); Thurnher, 'Examining autonomous weapon systems' (arguing that the IHL compliance challenges are 'not insurmountable' and that while AWS may not be able to be lawfully used in various 'complex battlefields', the 'frequency of such situations is likely to be diminished over time as the technology improves'); Schmitt, 'Autonomous weapon systems', 3 (criticizing HRW's report for failing 'to take account of likely developments in autonomous weapon systems technology'). See also P. Lin, G. Bekey and K. Abney, *Autonomous Military Robotics: Risk, Ethics, and Design*, report prepared for US Department of Navy, Office of Naval Research, 20 December 2008 (version 1.0.9), 50 (arguing that AWS 'would need to learn how to apply force proportionate to their goal . . . After testing, it is easy to imagine that robots could perform at least as well as humans in deploying no greater violent force than needed') and 53 (because eventually AWS 'should be able to do as well or better than a human operator in such discrimination', and because AWS could 'be more effective in preventing unintended deaths' the laws of war 'would permit or even demand that such autonomous robots be used' (italics in original); E. Jensen, presentation to the 2015 CCW Informal Meeting of Experts on Lethal

improvement is at least possible, especially when considered on a long time scale and, thus, should not be foreclosed by a pre-emptive ban or early judgments about potential legality.[17] While many ban opponents concede that programming in various areas could be very difficult[18] or that 'some conceivable autonomous weapon systems might be prohibited as a matter of law',[19] they argue that it is possible that other potentially developed systems might be legally compliant or could actually promote rights and civilian protection through greater targeting precision capacities.[20] Ban opponents thus conclude that the current uncertainty

Autonomous Weapons Systems, 15 April 2015 ('As technology emerges, I see this providing a much more discriminating weapons platform').

[17] Waxman and Anderson sometimes express agnosticism as to the direction of weapons development, and occasionally refer to what they describe as their cautious optimism. See, e.g., Anderson and Waxman, 'Law and ethics for autonomous weapon systems', 14. See also W. Boothby, presentation to the 2015 CCW Meeting of Experts on Lethal Autonomous Weapons Systems, 15 April 2015 ('It would in my view be a mistake to try to ban a technology on the basis of its current shortcomings, when in future it may actually enable the law to be complied with more reliably than now'); C. Grut, 'The challenge of autonomous lethal robotics to international humanitarian law', *Journal of Conflict and Security Law*, 18 (2013) 5, 22 (the author raises numerous concerns about AWS but argues: 'Given that some developments towards autonomy might result in more discriminatory systems, a blanket ban on autonomy ... would not be wise').

[18] See, e.g., Schmitt, 'Autonomous weapon systems', 16–17, 20 (noting that it will 'prove highly challenging' but would be 'theoretically achievable' to program the IHL rule that where there is doubt as to civilian status, the person should be presumed civilian; yet 'it is unlikely in the near future' that AWS could 'perform robust assessments of a strike's likely military advantage'); Anderson and Waxman, 'Law and ethics for autonomous weapon systems', 12 (noting the 'daunting' challenge of programming distinction, proportionality, and precautions in attack for a fully autonomous weapon); Boothby, presentation to the 2015 CCW Meeting of Experts, 3 ('offensive autonomous weapon systems that go out and choose their own targets are, judged by reference to currently available technology, generally going to fail a weapon review. The circumstances in which they could lawfully be used, discussed earlier, are very limited').

[19] Schmitt, 'Autonomous weapon systems', 3.

[20] Schmitt and Thurnher, '"Out of the loop"', 234, 262, 281. See also Thurnher, 'Examining autonomous weapon systems' (AWS 'may even be able to provide greater protection to civilians by delivering more precise and accurate strikes'); Schmitt, 'Autonomous weapon systems', 3, 25, 36 (arguing that to 'ban autonomous weapon systems altogether based on speculation as to their future form is to forfeit any potential uses of them that might minimize harm to civilians' and noting ways in which AWS might result in less collateral damage, by, e.g., being armed with non-lethal weapons or having more precise sensors); Anderson and Waxman, 'Law and ethics for autonomous weapon systems', 3, 21 (arguing that AWS may have humanitarian and civilian protection advantages); Waxman and Anderson, 'Don't ban armed robots in the US', *The New Republic* (17 October 2013), available at www.newrepublic.com/article/115229/armed-robots-banning-autonomous-weapon-systems-isnt-answer ('it is quite possible that autonomous machine decision-making may, at least in some contexts, reduce risks to civilians

about weapon developments makes it too soon to make broad legal assessments. Together with the potential for AWS benefits, including promoting national security interests by giving a state a 'technological edge' and 'minimizing the risk to their own forces',[21] they argue that a ban on AWS would be irresponsible, unnecessary and counter-productive.[22]

Some versions of the structure and control and technological development arguments appear overly optimistic, marginalizing and discounting well-known contrary expert views about the likely trajectory of AWS technologies and uses. Moreover, arguments that it would be premature to now draw firm legal conclusions about AWS and that AWS 'could' comply with the law sometimes slip into a conclusion that AWS 'can' do so. Others unhelpfully approach tautology (if future technologies could properly distinguish, they would comply with IHL) or rely on a thesis of inevitability ('the technological imperative'). Nevertheless, the future of weapons developments is undoubtedly uncertain and likely to continuously evolve. And it is not difficult to at least imagine autonomous systems that, if developed in certain ways or used within certain defined parameters, could comply with the conduct of hostilities rules in IHL. Concerns about whether AWS

---

by making targeting decisions more precise and firing decisions more controlled ... As a moral matter, states should strive to use the most sparing methods and means of war – and at some point that may involve [AWS] ... it would be morally wrong not to seek such gains as can be had'). See further Lokhorst and van den Hoven, while noting the general difficulty of converting the laws of war into precise rules for a robot, they argue that AWS could be 'morally superior' to humans because they could 'be designed to immobilize or disarm enemy forces, instead of killing them' – AWS could be programmed to temporarily incapacitate an enemy where a human 'would have no option but to kill'. G. Lokhorst and J. van den Hoven, 'Responsibility for military robots' in P. Lin, K. Abney and G. A. Bekey (eds.), *Robot Ethics: The Ethical and Social Implications of Robotics* (Cambridge, MA: MIT Press, 2012), 145, 148, 153. This argument also reveals 'AWS' definitional tensions. An AWS that was programmed to carry out non-lethal, or less-than-lethal, operations may be excluded from commonly used definitions of AWS, which generally focus on lethal force.

[21] Schmitt and Thurnher, '"Out of the loop"', 232.

[22] Schmitt, 'Autonomous weapon systems', 36–7; Boothby, presentation to the 2015 CCW Meeting of Experts, 3; Jensen, presentation to the 2015 CCW Informal Meeting of Experts, 3; Waxman and Anderson, 'Don't ban armed robots in the US'. See similarly A. Bolt, 'The use of autonomous weapons and the role of the legal advisor' in Saxon, *International Humanitarian Law*, 123, 124, n. 5 (the author, a legal officer for the Canadian Forces, argues that 'blanket determinations ... are inadvisable ... a case-by-case approach is preferable. It is very difficult to guess what a yet-to-be invented weapon [such as AWS] will look like and how it will perform').

could comply with IHL's use of force restrictions, which have driven much of the AWS debate, are extremely difficult to resolve in the abstract and for the future. Assessment as to whether an AWS would comply or whether its use was in compliance with international law, and answering the serious concerns raised by AWS sceptics and prohibitionists, would require knowledge of specific legal, policy and technical information, including whether the circumstances of lawful use put forward in ban opponents' structure and control and technological development arguments in fact come to exist, and whether increasingly autonomous weapons are being developed and deployed in accordance with the applicable rules, norms and interpretations agreed between states. Yet despite the importance of government-provided information for fact-based assessments, transparency has played only a very marginal role in AWS intergovernmental and civil society debates to date, and there has been almost no dialogue about the appropriate scope of transparency.

Towards an international dialogue about transparency for AWS

The dependence of assessments on future facts raises a series of crucial questions. How will a domestic public or the international community come to know if weapons have been developed from relatively innocuous or safe structured or controlled systems, to more paradigm shifting, ethically problematic or IHL-violating systems? How will human responsibility be secured for any errors or violations? Will we be able to know if weapons are used in compliance with a limited operating context, what that operating context is and whether a state's use restrictions comply with international law? If states agree to regulation, a norm of meaningful human control or an AWS prohibition, how will compliance be monitored and assured?

Transparency practices around many of these issues have historically been limited, and no already existing transparency architecture clearly sets out what kinds of AWS information should be disclosed. Secrecy has often been a feature of weapons development and the use of lethal force by states, and past practice suggests that many of the kinds of facts actually necessary for any external observer to make reasonable legal conclusions about AWS may in practice be kept secret on 'national security' grounds. Existing international legal norms around transparency, weapons and the use of lethal force are developing, but they are contested in key respects, as recently demonstrated by debates about how much and what type of information the United States should reveal about its targeted killings and drone strike practices.[23] Human rights treaty protections for the right to life contain no explicit requirement for transparency about violations or investigations, but certain types of transparency, including about government investigations into alleged violations of the right to life, have been instrumentally read into the treaties as necessary to secure substantive rights and are uncontroversial as a matter of human rights law.

However, similar instrumental arguments made for transparency requirements in IHL,[24] even in a limited version, have been met with strong opposition from some military and former military lawyers.[25] Current instrumental interpretations might also serve only to ground the publication of information about use of force investigations and violations and not the range of issues raised above.[26] In addition, while Article 36 of Additional Protocol I (or its customary equivalent) requires states to carry out legal reviews of new weapons, it does little to advance transparency.[27] While many might accept that customary international

---

[23] For a summary, see S. Knuckey (ed.), *Drones and Targeted Killings: Ethics, Law, Politics* (New York: iDebate Press, 2015), 333–88.

[24] Report of the Special Rapporteur on the promotion and protection of human rights and fundamental freedoms while countering terrorism, Doc. A/68/389, 18 September 2013, paras. 41–5. See further Turkel Commission, the Public Commission to examine the maritime incident of 31 May 2010, February 2013; P. Alston, 'The CIA and targeted killings beyond borders', *Harvard National Security Journal*, 2 (2011), 283; E. Lieblich, 'Show us the films: transparency, national security and disclosure of information collected by advanced weapons systems under international law', *Israel Law Review*, 45 (3) (2012), 459.

[25] See, e.g., M. Schmitt, 'Investigating violations of international law in armed conflict', *Harvard National Security Law Journal*, 2 (2011), 31, 81 ('Investigations need not be conducted publically or their results released'); E. Jensen, 'The report of the UN Special Rapporteur for extrajudicial executions: law or advocacy?', *Just Security* (23 October 2013), available at http://justsecurity.org/2414/guest-jensen-un-report/.

[26] The Tschwane Principles, e.g., generally support public disclosure of legal violations but specifically list ongoing defence capabilities and weapons systems capabilities and use as examples of information that may be withheld from the public on national security grounds. See Global Principles on National Security and the Right to Information (Tschwane Principles), available at www.opensocietyfoundations.org/sites/default/files/global-principles-national-security-10232013.pdf (2013), Principle 9. Transparency from the security sector to oversight bodies is subject to separate principles, which mandate 'unrestricted access' to information necessary for oversight (Principle 32).

[27] Protocol Additional to the Geneva Conventions of 12 August 1949, and Relating to the Protection of Victims of International Armed Conflicts (Additional Protocol I) 1977, 1125 UNTS 3.

law requires reviews to be conducted, there is little support for the view that the release of reviews is required.[28]

Weapons-specific treaties offer mixed precedents for information sharing between states and international oversight. Some contain no, or only very limited, compliance provisions.[29] Others contain provisions to promote bilateral or multilateral consultations, procedures such as inter-state dialogue in the event of disputes, annual conferences, the presenta-tion of annual state reports on treaty compliance or for the lodging of complaints with, for example, the UN Security Council.[30] The Chemical Weapons Convention contains stronger transparency and verification

---

[28] For analysis of Article 36, see ICRC, 'A guide to the legal review of new weapons, means and methods of warfare: measures to implement Article 36 of Additional Protocol I of 1977', *International Review of the Red Cross*, 88 (2006), 931, 956 (noting that 'there is no obligation on the reviewing state to make the substantive findings of its review public nor share them with other States'); W. H. Parks, 'Conventional weapons and weapons reviews', *Yearbook of International Humanitarian Law*, 8 (2005), 55, 135 ('Article 36 establishes no transparency obligation'); Wing Commander Blake and Lieutenant Colonel Imburgia, '"Bloodless weapons?" The need to conduct legal reviews of certain capabilities and the implications of defining them as "weapons"', *Air Force Law Review*, 66 (2010), 159, 162–72. See also I. Daoust, R. Coupland and R. Ishoey, 'New wars, new weapons? The obligation of states to assess the legality of means and methods of warfare', *International Review of the Red Cross*, 84 (2002), 345; J. McClelland, 'The review of weapons in accordance with Article 36 of Additional Protocol I', *International Review of the Red Cross*, 85 (2003), 397.

[29] See, e.g., Additional Protocol to the Convention on Prohibitions or Restrictions on the Use of Certain Conventional Weapons which May Be Deemed to Be Excessively Injurious or to Have Indiscriminate Effects (Protocol IV, entitled Protocol on Blinding Laser Weapons), 13 October 1995, 2024 UNTS 163.

[30] See, e.g., Protocol on Prohibitions or Restrictions on the Use of Mines, Booby-Traps and Other Devices as amended on 3 May 1996 (Protocol II) annexed to the CCW, 3 May 1996, 2048 UNTS 93, Articles 13 (annual report and conference) and 14 (intergovernmental consultation or through the UN Secretary-General to resolve disputes); Protocol on Explosive Remnants of War to the Convention on Prohibitions or Restrictions on the Use of Certain Conventional Weapons which May Be Deemed to Be Excessively Injurious or to have Indiscriminate Effects (Protocol V), 28 November 2003, 2399 UNTS 100, Articles 10 (annual conference) and 11 (intergovernmental consultation or through the UN Secretary-General); Convention on the Prohibition of the Use, Stockpiling, Production and Transfer of Anti-Personnel Mines and on Their Destruction, 18 September 1997, 2056 UNTS 211, Articles 7 (annual report submitted to the UN Secretary-General and transmitted by the UN to other states parties), 8 (states may request a clarification through the UN Secretary-General about another state's compli-ance, and a fact-finding mission may be authorized), 11 (regular conferences); Convention on Cluster Munitions, 30 May 2008, 2688 UNTS 39, Articles 7 (explicit 'transparency measures' include conferences and reporting obligations to the UN Secretary-General, 8 (states may submit requests for clarification through the UN Secretary-General), 11 (regular meetings of states parties); Convention on the Prohibition of the Development, Production and Stockpiling of Bacteriological

processes, including – in addition to procedures for bilateral and multi-lateral dispute resolution and annual reporting obligations – the creation of a technical secretary that can request information from states and carry out on-site verification inspections.[31]

Given the lack of one dominant arms control transparency model, and the patchwork of transparency rules, there is a need to systematically address how much and what kinds of transparency for emerging autonomous systems should be sought, provided or required. Transparency concerns thus far have usually only been expressed in general terms. Some NGOs supporting calls for a ban have asked states to 'explain in detail' how they would retain human control over weapons systems,[32] 'demonstrate' that the weapons comply with international law before any use[33] and make public their weapons legal reviews.[34] Reports by the UN Special Rapporteur on extrajudicial executions, which have raised concerns about AWS but ultimately been agnostic on the question of a legal ban, have noted the potential for such systems to promote transparency around the use of force, while also expressing concern about whether new systems will in fact be designed to record and monitor abuse.[35] A European Parliament policy study, adopting no position on a legal

---

(Biological) and Toxin Weapons and on Their Destruction, 10 April 1972, 1015 UNTS 163, Articles V (consultations between states), Article VI (complaints may be submitted to the Security Council, and states parties undertake to cooperate). For an analysis of the increased range and specificity of 'production of information' provisions in bilateral and multilateral arms control treaties (such as the Nuclear Non-Proliferation Treaty, the SALT treaties and the Limited Test Ban Treaty), see K. W. Abbott, '"Trust but verify": the production of information in arms control treaties and other international agreements', *Cornell International Law Journal*, 26 (1) (1993), 1.

[31] Chemical Weapons Convention (CWC), 3 September 1992, 1974 UNTS 45, Article VIII (setting out the Technical Secretariat), Article IX (consultation between states, procedures for requesting clarifications and challenge inspections), Annex on Implementation and Verification (procedures for inspections). While the CWC has one of the strongest verification procedures, some of its noted weaknesses may have particular relevance for any potential AWS regulation, including its lack of universal ratification, lack of clarity around some terminology, and verification difficulties due to dual use.

[32] Article 36, 'Structuring debate on autonomous weapons systems: memorandum for delegates to the Convention on Certain Conventional Weapons', November 2013, 3.

[33] Amnesty International, 'Moratorium on fully autonomous robotics weapons needed to allow the UN to consider fully their far-reaching implications and protect human rights', written statement to the twenty-third session of the UN Human Rights Council, 22 May 2013.

[34] HRW, *Losing Humanity*, 47.

[35] Report of the Special Rapporteur on extrajudicial, summary or arbitrary executions, Doc. A/HRC/23/48, 9 April 2013, para. 81; see also transparency-focused recommendations, paras. 111, 115, 120, 125.

ban and raising both potential concerns and benefits of AWS, advocates broadly for more transparency for unmanned systems and specifically for intergovernmental dialogue about AWS.[36] During the first and second AWS intergovernmental expert meetings of the states parties to the Convention on Certain Conventional Weapons, numerous governments also encouraged states to be more transparent about AWS developments and policies,[37] and the UN Secretary-General's Advisory Board on Disarmament Matters recommended that the Secretary-General encourage transparency.[38] In addition, some legal academics who have argued against a pre-emptive ban have also advised the United States to articulate standards and policies for AWS 'to the world', to participate in international dialogue and to 'resist its own impulses toward secrecy'.[39]

These initial statements indicate an emerging shared concern about transparency among those with otherwise conflicting substantive views about AWS. This apparent common ground around transparency also occurred in the current debates about (remotely piloted) drones. However, agreement among different kinds of actors about the need for more transparency for AWS should not be mistaken for necessary agreement about the interests driving transparency demands, or about the desired content or direction of information flows. In use of force debates generally, and recently in the drone debates, transparency as a concept has often been left unclarified and under-analysed, although it has been called for or argued against in general terms. This simplified treatment has led to a limited understanding about which information matters, why, and to whom it might be provided. Inattentiveness to disentangling the dimensions of transparency can cloud debate about how much information should be transparent, and inhibit the assessment of transparency efforts.

In an effort to deepen and clarify future AWS transparency discussions at the international level, I suggest here some preliminary ways to begin

---

[36] Melzer, *Human Rights Implications*, 44–5.

[37] See, e.g., S. Knuckey, 'Governments conclude first (ever) debate on autonomous weapons: what happened and what's next', *Just Security* (16 May 2014), available at http://justsecurity.org/10518/autonomous-weapons-intergovernmental-meeting/; Germany, statement on Transparency to the 2015 CCW Meeting of Experts on Lethal Autonomous Weapons Systems, 17 April 2015; Sweden, statement on Transparency and the Way Forward to the 2015 CCW Meeting of Experts on Lethal Autonomous Weapons Systems, 17 April 2015; Ghana, statement to the 2015 CCW Meeting of Experts on Lethal Autonomous Weapons Systems, 17 April 2015.

[38] UN Secretary-General, 'Work of the Advisory Board on Disarmament Matters', Doc. A/69/208, 30 July 2014, para. 9.

[39] Anderson and Waxman, 'Law and ethics for autonomous weapon systems', 23, 25.

to think through the elements and types of potential transparency in this context.[40] As a starting point, I offer an ordering of transparency along three basic dimensions: *information* (what should be released or kept secret), *relationships* (the directions of, and mechanisms and actors involved in, information flows) and *justifications* (the reasons for openness).

In the AWS context, information that might be debated for release or secrecy could include information in four broad categories.

First, law and policy information, which could include a state's intentions or policies governing any AWS development. An example of AWS transparency of this form would include the 2012 US Department of Defense Directive 3000.09 on Autonomy in Weapon Systems. Law and policy information might also include the results of Article 36 reviews, the legal rules programmed into the weapons or any programmed or governing policy restrictions on the parameters of their use or transfer.

Second, conduct information – information about the actual development and use of AWS. This could include public acknowledgement of when an autonomous system was used, the circumstances of any use, weapons transfers, statistical or aggregate information about use, pattern or practice data, use-specific information about whether or how a particular strike complies with legal and policy constraints or information about mistakes or errors in use.

Third, process and accountability information, including detail about the procedures in place to ensure human control over decisions or to permit autonomous targeting, the process for recording or monitoring a system's actions, processes to ensure the legal use of AWS, the location of individual and institutional responsibility, oversight mechanisms and accountability regimes, and investigation processes and results.

And, fourth, technological information about autonomous capacities, functions and limits, including how much autonomy the weapon had and with respect to what tasks. In the AWS context, as in all weapons contexts, technological information would be particularly sensitive, and much would be protected by states' national security interests.[41]

---

[40] The structure of this analysis and the concepts introduced here draw upon ongoing research by the author on the role of transparency in current debates about remotely piloted drones.

[41] A foreseeable and unique challenge in the AWS context will be how to balance these interests with the interest in limiting the danger of states' AWS systems interacting with each other in unpredictable and potentially dangerous ways.

'Transparency relationships' concern the direction and path of information demand or release.[42] To whom should information be provided and through what mechanism or process? Transparency relationships could exist along domestic and international, as well as horizontal (for example, state to state or executive to legislature) and vertical (for instance, state to the public or state to an international oversight mechanism), dimensions. An example of a domestic transparency relationship would be a legislative oversight committee's review of information provided by the state's defence department. The arms control mechanisms described earlier create international horizontal and vertical transparency relationships. Actors potentially demanding or receiving transparency about AWS could include members of a state's parliament or legislature; states, including allies or impacted states; UN officials and institutions, such as the Human Rights Council; the International Committee of the Red Cross; a monitoring or verification body set up via binational or multinational processes; civil society groups; the public; any victims of AWS use; or the press. Transparency could be demanded or provided through a variety of informal or formal methods and spaces, including litigation, legislative hearings, state-to-state bilateral processes or multilateral forums. At the international level, numerous states have already opted to participate, through the Convention on Certain Conventional Weapons, in state-to-state dialogue, and some have engaged in the voluntary ad hoc sharing or publication of selected AWS information.

A third general transparency dimension is the justification or basis for transparency about particular information and to particular actors. In the literature on transparency, a huge array of reasons are put forward for greater openness.[43] In the weapons and use of force

---

[42] Although there is no single agreed transparency definition, a principal insight of the academic transparency literature is that relationality is core to understanding transparency. See, e.g., M. Fenster, 'The opacity of transparency', *Iowa Law Review*, 91 (2006), 885, 888 (transparency is 'a governing institution's openness to the gaze of others'); T. N. Hale, 'Transparency, accountability, and global governance', *Global Governance*, 14 (2008), 73, 75 ('An institution is transparent if it makes its behavior and motives readily knowable to interested parties'); A. Florini, 'Introduction: the battle over transparency' in A. Florini (ed.), *The Right to Know: Transparency for an Open World* (Columbia University Press, 2007), 5; M. Bauhr and M. Grimes, 'What is government transparency? New measures and relevance for quality of government', The Quality of Government Institute, Working Paper Series, December 2012, 5.

[43] The transparency literature is immense, but see generally, e.g., J. E. Stiglitz, 'On liberty, the right to know, and public discourse: the role of transparency in public life', Oxford Amnesty Lecture, Oxford, 27 January 1999; B. I. Finel and K. M. Lord (eds.), *Power and*

contexts, four pro-transparency justifications are particularly promi-
nent: transparency is necessary (i) to check or account for illegality or
abuse; (ii) for democratic legitimacy; (iii) for international peace and
security; or (iv) for strategic reasons. Transparency about legal compliance serves primarily an instrumental role. It may prevent harm
through the disciplining effect of risk of exposure, prevent harm by
other states through positive precedent setting, expose conduct and
policies to external scrutiny and enable subsequent reform efforts or
enable victims to seek accountability. As would be expected, this justification has been the primary reason put forward for AWS transparency
by civil society groups. Transparency for democratic legitimacy rests on
the fundamental tenet of liberal democratic theory of a public that is
informed of, engaged in debate about, and ultimately consents to
government conduct and laws. International security transparency is
designed as a confidence-building measure between states and to
reduce misperceptions. Strategic transparency is transparency advocated for, or provided to serve, a state's foreign policy or national
security interests. It could include transparency designed to strengthen
diplomatic relationships, secure deterrence, increase a state's soft power
or norm influence around AWS use or to shore up the perceived
legitimacy of autonomous systems.[44]

Transparency for AWS should be understood and debated through the
relationships between these dimensions. Certain actors demand specific
kinds of information: an alleged victim's family or an NGO representing
them may demand information about a government's knowledge of
abuse associated with specific AWS, but have little need for technical
weapon information. Some justifications provide strong support for the
release of one form of information but weak support for another, and

Conflict in the Age of Transparency (Basingstoke: Palgrave Macmillan, 2002); K. M. Lord,
*The Perils and Promise of Global Transparency: Why the Information Revolution May Not
Lead to Security, Democracy, or Peace* (Albany: SUNY Press, 2006); C. Hood and D. Heald
(eds.), *Transparency: The Key to Better Governance?* (Oxford University Press, 2006);
T. N. Hale, 'Transparency, accountability, and global governance', *Global Governance*, 14
(2008), 73; M. Fenster, 'Seeing the state: transparency as metaphor', *Administrative Law
Review*, 62 (2010), 617; T. Erkkilä, *Government Transparency: Impacts and Unintended
Consequences* (Basingstoke: Palgrave Macmillan, 2012), 13.
[44] During the 2015 CCW meetings, the tensions between these various motives and justifications started to become visible. A number of states opposed to an AWS ban appeared
to be developing an interest in focusing future CCW AWS work on Article 36 reviews and
the sharing of review processes. Some civil society groups and states expressed concern
that a focus on transparency in this sense was a distraction from substantive concerns and
could be used to legitimate developing autonomy.

different kinds of actors deploy distinct justifications. Democratic legitimacy, for example, may provide a strong argument for the release of information to a state's specialist legislative oversight committees, but not to the international community at large. Or, it may ground the public release of general information about whether a state intends to develop AWS and the relevant legal frameworks for AWS use. Likewise, strategic transparency may justify the wide publication of general domestic policies for AWS use, Article 36 review best practices, the sharing of certain information with ally states but not with other actors or the public release of positive (but not reputation-harming) case-specific data.

In future transparency dialogues, these various elements should be disentangled, the limits and motives of justifications recognized, and clarity brought to bear on what kinds of information follow from which rationales and whether an information release would satisfy the stated purposes. In this context, as in other weapons and use of force contexts, many pro-secrecy rationales would be relevant in assessing the proper limits of AWS development and use transparency.[45] These include the obvious national security costs of the publication of many forms of information about new weapons or operational plans, as well as the reputational harm of admission of mistake or legal violation. A disentangling of transparency is thus also important for information-specific and relationship-specific weighing of transparency justifications against state interests in secrecy.

Conclusions

It is crucial that transparency enters the international dialogue around AWS and that assessment of whether and how to improve AWS transparency becomes a part of any path forward for how states respond to autonomous systems – whether new weapon developments are addressed through intergovernmental discussion, the formation of shared policies, regulation of use or a legal prohibition. Key to a productive transparency dialogue is the unpacking and maintaining of distinctions between the

---

[45] For discussion of secrecy's benefits, see, e.g., E. A. Posner and A. Vermeule, *The Executive Unbound: After the Madisonian Republic* (Oxford University Press, 2010), 19; G. Schoenfeld, *Necessary Secrets: National Security, the Media, and the Rule of Law* (New York: W. W. Norton, 2010); C. Sunstein, 'Government control of information', *California Law Review*, 74 (3) (1986), 889, 895–6; D. E. Pozen, 'Deep secrecy', *Stanford Law Review*, 62 (2010), 257, 277.

categories of AWS information and the levels and direction of information flows as well as clarity about information release justifications.

Two fundamental questions present fruitful lines of inquiry for both future scholarship and intergovernmental and civil society debate: first, assessment of how current international and domestic institutional and legal arrangements for information release and oversight might govern AWS in different countries as well as the extent to which existing gaps undermine shared principles and goals or are justified by legitimate state secrecy concerns; second, study of the potential modes and feasibility of improved transparency. At the international level, this could include consideration of various models of new mechanisms for transparency, such as a voluntary, but structured, sharing of information around core concerns (for example, best practices for Article 36 weapons reviews) or establishing reporting obligations up to an oversight body. The development of shared expectations for minimum information disclosure could also be beneficial and might include, for example, whether or not a state is intending to advance autonomy in critical functions and how a state intends to ensure human control and legal compliance as autonomy advances.

Legal debate around autonomous systems is relatively new, yet legal analysis has already set out many of the factors relevant to assessing potential legal implications. At this stage, it is difficult to move legal debate forward, absent actual AWS developments or new information about such systems. The international community should thus examine not only the possible future circumstances in which AWS might or might not be lawful, ethical and effective, but also whether those circumstances will be able to be known and by whom. In particular, to the extent that arguments for AWS rely on potential or hypothetical future use and development scenarios, it is critical to tackle the question of how the international community could know whether such scenarios actually come to exist. Absent such a discussion, the international community risks allowing autonomy to develop on the promise of future legality, but without adequate systems in place to monitor and ensure compliance.

9

A human touch: autonomous weapons, DoD Directive 3000.09 and the interpretation of 'appropriate levels of human judgment over the use of force'

DAN SAXON

Introduction

This chapter addresses the legal, policy and military context of the drafting of 'Autonomy in weapon systems', the United States Department of Defense (DoD) Policy Directive 3000.09.[1] More specifically, the author describes the development and interpretation of Directive 3000.09's requirement that autonomous weapons systems (AWS) be designed to allow commanders and operators to exercise 'appropriate levels of human judgment over the use of force'.[2] The chapter compares the Directive's standard with another conceptual vision for the development of autonomous functions and systems known as 'coactive design' or 'human–machine interdependence'. Finally, the author argues that the increasing speed of autonomous technology – and the concomitant pressures to advance the related values of military necessity and advantage – eventually will cause the Directive's standard

---

[1] A. Carter, US Department of Defense (DoD) Directive 3000.09, 'Autonomy in weapon systems', 21 November 2012, available at www.dtic.mil/whs/directives/corres/pdf/300009p.pdf.

[2] It is important to distinguish between 'automatic' and 'autonomous' weapons systems. 'Automatic' systems are fully pre-programmed and act repeatedly and independently of external influence or control.' DoD, *Unmanned Systems Integrated Roadmap FY2011–2036*, 43, available at www.usnwc.edu/getattachment/4e2b8777-63dd-4bdc-b166-cd19c24dd0de/Excerpts-from-UUV-and-USV-master-plans.aspx. By contrast, 'autonomous weapons' systems are self-directed as they choose their behaviour to achieve a human-determined goal. Thus, autonomous weapons systems are 'capable of a higher level of performance compared to the performance of a system operating in a predetermined manner'. *Ibid.*

of 'appropriate levels of human judgment over the use of force' to be ineffective and irrelevant.

Directive 3000.09

The US government has begun to develop formal – albeit somewhat vague – policies concerning the development and use of semi-autonomous and autonomous weapons.[3] In DoD Directive 3000.09, Ashton B. Carter, deputy secretary of defense for policy, defines 'autonomous weapon system' as a 'weapon system that, once activated, can select and engage targets without further intervention by a human operator'.[4] The drafters of the Directive defined 'autonomous weapon systems' as those that select and engage targets because the drafters wanted to focus on the most critical aspect of autonomy – the function of 'lethality' – where both human judgment and the law of armed conflict (currently) apply.[5] This chapter adopts this definition of autonomous systems for the purposes of the discussion.

[3] Directive 3000.09. For example, according to s. 4 (a), '[a]utonomous and semi-autonomous weapon systems shall be designed to allow commanders and operators to exercise appropriate levels of human judgment over the use of force.' The omission of any explanation of the scope of 'appropriate levels of human judgment over the use of force' may be strategic, as it provides time for autonomous weapon technology to develop further before such standards are defined precisely.

[4] This definition 'includes human-supervised autonomous weapon systems that are designed to allow human operators to override operation of the weapon system, but can select and engage targets without further human input after activation'. *Ibid.*, 13–14. By contrast, Directive 3000.09, part II, 'Definitions', 13, defines a 'semi-autonomous weapon system' as a 'weapon system that, once activated, is intended to only engage individual targets or specific target groups that have been selected by a human operator'. The UK armed forces employ a more cognitive-based definition of 'autonomy'. According to military doctrine from the United Kingdom, an 'autonomous system is capable of understanding higher level intent and direction. ... As such they must be capable of achieving the same level of situational awareness as a human.' An 'automated' or 'automatic' weapon system, however, is one that, in response to inputs from one or more sensors, is programmed to logically follow a pre-defined set of rules in order to provide a predictable outcome. UK military doctrine provides that 'the MOD currently has no intention to develop systems that operate without human intervention in the weapon command and control chain, but it is looking to increase levels of automation where this will make systems more effective'. 'The UK approach to unmanned aircraft systems', Joint Doctrine Note 2/11, 30 March 2011, paras. 205–6 and 508, available at www.gov.uk/government/uploads/system/uploads/attachment_data/file/33711/20110505JDN_211_UAS_v2U.pdf.

[5] Colonel R. Jackson, panel on 'Autonomous Weaponry and Armed Conflict', Annual Meeting of American Society of International Law, Washington, DC, April 2014.

The Directive defines 'semi-autonomous weapon system' as a 'weapon system that, once activated, is intended to only engage individual targets or specific target groups that have been selected by a human operator'.[6] Progressively, the categorization of 'semi-autonomous' versus 'autonomous' is becoming a distinction without a difference as the line between the two becomes more difficult to discern.[7] For example, the US military's new 'long range anti-ship missile' – a weapon the United States contends is semi-autonomous – can fly hundreds of miles after release by an aeroplane and identify and destroy a target without human oversight.[8]

In addition, at present, flying the aeroplane is now a secondary or tertiary task of fighter pilots.[9] The onboard digital flight control system controls steering and the plane's stability. Similarly, the engine digital control system adjusts the power level of the engine and remains within set limits, based on the pilot's input. This technology reduces the pilot's workload tremendously, and he/she can focus on other tasks, such as engaging with targets. Nevertheless, the pilot of contemporary jets such as the F-16 must 'fuse' (that is, interpret) different information provided by the aircraft's sensors and electronics that indicate whether an approaching object is an enemy fighter or a 'friendly' plane. Although the fusion process creates mental work for the pilot, it also can lead to more cautious behaviour prior to engaging a target. In the future, the new, more technologically advanced, F-35 fighter jet will fuse the different data and then present the best information to the pilot, thereby removing this 'judgment call' from the pilot's responsibility. 'Whether it's correct or not, I don't know. At least I don't have to spend time assessing information from multiple sources and worry about it.'[10]

In such situations, attempts to classify the F-35 as a semi-autonomous or autonomous weapons system are artificial as the pilot's real

[6] Directive 3000.09, 14.
[7] Author interview with Colonel Denny Traas, Chief Air Force Branch, Plans Directorate, Defence Staff, Netherlands Ministry of Defence, The Hague, 20 February 2015.
[8] J. Markoff, 'Fearing bombs that can pick whom to kill', *New York Times* (11 November 2014). 'BAE Sensor hits the mark in live long-range missile flight test: first of its kind autonomous missile test proves successful for DARPA', *Aerospace and Defence News*, available at www.asdnews.com/news-51520/BAE_Sensor_Hits_the_Mark_in_Live_Long-Range_Missile_Flight_Test.htm.
[9] Author interview with Colonel Denny Traas.
[10] *Ibid.* See, e.g., description of the M426S E-Scan IFF Interrogator, produced by SELEX ES, available at www.selex-es.com/-/m426s.

participation in targeting decisions can vary significantly.[11] Nevertheless, as described earlier, the consequences of these designations are significant as the Directive permits the development of semi-autonomous weapons systems as well as their exercise of lethal force.[12] The Directive describes who shall be responsible for, *inter alia*, the lawful design of semi-autonomous and autonomous weapons, their experimentation strategies, 'human–machine interfaces', operational standards, doctrine, training, hardware and software safety mechanisms and employment against adversaries.[13] The Directive confirms that persons who authorize the use of, direct the use of or employ semi-autonomous or autonomous weapons systems must do so with appropriate care and consistent with international humanitarian law (IHL), applicable treaties, weapons system safety rules and applicable rules of engagement (ROE).[14] Furthermore, the Directive anticipates that 'unintended engagements' (that is, the death and injury of civilians) will occur and obliges military and civilian leaders to design semi-autonomous or autonomous weapons

[11] 'Full autonomy exists where humans no longer exercise meaningful human control.' C. Heyns, 'Autonomous weapons systems: living a dignified life and dying a dignified death', Chapter 1 in this volume.

[12] To create more sophisticated and complex ('semi-autonomous') weapons systems, the US government has already begun a programme called 'SoSITE', which stands for 'system of systems integration technology and experimentation'. SoSITE will link together a network of manned and numerous unmanned aerial vehicles (also called a 'swarm') 'to enhance mission effectiveness'. The unmanned systems would enter enemy territory with weapons, electronic warfare systems and so on, while the manned platforms would 'control' the unmanned systems using information fused by the technology. The pilot of the manned aircraft will 'command' the swarm of unmanned vehicles, but he 'is relieved of control burdens through the use of advanced distributive battle management aids'. Prior to the pilot's decision to engage a target, 'only a limited amount of information' will be transmitted from the unmanned systems to the pilot. Thus, 'the planning of the engagement, selection and programming of weapons and generation of a targeted solution again [will be] conducted with minimal pilot burden'. 'New concept for air warfare: DARPA advancing system-of-systems open architectures for airborne assets', *AUVSI News* (31 March 2015), available at www.auvsi.org/blogs/auvsi-news/2015/03/31/darpasos.

[13] *Ibid.*, enclosure 4, 'Responsibilities,' parts 1–10. For the purposes of this chapter, the term 'human–machine interface' should be understood as the system of communication and distribution of functions, responsibilities and expectations between computers and their human supervisors or operators. See generally M. L. Cummings, 'Automation and accountability in decision support systems interface design', *Journal of Technical Studies*, 32(1) (2006), 10, available at http://dspace.mit.edu/handle/1721.1/90321.

[14] *Ibid.*, s. 4, b. Concurrent with its concerns about law of armed conflict issues, the DoD instructs the commanders of the US armed forces to 'identify warfighter priorities and operational needs that may be met by autonomous and semi-autonomous weapon systems'. *Ibid.*, enclosure 4, 'Responsibilities', parts 10, b, d and e.

systems so as to minimize the probability of such failures or of 'loss of control of the system'.[15]

Furthermore, Directive 3000.09 affirms that it is US DoD policy that: 'a. Autonomous and semi-autonomous weapons systems shall be designed to allow commanders and operators to exercise appropriate levels of human judgment over the use of force.'[16] The Directive initially limits the use of AWS to the application of non-lethal, non-kinetic force.[17] However, there is a 'loophole' to this restriction. AWS that operate differently – that is, that might apply lethal force – may be developed and deployed with approval from the under-secretary of defense for policy (USDP), the under-secretary of defense for acquisition, technology and logistics, and the chairman of the joint chiefs of staff (the principal military adviser to the president).[18] Before making the decision to commence the development of a lethal, kinetic AWS, however, these three officials must ensure that: '(1) The system design incorporates the necessary capabilities to allow commanders and operators to exercise appropriate levels of human judgment in the use of force.'[19] In addition, after development of a lethal, kinetic AWS, but prior to fielding, the same three DoD representatives must ensure:

> (1) System capabilities, human–machine interfaces, doctrine, TTPs, and training have demonstrated the capability to allow commanders and opera-tors to exercise *appropriate levels of human judgment in the use of force* and to employ systems with appropriate care and in accordance with the law of war, applicable treaties, weapon systems safety rules, and applicable ROE.[20]

Historical and military context of the directive

Depending on how one interprets technical specifications, it is arguable that AWS have been in use for decades. For example, the navies of many nations operate the 'Phalanx close-in weapons system' on their ships against urgent air warfare threats such as planes and missiles. The US Navy describes Phalanx as 'the only deployed close-in weapon system capable of autonomously performing its own search, detect, evaluation, track, engage and kill assessment functions'.[21] In addition, South Korea

---

[15] *Ibid.*, s. 4, a (1) (c).   [16] *Ibid.*, s. 4, a.   [17] *Ibid.*, s. 4, c (3).   [18] *Ibid.*, s. 4, d.

[19] *Ibid.*, enclosure 3, 'Guidelines for review of certain autonomous or semi-autonomous weapon systems', 1, A (1).

[20] *Ibid.*, 1, b (1) (emphasis added). 'ROE' is the acronym for 'rules of engagement'.

[21] Phalanx Close-In Weapons System, *About.Com: The United States Navy Fact File*, avail-able online at http://usmilitary.about.com/library/milinfo/navyfacts/blphalanx.htm.

and Israel have deployed AWS along their borders, the sensors of which can detect approaching soldiers or infiltrators and respond with force.[22] Certain classes of sea mines are programmed to identify and 'attack' particular kinds of ships.[23]

The crucial distinction is in the amount of freedom of manoeuvre that is delegated to the weapon system. For example, 'wide-area loitering munitions', such as Israel's 'Harpy', are designed to patrol large areas of terrain from the air, detect enemy installations and destroy them.[24] Thus, the last human decision is a determination to launch the missile rather than a targeting judgment. The deployment of sophisticated, lethal AWS, therefore, long predates the Directive.

However, to fully understand the publication of Directive 3000.09 in 2012, it is necessary to return to 2003 and the multinational military operation known as 'Operation Iraqi Freedom'. During the invasion of Iraq, the United States' electronic 'Patriot' missile defence system – designed to shoot down incoming ballistic missiles – was at the centre of three incidents of fratricide. On two occasions, Patriot missile batteries engaged friendly coalition aircraft, resulting in the deaths of three crew members. In a third incident, a US aircraft fired on a Patriot battery believed to be an Iraqi surface-to-air missile system.[25]

The US military devoted extensive time and resources to investigating the causes of these accidents and to recommending improvements in the design and operation of this sophisticated technology. A report issued by the DoD's Defense Science Board identified three essential weaknesses in the Patriot system. First, the system's ability to identify and distinguish friendly aircraft from enemy objects was poor. Astoundingly, this deficiency had been observed during many training exercises but never fixed.[26]

---

[22] J. Cho, 'Robo-soldier to patrol South Korean border', *ABC News* (29 September 2006), available at http://abcnews.go.com/Technology/story?id=2504508; E. Cohen, 'Robots on every scene', *Israel Defence* (2 December 2011), available at www.israelDefence.com/?CategoryID=411&ArticleID=688.

[23] See 'Stonefish (mine)', *Digplanet*, available at www.digplanet.com/wiki/Stonefish_(mine).

[24] Israel Aerospace Industries describes the Harpy Loitering Weapon as 'a "Fire and Forget" autonomous weapon, launched from a ground vehicle behind the battle zone'. Israel Aerospace Industries, available at www.iai.co.il/2013/16143-16153-en/IAI.aspx. The US 'harpoon' anti-ship missile system has similar capabilities, although more recent versions permit human control over the final attack on a target. 'Harpoon', WeaponSystems.net, available at http://weaponsystems.net/weapon.php?weapon=HH10+-+Harpoon.

[25] Report of the Defense Science Board Task Force on Patriot System Performance, Report Summary, Office of the Under-Secretary of Defense for Acquisition, Technology, and Logistics, January 2005, 2, available at www.dtic.mil/cgi-bin/GetTRDoc?AD=ADA435837.

[26] *Ibid.*

Second, there was insufficient communication and coordination between the Patriot missile batteries and the other sophisticated, electronic and (at least partly) AWS deployed to Iraq. The US Air Force operated airborne warning and control systems, which were designed to detect aircraft, ships and vehicles at long ranges and exercise command and control of the battle space.[27] Aegis, a ship-based AWS designed to track and destroy threats to naval vessels, was in operation as well.[28] However, the information accumulated by these disparate systems was not fully shared or assimilated by each domain.[29]

Third, the operating philosophy, procedures, human–machine interfaces and software of the Patriot system were poorly designed for the conditions of Operation Iraqi Freedom, where the vast majority of airborne objects were coalition aircraft rather than hostile missiles. The operating procedure was primarily automatic, and operators were trained to trust the Patriot's software, which left limited room for human judgment and control. This deficiency required changes in software, computer displays and training.[30] This last conclusion would resonate during the drafting process of Directive 3000.09. How much human supervision and control is necessary for sophisticated, automated or autonomous weapons systems? As J. Hawley explains, '[d]riven by advances in technology and mission changes, Patriot crewmembers' roles had evolved from traditional operators *to supervisors of automated processes*'.[31] Nevertheless, prior to 2003, the training of Patriot operators was piecemeal rather than holistic. This fragmented training resulted in a focus on individual tasks and components rather than on the development of expertise required to operate – that is, *supervise* – the weapons system in complex environments.

The scientists who studied the Patriot fratricides understood that the goals of training personnel for the use of modern weapons systems should be the development of broad expertise in the system's functions and capabilities rather than of superficial familiarity with the technology.[32]

---

[27] United States, E-3 AWACS (Sentry) Airborne Warning and Control System, available at www.airforce-technology.com/projects/e3awacs/.

[28] Lockheed Martin, Aegis Ballistic Missile Defence, available at www.lockheedmartin.com /us/products/aegis/aegis-bmd.html; report of the Defense Science Board Task Force on Patriot System Performance, 2.

[29] Report of the Defense Science Board Task Force on Patriot System Performance, 2.

[30] *Ibid.*

[31] J. Hawley, 'Patriot fratricides: the human dimension lessons of Operation Iraqi Freedom', *Field Artillery Journal*, 11 (2006), 18.

[32] J. Hawley, 'Patriot vigilance project: training and leader development for the future force', *Fires Bulletin* (2009), 36, 39.

Crucially, Patriot operators required the ability to recognize when to shift from automatic processing of information to critical thinking and problem solving.[33] Thus, some form of 'man-in-the-loop' or 'man-on-the-loop' weapons system, short of full automation or autonomy, was necessary.[34] The appropriate level of oversight would be 'a function of both system design and user training and professional development'.[35]

Thus, the Patriot accidents and ensuing studies generated discussions about standards such as 'appropriate levels of human judgment', which emerged in the Directive. In 2006, for example, one US Army colonel raised 'a point we must address. When and how much human intervention is required' in the use of weapons systems?[36] The Patriot system incidents and investigations helped to shape the views of the working group that produced the Directive.[37] The drafters reviewed the causes of errors in Iraq and considered measures that might prevent catastrophic events or mistakes with contemporary and future autonomous weapons.[38]

Policy and legal issues that influenced the drafters of the Directive

Between 2005 and 2011, the DoD produced a series of 'roadmaps' for unmanned weapons systems,[39] which, clearly in anticipation of the

[33] *Ibid.*, 37.   [34] Hawley, 'Patriot fratricides', 18.   [35] *Ibid.*, 19.

[36] Col. J. Haithcock Jr, TSM FATDS, Fort Sill, Oklahoma, letter to the Editor, *Field Artillery Journal*, January–February 2006, available at http://sill-www.army.mil/firesbulletin/archives/2006/JAN_FEB_2006/JAN_FEB_2006_FULL_EDITION.pdf.

[37] Author interview with P. Scharre, Senior Fellow, Center for a New American Security, Washington, DC, 9 April 2014.

[38] Jackson, panel on 'Autonomous Weaponry and Armed Conflict'. In addition to the Patriot fratricide incidents, the drafters reviewed the shooting down of a civilian Iranian airliner by the US *Vincennes* when operating in the Persian Gulf in 1988. The AEGIS missile defence system on board the Vincennes 'performed as designed'. However, the investigation report concerning the incident noted that AEGIS was incapable of identifying the type of aircraft being tracked by the warship. 'That decision is still a matter for human judgment', which, in this tragedy, led to a mistaken belief that the target was an incoming Iranian fighter jet. 'Stress, task fixation, and unconscious distortion of data may have played a major role in this incident.' DoD, *Investigation Report: Formal Investigation into the Circumstances Surrounding the Downing of Iran Air Flight 655 on 3 July 1988* (Washington, DC: DoD, 1988), ch. IV, 63. Furthermore, the report recommended that 'some additional engineering be done on the display system of AEGIS' to permit monitors to easily separate vital data from other information ('Second endorsement', 7–8).

[39] Not all unmanned weapons systems or 'platforms' will be autonomous. Directive 3000.09 defines an 'unmanned platform' as an '[a]ir, land, surface, subsurface, or space platform that does not have the human operator physically aboard the platform'. Directive 3000.09, part II 'Definitions', 15. E.g., the Predator and Reaper 'drones' are unmanned surveillance

possible fielding of AWS in the future,[40] articulated the US military's vision for the future role of unmanned weapons in meeting security needs.[41] One of the goals of these roadmaps was to foster 'the development of policies, standards, and procedures that enable safe and timely operations and the effective integration of manned and unmanned systems'.[42] In addition, the roadmaps supported better validation and testing processes for new weapons systems and the implementation of standardized control measures for unmanned systems.[43]

Not least, especially for weapons manufacturers and technology developers, the roadmaps summarized the 'direction for future investments intended to produce common hardware and software'[44] that would facilitate the design and employment of unmanned systems, including the use of autonomy. 'The overarching goal' of the 2009–34 roadmap, for example, was 'to focus military departments and Defense agencies towards investments in unmanned systems and technologies that meet the prioritized capability needs of the Warfighter'.[45] Thus, this roadmap describes the performance characteristics for unmanned systems that the *industrial base* must achieve to develop technologies supportive of the US armed forces.[46]

By 2009, at least one such roadmap foreshadowed Directive 3000.09's focus on appropriate levels of human judgment and autonomy:

and weapon platforms that are operated by ground-based pilots using remote-control technology.

[40] M. Schmitt and J. Thurnher, '"Out of the loop": autonomous weapon systems and the law of armed conflict', *Harvard National Security Journal*, 4 (2013), 231, 237.

[41] See *Unmanned Aircraft Systems Roadmap 2005–2030*, available at http://fas.org/irp/program/collect/uav_roadmap2005.pdf; *Unmanned Systems Roadmap 2007–2032*, 7 December 2007, available at www.globalsecurity.org/intell/library/reports/2007/dod-unmanned-systems-roadmap_2007–2032.pdf; *Unmanned Systems Integrated Roadmap FY2009–2034*, 6 April 2009. *Unmanned Systems Integrated Roadmap FY2011–2036*. In 2009, the US Air Force issued its *Unmanned Aircraft Systems Flight Plan 2009–2047*, 18 May 2009 available at http://fas.org/irp/program/collect/uas_2009.pdf. Not to be outdone, in 2010, the US Army published its *Eyes of the Army: US Army Unmanned Aircraft Systems Roadmap 2010–2035*, available at http://fas.org/irp/program/collect/uas-army.pdf.

[42] *Unmanned Systems Roadmap 2007–2032*, ii.

[43] *Ibid.*, ii and 17; *Unmanned Systems Integrated Roadmap FY2009–2034*, 10–11.

[44] *Unmanned Systems Roadmap 2007–2032*, 48–54.

[45] *Unmanned Systems Integrated Roadmap FY2009–2034*, xiii.

[46] *Ibid.*, 1 (emphasis added). In an effort to better inform future investments into robotics technology and better focus industry efforts to create robotic vehicles suitable for military missions, the DoD and a consortium of eighty defence contractors, 'non-traditional contractors' and universities signed an agreement that enabled the defence industry to participate in the DoD technology assessment process. *Ibid.*, 3.

Assuming the decision is reached to allow some degree of autonomy, *commanders must retain the ability to refine the level of autonomy* the systems will be granted by mission type, and in some cases by mission phase, just as they set rules of engagement for the personnel under their command today. *The trust required for increased autonomy of systems will be developed incrementally.* The systems' programming will be based on human intent, with humans monitoring the execution of operations and retaining the ability to override the system or change the level of autonomy instantaneously during the mission.[47]

This incremental development of autonomous military technology is evident in the US military's current development of unmanned systems for non-combat purposes such as surveillance, bomb disposal and logistics supply as opposed to the engagement of targets.[48] In its *Unmanned Systems Integrated Roadmap FY2011–2036*, the DoD framed the concept of 'level of autonomy' in terms of the interdependence of humans and machines:

> [A]utonomy must be developed to support natural modes of interaction with the operator. These decision-making systems must be cognitively compatible with humans in order to share information states and to allow the operator and the autonomous system to interact efficiently and effectively. The level of autonomy should be dynamically adjust [sic] based on workload and the perceived intent of the operator. Common terms used for this concept are *sliding autonomy* or *flexible autonomy*.[49]

In the same roadmap, the DoD noted additional challenges in the development and fielding of AWS: 'The introduction of increased unmanned system autonomy must be mindful of affordability, operational utilities, technological developments, policy, public opinion, and their associated constraints.'[50] No mention was made of the constraints that IHL and/or international human rights law might impose on autonomous weapons. In addition to these challenges, the Pentagon concluded that AWS require the capacity to understand and adapt to their environment, one of the great technological challenges of robotics.[51] At the procurement level, the military will need new 'verification and validation' methods to ensure that the new technology fulfils its intended purpose.[52] According to the DoD's vision, after procurement, robust operational training programmes would ensure that AWS perform properly.[53] Finally, this

---

[47] *Unmanned Aircraft Systems Flight Plan 2009–2047*, 41 (emphasis added).
[48] Email message from P. Scharre, 31 October 2014 (copy in author's possession).
[49] *Unmanned Systems Integrated Roadmap FY2011–2036*, 46 (emphasis in original).
[50] *Ibid.*, vi.   [51] *Ibid.*, 45.   [52] *Ibid.*, 50.   [53] *Ibid.*, 48.

roadmap acknowledged the need for 'policy guidelines' for AWS capable of selecting and engaging targets with lethal force.[54] Importantly, the road-maps predict how AWS will increase the speed of battle space decision making and performance, thereby providing strategic, operational and tactical advantages to the militaries that field them:

> Advances in computing speeds and capacity will change how technology affects the OODA loop.[55] Today the role of technology is changing from supporting to fully participating with humans in each step of the process. *In 2047 technology will be able to reduce the time to complete the OODA loop to micro or nano-seconds.* Much like a chess master can outperform proficient chess players, [AWS] will be able to react at these speeds and therefore this loop moves toward becoming a 'perceive and act' vector. Increasingly humans will no longer be 'in the loop' but rather 'on the loop' – monitoring the execution of certain decisions. Simultaneously, advances in [artificial intelligence] will enable systems to make combat decisions and act within legal and policy constraints without necessarily requiring human input.[56]

The publication of these roadmaps has led to a tipping point within the DoD. The office of the USDP began to receive queries about legal and ethical issues concerning the development and deployment of autono-mous weapons, while the different military branches adopted inconsis-tent positions. The US Army initially asserted that it 'will never delegate use-of-force decisions to a robot'.[57] The US Air Force took a different view.[58] In 2010, the DoD funded an internal survey of current technology and its level of autonomy and new technologies in development. However, this study was 'hyper-technical' and 'all over the place' and

---

[54] *Ibid.*, 50. In 2009, the US Air Force observed that '[a]uthorizing a machine to make lethal combat decisions is contingent upon political and military leaders resolving legal and ethical questions. These include the appropriateness of machines having this ability, under what circumstances it should be employed, where responsibility for mistakes lies and what limitations should be placed upon the autonomy of such systems.' *Unmanned Aircraft Systems Flight Plan 2009–2047*, 41.

[55] 'OODA' stands for 'observe, orient, decide and act', a decision cycle developed by John Boyd, a US Air Force colonel and military strategist. The faster a military unit can complete this cycle and react to an event, the greater its success. R. Thomas Jr, 'Colonel John Boyd is dead at 70; advanced air combat tactics', *New York Times* (13 March 1997), available at www.nytimes.com/1997/03/13/us/col-john-boyd-is-dead-at-70-advanced-air-combat-tactics.html.

[56] *Unmanned Aircraft Systems Flight Plan 2009–2047*, 41 (emphasis added). As Schmitt and Thurnher observe, '[f]uture combat may therefore occur at such a high tempo that human operators will simply be unable to keep up' ('"Out of the loop"', 238). Militaries that do not field autonomous weapons systems will cede initiative in the battlespace. *Ibid.*

[57] Author interview with P. Scharre.   [58] *Ibid.*, Air Force UAS Flight Plan, 45 and 51.

not very useful.[59] When certain AWS did reach the field, commanders refused to trust them since command-and-control lapses raised questions about the weapon's safety.[60] By 2011, it was evident that clearer guidance on the development and use of autonomous weapons was necessary, and the USDP commenced work on the Directive.

Within the DoD, two general concerns motivated the production of Directive 3000.09. First DoD officials understood that the lack of a clear policy concerning AWS might result in the development or deployment of weapon systems that are unsafe, illegal and/or unethical.[61] For example, in any combat environment, commanders are expected to maintain and exercise control over their subordinate units in order to preserve discipline, efficiency and proper conduct.[62] Increased autonomy of weaponry and the speed of decision making offered by autonomous weapons present obvious challenges to the exercise of command and control.[63] The drafters determined, however, that the design of new AWS must permit commanders to retain explicit control over them.[64] Indeed, the Directive instructs commanders of the US military's 'combatant commands'[65] to '[e]mploy

---

[59] Author interview with P. Scharre.

[60] S. Magnuson, 'Armed robots sidelined in Iraqi fight', *National Defence* (May 2008), available at www.nationaldefensemagazine.org/archive/2008/May/Pages/Armed2265.aspx. To be effective in combat situations, autonomous weapons systems (AWS) must 'achieve a level of trust approaching that of humans charged with executing missions'. Air Force UAS Flight Plan, 41.

[61] *Ibid.*

[62] The term 'command' refers to the legal authority accorded to a soldier by his superiors to direct, coordinate or control armed forces. The exercise of command includes the process by which a commander makes decisions, transmits his intentions to and impresses his will on his subordinates to achieve objectives. NATO, 'Command and control at the operational level', Doc. AJP-01(C), *Allied Joint Doctrine* (March 2007), paras. 0501 and 0606. 'Control', which is an aspect of 'command', is the authority exercised by a commander and is the process through which a commander, assisted by staff, organizes, directs and coordinates the activities of the forces assigned to implement orders and directives. Directorate General Development and Doctrine, 'Land operations', *UK Army Doctrine Publications* (May 2005), para. 0502(b).

[63] However, as M. Sassóli observes, autonomy may provide certain advantages for command and control. The real-time video and other communication options 'designed in' to autonomous weapons systems, as well as their electronic 'footprints', could facilitate a commander's control over subordinates in certain situations. M Sassóli, 'Autonomous weapons and IHL: advantages, questions and issues', *International Law Studies*, 90 (308) (2014), 326 and 338. Furthermore, commanders and their subordinates may be able to adjust remotely future autonomous weapons systems during ongoing operations to account for changing circumstances. Schmitt and Thurnher, '"Out of the loop"', 264.

[64] Author interview with P. Scharre.

[65] The DoD 'has nine unified combatant commands, each with responsibilities for a geographic region or functional area in support of U.S. strategic objectives. Their

autonomous and semi-autonomous weapon systems with appropriate care
and in accordance with the law of war, applicable treaties, weapon system
safety rules, and applicable rules of engagement'.[66]

Furthermore, as mentioned earlier, the development of autonomous
or semi-autonomous weapon systems intended for the use of lethal force
must receive the prior approval of three high-ranking members of the
DoD: the USDP, the under-secretary of defense for acquisition, technology and logistics and the chief of the joint chiefs of staff. Approval of the
new system must be repeated prior to fielding.[67] These requirements
illustrate the significant degree of responsibility that the United States
intends to exert over the development and use of lethal AWS during the
coming five to ten years.[68] Indeed, Geoffrey Corn argues that the decisive
point in the process of ensuring that an AWS is used in accordance with
IHL will shift from the tactical phase (as is usually the case with 'traditional' weapons) to the development and procurement phase.[69]

The second DoD concern was perceived constraints to the research and
development of new kinds of autonomous technologies. As described
earlier, modern militaries already incorporate some autonomous features
in certain weapons. Nevertheless, as described elsewhere in this volume,
the introduction of greater autonomy in weapons systems raises complex
legal, moral and ethical issues. In the absence of government policy direction addressing the development and deployment of weapon systems with
greater autonomy, researchers and developers were hesitant to develop
autonomous functions that might be constrained by these challenges.
Thus, the Directive's guidelines were intended to provide clarity so that
researchers and developers could incorporate autonomous functions in
weapons system within legal and ethical boundaries.[70]

<hr/>

mission is to maintain command and control of U.S. military forces around the world in
peacetime as well as in conflict.' DoD, *United States Combatant Commands*, available at
www.defense.gov/Sites/Unified-Combatant-Commands; the nine combatant commands
are Northern Command, Southern Command, European Command, Africa Command,
Central Command, Pacific Command, Transportation Command, Special Operations
Command and Strategic Command. *Ibid.*

[66] Directive 3000.09, 'Responsibilities', s. 10, b.   [67] *Ibid.*, 4 (Policy) d.

[68] Jackson, Panel on 'Autonomous Weaponry and Armed Conflict'. Directive 3000.09
stipulates that it must be reissued, cancelled or certified current within five years of its
issuance in November 2012. If not, the Directive will expire on 21 November 2022.
Directive 3000.09, s. 7, 'Effective date', 4.

[69] G. S. Corn, 'Autonomous weapons systems: managing the inevitability of "taking the man
out of the loop"', Chapter 10 in this volume.

[70] Author interview with P. Scharre; email message from P. Scharre, 31 October 2014.

Hence, the Directive's neutral language and parameters for the design and use of AWS is intended to encourage the development of new autonomous technologies.[71] Although the Directive creates high compliance standards for the development, procurement and deployment of (lethal) AWS (discussed later in this chapter), it does not prohibit them. The Directive's neutral tone balances different perspectives within the DoD regarding AWS – officials who wished to slow or limit the development of such weapons and others who believed that any self-imposed restrictions on the US military's procurement and use of the weapons would be a mistake.[72] In doing so, Directive 3000.09 removes political-bureaucratic obstacles to the development of AWS.

The individuals who prepared and drafted Directive 3000.09 considered that four principles should guide the development and use of AWS. First, the system must be capable of accomplishing the military mission.[73] This is uncontroversial as it would be absurd for any state intentionally to develop and field weapons that are ineffective. Consequently, the drafters intended Directive 3000.09 to create a robust 'validation and verification' process that would ensure the procurement and fielding of only reliable AWS. Therefore, the Directive includes a series of technical testing and training requirements to ensure that the weapons and their autonomous functions will perform as designed. For example, new autonomous systems must receive rigorous hardware and software testing in realistic conditions to ensure that they perform 'as anticipated in realistic operational environments against adaptive adversaries'.[74] Moreover, the validation and verification process must ensure that the new system will complete engagements in a timely manner 'consistent with commander and operator intentions and, if unable to do so, terminate engagements or seek additional human input before continuing the engagement'.[75]

Second, the system must be robust against failures and hacking. This principle speaks to a real danger of AWS. Fundamentally, they rely on computer software for their artificial intelligence, and computer software is vulnerable to interference and re-programming by the enemy.[76] The Directive asserts that AWS must be 'sufficiently robust to minimize failures that could lead to unintended engagements or loss

[71] Author interview with P. Scharre.
[72] Author interview with P. Scharre; email message from P. Scharre, 31 October 2014.
[73] Author interview with P Scharre.   [74] Directive 3000.09, 'Policy', 4, a (1) (a) and (b).
[75] *Ibid.*, enclosure 3, 1, a (2).   [76] Schmitt and Thurnher, "Out of the loop", 242.

of control of the system to unauthorized parties'.[77] To ensure such robustness, the Directive insists that the hardware and software of AWS must contain 'appropriate' safety and 'anti-tamper mechanisms' and '[h]uman machine interfaces and controls'.[78] The Directive provides some guidance on the standards required for an appropriate 'interface between people and machines' that will permit 'operators to make informed and appropriate decisions in engaging targets'.[79] First, the interface should be easily understandable to trained operators. Second, it should provide traceable information on the status of the weapons system. Last, the interface should provide clear procedures for trained operators to activate and deactivate functions of the weapons system.[80] While these criteria may be appropriate for semi-autonomous weapons systems, Directive 3000.09 does not explain how, or in what circumstances, human 'operators' will override the capabilities of AWS and decide whether and how to engage targets. Furthermore, as discussed further below, as the speed of decision making by autonomous weapons increases, the ability for humans to deactivate particular functions to avoid 'unintended engagements' is bound to decrease.

The third general principle adopted by the drafters of the Directive is that the system must be capable of lawful use.[81] For example, military commanders who employ weapon systems with autonomous functions must continue to perform the decision-making processes required by IHL: 'Commanders must ensure that autonomous weapons will be employed in a discriminate manner consistent with proportionality analysis.'[82] Alternatively, commanders must understand the capabilities of the system sufficiently to assess whether discrimination and proportionality determinations programmed into its computer software can meet IHL standards in the circumstances in which it is employed.[83] Crucially, 'the Directive does not change the individual responsibility of commanders operating autonomous weapon systems'.[84] Similarly, during the 'legal reviews' of new AWS pursuant to Article 36 of

---

[77] Directive 3000.09, 'Policy', 4, a (1) (c). 'Unintended engagements' would include, e.g., attacks against civilians.

[78] Ibid., 'Policy', 4, a (2) (a) and (b).   [79] Ibid., 'Policy', 4, a (3).

[80] Ibid., 'Policy', 4, a (3) (a) (b) and (c).   [81] Author interview with P. Scharre.

[82] Jackson, panel on 'Autonomous Weaponry and Armed Conflict'.

[83] Email message from R. Jackson, Special Assistant to the US Army Judge Advocate General for Law of War Matters, 7 May 2014 (copy in author's possession).

[84] Jackson, panel on 'Autonomous Weaponry and Armed Conflict'.

Additional Protocol I,[85] weapons manufacturers must demonstrate that their new weapons systems will comply with the IHL rules concerning distinction, proportionality and precautions before and during attack.[86]

Fourth, the system must employ the proper balance of autonomy and human supervision vis-à-vis other criteria such as military professionalism, ethics and the public perception of such systems.[87] This principle, reflected in the standard repeated several times in the Directive – appropriate levels of human judgment over the use of force – is probably the most controversial – and undefined – piece of the DoD's policy. Absent in the Directive is a definition or explanation of this crucial guideline for the employment of lethal AWS: what are the appropriate levels of human judgment – if any – that should be exercisable, and exercised, by military commanders and operators of AWS before, during and after the use of lethal force by autonomous machines in armed conflict?

The standard of 'appropriate levels of human judgment over the use of force' and alternative visions for autonomy

The authors of the Directive decided not to include an explicit definition of 'appropriate levels of human judgment over the use of force' in the document, nor did they treat this guideline as a precise concept. The drafters believed that the 'appropriateness' standard for levels of human judgment over the use of force requires the balancing of multiple interests, including military necessity.[88] Thus, what is 'appropriate' – for the DoD – will vary

---

[85] Protocol Additional to the Geneva Conventions of 12 August 1949, and Relating to the Protection of Victims of International Armed Conflicts (Additional Protocol I) 1977, 1125 UNTS 3, Art. 36 obliges states, before fielding new weapons or methods of warfare, to 'determine whether its employment would, in some or all circumstances, be prohibited' by any rule of international law applicable to the state. Prior to fielding a new AWS, the guidelines to the Directive require that the General Counsel of the DoD, in coordination with the chairman of the joint chiefs of staff, the under-secretary of defense for policy and the under-secretary of defense for acquisition, technology and logistics, complete a legal review. Directive 3000.09, s. 1, b, (6).

[86] Jackson, panel on 'Autonomous Weaponry and Armed Conflict'.

[87] Author interview with P. Scharre. The authors considered that principle (iv) should be applied more flexibly than the first three criteria.

[88] Francis Lieber defined military necessity as 'those measures which are indispensable for securing the ends of the war and which are lawful according to the modern laws and usages of war'. General Orders no. 100: The Lieber Code, 1863, available at http://avalon.law.yale.edu/19th_century/lieber.asp#art14. In a more nuanced version, the United Kingdom asserts that 'military necessity permits a state engaged in armed conflict to use only that degree and kind of force, not otherwise prohibited by the law of armed conflict, that is required in order to achieve the legitimate purpose of the conflict, namely the complete or partial submission of

according to the circumstances.[89] According to one of the authors of
Directive 3000.09 – a leading IHL expert in the US military – the drafters
intended the language 'appropriate levels of human judgment' to refer to the
levels of supervision required to ensure compliance with the standards
prescribed by the law of armed conflict – that is, 'distinction', 'proportionality' and whether the AWS is, by its nature, an indiscriminate weapon.[90]
As Richard Jackson explains, '[w]e still expect military commanders
employing a system with autonomous functions to engage in the decision-
making process that is required by IHL'.[91] Consequently, the Directive does
not affect the individual criminal responsibility of commanders who operate
AWS. As noted earlier, commanders must ensure that AWS are employed
in a manner that is discriminate, consistent with proportionality analysis.
If that is not possible, the commander must understand the capabilities of
the weapons system sufficiently to assess whether the machine(s) can make
discrimination and proportionality determinations consistent with IHL at
the time and in the conditions where it is employed.[92]

It is important to note that, depending on the conditions, the phrase
'appropriate levels of human judgment over the use of force' exercised by
commanders and operators of AWS can include the exercise of no
human judgment at all. In this respect, the Directive's benchmark for
human supervision of autonomous weapons differs from the exercise of
'meaningful human control' standard articulated by other institutions
and individuals.[93] Philosopher Peter Asaro argues that 'meaningful

the enemy at the earliest possible moment with the minimum expenditure of life and
resources'. Joint Doctrine and Concepts Centre, Ministry of Defence, *Joint Service Manual
of the Law of Armed Conflict*, JSP 383 (2004), para. 2.2, available at www.gov.uk/government/
uploads/system/uploads/attachment_data/file/27874/JSP3832004Edition.pdf. In essence, as
a legal principle, military necessity 'forbids acts unnecessary to secure a military advantage'.
A. P. V. Rogers, *Law on the Battlefield*, 2nd edn (Manchester University Press, 2004), 6, citing
M. Schmitt, 'War and the environment: fault lines in the prescriptive landscape' in J. Austin
and C. Bruch (eds.), *The Environmental Consequences of War* (Cambridge University Press,
2000), 101.
[89] Author interview with P. Scharre.
[90] Jackson, panel on 'Autonomous Weaponry and Armed Conflict'.
[91] *Ibid.* Consequently, during 'Article 36 Legal Reviews' of new AWS prior to fielding, DoD
lawyers will expect developers and manufacturers to demonstrate that their new technology, when used as intended, complies with the rules of IHL. *Ibid.*
[92] *Ibid.*; email message from R. Jackson, 7 May 2014.
[93] N. Sharkey, audio presentation to Convention on Certain Conventional Weapons Meeting of
Experts on Lethal Autonomous Weapons Systems, 13–16 May 2014, available at www.unog
.ch/80256EE600585943/(httpPages)/6CE049BE22EC75A2C1257C8D00513E26?
OpenDocument. C. Heyns, 'Human rights law issues', presentation to Convention on Certain
Conventional Weapons Meeting of Experts on Lethal Autonomous Weapons Systems, 13–16

human control' requires sufficient opportunity for human supervisors to perform moral reasoning and deliberation prior to 'each and every use of violent force'.[94] Computer scientist Noel Sharkey proposes that 'meaningful human control' over a weapons system might include the following components:

1. a commander or operator has full contextual and situational awareness of a target area of a specific attack;
2. he/she is able to perceive and react to any change or unanticipated situations that may have arisen since planning the attack;
3. there must be active cognitive participation in the attack and time for deliberation on the significance of the target in terms of necessity and appropriateness of the attack and the likely incidental and possible accidental effects of the attack;
4. there must be a means for the rapid suspension or abortion of the attack.[95]

The US government rejects the 'meaningful human control' standard for AWS as it threatens the US desire to maximize available options in the interests of military necessity: 'This formulation does not fully capture the full range of human activity that takes place in weapon system development, acquisition, fielding and use, including a commander's or operator's judgment to deploy a particular weapon to achieve a particular effect on a particular battlefield.'[96] By choosing not to define its standard

May 2014, available at www.unog.ch/80256EE600585943/(httpPages)/ 6CE049BE22EC75A2C1257C8D00513E26?OpenDocument. P. Asaro, Assistant Professor of Media Studies, presentation to Convention on Certain Conventional Weapons Meeting of Experts on Lethal Autonomous Weapons Systems, 13–16 May 2014, 12, available at www .unog.ch/80256EDD006B8954/(httpAssets)/79F6199F74DC824CC1257CD8005DC92F/ $file/Asaro_LAWS_ethical_2014.pdf.

94 P. Asaro, 'Ethical questions raised by military application of robotics', presentation to Convention on Certain Conventional Weapons Meeting of Experts on Lethal Autonomous Weapons Systems, 13–16 May 2014, available at www.unog.ch /80256EE600585943/(httpPages)/6CE049BE22EC75A2C1257C8D00513E26? OpenDocument.

95 N. Sharkey, Professor of Artificial Intelligence and Robotics, PowerPoint presentation to Convention on Certain Conventional Weapons Meeting of Experts on Lethal Autonomous Weapons Systems, 13–16 May 2014, available at www.unog.ch /80256EDD006B8954/(httpAssets)/78C4807FEE4C27E5C1257CD700611800/$file/ Sharkey_MX_LAWS_technical_2014.pdf.

96 S. Towncey, US Delegation to Expert Meeting on Lethal Autonomous Weapons, 16 May 2014, available at www.unog.ch/80256EE600585943/(httpPages)/ 6CE049BE22EC75A2C1257C8D00513E26?OpenDocument.

of 'appropriate levels of human judgment over the use of force', the United States keeps alive all possible options for the exercise of a commander or operator's judgment as long as they fall within the bounds of IHL.[97] One of the difficulties with phraseology such as 'appropriate levels of human judgment' is that it reveals little about the challenges faced by persons and/or machines in understanding their environment, particularly during armed conflict where the need for human judgment is constantly shifting.[98]

Conversely, the 'meaningful human control' frameworks proposed by Asaro and Sharkey resemble a vision of autonomy referred to as 'coactive design' or 'human–machine interdependence'. Some computer and robotics scientists contend that this perspective is a more effective concept for human interaction with AWS than a focus on 'appropriate levels'. The coactive design model attempts to leverage and integrate the different strengths of humans and machines in order to maximize the performance of weapons systems.[99] For example, it is true that computers can outperform humans in tasks such as the collection and filtering of information. However, 'for decisions that matter, human judgment is better and faster'[100] because humans have greater ability to recognize context[101] and apply inductive reasoning for creative thinking.[102] Thus, under this perspective of autonomy, it is shortsighted to suggest that human factors and

---

[97] It is certainly possible that political, as well as legal, constraints will impact the interpretation of the 'appropriate level' standard. Currently, e.g., because political elites prefer to minimize risks such as the deaths of civilians and armed forces personnel, the autonomy of human soldiers on the battlefield is decreasing due to real-time communication links to their commanders. Lieutenant Colonel Olivier Madiot, French Joint Staff, remarks to the Expert Meeting on Lethal Autonomous Weapons, 16 May 2014, available at www.unog.ch/80256EE600585943/(httpPages)/6CE049BE22EC75A2C1257C8D00513E26?OpenDocument.

[98] The form and substance of communications between humans and autonomous weapons systems may also evolve in ways that are difficult to foresee today. Robotic scientists have observed that, as interactions between humans and robots increase, the two entities begin to develop their own language. L. Steels, 'Ten big ideas of artificial intelligence', Twenty-Fifth Benelux Conference on Artificial Intelligence, Delft University of Technology, 8 November 2013.

[99] Author interview with J. Bradshaw, Senior Research Scientist, Florida Institute for Human and Machine Cognition, Leiden, Netherlands, 10 June 2014.

[100] Author interview with M. Johnson, Research Scientist, Florida Institute for Human and Machine Cognition, Leiden, Netherlands, 10 June 2014.

[101] Author interview with J. Bradshaw.

[102] M. L. Cummings, 'Man versus machine or man + machine?' 12 (unpublished draft; copy in author's possession). Research efforts are underway to mimic human reasoning and judgment processes in machines. One example is KEEL technology. KEEL stands for 'knowledge-enhanced electronic logic'. Email message from Tom Keeley, President,

input can be minimized in the design and fielding of machines.[103] Priority should be given to the reinforcement of human–machine teamwork rather than to the separation of duties between humans and machines.[104] Thus, autonomy can be viewed not as an end in itself but, rather, as a tool to accomplish particular objectives.[105]

Accordingly, the coactive design model contends that as autonomous technologies improve, the interdependence between humans and machines will increase.[106] More advanced coactive weapons systems with autonomous functions will create opportunities to accomplish more complex tasks.[107] Indeed, just months before the publication of Directive 3000.09, the US Defense Science Board issued a report entitled 'The role of autonomy in DoD systems'.[108] The report argues that efforts to provide definitions of levels of autonomy (as the Directive suggests) are counter-productive and create confusion among stakeholders.[109] The report contends that '[a]utonomy is better understood as a capability (or a set of capabilities) that enables the larger human–machine system to accomplish a given mission'.[110] Thus,

---

Compsim LLC, 2 and 13 June 2014 (copy in author's possession). See 'Keel technology for complex problems', available at www.compsim.com.

[103] J. Bradshaw *et al.*, 'The seven deadly myths of "autonomous systems"', *Human-Centred Computing* (May–June 2013), 57, available at www.jeffreymbradshaw.net/publications/IS-28-03-HCC_1.pdf.

[104] *Ibid.*, 58–60. As a team, humans and computers are far more powerful than either alone, especially under uncertainty. M. L. Cummings, 'Man versus machine or man + machine?', 12. E.g., if autonomous weapons systems can exercise 'self-recognition' – i.e., the capacity of the machine to detect that it is operating outside the conditions for which it was designed – the machine will call on humans for increased supervision. Author interview with M. Johnson.

[105] Author interview with Gianfranco Visentin, Head, Automation and Robotics Section, European Space Research and Technology Centre, European Space Agency, Noordwijk, the Netherlands, 4 November 2013.

[106] *Ibid.*

[107] As several leading proponents of the coactive design model argue: '[T]he property of autonomy is not a mere function of the machine, but rather a relationship between the machine and a task in a given situation.' M. Johnson *et al.*, 'Beyond cooperative robotics: the central role of interdependence in coactive design', *Human-Centred Computing* (May–June 2011), 84, available at www.ihmc.us/users/mjohnson/papers/Johnson_2011_HCC_BeyondCooperativeRobotics.pdf.

[108] DoD, Office of the Under-Secretary of Defense for Acquisition, Technology and Logistics, *The Role of Autonomy in DoD Systems*, July 2012, 21, available at http://fas.org/irp/agency/dod/dsb/autonomy.pdf.

[109] *Ibid.*, 23. See, e.g., 'Table 3: four levels of autonomy', in DoD, *Unmanned Systems Integrated Roadmap FY2011–2036*, 46.

[110] *Ibid.*, 21. The Defense Science Board report argues that 'there are no fully autonomous systems just as there are no fully autonomous soldiers, sailors, airmen or Marines'. *Ibid.*, 24.

the Defense Science Board recommended that the DoD abandon its use of 'levels of autonomy' and replace this concept with a framework that focuses design and development decisions on the explicit allocation of cognitive functions and responsibilities between humans and machines to achieve specific capabilities.[111]

Thus, on their face, the Directive and the Defense Science Board's report unhelpfully appear to diverge conceptually on the nature of autonomy and AWS. However, according to Paul Scharre, who coordinated the Directive's drafting process, 'while we used the term "level" of human judgment, I think it's fair to say that we meant "level" in a very general sense'.[112] By focusing the Directive on a particularly important task, the use of AWS for the selection and engagement of targets, the drafters arguably included some of the human–machine interdependence concepts contemplated by the Defense Science Board.[113]

Nevertheless, the inconsistent language used by the two documents, particularly when published within months of each other,[114] casts confusion on the appropriate design, development and use of AWS. The use of 'levels of human judgment' terminology suggests a fixed, calculated predetermination of human supervision over AWS instead of an emphasis on effective human–machine collaboration.[115] 'Effective' in this context includes the ability of the system – both humans and machines – to comply with international law. Furthermore, a danger exists that, eventually, the current debates about the merits of conceptual frameworks of 'levels' of autonomy versus coactive design and human–machine interdependence will begin to lose their relevance. When weapons developers submit options to the military for new weapons systems, the key question for the individuals making procurement decisions is: '[w]ill it enhance my

---

[111] Ibid., 4. The Defense Science Board would impress upon commanders 'that all machines are supervised by humans to some degree, and the best capabilities result from the coordination and collaboration of humans and machines'. Ibid., 21.

[112] Email message from P. Scharre, 7 July 2014 (copy in author's possession).   [113] Ibid.

[114] A complete or nearly complete draft of Directive 3000.09 was produced by 23 May 2012 – that is, six months before it was issued and two months prior to the publication of the Defense Science Board's report. This draft was coordinated by the Autonomy Working Group of the Office of the Secretary of Defense of the DoD and circulated for comment. 'Action Processing Sheet', Subject: Draft DoD Directive 3000.ii (Autonomy in Weapons Systems, United States Strategic Command, 23 May 2012, obtained pursuant to requests made under the US Freedom of Information Act, 10 September 2013 (copies in the author's possession)). Thus, the language in the Directive was 'fairly settled' prior to the issuance of the Defense Science Board's report. email message from P. Scharre, 7 July 2014.

[115] Johnson et al., 'Beyond cooperative robotics', 83.

ability to carry out my strategic, military objective?'[116] Military interests require timely decision making.[117] Consequently, as the speed of new autonomous technologies and weapons systems develops, entreaties on designers, engineers, commanders and operators, as well as individuals participating in Article 36 legal reviews, will inevitably increase to reduce the levels of human supervision on these systems so as to achieve the greatest possible military advantages and fulfil the demands of military necessity.[118] Put differently, the development of increasingly powerful and fast AWS will force armed forces to choose between the potential for greater speed of action and the maintenance of human command and control.

The speed of military action and decision-making processes often plays a determinative role in the outcome of battles at the tactical level[119] and in the resolution of armed conflict at the strategic level.[120]

---

[116] G. S. Corn, remarks at 'Autonomous Weapon Systems: Law, Ethics and Policy', Conference at European University Institute, Academy of European Law, 24 April 2014.

[117] W. Boothby, *The Law of Targeting* (Oxford University Press, 2012), 122.

[118] 'The pressure on states to embrace this technology will be overwhelming.' Corn, remarks at 'Autonomous Weapon Systems'. See exchange between the author and R. Jackson during panel discussion 'Autonomous Weaponry and Armed Conflict', Annual Meeting of American Society of International Law, 10 April 2014, available at www.youtube.com /watch?v=duq3DtFJtWg&index=3&list=PLYp0ZUypbrnevQlBfMUSDG0IanrvJ3J6z. Cummings, an engineer and former US Navy fighter pilot, observes that '[m]any controls engineers see the human as a mere disturbance in the system that can and should be designed out' ('Man versus machine or man + machine?', 2).

[119] During the American Civil War, field communications were so primitive that orders had to be delivered personally, through couriers. This process 'could require up to an hour between army headquarters and corps headquarters, another thirty minutes from corps to division, and another twenty from division to the fundamental unit of Civil War combat, the brigade'. A. Guelzo, *Gettysburg: The Last Invasion* (New York: Vintage Books, 2013), 37. In March 1944, after conditions on the Eastern Front turned in favour of the Soviet Union, journalist Vasily Grossman commented on the important attention to speed and time that had become characteristic of the army officers of the Soviet Union: 'They have learned to hurry but it isn't their motto, it is just in everyone's blood. ... The speed of pursuit matches the speed of the enemy's retreat.' A. Beevor and L. Vinogradova (eds.), *A Writer at War: Vasily Grossman with the Red Army 1941–1945* (London: Pimlico, 2006), 266. During the first Gulf War, the faster American armoured vehicles disoriented their Iraqi foes: 'The Iraqis could not imagine armoured forces, this big, this powerful, moving at them as fast as they were.' *The Tank of Desert Storm: The Gulf War*, History Channel, available at www.youtube.com/watch?v=ulZui5iRaPQ.

[120] In his memoirs of the US Civil War, General Ulysses S. Grant observed that, had the Confederacy succeeded in prolonging the war for an additional year beyond 1865, the circumstances 'would probably have exhausted the North to such an extent that they might then have abandoned the contest and agreed to a separation'. *Personal Memoirs of General Ulysses S. Grant*, part IV, ch. XLIX, available at www.gutenberg.org/files/5863/ 5863-h/5863-h.htm.

As Geoffrey Corn observes, '[s]o many decisions on the battlefield are time-sensitive, to engage with the enemy and destroy them.'[121] Indeed, for years, the DoD has anticipated the advantages arising from faster, more autonomous weaponry: 'Autonomously coordinated unmanned systems may be capable of faster, more synchronized fire and maneuver than would be possible with remotely controlled assets.'[122] Decisions about the design and development of new automated and autonomous technologies are really 'about speed of service. The better the automated system, the faster we can accomplish the mission. That is not the only consideration, but it is the main one.'[123] More than a decade ago, a US DoD report predicted that 'the future will require that more of our people do new and much more complicated cognitive tasks more rapidly and for longer continuous periods than ever before'.[124] Consequently, during the stress of warfare, there will be an inexorable pressure on the human 'operator' to permit (or encourage) the AWS to act as rapidly as possible. The Directive, however, does not specifically address the pressures and imperatives of speed and time.

Colonel Richard Jackson, the special assistant to the US Army judge advocate for law of war matters and a member of the DoD working group that drafted the Directive, described the challenge of balancing the speed of new autonomous technologies with the policy of maintaining appropriate levels of human supervision as 'a huge focus of our working group'.[125] The drafters sought to alleviate risks of 'machine bias' – that is, human over-reliance on a computer's decision-making ability,[126] by emphasizing the proper training of operators as well as the strong 'validation and verification approach' during the acquisition phase of new AWS: 'These guidelines have been developed more broadly to make sure that we don't have the individual relying too much on the decision-making capability of the machine.'[127]

---

[121] Corn, remarks at 'Autonomous Weapon Systems'.

[122] *Unmanned Systems Integrated Roadmap FY2011–2036*, 49.

[123] Colonel John L. Haithcock Jr, letter to the editor.

[124] Defense Science Board Task Force on Training for Future Conflicts, Final Report, 9 July 2003, 6, available at www.acq.osd.mil/dsb/reports/ADA429010.pdf.

[125] Jackson, panel on 'Autonomous Weaponry and Armed Conflict'.

[126] Cummings uses the term 'moral buffer' to describe the sense of distance and remoteness that computer interfaces create for their users. It is this moral buffer that permits individuals 'to morally and ethically distance themselves from their actions' while 'operating' machines. Cummings, 'Automation and accountability in decision support systems'.

[127] Jackson, panel on 'Autonomous Weaponry and Armed Conflict'.

This is a laudable effort. Nevertheless, even with the best training of human operators, the challenge of maintaining appropriate levels of human judgment and/or human–machine collaboration and teamwork will become increasingly difficult as decision-making cycles of AWS shrink to micro-seconds.[128] Common sense suggests that in situations where lives depend on the fastest possible actions and reactions, the likelihood that human supervisors and operators will intervene with AWS will be even less. A danger exists, therefore, that 'appropriate levels of human judgment over the use of force' will be reduced eventually to very little or nothing. When we reach that moment, the capacity of the current IHL framework to guide the conduct of AWS will be in question. To preserve the law's relevance, validation and verification of the system's compliance with international law must occur before deployment of the weapon.[129]

Conclusions

The military advantages achieved by states and organized armed groups in possession of autonomous weapons technologies and capabilities will lead, inexorably, to the increasing use of autonomous functions and AWS.[130] Although less than perfect, Directive 3000.09 represents one of the few national attempts to articulate autonomous weapons policy. In this sense, and in its emphasis on compliance with international law, the Directive represents 'a demonstration of state responsibility to a degree that is unprecedented'.[131] While the Directive admirably sets high standards for validation and verification during the procurement process and requires realistic training scenarios and compliance with IHL, it also contains troubling lacunae. The vague and undefined standard of 'appropriate levels of human judgment over the use of force' leaves broad discretion to designers, acquisition officers, commanders and operators, particularly as the advancing speed of AWS provides opportunities to achieve military advantages.

---

[128] Indeed, it is not difficult to envision future generations of autonomous weapons systems that will communicate between each other much more quickly than with humans.

[129] Corn, 'Autonomous weapons systems'.

[130] As one unnamed DoD official observed during the review process of Directive 3000.09, '[i]t is better to keep up than to catch up'. Names withheld, internal email message from Deputy Inspector General for Auditing, Readiness, Operations, and Support Directorate, DoD, to Office of the Inspector General, Policy and Oversight, DoD, 24 May 2012 (copy in the author's possession); Pavlik, 'Response from Inspector General DoD'.

[131] Jackson, panel on 'Autonomous Weaponry and Armed Conflict'.

10

Autonomous weapons systems: managing the inevitability of 'taking the man out of the loop'

GEOFFREY S. CORN

Introduction

War and technological development have been indelibly linked for centuries.[1] Military leaders will constantly seek both the means (weapons) and the methods (tactics) of warfare to maximize their full-spectrum dominance over their adversaries. When assessing the value of emerging weapons technologies, mitigating risk to friendly forces has always been perceived as a key benefit. This aspect of weapons technology is increasingly valued in an era of all volunteer forces and a general perception among strategic decision makers that the public is generally averse to friendly casualties,[2] even when force is employed to achieve vital national or international objectives. At the operational level, all commanders seek to husband resources while achieving precision effects,[3] and, therefore, technologies that facilitate producing such effects with limited risk to friendly forces will be highly coveted.

Willingness to accept mortal risk in pursuit of important objectives is, of course, a core ethos of a professional military. One of the greatest burdens of military command is the authority and responsibility to send subordinates into harm's way to achieve such goals, knowing full well that many may lose their lives or be seriously injured while obeying these

---

[1] See Levin Institute, *Modern Warfare: Globalization 101*, available at www.globalization101
.org/modern-warfare/.

[2] See Lieutenant Colonel R. A. Lacquement Jr, *The Casualty-Aversion Myth: US Army Professional Writing Collection*, available at www.usnwc.edu/getattachment/82192134-8122-404a-a139-2fcc2de2fe38/Casualty-Aversion-Myth,-The–Lacquement,-Richard-.

[3] See Joint Chiefs of Staff, *Joint Publication 3–0: Joint Operations I-13-14*, 11 August 2011, available at www.dtic.mil/doctrine/new_pubs/jp3_0.pdf (stating that a commander's job at the operational level is to design, plan and execute all details of the operation).

orders.[4] Issuing such orders and subjecting subordinates to mortal risk is, however, a key aspect of military command. But when technology can empower a commander to accomplish tactical and operational objectives with little or no risk to friendly forces, it should be self-evident why commanders at all levels covet such options.

However, there have always been inherent limits on the extent to which technology may be used as an effective substitute for human action. To date, these limits have generally focused on the ability to control the effects of a weapon system once employed. Thus, the law prohibits use of such weapons as chemicals and other poison gas, air-delivered incendiaries in populated areas and any other weapons that cannot be directed with any reasonable certainty to strike an intended target.[5] Autonomous weapons – weapons with the capacity to utilize

---

[4] 'It doesn't take a hero to order men into battle. It takes a hero to be one of those men who goes into battle' – General Norman Schwarzkopf.

[5] See Convention on the Prohibition of the Development, Production, Stockpiling and Use of Chemical Weapons and on Their Destruction, 13 January 1993, 1974 UNTS 317; Protocol on Prohibitions or Restrictions on the Use of Incendiary Weapons, 10 October 1980, 1342 UNTS 137, Article 2: 'It is prohibited in all circumstances to make any military objective located within a concentration of civilians the object of attack by air-delivered incendiary weapons'; Protocol Additional to the Geneva Conventions of 12 August 1949, and relating to the Protection of Victims of International Armed Conflicts (Additional Protocol I), 8 June 1977, 1125 UNTS 3, Article 51; International Committee of the Red Cross (ICRC), *Commentary to the Additional Protocols of 8 June 1977 to the Geneva Conventions of 12 August 1949 (AP I Commentary)* (Geneva: ICRC, 1987) 613–28. Additional Protocol I to the Geneva Conventions defines indiscriminate attacks:

4. Indiscriminate attacks are prohibited. Indiscriminate attacks are:
   (a) those which are not directed at a specific military objective;
   (b) those which employ a method or means of combat which cannot be directed at a specific military objective; or
   (c) those which employ a method or means of combat the effects of which cannot be limited as required by this Protocol; and consequently, in each such case, are of a nature to strike military objectives and civilians or civilian objects without distinction.

5. Among others, the following types of attacks are to be considered as indiscriminate:
   (a) an attack by bombardment by any methods or means which treats as a single military objective a number of clearly separated and distinct military objectives located in a city, town, village or other area containing a similar concentration of civilians or civilian objects; and
   (b) an attack which may be expected to cause incidental loss of civilian life, injury to civilians, damage to civilian objects, or a combination thereof, which would be excessive in relation to the concrete and direct military advantage anticipated. (Additional Protocol I, Article 51)

artificial intelligence to replicate human cognitive reasoning[6] – present an entirely new dilemma to the regulation of armed conflict.

The rapid advancement in the technologies enabling the development and fielding of such weapons is apparent, and humanitarian law experts are increasingly focused on the capacity of artificial intelligence to replicate human judgment as the most significant concern associated with the development of such weapons.[7] Certainly, this is a critical aspect of assessing the propriety of using technology in warfare. However, from an operational perspective, an arguably more significant consideration is the capacity of the technological substitute to produce a desired tactical effect in a manner that replicates the level of legal compliance expected from the human actor – the soldier.[8] In the context of employing lethal (or even less than lethal) combat power in any situation involving risk to civilians and/or civilian property, the concept of legal compliance involves executing combat operations consistent with the principles of distinction, proportionality and precautionary measures under the fundamental law of armed conflict (LOAC). These principles are further implemented by codified and customary LOAC rules, such as the rule of military objective, the prohibition against indiscriminate attacks and the requirement to consider specific precautions prior to launching an attack that places civilians at risk.

Professional armed forces prepare soldiers to comply with these obligations through training and rely on responsible command to create a high probability of such compliance during mission execution.[9] But no amount of training or supervision can eliminate a very basic reality of

[6] See K. Anderson and M. C. Waxman, 'Law and ethics for autonomous weapons systems: why a ban won't work and how the laws of war can', Jean Perkins Task Force on National Security and Law Essay Series, Research Paper no. 2013–11 (2013), 1, available at http:// media.hoover.org/sites/default/files/documents/Anderson-Waxman_LawAndEthics_ r2_FINAL.pdf.

[7] See ibid., 3–4; See also ICRC, 'Autonomous weapons: what role for humans?', 12 May 2014, www.icrc.org/eng/resources/documents/news-release/2014/05-12-autonomous-weapons-ihl.htm: 'The central issue is the potential absence of human control over the critical functions of identifying and attacking targets, including human targets. There is a sense of deep discomfort with the idea of allowing machines to make life-and-death decisions on the battlefield with little or no human involvement' (internal quotation marks omitted).

[8] The term 'soldier' is used throughout this chapter generically to indicate any belligerent operative, no matter the operatives' military branch of service or whether the operative is subordinate to state or non-state authority.

[9] See Major D. I. Grimes et al., Law of War Handbook (Charlottesville, VA: International and Operational Law Department, Judge Advocate General's Legal Center and School, 2005), 218–22, available at www.loc.gov/rr/frd/Military_Law/pdf/law-war-handbook-2005.pdf; UK

human operatives: they are, and have always been, 'autonomous' weapons systems, because all soldiers must exercise cognitive reasoning in the execution of their battlefield tasks. Characterizing a soldier as an autonomous weapon system (AWS) may appear inhuman, but it is in fact quite accurate. The soldier, when coupled with the means of warfare entrusted to his control, becomes a combat system. And, as a human, the soldier is obviously capable of exercising autonomous judgment and decision making. Indeed, the efficacy of the soldier as a combat system is linked to that autonomous reasoning capacity. Soldiers are trained extensively to prepare them to respond effectively to a wide variety of combat challenges, but no training can replicate the demands of combat or all of the variables that will arise. Training is therefore used to enable the soldier to develop judgment skills that will maximize the likelihood that his or her autonomous judgment will be exercised in a manner that contributes to the overall tactical, operational and strategic objectives of his or her command.

Thus, it is impossible to have absolute 'compliance confidence' for even this 'weapon system' – the weapon system with the most advanced capacity to engage in cognitive reasoning and apply that reasoning to the decision-making process related to unleashing lethal and destructive combat power. Nonetheless, the legality of employing the human 'autonomous' weapon is beyond question. Why is this so? The answer seems clear: because of the presumption that their human autonomous reasoning will be exercised in accordance with the standards imposed by responsible command, which, in turn, indicate an exercise of autonomous reasoning framed by the obligations imposed by the LOAC.

This consideration – the confidence that autonomous judgment will be exercised consistently with LOAC obligations – seems to explain the demarcation line between fielded versus conceptual technological substitutes for human battlefield action and is therefore a potentially critical consideration when exploring the evolution and legality of AWS. As will be explained in this chapter, this consideration undermines the credibility of demands for adopting a per se prohibition against autonomous weapons. However, it also necessitates a creative regulatory focus that ensures these future weapons are fielded only if and when it is possible to validate their ability to produce a level of LOAC compliance confidence that is analogous to – or perhaps even greater than – that of the human soldier.

Ministry of Defence, *The Manual of the Law of Armed Conflict* (*UK LOAC Manual*) (London: Ministry of Defence, 2004).

The centrality and logic of this 'LOAC compliance confidence' focus is illustrated by considering the existing demarcation line between permissible and impermissible technological substitutes for human target engagement judgment. It also reveals that where the technology has been unable to produce a desired tactical effect analogous to that of a human actor, the utility of such weapons has been questioned not from a humanitarian perspective but, rather, from a military operational perspective. A prime example of this phenomenon is the anti-personnel landmine. By relying on rudimentary technology – weight or movement activation – this weapon is quintessentially autonomous.[10] Once an anti-personnel landmine is emplaced, it operates solely on its own to decide when to produce its deadly effect. However, because it is incapable of distinguishing between friend, foe, or civilian in a manner analogous to a human actor, these weapons are widely condemned as unlawful.[11] Of equal significance for the purposes of this chapter, the tactical benefit produced by anti-personnel landmines is widely perceived by military leaders as insufficient to justify the risk of injury to civilians and friendly forces as the result of the weapons' inability to engage in anything close to the type of cognitive reasoning expected of a soldier.[12]

What then explains the persistence of some states, the United States most notably, in retaining anti-personnel landmines for use as a permissible weapon of war? The answer seems to be the intersection of technology, operational necessity and desired effect. US commitment to the approach of the Convention on Conventional Weapons to regulating anti-personnel landmines[13] indicates a commitment to leverage

[10] See US Department of Army, *Operator's and Unit Maintenance Manual for Land Mines*, Technical Manual 9-1345-203-12, October 1995, 1–4, available at http://mines.duvernois .org/LandMines.pdf (describing the function of a landmine).

[11] See Convention on the Prohibition of the Use, Stockpiling, Production and Transfer of Anti-Personnel Mines and on Their Destruction, 18 September 1997, 2056 UNTS 211, Article 1, 242; See also D. Crane, 'Smart mines: yep, that's the ticket', *Defense Review* (10 April 2004), available at www.defensereview.com/smart-mines-yep-thats-the-ticket/ (explaining that the Bush administration's reasoning for declining to sign the global treaty banning landmines is the United States' policy of using 'smart' mines that self-destruct within a relatively short time period).

[12] See Human Rights Watch, 'Retired generals renew call for total antipersonnel mine ban', 22 July 1997, www.hrw.org/fr/news/1997/07/20/retired-generals-renew-call-total-antipersonnel-mine-ban.

[13] See Protocol on Prohibitions or Restrictions on the Use of Mines, Booby-Traps and Other Devices, 3 May 1996, 2048 UNTS 93; see also US Department of State, US Landmine Policy, available at www.state.gov/t/pm/wra/c11735.htm. Convention on Prohibitions or Restrictions on the Use of Certain Conventional Weapons Which May Be Deemed to Be Excessively Injurious or to Have Indiscriminate Effects, 1990, 19 UNTS 1823.

technological advances that create a high probability of producing desired tactical effects in a manner that effectively distinguishes lawful from unlawful targets. This technology, coupled with restrictions on where anti-personnel landmines may be utilized and conditions related to such use, sufficiently offsets the risk of unintended effect to justify continued reliance on this weapon system.[14] Furthermore, the fact that the United States has chosen not to join or endorse the absolute ban on anti-personnel landmines indicates the tactical and operational value the United States believes is still inherent in this weapon system, so long as the technology is sufficiently advanced to mitigate the risk of unintended effects.

Another oft-cited example of an existing weapon relying on technology as a substitute for human target engagement judgment is the Phalanx anti-missile system.[15] This system functions autonomously to intercept missiles directed against US warships, relying on artificial intelligence to trigger the engagement process.[16] Like the anti-personnel landmine, the Phalanx lacks any meaningful capacity to exercise cognitive reasoning to distinguish between a lawful object of attack and civilians and/or civilian property, nor to distinguish between enemy assets and friendly assets. Nonetheless, the system was fielded based on an apparent determination that it was capable of producing an important tactical effect with minimal risk of error – not because of technical capacity but, instead, because the context in which it is anticipated to be employed will rarely, if ever, implicate a risk that such judgment is necessary to comply with the LOAC. Since the nature of the target engagement the weapon is designed for involves reaction to a high-speed, low-flying missile at sea, the likelihood of something other than an imminent attack on the ship it protects triggering Phalanx engagement is extremely remote, as is the risk that such engagement will create a serious risk of civilian collateral damage or incidental injury. Accordingly, the system is embraced because it is capable of producing the desired tactical effect with minimal risk of error, implicating LOAC compliance.

This provides an interesting contrast. For the landmine, this inability accounts for its widespread condemnation and the decision by so many

---

[14] See Major G. S. Musselman, *Law of War Deskbook* (Charlottesville, VA: International and Operational Law Department, Judge Advocate General's Legal Center and School, 2011), 160–2, available at www.loc.gov/rr/frd/Military_Law/pdf/LOW-Deskbook-2011.pdf.

[15] See Anderson and Waxman, 'Law and ethics for autonomous weapons systems', 1.

[16] See Federation of American Scientists, 'MK 15 Phalanx close-in weapons system (CIWS)', available at www.fas.org/man/dod-101/sys/ship/weaps/mk-15.htm.

states to join the absolute ban on use. No analogous consternation has been triggered by the Phalanx or similar autonomous seaborne anti-missile systems. What explains this distinction? Clearly, it is the fact that the conditions of employment for the Phalanx indicate an insignificant risk of erroneous engagement, resulting from the fact that, unlike the anti-personnel landmine, the geographic and tactical contexts for such employment suggest that only genuine threats would present themselves in a manner triggering engagement.

Neither of these weapon systems, however, has the capacity to replicate human cognitive reasoning or exercise the type of judgment required to distinguish between lawful and unlawful objects of attack.[17] With anti-personnel land mines, this largely explains their widespread condemnation; for the Phalanx, it is largely irrelevant as the context of employment mitigates the negative consequences of this incapacity. However, it seems that the proverbial game is on the verge of changing dramatically. As numerous experts have noted, the rapid evolution of artificial intelligence renders these examples simplistic compared to what is on the weapons horizon.[18] What is anticipated, and what causes so much consternation, is the prospect of an AWS designed to exercise a level of cognitive reasoning analogous to – or, in the view of some, superior to – that of humans.[19]

Many artificial intelligence experts question whether the development of truly autonomous weapons – what some have labelled 'killer robots' – is even conceptually feasible. Based on publicly available information, it does not seem that such weapons will be available for military procurement in the foreseeable future. Indeed, this most likely provides some explanation for the current US Department of Defense (DoD) policy on autonomous weapons requiring some human involvement in the targeting loop, a limitation that seems consistent with an expectation that this requirement will align with the inherent limitations on the foreseeably available technology.

However, if the availability of such weapons does move from the realm of speculation to reality, it is very likely that states, and, more specifically, military leaders, will be attracted by the opportunities they offer to maximize the effects of combat power while mitigating risk to friendly forces. This does not mean that all states will embrace this opportunity.

[17] See Additional Protocol I, Articles 50–1; see also G. S. Corn *et al.*, *The Law of Armed Conflict: An Operational Approach* (New York: Aspen, 2012).
[18] See Anderson and Waxman, 'Law and ethics for autonomous weapons systems', 1.
[19] See *ibid.*, 2.

Even assuming a proposed weapons system offers the capacity to sub-stantially contribute to the achievement of targeting priorities, there may be reluctance – especially among military leaders – to field lethal cap-abilities that substitute artificial intelligence for human judgment. This reluctance might arise from what may be emerging as a somewhat ironic inverse relationship between the capacity of technology to offer such substitutes and the perceived importance of human judgment in relation to the execution of military operations. This potential tension between the theoretical advantages offered by autonomous weapons and the perception that removing human judgment from the target engagement process will be addressed in more detail below.

How military leaders will respond to the opportunities offered by emerging weapons technology is ultimately speculative. Even consider-ing what might be considered negative consequences of increasingly sophisticated automation, it is still not difficult to imagine that military leaders, and, in turn, their nations, will be tempted to embrace these advances. While critics of truly autonomous weapons believe they pose immense risk to humanity,[20] the perception and reaction of military and civilian leaders and experts will undoubtedly influence how their states react to this concern. As a result, interests of humanity will certainly not be the exclusive consideration influencing the reaction to these weapons and perhaps not even the dominant consideration. Instead, the response to the opportunity to develop and field increasingly autonomous weap-ons capability will most likely focus on a very different question: whether the positive tactical and operational potential of these weapons can be achieved without a serious risk of unintended unlawful consequences.

This question will only be answered with time, as weapons developers ply their wares to military consumers. However, the risk of development to outpace legal compliance validation is genuine and most likely explains policies such as that adopted by the DoD, which establishes strict oversight requirements related to autonomous weapons develop-ment and procurement. Discussed in greater detail later in this chapter, such policies demonstrate the importance of ensuring that military goals, technology and legal oversight are each completely engaged in this development process. Such a process will advance the important interest of ensuring that both developers and consumers of weapons technology understand and demand that the ability to discriminate between lawful and unlawful objects of attack, with minimal risk of error, is a central

---

[20] Ibid.

component to the artificial intelligence responsible for any autonomous engagement decision. In fact, if this consideration does drive autonomous weapons development, it is unrealistic to demand or expect their outright prohibition. It is equally unrealistic to expect that international law will in some manner effectively prohibit autonomous weapons development or substantially circumscribe the use of such weapons (for example, by prohibiting use in proximity to civilians or civilian property). The combined effect of market forces (the immense profit potential associated with the development and marketing of highly advanced weapons systems), casualty aversion (the desire of strategic leaders to minimize the risk to friendly forces when conducting military actions against enemy personnel and capabilities) and rapid crisis management (the interest in addressing emerging threats at the nascent stage) make the development, procurement and utilization of autonomous weapons a very likely evolution of modern warfare.

Those who press for international legal prohibitions on the development and fielding of AWS must recognize the potential tactical and operational value inherent in these weapons. Prohibiting the use of autonomous weapons, even if they can function consistently with LOAC principles, will be considered by many as a further step in the already troubling attenuation between conflict regulation and strategic, operational and tactical realities. In this regard, such prohibitions may undermine the credibility of the law itself. Indeed, even the alternative characterization for the LOAC – international humanitarian law – highlights this concern. For several decades, there has been an ongoing debate over the proper characterization for this branch of international conflict regulation law.[21] While this debate is in large measure now stale, it represents a consistent and continuing concern that the very title of this branch of international law suggests a primary humanitarian objective.[22] For proponents of the LOAC characterization, this is a distortion of the historic foundation and purpose of the law. Instead, they believe, the humanitarian component of the law is only one aspect of the regulation of conflict and that, when considered in proper context, the entire

---

[21] See US Department of Defense (DoD) Directive 2311.01E, 'DoD law of war program', 9 May 2006, available at www.dtic.mil/whs/directives/corres/pdf/231101e.pdf; See also ICRC, *What Is International Humanitarian Law?* (Geneva: ICRC, July 2004): 'International humanitarian law is also known as the law of war or the law of armed conflict.'

[22] See ICRC, *What Is International Humanitarian Law* (explaining that international humanitarian law exists to protect civilians during armed conflict between nations).

body of law should not be characterized in a manner inferring that it is the law's predominant purpose.[23]

However, this debate, stale as it may be, highlights a much more significant underlying concern, which is the risk that the law will evolve in a manner that may not adequately account for the legitimate interests of armed forces.[24] Humanitarian restraint is undoubtedly a noble goal, but this law ultimately must account for the pragmatic interests of those called upon to engage in mortal combat. Armed conflict involves the inevitable reality that belligerents will seek to impose their will on each other through the application of deadly combat power and that they will do so in the most efficient and effective manner. Humanitarian constraints are, as they have always been, essential to mitigate the suffering caused by this contest, but when these constraints are perceived as prohibiting operationally or tactically logical methods or means of warfare, it creates a risk that the profession of arms – the very constituents who must embrace the law – will see it as a fiction at best or, at worst, that they will feign commitment to the law while pursuing *sub rosa* agendas to sidestep obligations.

As I argued in a prior article, this is why those responsible for advancing the law must be vigilant in preserving the historic symmetry between

---

[23] See Grimes, *Law of War Handbook*, 2–15 (describing the historical development of the law of armed conflict (LOAC) and its functions to protect human dignity and morality amidst the necessity of war in a civilized society).

[24] This is obviously a highly subjective concern. However, there are indications that concerns over civilian protections may be increasingly distorting the balance between military necessity and humanity. Reluctance by significant military powers to commit to treaties banning certain weapons – such as cluster munitions – reflects some level of inconsistency between the perceived legitimacy of the balance of interests reflected in these treaties. International jurisprudence, and scholarly commentary, also influence the evolution of the law and should be considered in this regard. One such illustration was the International Criminal Tribunal for the former Yugoslavia Trial Chamber judgment in *Prosecutor* v. *Gotovina*, case no. IT-06-90-T, Judgment, 15 Apr. 2011. The response from a group of military experts explicitly raised the concern that the evidentiary foundation for condemning General Gotovina risked imposing a standard of conduct that was incompatible with the reality of military operations. Other examples of this trend include the ongoing assertion of a least-harmful means obligation in relation to targeting enemy belligerents and some of the interpretations of the 'warning obligation' asserted in response to the Israeli Operation Protective Edge in Gaza. See 'Soldiers and human rights: lawyers to the right of them, lawyers to the left of them', *The Economist* (9 August 2014), available at www.economist.com/news/britain/21611096-army-increasingly-feels-under-legal-siege-lawyers-right-them-lawyers-left-them?fsrc=rss|btn# (describing an increase in civil litigation in Britain attempting to harmonize the human rights laws with the LOAC).

military logic and humanitarian constraints.[25] This does not mean that
the plight of innocent victims of war – whose numbers do not seem to
have abated as the nature of means of warfare have increased in sophistication, precision and lethality[26] – should be subordinated to the military necessities. What it does mean, however, is that these necessities
must be carefully assessed to determine the demarcation line between
actual military logic and demands for overly broad operational freedom
of action.

There are probably no aspects of conflict regulation where this need is
more acute than in the development of autonomous weapons.[27]
International law experts must be involved in this development process,
but they must also be cognizant of the enormous appeal such weapons
will present to military leaders. However, military leaders and those
responsible for procuring and fielding weapons must also recognize the
inherent risk associated with pursuing weapons systems that cannot
produce both tactical and strategic benefit. History has demonstrated
time and again that there is simply no military utility – and, in fact,
immense disutility – in any military measure incapable of producing
tactical benefit without ensuring LOAC compliance. This idea applies
equally to both tactics (methods of warfare) and weapons systems (means
of warfare). Accordingly, no matter how appealing the tactical benefit of
an autonomous weapon may appear, its value is illusory unless it can
effectively distinguish between lawful and unlawful objects of attack.
With military leaders increasingly cognizant of the link between legal
compliance, perceptions of legitimacy and strategic success,[28] military
leaders should embrace strict limitations on the fielding of these future
weapons in order to ensure sufficient LOAC compliance capability. Thus,
the ultimate thesis of this chapter reflects the inherent balance of the
LOAC itself: humanitarian advocates must avoid the temptation of

[25] See generally G. S. Corn, 'Mixing apples and hand grenades: the logical limit of applying
human rights norms to armed conflict', *Journal of International Humanitarian Legal
Studies*, 1 (2010), 52.
[26] See E. T. Jensen, 'The future of the law of armed conflict: ostriches, butterflies, and
nanobots', *Michigan Journal of International Law*, 35 (2014), 253 (analysing how the law
of armed conflict will evolve to address the challenges of evolving weapons technology).
[27] See Anderson and Waxman, 'Law and ethics for autonomous weapons systems', 11–12;
see also Jensen, 'The future of the law of armed conflict'.
[28] See US Department of Army, TRADOC Pam 525-3-1: 'The US Army operating concept',
19 August 2010, 28, available at www.tradoc.army.mil/tpubs/pams/tp525-3-1.pdf (indicating the importance of civilian and military leaders operating in unity with a clear
understanding of the legal limitations of war).

unrealistic autonomous weapons per se prohibitions, and military leaders must avoid the seductive effect of emerging technology.

Rethinking the locus of compliance validation

Demanding integration of technical characteristics that produce a high level of confidence that the weapon will comply with the LOAC is vital, because the very nature of autonomous weapons inverses the normal locus of human involvement in the weapon utilization process. Article 36 of Additional Protocol I[29] establishes an obligation that all new weapons systems be reviewed to ensure LOAC compliance, but it provides very little guidance on the nature of this review.[30] The review must, however, assess the compatibility of the proposed weapon system with LOAC standards when the weapon is used as intended.[31] For most weapons, this is only a preliminary step in ensuring ultimate employment complies with the LOAC. This is because it is the human involvement in that employment – the exercise of human judgment as to when, where and how to employ the weapon – that will often be far more decisive in ensuring such compliance. In contrast, for truly autonomous weapons, the focal point of LOAC compliance will shift to the development/procurement phase. This is because tactical employment will have a significantly reduced influence on LOAC compliance: tactical commanders will employ these weapons pursuant to established use criteria, but beyond that they will have very little influence on how the weapon executes combat operations. It is therefore essential to reconceive the LOAC compliance model when contemplating the procurement, production and employment of AWS. The process of mitigating the risk of failures in this cognitive process must be tailored to address this inversion of the LOAC compliance influence between the procurement and employment phases of utilization. Doing so will focus compliance efforts at the decisive point in this process: the procurement phase.

---

[29] See Additional Protocol I, Article 36.

[30] See ICRC, *A Guide to the Legal Review of New Weapons, Means and Methods of Warfare: Measures to Implement Article 36 of Additional Protocol 1 of 1977* (Geneva: ICRC, 2006), 933, available at www.icrc.org/eng/assets/files/other/irrc_864_icrc_geneva.pdf: 'Article 36 does not specify how a determination of the legality of weapons, means and methods of warfare is to be carried out.'

[31] See, e.g., US Department of Defense (DoD) Directive 3000.09, 'Autonomy in weapon systems', 21 November 2012, available at www.dtic.mil/whs/directives/corres/pdf/300009p.pdf.

This reconception should begin by acknowledging an undeniable reality: that soldiers are themselves AWS. The soldier, like the hypothe-sized and arguably speculative AWS, is capable of exercising cognitive reasoning. This is obviously inherent in any human being. However, the soldier is not an unconstrained 'autonomous actor'; he/she does not exercise judgment with no parameters. Instead, the soldier operates as an agent of responsible command and, in that capacity, must frame his/her decision-making process within the parameters established by super-ior command. How the soldier is developed and prepared to exercise this inherently autonomous cognitive capacity without becoming an auton-omous actor therefore provides a logical template for the 'preparation' of a weapon system with autonomous cognitive capacity. The goal must ultimately be to ensure the autonomous weapon functions in a manner that, like the soldier, is subordinated to the will and parameters imposed by responsible command. The ability to employ combat power consistent with LOAC obligations is inherent in that superior–subordinate relationship.

Preparing the 'weapon' for legally sound employment

Soldiers, or perhaps more accurately the soldier mentality, are in many ways 'produced' through a development process. Much of the focus of initial entry training is to develop in the soldier a sense of discipline that results in a high degree of confidence that the soldier will be capable of adjusting to the demands of military society. First and foremost among those demands is subordination to the orders of superior leaders. This superior–subordinate relationship is the essence of a military organiza-tion and involves the willingness to not only obey orders to employ deadly force on command but also to obey orders to refrain from using such force when individual instinct may be dictating the exact opposite response to a given situation.[32]

Preparing soldiers to obey orders that require them to subordinate their personal self-interest for the greater good of the military unit and mission is a primary responsibility of military leadership. Intrinsic to this preparation process is developing soldiers to obey orders that are

---

[32] See G. Klein et al., *Enhancing Warrior Ethos in Soldier Training: The Teamwork Development Course* (Research Institute for the Behavioral and Social Sciences, US Department of the Army, 2006); G. Riccio et al., *Warrior Ethos: Analysis of the Concept and Initial Development of Applications* (Washington, DC: Research Institute for the Behavioral and Social Sciences, US Department of the Army, 2004).

intended to ensure respect for, and compliance with, the LOAC. Ensuring that a military unit employs collective violence only for lawfully permissible purposes is therefore equally central to the notion of responsible command.[33] It is therefore unsurprising why operating pursuant to 'responsible command' as part of an organization that complies with the laws and customs of war has been the historic *sine qua non* of qualification for lawful belligerent status.[34]

The link between responsible command, LOAC compliance and lawful combatant status reveals a ground truth about the law: only those individuals capable of autonomous reasoning who have been incorporated into an organization capable of managing the exercise of that reasoning should be granted the privilege of engaging in hostilities.[35] It is through this command–subordinate relationship that the law establishes a high degree of confidence that the 'autonomous human' will not use the power entrusted to him/her in a truly unconstrained manner but, rather, will instead exercise that autonomy within the boundaries imposed by superior authority and intended to ensure mission accomplishment within the LOAC legal framework.

The process of influencing and framing the exercise of cognitive reasoning will function much differently for autonomous weapons than for the soldier. As a result, the superior–subordinate relationship will not produce an analogous effect on the autonomous weapon. For the soldier, initial training prior to 'fielding' merely lays the foundation for the ongoing process of framing or shaping the exercise of cognitive reasoning and independent judgment.[36] Unit commanders then build upon this foundation by exercising their responsibility to further develop the soldier through the continuation of the training process. Of equal

---

[33] See Additional Protocol I, Article 87; see also *In re Yamashita*, 327 US 1, 16–17 (1946); see also ICRC, *AP I Commentary*, 1005–16.

[34] See Additional Protocol I, Article 43; Convention (IV) Respecting the Laws and Customs of War on Land and Its Annex: Regulations Concerning the Laws and Customs of War on Land, 18 October 1907, 32 Stat 1803, Articles 1–3; see also ICRC, *Commentary: Protocol Additional to the Geneva Conventions of 12 August 1949, and relating to the Protection of Victims of International Armed Conflicts* (Geneva: ICRC, 1987); see generally G. S. Corn, 'Unarmed but how dangerous? Civilian augmentees, the law of armed conflict, and the search for a more effective for permissible civilian battlefield functions', *Journal of National Security Law and Policy*, 2 (2008), 257.

[35] See Additional Protocol I, Article 87; see also ICRC, *AP I Commentary*, 1017–23.

[36] See US Department of Army, *Soldier's Manual of Common Tasks STP 21-24-SMCT: Warrior Leader Skills Level 2, 3, and 4*, September 2008, available at www.milsci.ucsb .edu/sites/secure.lsit.ucsb.edu.mili.d7/files/sitefiles/resources/STP%2021-24-SMCT,% 20Warrior%20Leader%20Skills,%20Level%202,%203,%20and%204.pdf.

importance, these commanders are expected to establish a command culture that emphasizes not only tactical aggressiveness, but also humanitarian constraint derived from LOAC obligation. The significance of these dual responsibilities is reflected in the doctrine of command responsibility, which holds commanders criminally accountable for subordinate war crimes for failure to effectively execute these two aspects of command responsibility.[37]

Field commanders will not, however, have a meaningful opportunity to influence the exercise of cognitive reasoning and judgment by truly autonomous weapons. Instead, they will merely unleash these weapons when a situation indicates that the purported capability will produce a desired effect.[38] In this regard, the autonomous weapon is perhaps more like the brand new replacement soldier, fresh out of initial entry training, who is fielded and deployed into combat with no opportunity to undergo unit training. In such a situation, the employing commander will rely almost exclusively on the expectation that the initial training effectively prepared the soldier for the complex battlefield judgments he or she will

---

[37] See Additional Protocol I, Article 87; see also US Department of Army, *Field Manual 27–10: The Law of Land Warfare*, 18 July 1956, para. 2, available at armypubs.army.mil/doctrine/DR_pubs/dr_a/pdf/fm27_10.pdf (the purpose of the law of war 'is inspired by the desire to diminish the evils of war by: (a) Protecting both combatants and noncombatants from unnecessary suffering; (b) Safeguarding certain fundamental human rights of persons who fall into the hands of the enemy, particularly prisoners of war, the wounded and sick, and civilians; and (c) Facilitating the restoration of peace'); *UK LOAC Manual*. See also V. Hansen, 'What's good for the goose is good for the gander – lessons from Abu Ghraib: time for the United States to adopt a standard of command responsibility towards its own', *Gonzaga Law Review*, 42 (2007), 335; Y. Shany and K. R. Michaeli, 'The case against Ariel Sharon: revisiting the doctrine of command responsibility', *New York University Journal of International Law and Policy*, 34 (2002), 797 (summarizing the history of command responsibility).

[38] It is self-evident that a commander employing such a weapon will have the ability to employ the weapon unlawfully. This is inherent in every weapon system and every soldier entrusted to the commander's responsibility. When commanders utilize methods and means of warfare with the intent to violate the LOAC, they will be personally responsible for the ensuing violation under any conception of principal liability. However, methods and means of warfare are normally employed in a manner intended to comply with the LOAC. The much more complex question of command liability (responsibility) arises when the commander does not intend an unlawful outcome, but such an outcome results from subordinate misconduct, which may be the result of employing a lawful weapon system in an unlawful manner. As will be discussed below, liability may also arise when such violations are foreseeable consequences of a leadership failure. This presupposes the commander to whom liability is imputed could have influenced the subordinate in a manner that would have averted the violation. It is the inability to produce this type influence on subordinate reasoning and judgment that distinguishes the truly autonomous weapon from the soldier.

have to make. And even this comparison is somewhat inapposite, as even this brand new member of the unit will be capable of perceiving and internalizing the command culture. Of equal importance, the moment that soldier joins the unit he or she will be subjected to the leadership actions of his superiors, which, even in the shortest period of time, can contribute to shaping the soldier's cognitive reasoning and thereby contribute to either respect for, or aversion to, the LOAC.

Field commanders will have no analogous shaping or influencing opportunity on the artificial intelligence that will dictate the reasoning of an autonomous weapon. Instead, the fielding commander must essentially take on faith the capacity of the weapon to exercise cognitive judgment in a manner that ensures LOAC compliance and, in turn, respect for what is hopefully the command culture. Accordingly, it is the development phase – analogous to the initial training phase for a soldier – that is the decisive point in establishing parameters to ensure cognitive autonomy is exercised within the parameters that ensure LOAC compliance, and in turn both the tactical and strategic interests of the fielding force. As a result, the inputs of military procurement managers, weapons developers and legal advisors must be fully engaged in the weapons development process to ensure the commander employing such a weapon system may do so with genuine confidence that the system will exercise cognitive reasoning consistent with LOAC requirements and at least as effectively as should be expected of the best-trained soldier.

The three LOAC compliance confidence enablers

Accomplishing this goal will require emphasis on three LOAC compliance enablers. First, the military command seeking autonomous weapon capability must carefully and precisely define the tactical effect it seeks to achieve with the weapon, the desired method by which the weapon will produce that effect and any limitations that will be imposed on use of the weapon. In very general terms, this is nothing more than an articulation of the anticipated 'task and purpose' for the weapon, which will in turn define the permissible use of the weapon and, in so doing, facilitate LOAC compliance validation.

This approach is commonly used when issuing tactical orders to subordinate units. One somewhat simplified example is the mantra that the mission of the infantry is to 'close with and destroy' the enemy: the task is to confront the enemy; the purpose is to destroy the enemy. In fact, 'task and purpose' is normally far more refined. For example, for a unit of soldiers, the commander might indicate that the 'task' is to breach an obstacle, while the 'purpose' is to enable friendly movement to contact with the enemy. Translating this methodology to the autonomous weapon, for example, might result in a 'task' of close with and attack enemy ground forces in a populated area, with the 'purpose' of subduing enemy forces without having to endanger friendly forces. Other illustrations might include: identify and suppress enemy air defence capabilities; identify and suppress enemy fire support capabilities; acquire and engage with indirect fires enemy command and control in order to disrupt such capability; conduct counter-surveillance acquisition and disable enemy surveillance assets. Although it need not take the precise form of 'task and purpose', maximizing the articulation of the intended tactical function for the AWS will inevitably facilitate the capacity of legal advisors responsible for vetting the weapon system to assess the capacity to comply with the LOAC in the tactical context in which use of the weapon is intended.

This is an important first step in the compliance process, because this articulation will enable those providing operational and legal review and oversight of the development process the ability to assess the inherent risk of LOAC violation associated with the weapon. In other words, this will define the weapon's intended use, which will be the focus of both legal compliance review and employment parameters. This, in turn, will enable the integration of LOAC violation mitigation measures with the weapon system itself or through employment parameters established prior to fielding the weapon.

Such a 'task and purpose' foundation is actually analogous to the preparation of military units for various missions. By training a unit to function in a specific operational and tactical environment, commanders enhance their confidence in legally compliant mission execution.[39] Furthermore, those responsible for task-organizing military units for specific missions are able to enhance the likelihood of legal compliance by refraining, when feasible, from committing a unit trained to participate in one operational context (for example, high-intensity conflict) into a context the unit has not been well prepared for (for example, a peace-keeping mission).[40] Thus, defining the task and purpose of the weapon

[39] See US Dept of Army, *Field Manual 7-0: Training for Full Spectrum Operations* para. 1-30 (12 December 2008) (explaining that the legal complexity of war means that soldiers trained specifically in certain areas, such as stability tasks, will be ineffective when involved in other tasks, such as civil support).

[40] See 'Inquiry into abuse by GI's in Kosovo faults training', *New York Times*, 19 September 2000, www.nytimes.com/2000/09/19/world/19MILI.html.

system will ideally enable the integration of LOAC compliance criteria tailored to that task without undermining the ability to achieve the intended purpose. Or, in the alternative, it will inform field commanders of the situations in which the system may be permissibly used and those where it may not.

Second, LOAC 'compliance standards' must be established at the national level and integrated into the procurement and development process, and it must be clear that no autonomous weapon may be fielded without satisfying these standards. These standards must be imposed to effectuate a level of 'compliance confidence' greater than that of an actual soldier who has passed through the pre-deployment development process. This is because, unlike the soldier, it will be impossible to 'downstream' the fulfilment of this development process to the commander and unit responsible for tactical employment. Integrating compliance mechanisms into the development of the system, and prohibiting the fielding of systems that fail to satisfy these strict requirements, should produce confidence that the system will function consistently with the standards of the 'responsible' tactical or operational command.

This is an apparent focal point within the US DoD as it begins to contemplate the procurement, development and fielding of autonomous systems, as illustrated by the relatively recent DoD Directive 3000.09.[41] This Directive reflects the commitment to establishing LOAC compliance confidence at the pre-fielding phase of employment for any AWS. Most significantly, the Directive requires that any AWS be capable of exercising judgment analogous to that of a human when the consequence of employment implicates LOAC targeting norms, such as distinction and proportionality. Thus, the Directive requires that any future autonomous weapon:

- function pursuant to LOAC requirements, to wit:
  - requirement for proportionality and discrimination
  - can be built into system design or employed only narrowly
- include fail-safes to provide robust protection against possible failures:
  - 100 per cent error free operation not required, but system design must allow for human intervention before unacceptable levels of damage occur
  - robustness harder to ensure than simply ethical decision making?
- is capable of accomplishing military mission.[42]

---

[41] See DoD, Directive 3000.09.   [42] See *ibid.*

How such requirements will be validated, much less developed, is certainly a complex question. But that question is beyond the scope of assessing the potential legality of employing such weapons. Quite simply, if the technology cannot meet these requirements, or there is no way to effectively validate assertions that they have been met, the weapon must not be fielded. Any other decision would be analogous to deploying a soldier so poorly trained that he/she is incapable of navigating the complex environment of battle with any degree of confidence that he/she will do so consistently with the requirements of the mission and the law.

The third critical enabler for ensuring legally compliant use of these weapons is the legal review process. Article 36 of Additional Protocol I has required since 1977 that:

> In the study, development, acquisition or adoption of a new weapon, means or method of warfare, a High Contracting Party is under an obligation to determine whether its employment would, in some or all circumstances, be prohibited by this Protocol or by any other rule of international law applicable to the High Contracting Party.[43]

This new weapon review requirement is arguably a customary international law obligation[44] and was implemented by the United States (which is not a party to Additional Protocol I) two years prior to 1977.[45] Unfortunately, very few states have implemented a robust programme to meet this obligation.[46] One explanation for this gap between obligation and implementation is the reality that most conventional weapons fielded in the three decades following Additional Protocol I coming into force were produced by a relatively small number of nations. Perhaps states procuring such weapons did so on the assumption that if they were produced for the armed forces of the state of production, by implication, they satisfied the legal requirements.

This explanation, of course, is problematic in the abstract, as individual states bear responsibility for independently ensuring newly fielded weapons comply with the LOAC. However, because LOAC compliance

---

[43] See Additional Protocol I, Article 36.

[44] See ICRC, *Guide to the Legal Review of New Weapons*, 933; See also J. Henckaerts and L. Doswald-Beck, *Customary International Humanitarian Law* (Geneva: ICRC, 2005), 250 available at www.icrc.org/eng/assets/files/other/irrc_864_icrc_geneva.pdf.

[45] See DoD Directive 3000.09; DoD Directive 5000.01: 'The defense acquisition system', 12 May 2012, available at www.dtic.mil/whs/directives/corres/pdf/500001p.pdf.

[46] See J. McClelland, 'The review of weapons in accordance with Article 36 of Additional Protocol I', *Current Issues and Comments*, 85 (2003), 398, available at www.icrc.org/eng/assets/files/other/irrc_850_mcclelland.pdf.

will be dictated almost exclusively during the weapons development process, the entire legal review process must take on a fundamentally different emphasis in relation to autonomous weapons. Unlike most new weapons systems, autonomous weapons will involve an inherent reduction in the expectation that the tactical employment of the weapon will substantially influence LOAC compliance. Instead, the development phase must be understood as decisive in establishing a high degree of LOAC compliance confidence.

This will present a number of complexities. First among these will be the challenging intersection of law and technology.[47] Lawyers reviewing weapons system legality must understand the nature of the weapon. As artificial intelligence evolves to provide mechanical devices with cognitive capability, it is essential that the technical characteristics of this capability be translated into terms that can be meaningfully understood and critiqued during the legal review process. This is also another aspect of the development and fielding process where the contribution of a clear and carefully defined task and purpose becomes apparent. The legal advisor will ultimately be responsible for advising the procuring commander with an opinion that the capacity of the artificial intelligence satisfies the intended task and purpose with minimal risk of unacceptable error.

This 'LOAC risk' analysis will be central to the credibility of any legal review. Critics of developing and fielding autonomous weapons focus on the inherent risk that these weapons will be incapable of complying with the fundamental LOAC targeting rules, most notably distinction and proportionality.[48] LOAC compliance, however, does not require a zero risk standard. Such a standard would be inconsistent with the requirements related to the most advanced AWS currently fielded: the soldier. Deploying a soldier into hostilities always involves some risk that the soldier will exercise his/her autonomous judgment in a manner that results in an LOAC violation. Demanding that nations guarantee that this will never occur is unrealistic. For the soldier, this risk is mitigated through the training, guidance and the discipline process – the very

---

[47] See Anderson and Waxman, 'Law and ethics for autonomous weapons systems', 9–11.
[48] See Human Rights Watch, *Losing Humanity: The Case against Killer Robots* (New York: Human Rights Watch, 2012), 30–4, available at www.hrw.org/sites/default/files/reports/arms1112ForUpload_0_0.pdf; See also J. Foy, 'Autonomous weapons systems: taking the human out of international humanitarian law', *Dalhousie Journal of Legal Studies*, 23 (2014), 61–5.

essence of leadership. For the autonomous weapon, it must be mitigated through technology validation.

However, I do believe that it is appropriate to demand that the process of reviewing the weapon's capability produces a higher degree of LOAC compliance confidence than that demanded of the soldier. I believe two considerations justify this more demanding standard. First, it is almost impossible to completely assess such risk in humans. While it is undeniable that any human is susceptible to deviations from expected and demanded standards of judgment, this susceptibility is often latent and imperceptible until it unfortunately manifests itself. Examples of latent defects in human judgment producing LOAC violations are unfortunately too common; US Army Staff Sergeant Robert Bales is, perhaps, a prime example of this problem.[49] In contrast, technical aspects of artificial intelligence are susceptible to objective critique and assessment. Information technology experts should be able to 'debug' the artificial intelligence associated with autonomous weapons to a degree of certainty that substantially exceeds that which is possible for human actors. Second, a more demanding standard for LOAC compliance is necessary to provide fielding commanders with a level of confidence that the weapons they employ, but have very little opportunity to influence, will not compromise either their tactical or strategic objectives. Since the fielding commander, unlike the soldier, will have virtually no ability to influence the exercise of autonomous weapons judgment as it relates to LOAC compliance, the degree of compliance confidence prior to ever fielding the weapon should be substantially higher than that of the new soldier.

These considerations must permeate the weapons review process. First, any state contemplating developing and fielding autonomous weapons must, if it has not already done so, implement a formal weapons review programme. Second, only legal advisors with a high degree of competence in LOAC and international law practice should be detailed to conduct weapons reviews. Third, these legal advisors must be provided the opportunity to develop in-depth understanding of the nature of the artificial intelligence that will be at the proverbial 'heart and mind' of the system. Fourth, the state (normally acting through senior levels of the armed forces) must establish review and validation standards that provide a high level of LOAC compliance confidence prior to fielding the system.

[49] See 'How it happened: massacre in Kandahar', *BBC News* (17 March 2012), www.bbc.com/news/world-asia-17334643.

Reconceiving the concept of command responsibility

This review process, if properly conducted and based on clearly established standards that define the degree of accuracy necessary for validating an autonomous system is capable of LOAC compliance, should produce a sufficient level of confidence in the system to justify fielding and employment. The level of LOAC compliance confidence must, in turn, dictate the extent of permissible lethal force capability fielded in the form of an AWS. In this regard, there is no conceptual justification for imposing a per se requirement that autonomous weapons employ only less than lethal force. Instead, the test for when such weapons should be permitted to employ lethal force should in theory be no different than the test for when a human soldier may employ such force.[50]

Armed conflict involves a contest between organized belligerent groups. The objective of employing force in this contest is to bring about the complete submission of the enemy efficiently through the lawful use of violence. The essential distinction between a use of force in this context and in a peacetime context is that it is the enemy in the collective sense, and not the individual enemy operatives, who is the object of this effort. As a result, use-of-force authority is based on the presumptive threat posed by members of the enemy group and not on individualized conduct-based threat validation. Since such members represent a presumed threat unless and until rendered *hors de combat*, attacking forces are legally justified in employing deadly combat power against such members as a measure of first resort. This protects these forces from the inherent risk of tactical hesitation and serves the legitimate objective of imposing their will on the enemy in the collective sense.[51]

There is no theoretical reason to deprive autonomous weapons of analogous authority. As weapons systems, they, like soldiers, should be

---

[50] Nor should considerations of 'combatant privilege' be interjected in the analysis of permissible lethal force capability. Indeed, this privilege is simply an irrelevant concept in this assessment, as it relates more to the protection of the lawful combatant from criminal sanction for a lawful conduct during hostilities than it does to the permissibility of engaging in hostilities. An autonomous weapon, unlike a human, is a piece of equipment, and like all other military equipment will be subject to confiscation and either destruction or use by a capturing enemy so long as distinctive markings are properly substituted.

[51] See L. Blank et al., 'Belligerent targeting and the invalidity of a least harmful means rule', available at papers.ssrn.com/sol3/papers.cfm?abstract_ibid=2271152; see also G. S. Corn, 'Mixing apples and hand grenades: the logical limit of applying human rights norms to armed conflict', available at http://papers.ssrn.com/sol3/papers.cfm?abstract_ibid=1511954.

employed in a manner to produce maximum effect on the collective ability of an enemy to resist friendly forces. It is certainly true that, unlike with human soldiers, there is no genuine concern that tactical hesitation may result in mortal danger. However, this is only one aspect of the justification for employing deadly force as a measure of first resort against enemy belligerents. Equally significant is the tactical and strategic effect inherent in such authority. Subjecting enemy forces to the risk of status-based targeting contributes to seizing and retaining operational initiative and setting the tempo of battle. Granting the enemy an automatic reprieve from the full scope of this authority simply because the weapons system employing force is not human provides the enemy with an unjustified windfall and potentially cedes this initiative to the enemy. It also potentially enables the enemy to leverage this constraint to economize a commitment of resources against these assets and mass resources where the enemy believes more robust use-of-force authority may be leveraged.

Of course, as with a human soldier, there may be reasons related to mission accomplishment that warrant restraining the full scope of belligerent targeting authority and imposing an 'attempt-to-capture' restriction on autonomous weapons. As a result, it seems essential that the cognitive capacity of the weapon includes not only an ability to assess when a human subject to lawful attack is rendered *hors de combat* and, hence, protected from further violence but also an ability to assess when such an individual should be offered the opportunity to surrender prior to that point of incapacity. This will enable the employing commander to tailor the weapon's effects to the needs of the mission.

Another issue related to this concern is whether autonomous weapons will ever be able to conduct the nuanced balancing necessary to comply with the targeting principle of proportionality. The impact of this concern may very well turn on the nature of the weapon and will certainly be impacted by the established parameters of permissible use. For example, this would be a minimal concern for a weapon authorized for use only in areas with minimal to no civilian presence, whereas authorizing use of the weapon in a civilian population centre would require a very different cognitive capacity. It should also be noted that the nature of the attack parameters should influence this concern. Thus, an AWS developed as a substitute for human soldiers engaged in close combat will certainly require a capacity to engage in split-second distinction judgments but not necessarily in sophisticated proportionality balancing. The reality of combat indicates that soldiers engaged in close combat cannot engage in the type of deliberate and sophisticated proportionality assessments that are expected from a battle staff involved in deliberate targeting decisions. Instead, their judgments are by nature swift and ad hoc and will almost inevitably gravitate towards the distinction component of lawful targeting. Perhaps artificial intelligence will actually enable commanders to enhance the proportionality component of this equation, which would be ideal. However, there is no reason to demand more from the autonomous weapon than is demanded of the human soldier.

Developing artificial intelligence capable of this type of sophisticated human judgment may well be impossible. If so, no military or civilian leader may authorize the procurement and fielding of such a weapon. However, once it is determined that an AWS is capable of such efforts, there is no compelling justification for subjecting these systems to a use-of-force regime more restrictive than that imposed on human soldiers. The complete removal of human judgment from the target decision-making process, however, does justify the prioritization of the development phase of fielding over the employment phase as the necessary LOAC compliance focal point. Furthermore, the nature of such potential weapons also necessitates reconsideration of another critical LOAC compliance mechanism: command responsibility. This reconception should, like the process of fielding autonomous weapons writ large, produce a modification or evolution of the focus of command responsibility from the field commander who employs the weapon to the commander responsible for the procurement and fielding decision.

This will undoubtedly present significant conceptual obstacles. The doctrine of command responsibility is obviously premised on responsibility being linked to command and rarely will a procuring official be in a position of command. Even as it is extended to civilian superiors, the doctrine is still premised on the individual possessing directive authority over the subordinates whose LOAC violations are imputed to the leader. Thus, as currently conceived, the foundation of the doctrine will not support the weight of shifting the focus of imputed criminal liability to a procurement official.[52]

However, this need not function as an absolute impediment to such a reconception. Instead, a focus on the underlying rationale of the doctrine suggests that extension to procurement officials, what I call procurement

---

[52] See Rome Statute of the International Criminal Court (Rome Statute), UN Doc. A/CONF.183/9 (1998); see also Corn, *The Law of Armed Conflict*, 530–1; see generally Hansen, 'What's good for the goose'; Shany and Michaeli, 'The case against Ariel Sharon'.

responsibility, is indeed viable. Ultimately, command responsibility involves two distinct theories of criminal liability. The first is uncontroversial: traditional accomplice liability. Where a commander shares a criminal *mens rea* and acts in a manner (either by commission or omission) that contributes or facilitates a LOAC violation at the hands of a subordinate, liability is attributed to the commander, as it would be to any other individual under the doctrines of accomplice liability.[53]

The second theory subjects commanders to individual criminal liability for the foreseeable LOAC violations committed by subordinates even when there is no evidence that the commander shared the culpable *mens rea* with the subordinate. This is the well-known 'should-have-known' theory of command responsibility: commanders are responsible for LOAC violations that they 'should have known' would occur even if they did not affirmatively encourage or condone those violations. First enunciated in the seminal US Supreme Court *Yamashita* decision,[54] and controversial since that date,[55] this theory of command responsibility creates a powerful incentive for commanders to maintain awareness of the conduct of subordinates and to respond promptly to indicators of misconduct within the ranks. In so doing, the commander discharges his/her responsibility and, in so doing, renders subsequent LOAC violations objectively unforeseeable.[56]

Exploring the complexities of each of these theories of command responsibility is well beyond the scope of this chapter. It suffices that even the more expansive theory is premised on the culpable failure to prevent objectively foreseeable LOAC violations. This is the seed from which an extension of the doctrine to procurement officials should blossom. Indeed, for autonomous weapons, it is the significance of the procurement phase of fielding that makes shifting the liability lens from the employing commander to the procuring official both logical and equitable.

One conceptual obstacle to analogizing autonomous weapons with soldiers is related to the requirement that armed forces operate under responsible command. As noted earlier, key among the responsibilities of

---

[53] See Rome Statute, Article 28; see also Corn, *The Law of Armed Conflict*, 530–1; see generally Hansen, 'What's good for the goose'; Shany and Michaeli, 'The case against Ariel Sharon'.
[54] See *In re Yamashita*, 16–17. [55] See *ibid.*, 34–41 (Murphy, J, dissenting).
[56] See Rome Statute, Article 28; see also Corn, *The Law of Armed Conflict*, 530–1; see generally Hansen, 'What's good for the goose'; Shany and Michaeli, 'The case against Ariel Sharon'.

command is training and preparing the soldier for the exercise of combat judgments – developing combatants who are capable of exercising autonomous judgment as to what is and what is not a lawful use of combat power. By subjecting commanders to imputed criminal responsibility for subordinate LOAC violations that they 'should have known' would occur, the doctrine of command responsibility creates a powerful disincentive for commanders to fail in this responsibility. This doctrine is therefore integral to the high level of confidence that these human 'weapon systems' will, in fact, properly exercise battlefield judgment.[57]

Accordingly, this doctrine is vital in ensuring that the resources committed to conflict are properly prepared and supervised in order to minimize the risk of LOAC violations. For the soldier, the focal point of this responsibility is the fielding commander. This is logical, as history demonstrates that LOAC violations are usually attributable to unit climate, the nature of orders and directives, and the disciplinary response to indications that the unit is descending into the abyss of disrespect for the law. The role of the commander and the doctrine of criminal responsibility derived from that role provide the genuine lynchpin between fielding armed forces with the explicit task of unleashing deadly combat power and limiting the harmful consequences of that power in accordance with the LOAC.[58]

An analogous concept of criminal responsibility should also become an essential component to ensure AWS comply with LOAC norms. The focus of command accountability must shift, however, from the field commander to the military and/or civilian officials responsible for procuring and fielding these weapons systems. This is a logical outgrowth of the relationship between command responsibility and mitigating the humanitarian risks associated with autonomous weapons. Modifying the doctrine to apply to procurement officials, and not only to fielding commanders, will emphasize that it will ultimately be decision-making officials, and not technicians or legal advisers, who must validate the capability of the emerging technology. Knowing that they bear responsibility for objectively foreseeable technological failures should make these decision makers cautious to field such capability, which

---

[57] See Rome Statute, Article 28; see also Corn, *The Law of Armed Conflict*, 530–1; see generally Hansen, 'What's good for the goose'; Shany and Michaeli, 'The case against Ariel Sharon'.

[58] See Rome Statute, Article 28; see also ICRC, *AP I Commentary*, 1017–23; Corn, *The Law of Armed Conflict*, 530–1; see generally Hansen, 'What's good for the goose'; Shany and Michaeli, 'The case against Ariel Sharon'.

will, in turn, mitigate the risks associated with taking human judgment out of the actual target engagement decision.

Accordingly, these officials must understand they will be accountable for objectively foreseeable failures of the weapon review and compliance validation process: if a fielded weapon produces a LOAC violation, and it is determined that the procurement process was objectively insufficient to ensure LOAC compliance, the official who approved the weapon will bear responsibility for the violation. This process should logically result in demands for the highest level of confidence that the nature of the weapon system is capable of effectively implementing obligations of distinction, proportionality and precautionary measures if and when employed.

In short, not just the employment but also the development and procurement of autonomous weapons must fit squarely within this complex interrelationship between the lawful combatant status – the status that provides the international legal privilege to participate in hostilities – and the requirement for such participants to operate under responsible military command. Lawful combatant status is established by compliance with the four criteria incorporated into the Third Geneva Convention's prisoner of war qualification provision, which collectively indicate the link between the responsibility of commanders and the legally sanctioned exercise of combatant judgment.[59] Indeed, it is the influence of responsible command on subordinates that distinguishes 'combatant' – individuals authorized to engage in hostilities – from others who, although entitled to prisoner of war status upon capture, are not vested with this authority.[60]

The importance of the link between responsible military command and combatant qualification is not a novel concept. Requiring subordination to responsible command as a condition for qualifying as a

---

[59] Geneva Convention Relative to the Treatment of Prisoners of War (Third Geneva Convention) 1949, 75 UNTS 135.

[60] This dichotomy is revealed by considering the extension of prisoner of war status to civilians who provide field support to the armed forces. Three of the four combatant qualification requirements could easily and routinely be satisfied by these civilians: carrying arms openly; wearing a fixed and distinctive symbol and complying with the LOAC. But these individuals, although entitled to prisoner of war status upon capture, are not considered combatants within the meaning of the law. The true distinguishing factor between members of the regular armed forces and associated militia groups, on the one hand, and civilian augmentees, on the other, is therefore operating within the context of the type of command relationship that is essential to ensure LOAC compliance: operating under 'responsible command'.

combatant is tethered back to the 1899 and 1907 Hague Regulations.[61] This connection was finally codified in 1977 when Additional Protocol I defined the term combatant. Article 43 of Additional Protocol I explicitly establishes the existence of military command and discipline as a condition for recognizing combatant status:

> Article 43 – Armed forces
> 1. The armed forces of a Party to a conflict consist of all organized armed forces, groups and units which are under a command responsible to that Party for the conduct of its subordinates, even if that Party is represented by a government or an authority not recognized by an adverse Party. *Such armed forces shall be subject to an internal disciplinary system which, 'inter alia', shall enforce compliance with the rules of international law applicable in armed conflict.*[62]

The rationale for this requirement seems clear: in order to ensure compliance with the LOAC, only those individuals subject to military command and discipline should be permitted to perform functions involving the type of discretion that, if abused, might result in LOAC violations. This is reinforced by the commentary to Article 43:

> This requirement [the link between combatant status and internal command discipline and control structure] is rendered here with the expression 'internal disciplinary system', which covers the field of military disciplinary law as well as that of military penal law ... The principle of the inclusion of this rule in the Protocol was from the beginning unanimously approved, as it is clearly impossible to comply with the requirements of the Protocol without discipline ... *Anyone who participates directly in hostilities without being subordinate to an organized movement under a Party to the conflict, and enforcing compliance with these rules, is a civilian who can be punished for the sole fact that he has taken up arms, unless he falls under one of the categories listed under (2) and (6) of Article 4A of the Third Convention (categories (1) and (3), which cover the regular armed forces, should automatically fulfil these requirements).*[63]

The commentary omits any reference to individuals entitled to prisoner of war status by operation of Article 4A(4) of the Third Geneva Convention – civilians who support the forces in the field. The significance of this omission is obvious: the definition of combatant – individual entitled to participate in hostilities – conclusively presumed that

---

[61] See L. Green, *The Contemporary Law of Armed Conflict* (Melland Schill Studies in International Law), 2nd edn (Manchester University Press, 2000), 102–9.
[62] See Additional Protocol I, Article 43 (emphasis added).
[63] See ICRC, *AP I Commentary*, 513–14 (emphasis added).

individuals not fully incorporated into the military command-and-control structure (not 'part of the armed forces') could not engage in combatant activities. As Michael Schmitt notes:

> There are but two categories of individuals in an armed conflict, combatants and civilians. Combatants include members of a belligerent's armed forces and others who are directly participating in a conflict. As noted, the latter are labeled unlawful combatants or unprivileged belligerents; they are either civilians who have joined the conflict or members of a purported military organization who do not meet the requirements for lawful combatant status. Everyone else is a civilian, and as such enjoys immunity from attack.[64]

In Schmitt's continuum, civilian support personnel may not be considered combatants. This conclusion reflects the LOAC's essential linkage between being incorporated into a military unit, subject to responsible command, and the legal privilege of operating as a combatant. This link serves the interests of LOAC compliance by emphasizing to the military commander – the individual with the most direct and meaningful opportunity to ensure respect for the law – that violations jeopardize not only state and international interests but also the commander's personal interest of avoiding imputed criminal responsibility for foreseeable subordinate misconduct. It also suggests that legitimate combatant status is contingent not simply on whether or not an individual will take a direct part in hostilities, or wears distinguishing clothing and equipment, but, instead, on the expectation that the individual is subject to the fundamental compliance mechanism of the LOAC – a military command–subordinate relationship. Thus, for the human warrior, the true *sine qua non* for determining the limits on authority that may be exercised in armed conflict is whether performance of the function requires an exercise of judgment implicating LOAC compliance.

This connection also reveals that the LOAC has historically relied on the loyalty and discipline inherent in the command–subordinate relationship, bolstered by the proscriptive and disciplinary authority over combatants, to maximize confidence that individual human actors exercise judgment in accordance with the law. It is therefore no surprise that operating under responsible command is an essential element for qualifying as a lawful combatant. Military command authority over subordinates is relied upon to emphasize compliance obligations and ensure proper LOAC training

---

[64] See M. Schmitt, 'Humanitarian law and direct participation in hostilities by private contractors or civilian employees', *Chicago Journal of International Law*, 5 (2004–5), 522.

and individual preparation for the exercise of combatant judgment.[65] Being a member of a military unit is also expected to produce a high degree of loyalty to the military commander, often referred to as the concept of unit cohesion. This bond of obedience and loyalty is a unique and critical aspect of military organizations. It is unquestionable that the military command relationship, to include the proscriptive and disciplinary authority inherent in that relationship, is an essential element in the scheme of LOAC compliance mechanisms.

Subjecting commanders to criminal responsibility for LOAC violations that they 'should have known' would occur enhances confidence that individual soldiers will comply with the LOAC.[66] Subjecting commanders to imputed criminal liability for foreseeable subordinate LOAC violations that did not evolve as an aberration ensures, instead, that commanders diligently execute their responsibilities to ensure subordinate LOAC compliance. These responsibilities include training subordinates in their legal obligations; involving legal advisers in operational decision making; establishing a command atmosphere that emphasizes good faith compliance with the law and taking swift disciplinary action in response to any breach of the law.[67]

This relationship between responsible command and the exercise of human judgment is logical and critical as a LOAC violation risk mitigation measure. However, when pre-established artificial intelligence dictates the exercise of judgment, this relationship cannot have its desired effect. It is therefore essential to ensure that the application of the doctrine of command responsibility focuses on the command level with genuine 'responsibility' for the exercise of judgment. This level is not the field or employing commander but, rather, the procuring commander. Only by emphasizing that it is this level of command that is subject to imputed criminal responsibility for objectively foreseeable failures of autonomous weapon LOAC compliance capability will the rational of the doctrine properly align with this emerging technology.

The intangible 'force multiplication' effect of the human warrior

The conclusion that truly autonomous weapons will evolve to a point where they may be employed with a sufficient degree of LOAC

[65] See Green, *The Contemporary Law of Armed Conflict*, 280–6.
[66] See generally *In re Yamashita*.
[67] See Green, *The Contemporary Law of Armed Conflict*, 277–83.

compliance confidence undermines a purely humanitarian-based demand for a per se prohibition. However, this conclusion does not indicate that military leaders will perceive employment of such weapons as desirable. Ultimately, such employment will depend on both the validation that these weapons comply with LOAC obligations and the determination that the contribution they make to effective military operations justifies this next step in the evolution of the means of warfare.

It is not self-evident that this will be the case. Conceptually, fielding the truly autonomous weapon would result in a quantum leap in military affairs. While military organizations seem eager to embrace technology as a supplement to human action, the notion of using technology as a substitute presents very different considerations. This is because such a development would be truly inconsistent with the perception of the well-trained soldier, capable of engaging in human reasoning to navigate the most complex battlefield decisions, as the most valuable and effective weapons system available for a commander to employ.

Military commanders understand perhaps better than anyone that well-trained soldiers led by quality leaders will often prove decisive in combat. This is not because these soldiers are viewed as 'robots' who simply follow orders without question. Instead, it is the sophisticated reasoning of soldiers that equips them to lead and follow effectively in a manner that advances mission accomplishment. In fact, the very concept of 'mission command' – a concept that is absolutely central to the planning and execution of US (and other nations') military operations – is premised on the expectation of subordinate initiative to advance the commander's intent. US Army Doctrinal Publication 6–0 (GDP 6.0) is devoted to this concept and defines mission command as 'the exercise of authority and direction by the commander using mission orders to enable disciplined initiative within the commander's intent to empower agile and adaptive leaders in the conduct of unified land operations'.[68] More specifically, mission command is explained as follows:

> The exercise of mission command is based on mutual trust, shared understanding, and purpose. Commanders understand that some decisions must be made quickly at the point of action. Therefore, they concentrate on the objectives of an operation, not how to achieve it. Commanders provide subordinates with their intent, the purpose of the operation, the key tasks, the desired end state, and resources. Subordinates then exercise

[68] US Department of Army, *Mission Command*, Doctrine Publication no. 6–0, 17 May 2012; C1, 10 September 2012; C2, 12 March 2014, para. 2, available at http://armypubs.army .mil/doctrine/DR_pubs/dr_a/pdf/adp6_0.pdf.

disciplined initiative to respond to unanticipated problems. Every Soldier must be prepared to assume responsibility, maintain unity of effort, take prudent action, and act resourcefully within the commander's intent.[69]

The publication then explains that:

> An effective approach to mission command must be comprehensive, without being rigid, because military operations as a whole defy orderly, efficient, and precise control. Military operations are complex, human endeavors characterized by the continuous, mutual give and take, moves, and countermoves among all participants. The enemy is not an inanimate object to be acted upon. It has its own objectives. While friendly forces try to impose their will on the enemy, the enemy resists and seeks to impose its will on friendly forces. In addition, operations occur among civilian groups whose actions influence and are influenced by military operations. The results of these interactions are often unpredictable – and perhaps uncontrollable.[70]

Then, in an explicit invocation of the significance of human judgment in the implementation of mission command, the publication provides:

> A   HUMAN   SOLUTION   TO   COMPLEX   OPERATIONAL CHALLENGES
> To overcome these challenges, mission command doctrine incorporates three ideas: the exercise of mission command, the mission command philosophy, and the mission command warfighting function. In this discussion, the 'exercise of mission command' refers to an overarching idea that unifies the mission command philosophy of command and the mission command warfighting function – a flexible grouping of tasks and systems. The exercise of mission command encompasses how Army commanders apply the foundational mission command philosophy together with the mission command warfighting function. The principles of mission command guide commanders and staffs in the exercise of mission command.[71]

It is difficult to imagine a more emphatic indication of the importance of human judgment in the execution of military operations, not merely because such judgment is important for the implementation of LOAC obligations but also because it is central to the effective execution of a commander's intent. It is very likely that effective commanders will be reluctant to embrace technological substitutes for human subordinates

---

[69] Ibid., para. 5. See generally General M. E. Dempsey, 'Mission command', Army Magazine, 61 (43) (2011), 43–4 (discussing both philosophical and definition changes for what defines mission control), available at www.ausa.org/publications/armymagazine/archive/2011/1/Documents/Dempsey_0111.pdf.
[70] Doctrine Publication no. 6-0, para. 3.   [71] Ibid., para. 4.

not merely because of concerns related to LOAC compliance but also perhaps because of the more significant concern that these substitutes cannot function with the type of human intellectual nuance necessary to fit within this mission command model.

Indeed, the rationale for asserting a shift from command responsibility to procurement responsibility – that fielding commanders will be incapable of asserting any meaningful influence on the cognitive reasoning of these weapons – may be the operational Achilles heel that results in the hesitation to pursue them. This is because developing a relationship of trust and confidence between commander and subordinate is central to mission command – or perhaps even the broader concept of 'responsible command'. As Doctrine Publication no. 6–0 notes, building 'cohesive teams through mutual trust' is the first principle of effective mission command and:

> [e]ffective commanders understand that their leadership guides the development of teams and helps to establish mutual trust and shared understanding throughout the force. Commanders allocate resources and provide a clear intent that guides subordinates' actions while promoting freedom of action and initiative. Subordinates, by understanding the commander's intent and the overall common objective, are then able to adapt to rapidly changing situations and exploit fleeting opportunities. When given sufficient latitude, they can accomplish assigned tasks in a manner that fits the situation. Subordinates understand that they have an obligation to act and synchronize their actions with the rest of the force. Likewise, commanders influence the situation and provide direction, guidance, and resources while synchronizing operations. They encourage subordinates to take bold action, and they accept prudent risks to create opportunity and to seize the initiative.[72]

This brief discussion of the relationship between human judgment and mission command is really just the tip of the proverbial iceberg in relation to the significance of human reasoning as an essential element of effective military operations. However, even this cursory discussion illustrates a critical point: analogizing an autonomous weapon to a human soldier for the purposes of assessing LOAC compliance confidence is not intended to indicate that technology and humans are simply interchangeable. There are other aspects of effective military operations where even the type of conceptually advanced artificial intelligence that could produce LOAC compliance confidence would be insufficient to justify treating the autonomous weapon as a human substitute.

---

[72] *Ibid.*, para. 6.

Opponents of these weapons may therefore be pleasantly surprised by a lack of enthusiasm for these weapons among military leaders; perhaps not for the reasons they advocate, but because of an unwillingness to entrust mission execution to anything other than a human subordinate.

Conclusion

Whether it is possible to develop the sophisticated artificial intelligence needed to enable a weapon to operate with a level of cognitive reasoning analogous to that of a human soldier is yet to be seen. However, it is almost inevitable that attempts to achieve this goal will gain momentum. If this comes to fruition, there is no normative infirmity with allowing the use of such weapons during armed conflict. Accordingly, instead of pursuing a per se prohibition against autonomous weapons, core concepts related to ensuring human actors comply with LOAC obligations must be adjusted to address the realities of these weapons. Doing so will preserve the historic animating purpose of the law: facilitate military mission accomplishment while mitigating the human suffering associated with war.

PART V

New frameworks for collective responsibility

11

The obligation to exercise discretion in warfare: why autonomous weapons systems are unlawful

ELIAV LIEBLICH AND EYAL BENVENISTI

Introduction

The question of 'killer robots', or autonomous weapons systems (AWS), has garnered much attention in recent discourse. While officials often downplay the prospect of such systems making targeting and other crucial decisions, their own statements reveal the possibility that such capabilities would be developed in the near future.[1] For instance, in late 2012, the US Department of Defense (DoD) imposed a de facto moratorium on the development of fully autonomous weapons systems, by emphasizing that weapons 'shall be designed to allow commanders and operators to exercise appropriate levels of human judgment over the use of force'.[2] From the mere fact that the DoD felt the need to constrain the development and use of AWS for the time being and in several ways,[3] we can learn that the prospect of such weapons is realistic. Indeed, DoD Directive 3000.09 includes a bypass clause in which deviations from its

The authors wish to thank Rebecca Crootof, Daniel Hessel, Itamar Mann, Adam Shinar and Keren Yalin-Mor for their thoughtful insights on previous drafts and Rabea Eghbariah for his diligent research assistance. We acknowledge the support of the European Research Council Advanced Grant (grant no. 323323).

[1] Human Rights Watch and International Human Rights Clinic at Harvard Law School, *Losing Humanity: The Case against Killer Robots* (New York: HRW, 2012).

[2] US Department of Defense (DoD) Directive 3000.09, 'Autonomy in weapon systems', 21 November 2012, available at www.dtic.mil/whs/directives/corres/pdf/300009p.pdf.

[3] Beyond insisting that weapons allow for appropriate human judgment, the Directive requires, for instance, that systems do not operate too fast for human scrutiny (para. 4.a (1)(b)) and that they have understandable user interfaces (para. 4.a (3)(a)). Importantly, the Directive distinguishes between 'semi-autonomous' and 'human-supervised autonomous' weapons for the sake of targeting: while the former can be used as lethal weapons, the latter cannot be used for the selection and engagement of human targets, and can only be used as static defence of manned installations or platforms, 'for local defense to intercept attempted time-critical saturation attacks' (para. 4.c).

requirements can be approved by high-ranking officials through special procedures.[4] There is therefore a consensus, among commentators, that the motivation to develop and deploy AWS will eventually overcome these temporary constraints.[5] This makes the discussion of AWS a timely one.

When discussing the legality and legitimacy of such weapons, the claim that machines should not be making 'decisions' to use lethal force during armed conflict is an intuition shared by many. However, the current discussion as to just why this is so is rather unsatisfying. The ongoing discourse on AWS is comprised of nuanced approaches found between two extremes, arguing against each other roughly along consequentialist and deontological lines. On one side of the spectrum is the approach that if AWS could deliver good results, in terms of the interests protected by international humanitarian law (IHL), there is no reason to ban them. On the contrary, as the argument goes, if we take humanitarian considerations seriously, we should encourage the development and use of such weapons. Of course, proponents of this approach envision technological advancements that would actually make such results possible. Found on the other side of the spectrum are those that claim that even if AWS could, in terms of outcomes, adhere to the basic norms of IHL, their use should still be prohibited, whether on ethical or legal grounds. Usually, those holding this position are also sceptical that technology would ever be able to produce such benevolent systems. The discussion, thus, is caught in a loop of utilitarian arguments and deontological retorts. In essence, the current debate on AWS is a manifestation of the circular argument between technological optimists and pessimists found in other contexts.[6]

In this chapter, we do not attempt to prove any approach within this spectrum 'wrong'. We likewise do not aim to propose all-encompassing solutions to the problem of AWS. Rather, we aim to suggest a framework

---

[4] *Ibid.*, para. 4.c.1, enclosure 3.

[5] See N. Sharkey, 'The evitability of autonomous robot warfare', *International Review of the Red Cross*, 94 (2012), 787–99, 788; M. N. Schmitt and J. S. Thurnher, '"Out of the loop": autonomous weapons systems and the law of armed conflict', *Harvard National Security Journal*, 4 (2013), 232–81, 237; R. Crootof, 'The killer robots are here: legal and policy implications', *Cardozo Law Review*, 36 (2015), 1837–1915.

[6] In another context, see J. E. Krier and C. P. Gillette, 'The un-easy case for technological optimism', *Michigan Law Review*, 84 (1985), 405–29; A. D. Basiago, 'The limits of technological optimism', *Environmentalist*, 14 (1994), 17–22; C. E. Harris *et al.*, *Engineering Ethics: Concepts and Cases*, 4th edn (Belmont, CA: Wadsworth, 2013), 80–6 (explaining the notions of technological determinism, optimism and pessimism).

that explains better some of the objections to such weapons. We suggest, therefore, another prism through which the question should be analysed, one flowing from an administrative perception of warfare. In essence, we offer to approach the emerging phenomenon of AWS as an exercise of state power against individuals through a computerized proxy. As such, we suggest that such interactions should be analysed according to basic notions of administrative law, chiefly the obligation to exercise proper administrative discretion.

This understanding bridges a gap between the administrative (or regulatory) realm, on the one hand, and the realm of warfare, on the other. Although, as we will point out, modern IHL already includes an administrative law aspect in its rules concerning target selection and the need to take 'constant care' to spare the civilian population, this aspect has never been explicitly articulated, and, hence, the two realms have traditionally been viewed as being unconnected. As we see it, however, the administrative law view becomes apparent when discussing the legality of AWS since it provides the missing link between some often-made objections to AWS and the question of how states should act during armed conflict.

Specifically, the administrative perception can explain why notions of 'due process' or 'procedural justice' – which are usually reserved for peacetime relations between a state and its citizenry – are also relevant to the relations between belligerents (and between them and non-combatants) during armed conflict and, thus, affect the legality of the use of AWS. As we claim, administrative law thinking is not simply another way to argue for the application of international human rights law (IHRL) during armed conflict, although these realms are mutually reinforcing. Rather, administrative law adds to our understanding of the requirements of IHRL, by its emphasis on the proper process of decision making rather than simply on the outcome of the decision, as much of the current discourse does.

Thus, discussing the issue of AWS through the administrative prism can assist us to better understand and articulate existing objections to AWS and can serve as an interpretive or complementing source of principles when analysing positive IHL (and obviously IHRL). Importantly, this approach allows us to assess the issue of AWS even under the assumption that such weapons could, in due time, perform reasonably, in terms of immediate results.

The discussion proceeds as follows. The first part of the chapter defines autonomy for the sake of our discussion, laying down the distinction between 'technical' and 'substantive' autonomy. The second part outlines the 'circular' debate on AWS, caught between the instrumentalist and deontological discourses. The third part suggests analysing the problem of AWS through the prism of administrative law, which exposes key problems relating to their use – both in relation to non-combatants and, perhaps – and here we make a preliminary argument – also to enemy combatants. Namely, we argue that owing to the administrative–legal duty to exercise constant discretion, any final decision to use lethal force must be taken in real time only by a human being. Furthermore, when considering their deployment against combatants, we raise the concern that AWS may diminish the option of surrender, an option that should be promoted rather than restricted.

Technical versus substantive autonomy

Before we delve into our analysis, we must define what we mean when referring to autonomous weapons. Indeed, as evident from the 2014 meeting on lethal AWS of the high contracting parties to the Convention on Prohibitions or Restrictions on the Use of Certain Conventional Weapons Which May Be Deemed to Be Excessively Injurious or to Have Indiscriminate Effects (CCW), any attempt to offer an elaborate definition is slippery and, in any case, likely to be highly technical.[7] Since autonomy is a spectrum, rather than an absolute term,[8] discussing autonomy without offering a simplified definition is like aiming at a moving target. For the purpose of this chapter, therefore, we offer a simple working distinction between substantive and technical autonomy and focus our analysis strictly on the latter.

Substantive autonomy assumes machines with complete 'sentient' abilities. If the prospect of such machines was our point of departure, our discussion would quickly cross the lines to a philosophical debate concerning the essential components of humanity. Are sentient machines robots or quasi-humans? If they are, are there grounds to treat them differently in

---

[7] See, e.g., report of the 2014 Informal Meeting of Experts on Lethal Autonomous Weapons ('Autonomous weapons report'), Advanced Version, 16 May 2014, paras. 19–20; see also A. Krishnan, *Killer Robots: Legality and Ethicality of Autonomous Weapons* (Aldershot: Ashgate, 2009), 33–61. Convention on Prohibitions or Restrictions on the Use of Certain Conventional Weapons Which May Be Deemed to Be Excessively Injurious or to Have Indiscriminate Effects (CCW) 1990, 19 UNTS 1823.

[8] See, e.g., Krishnan, *Killer Robots*, 4: 'The smaller the need for human supervision and intervention, the greater the autonomy of the machine.'

terms of law? We leave such questions to others.[9] Likewise, our analysis is not concerned with 'singularity' scenarios,[10] in which humanity and technology become enmeshed, nor with apocalyptic 'Terminator'-type debacles where machines become the dominant 'life form' on Earth.[11] In this chapter, we are concerned with reasonably foreseeable developments, which assume an interim perception of technical autonomy.[12]

Technically autonomous weapons, according to a widely accepted definition, are systems that 'once activated, can select and engage targets without further intervention by a human operator'.[13] The system therefore possesses the capability of autonomous choice, in the sense that it is able to take 'targeting decisions' with humans 'out of the loop'.[14] However, the definition stops short of assuming the sentiency that constitutes substantive autonomy.[15] The latter is negated because the human remains in the 'wider loop' of the weapons' actions: humans predetermine their actions – even if they do not per se control them – by programming their algorithms.[16]

---

[9] See, e.g., N. Haslam *et al.*, 'Subhuman, inhuman, and superhuman: contrasting humans with nonhumans in three cultures', *Social Cognition*, 26 (2008), 248–58.

[10] See generally R. Kurzweil, *The Singularity Is Near: When Humans Transcend Biology* (London: Penguin, 2005).

[11] See generally K. Warwick, *March of the Machines: The Breakthrough in Artificial Intelligence* (University of Illinois Press, 1997).

[12] We are aware that by ruling out substantive autonomy we too are making a 'sceptical' assumption regarding technological developments. However, we do not derive normative conclusions from this scepticism – we simply refer to it as a given, 'realistic' scenario.

[13] DoD Directive, 13; Human Rights Watch, *Losing Humanity*, 2; C. Heyns, report of the Special Rapporteur on extrajudicial, summary or arbitrary executions, UN Doc.A/HRC/23/47, 9 April 2013, para. 38.

[14] Heyns, report of the Special Rapporteur, paras. 27, 39.

[15] It should be noted that technically autonomous weapons differ from 'automated' or 'semi-autonomous' weapons, since the latter still operate under direct control or at least constant real-time supervision. We set such systems aside since if 'autonomy' is limited by the constant oversight of a 'human in the loop', then the weapons do not, at large, raise questions different from those raised by remote-controlled weapons such as drones. See P. Asaro, 'On banning autonomous weapon systems: human rights, automation, and the dehumanization of lethal decision-making', *International Review of the Red Cross*, 94 (2012), 687–709, 690; DoD Directive, Glossary; Schmitt and Thurnher, '"Out of the loop"', 234–6. It should be borne in mind, however, that a valid question is whether automated or semi-autonomous systems create bias in the sense that the human operator believes these are error-proof. See D. Keats Citron, 'Technological due process', *Washington University Law Review*, 85 (2008), 1249–1313, 1254, 1271 (discussing literature that highlights that human supervision over machines is ineffective since they tend to believe that machines are error-proof).

[16] Heyns, report of the Special Rapporteur, para. 39. Autonomous weapons with a human in the 'wider loop' may or may not be subject also to a human 'on the loop', meaning

Since a technically autonomous machine is incapable of altering its algorithms through a process that could be equated to human learning, we cannot claim that it engages in a true process of discretion – its 'inner deliberation' is controlled by determinations made *ex ante* by humans. Risking oversimplification – and ongoing research notwithstanding – it is safe to say that computers are generally unable to engage in 'thinking about thinking' or metacognition.[17] In general, metacognition comprises a 'knowledge of cognition', which refers to several aspects of knowledge of one's own cognition or about cognition at large,[18] and 'regulation of cognition', which refers to how humans control their learning.[19] For our purposes, we presume that both levels are required in order to exercise human-like discretion, especially in complex circumstances – a capacity that technically autonomous weapons do not possess.

Before moving on, a clarification must be made. One can argue that by focusing on human discretion, we are placing it on an essentialist pedestal. After all, the application, by a computer, of highly developed algorithms could amount, for all practical matters, to an exercise of discretion.[20] However, since we focus on 'technical' autonomy, we exclude scenarios in which AWS actually achieve such human-like capacities and thus refrain from judging them. Nonetheless, the critique from essentialism can be augmented by a determinist outlook, arguing that human discretion is also pre-bound since there is no such thing as human-free action.[21] Regarding this claim, we simply presume that

a human that can override the robot's 'decisions'. This option was criticized as being unrealistic in the sense that robots make decisions faster than humans, and, therefore, such 'supervised autonomy' would be ineffective. See 'Autonomous weapons report', para. 41. Human Rights Watch, e.g., views systems with humans 'on the loop' as fully autonomous. Human Rights Watch, *Losing Humanity*, 2. For this reason, for instance, the DoD requires that any weapons' system will 'complete engagement in a timeframe consistent with the commander and operator intentions' – in order to allow human intervention. DoD Directive, para. 1(b).

[17] For a general overview, see M. T. Cox, 'Metacognition in computation: a selected research review', *Artificial Intelligence*, 169 (2005), 104–41.

[18] G. Schraw, 'Promoting general metacognitive awareness', *Instructional Science*, 26 (1998), 113–25, 114 (describing 'cognition of knowledge' as consisting of 'declarative', 'procedural' and 'conditional' knowledge).

[19] *Ibid.*

[20] T. J. Barth and E. F. Arnold, 'Artificial intelligence and administrative discretion: implications for public administration', *American Review of Public Administration*, 29 (1999), 334–6.

[21] See generally C. Hoefer, 'Causal determinism', in E. N. Zalta (ed.), *The Stanford Encyclopedia of Philosophy* (2010), available at http://plato.stanford.edu/entries/determinism-causal/.

imputation of responsibility to human beings is possible,[22] if only because its negation results in ruling out the mere possibility of normative judgment, and, thus, of law, to begin with.[23]

Thus, our focus on technical autonomy, combined with the realization that such autonomy excludes the exercise of discretion, has both a methodological and a normative importance. Methodologically, it allows us to shift the discussion from the metaphysics of substantive autonomy to the more earthly issue of the process of decision making. Normatively, as we shall see, it has ramifications when considering the use of AWS under notions of administrative law: this is because the rigid structuring of decision making, through programming, is comparable to the 'pre-binding' of administrative discretion.

The circular debate on AWS

As mentioned earlier, the contemporary discussion of AWS is a classic debate between consequentialists (or instrumentalists) and deontologists – between technological optimists and pessimists. Our discussion is at once wider and narrower than both lines of argument. It is wider since it places the challenges emanating from AWS as part of the general phenomenon of the exercise of state power in relation to the individual. It is narrower in the sense that it proposes to view the problem from an administrative-discretion point of view, which avoids the key pitfalls of the instrumental argument and the inconveniences of the deontological approach. Before proceeding, we briefly demonstrate the circular nature of the current debate.

The instrumentalist discourse

The instrumentalist debate regarding AWS is generally focused on their direct results in relation to the protection of individuals; on the problem of assigning responsibility for their 'decisions' *ex post* and on their potential to diminish restraints on the resort to force by lowering the price of warfare in terms of human lives.[24] While the issues of

---

[22] For a detailed discussion of determinism and moral responsibility, see A. Eshleman, 'Moral responsibility', in Zalta, *Stanford Encyclopedia of Philosophy*.

[23] For a classic statement of the constitutive role of imputability in the legal system, see H. Kelsen, *Introduction to the Problems of Legal Theory*, trans. B. Litschewski Paulson and S. L. Paulson, new edn (Oxford: Clarendon Press, 1997), paras. 15–16.

[24] For a useful summary of such objections, see generally 'Autonomous weapons report'.

responsibility and *jus ad bellum* are of much significance, we focus here on the more primordial issue of protecting victims of war.

The instrumental discourse is essentially an argument about optimistic or pessimistic perceptions of technology, coupled with optimistic or pessimistic perceptions of human nature. At the heart of the pessimist objections is deep scepticism regarding the ability of computers to ever achieve a level of sophistication required to apply the complex legal standards prevalent in modern IHL.[25] While some concede – although this is in itself doubtful[26] – that AWS might sufficiently distinguish between civilians, combatants and persons *hors de combat* during 'traditional' armed conflicts, virtually all pessimists argue that it is impossible to imagine a system capable of achieving good results when applying vaguer norms.

If placing the pessimistic approach in jurisprudential terms, the claim is that while it is possible to envision computers applying rules, it is difficult to imagine them applying standards, which per se do not aim to predict the right legal outcome in any given situation.[27] The distinction between rules and standards is helpful, as it allows us to explain better common intuitions as to why some computerized processes seem acceptable while others seem objectionable – even in the context of 'life-and-death' decisions. For this reason, for instance, most people do not find it especially problematic that computers are delegated the power to calculate artillery trajectories,[28] which essentially amounts to applying a set of rules derived from geography and meteorology combined with safety-parameter rules. Yet it seems harder to accept computers making decisions regarding direct participation in hostilities[29] or on *jus in bello*

---

[25] See, e.g., Sharkey, 'Evitability of autonomous robot warfare', 788–90.

[26] See N. Sharkey, 'Cassandra or false prophet of doom: AI robots and war', *IEEE Intelligent Systems*, 23 (2008), 14–17; Asaro, 'On banning autonomous weapon systems', 697.

[27] See L. Kaplow, 'Rules versus standards: an economic analysis', *Duke Law Journal*, 42 (1992), 557–629. On rules and standards in the context of international humanitarian law (IHL), see A. Cohen, 'Rules and standards in the application of international humanitarian law', *Israel Law Review*, 41 (2008), 4–67; see also Asaro, 'On banning autonomous weapon systems' (distinguishing between computers' ability to apply 'chess' type rules versus legal norms that require 'interpretation').

[28] See, e.g., http://udcusa.com/product-development-technical-services/indirect-fire-direction/.

[29] The determination of direct participation in hostilities is complex and shrouded in controversy. Compare N. Melzer, *Interpretive Guidance on the Notion of Direct Participation in Hostilities under International Humanitarian Law* (Geneva: ICRC, 2009), with K. Watkin, 'Opportunity lost: organized armed groups and the ICRC direct participation in hostilities interpretive guidance', *NYU Journal of International Law and*

proportionality,[30] precisely because such decisions are evaluated in light of legal standards rather than of rules.

This is especially true regarding proportionality, which essentially requires an ethical decision between the value of a military advantage and the expected civilian harm. It has been labelled a profoundly human qualitative decision,[31] not least because it is judged in terms of 'common sense' and the 'reasonable military commander', which are classic legal standards that seem incompatible with technical autonomy.[32] Naturally, these problems are exasperated in the 'fog of war', where unforeseen factual combinations can fall outside the pre-programmed 'design parameters' of AWS and where the latter, lacking human 'common sense', will be unable to adapt.[33] The pessimism regarding technology is usually accompanied with pessimism regarding programmers. Even if complex ethical and legal standards could be embedded in computer software, they are likely to be distorted by programmers, at best because they are not themselves knowledgeable in the intricacies of the field.[34]

While we sympathize with these concerns, the problem with the instrumental objections to AWS is that they can always be countered, at least analytically, by resort to optimistic hypotheticals regarding future technologies. Such arguments assume that the development of artificial intelligence capable of delivering good results is possible, likely or even inevitable.[35] Not only is this development possible, but it could also be, as

Politics, 42 (2010), 641–95. According to some, determination of direct participation is especially problematic when AWS are concerned, since it requires the ability to assess intentions, which autonomous weapons are highly unlikely to have. See Asaro, 'On banning autonomous weapon systems', 697–8.

[30] Heyns, report of the Special Rapporteur, paras. 70–3; Asaro, 'On banning autonomous weapon systems', 697; Human Rights Watch, *Losing Humanity*, 30.

[31] Sharkey, 'Evitability of autonomous robot warfare', 789–90; Asaro, 'On banning autonomous weapon systems', 700 ('applying IHL requires multiple levels of interpretation in order to be effective in a given situation').

[32] 'Autonomous weapons report', paras. 70–3; Human Rights Watch, *Losing Humanity*, 32–3.

[33] See Asaro, 'On banning autonomous weapon systems', 691–2 (and sources cited therein).

[34] Keats Citron, 'Technological due process', 1261.

[35] See, e.g., K. Anderson and M. Waxman, 'Law and ethics for robot soldiers', *Policy Review*, 176 (2012), available at www.hoover.org/publications/policy-review/article/135336 (suggesting that even though it is debatable whether AWS could ever be advanced enough to satisfy the ethical and legal principles of distinction and proportionality, the possibility should not be ruled out when discussing the normative approach towards autonomous weapons); Schmitt and Thurnher, '"Out of the loop"', 239–40, 262; see also R. C. Arkin, *Governing Lethal Behavior in Autonomous Robots* (Boca Raton, FL: CRC Press, 2009), 65–6 (suggesting the theoretical possibility that the

the arguments go, a positive one. Indeed, like the instrumental objections to AWS, the optimists also rely on consequentialist reasoning, focusing on the possible results of the deployment of AWS.

Thus, instrumental supporters of AWS point out the fact that if done right, autonomous technology will be much better than humans in alleviating death and suffering at war.[36] Indeed, excluding human beings from the battleground will diminish the need for 'force protection', which might in turn lower collateral damage inflicted on civilians.[37] In any case, the circular debate goes on and on. Confronting the optimistic assumptions regarding future technology, pessimists claim that relying on technological hypotheticals should not inform our normative debate today.[38]

On the legal level, Michael Schmitt and Jeffrey Thurnher offer a robust instrumental defence of AWS, arguing that there is nothing per se unlawful in the process of autonomous targeting, assuming that its deployment and results correspond with IHL. As they claim, it is possible to envision algorithms that apply the principle of distinction and are flexible enough to reasonably perform complex proportionality calculations.[39] Emphasizing outcomes, they remind us that humans, too, are less than perfect in applying IHL's difficult standards.[40]

However, they also concede that in the near future there will be no choice but to leave the 'proportionality decision' – and other complex determinations – to humans. This human involvement, however, can be

---

most complex standards of IHL – and even utilitarian or Kantian ethics – can be applied by artificial intelligence software through the employment of what he calls an 'ethical governor'); J. O. McGinnis, 'Accelerating AI', *Northwestern University Law Review*, 104 (2010), 1253–69, 1256–60; compare Asaro, 'On banning autonomous weapon systems', 699: 'The empirical question is whether a computer, machine, or automated process could make each of these decisions of life and death and achieve some performance that is deemed acceptable. But the moral question is whether a computer, machine or automated process ought to make these decisions of life and death at all. Unless we can prove in principle that a machine should not make such decisions, we are left to wonder if or when some clever programmers might be able to devise a computer system that can do these things.'

[36] See, e.g., McGinnis, 'Accelerating AI', 1265–7.   [37] *Ibid.*, 1266.

[38] Asaro, 'On banning autonomous weapon systems', 703 (describing the hypothetical technology argument as 'rhetorical strategy'); see also Human Rights Watch, *Losing Humanity*, 27–8; Sharkey, 'Evitability of autonomous robot warfare'.

[39] Schmitt and Thurnher, '"Out of the loop"', 243–50 (arguing, inter alia, that an autonomous weapon system is only unlawful per se if there are no circumstances in which it can be used discriminately); 250–7 (discussing the prospects of autonomous systems capable of adhering to the principles of distinction and proportionality); 262–5 (discussing cases of doubt).

[40] *Ibid.*, 257.

manifested in the mere decision to deploy the system in specific circumstances.[41] Indeed, much of Schmitt and Thurnher's reasoning shifts back the point of assessment to the decision to deploy the weapon.[42] Needless to say, this claim assumes that the deploying officer can fully anticipate the system's actions, which is in itself a debatable contention.[43]

In our eyes, the discussion of AWS should be guided neither by optimistic prophecies regarding the immediate results that can be achieved by new technologies nor by unrelenting pessimism. Indeed, some humility is called for when attempting to predict future technologies.[44] Therefore, a substantive discussion of AWS must transcend the circular and speculative discourse regarding their ability to deliver end results.[45]

The instrumental arguments concerning AWS talk beyond each other not only with regard to future technology but also concerning the putative effects of 'human nature' on battlefield outcomes. Interestingly, instrumentalists that support AWS are as pessimistic regarding human conduct as they are optimistic about technology's power; while those that are pessimistic regarding technology romanticize human behaviour on the battlefield. Thus, the optimists claim that humanity will be better off with AWS, since the latter would be immune to negative aspects of the human psyche such as the tendency for revenge, prejudice or sadism[46] as well as the natural fear and panic that can result in material risk to civilians.[47] As phrased by John McGinnis, it is

---

[41] *Ibid.*, 257, 267.

[42] For instance, if a weapon that cannot distinguish between combatants and civilians is deployed in a mixed environment, the deploying commander could commit the crime of indiscriminate attack. *Ibid.*, 278.

[43] Some argue that due to the sheer complexity of modern computing 'no individual can predict the effect of a given command with absolute uncertainty'. See P. Lin, G. Bekey and K. Abney, *Autonomous Military Robotics: Risk, Ethics, and Design*, report prepared for the US Department of Navy, Office of Naval Research (2008), para. 6 (also stating that the notion that robot behaviour is fully predictable as 'a common misconception'). Thus, their acts can become unpredictable in chaotic situations such as armed conflicts. See 'Autonomous weapons report', para. 42.

[44] See W. Wulf, 'Observations on science and technology trends' in A. G. K. Solomon (ed.), *Technology Futures and Global Power, Wealth and Conflict* (Ottawa: Canadian Security Intelligence Service, 2005), 10–16. As candidly admitted by Noel Sharkey – one of the key critics of autonomous weapons – the possibility of a 'black swan event' in which new technology will allow autonomous weapons to apply complex standards well enough cannot be theoretically precluded. Sharkey, 'Evitability of autonomous robot warfare'.

[45] Asaro, 'On banning autonomous weapon systems', 699.

[46] Heyns, report of the Special Rapporteur, para. 54.   [47] *Ibid.*, para. 70.

'mistaken' to assume that artificial intelligence would 'worsen, rather than temper, human malevolence'.[48] However, pessimists are quick to retort that the elimination of the human factor from the field does not only neutralize adverse human traits but also positive ones such as common sense or compassion, which might allow humans to act mercifully even when they could lawfully kill.[49] Paradoxically, both pessimists and optimists disregard the fact that human nature – whether good or bad – is also behind the development of technology itself, which can therefore (potentially) reflect either humanity's benevolence or its malevolence.

It becomes clear that, as always, assumptions about human nature are mutually offsetting and are likely to remain inconclusive[50] and thus cannot carry the debate forward. Thus, any attempt to decide whether the elimination of negative human traits from the battlefield is instrumentally positive, in terms of immediate results, is speculative and prone to arbitrariness.

The deontological discourse

The second level of the debate on AWS is concerned with deontological ethics. Arguments of this order posit that even if AWS could overcome the instrumental concerns discussed earlier – a possibility concerning which deontologists are of course pessimistic – and could therefore, in terms of results, perform well in relation to the values that IHL sets out to protect, there is still something inherently wrong in subjecting humans to machine-made 'decisions' to use lethal force.

At large, the deontological arguments are variations of two basic claims. The first has to do with the nature of war and, specifically, the

---

[48] McGinnis, 'Accelerating AI', 1254; see also Schmitt and Thurnher, '"Out of the loop"', 249.

[49] Human Rights Watch, *Losing Humanity*, 37–9.

[50] See, e.g., N. Chomsky and M. Foucault, *Human Nature: Justice vs Power – The Chomsky-Foucault Debate*, new edn (New York: New Press, 2006); Peter Loptson, *Theories of Human Nature* (Guelph, Ont.: Broadview Press, 1995), 19–29. Arguments (and counter-argumemts) regarding 'human nature' have accompanied the discourse of international law at least since Hobbes, Machiavelli and Grotius, the latter claiming, contra the former, that human beings are naturally inclined 'to follow the direction of a well-tempered judgment, being neither led astray by fear or the allurement of immediate pleasure, nor carried away by rash impulse'. Hugo Grotius, *On the Laws of War and Peace* (Oxford: Clarendon Press, 1925), vol. II, 13; see also H. Lauterpacht, 'The Grotian tradition in international law', *British Yearbook of International Law*, 23 (1946), 1–53, 24–6.

expectation that it would involve some element of mutual risk; as the argument goes, in order to distinguish it from one-sided killing, war must involve some measure of self-risk.[51] According to this view, killing in war is not immoral, if war is understood as a series of individual self-defence actions undertaken by combatants against each other.[52] Killing through AWS is therefore unjustified unilateral killing.[53] However, this objection does not capture the salient dilemma of AWS because it could equally apply also to other methods and tactics of warfare such as drones, cruise missiles and high-altitude bombing – and, in the past, to crossbows, rifles and artillery.[54] However, nobody seriously suggests, nowadays, a complete, deontological ban on the latter. This must mean that there is something additionally vexing in the concept of AWS.

The second type of deontological argument concerns the nature of the mechanized decision maker, on the one hand, and the human dignity of potential victims, on the other. Arguments of this order point out the distance that AWS create between human beings and the consequences of their actions. As phrased by Special Rapporteur Christof Heyns, AWS create a 'new dimension' in this distance – not only will humans be removed physically from the battlefield, as drones already allow, but they also become detached mentally from decisions to kill.[55] Precisely for this reason, for instance, the International Committee for Robot Arms Control (ICRAC) asserts that 'machines should not be allowed to make the decision to kill people'.[56]

From the outset, it is worthwhile to recall that, as always, deontologists are placed in an awkward position when confronted by extreme hypotheticals. Again, instrumentalists are likely to point out that if the ultimate objective of law in armed conflict is to protect civilians, and assuming that AWS could actually be better than humans in doing so, the deontologist has three main (and unattractive) ways out of the dilemma: either to deny the plausibility of the hypothetical; to withdraw in some form from

---

[51] 'Autonomous weapons report', para. 60.

[52] P. W. Kahn, 'The paradox of riskless warfare', *Philosophy and Public Policy Quarterly*, 22 (2002), 2–8.

[53] It should be noted that such arguments can have an instrumental version as well. Kahn, e.g., argues that the immorality of riskless warfare will ultimately increase the adversaries' attacks against the civilian population, for lack of other options. See Kahn, 'The paradox', 2, 6.

[54] It was in this context that the argument was initially made. See, e.g., *ibid.*

[55] Heyns, report of the Special Rapporteur, paras. 26–7.

[56] Mission statement of the International Committee for Robot Arms Control (2009), available at http://icrac.net/statements/.

his or her absolute position (threshold deontologism); or – in our context, it is indeed a fitting phrase – to 'bite the bullet' and accept that greater loss of life is preferable to lesser loss of life, only because a machine is involved in the process.[57]

The argumentation of Peter Asaro, a founding member of the ICRAC, represents a sophisticated deontological position, based on considerations emanating from IHL and supplemented from ethics. Asaro's basic claim revolves around the principle that 'the authority to decide to initiate the use of lethal force cannot be legitimately delegated to an automated process'.[58] He grounds these notions on positive IHL, claiming that the latter 'explicitly requires combatants to reflexively consider the implications of their actions, and to apply compassion and judgement in an explicit appeal to their humanity'.[59] As he argues, what matters under IHL – for instance, in the context of proportionality – is not necessarily the 'specific calculation' but, rather, the ultimate 'deliberate consideration' undertaken by humans before using lethal force.[60] Thus, Asaro asserts that 'justice cannot be automated: when computer processes replace human agents, due process is fundamentally compromised, as human judgment is constitutive of any system of justice'.[61]

This reasoning brings us closer to a satisfying discussion of the dilemma of AWS, as it alludes to an understanding of warfare as an executive action. However, it still requires us to make a broader theoretical claim about the relations between warfare and public law. Absent such a claim, it is unclear to what extent IHL alone would require such a 'residual' possibility of human discretion, assuming an autonomous system that otherwise delivers reasonable results. Namely, Asaro's approach does not provide a sufficient theoretical link between the norms regulating armed conflict, in which hostilities are conducted against an adversary, and concepts of procedural justice or fairness such as 'due process' that are usually reserved for domestic law. In short, arguments of this order tell us why AWS might jeopardize concepts of procedural justice such as due process; but they do not tell us why these are relevant, as such, in situations of warfare.

---

[57] See L. Alexander and M. Moore, 'Deontological ethics', in Zalta, *Stanford Encyclopedia of Philosophy*.

[58] Asaro, 'On banning autonomous weapon systems', 689.   [59] *Ibid.*, 700.   [60] *Ibid.*

[61] *Ibid.*, 700–1. This is because, according to Asaro, the essence of due process is 'the right to question the rules and appropriateness of their application in a given circumstance, and to make an appeal to informed human rationality and understanding'. *Ibid.*, 700.

In sum, as we have demonstrated earlier, neither the instrumental, nor the deontological discourses – in their various forms – are entirely satisfying. In the next part of this chapter, we attempt to offer a third prism through which to analyse the complex question of AWS. In particular, this prism can serve as a theoretical bridge between warfare and administrative concepts of justice and due process.

Reframing the debate: warfare as an exercise of administrative power

War as governance

As mentioned earlier, some of the deontological arguments about AWS refer to ideas of procedural justice and due process. However, their shortcoming lies precisely in that they fail to demonstrate how, or to what extent, this framework is relevant to the law regulating wars. In order to argue that notions such as due process apply during war, we thus have to also make an argument about war itself. As we argue, war under contemporary international law must be understood as a form of governance[62] – a fact that spawns, as we demonstrate, administrative-legal obligations.

Justice and due process seem foreign to the traditional idea of war. Indeed, in the past, the laws of war were quite explicit in their obliviousness to these ideals, as we understand them in domestic law.[63] For instance, the 1863 Lieber Code bluntly stated that '[t]he citizen or native of a hostile country is thus an enemy, as one of the constituents of the hostile state or nation, and as such is subjected to the hardships of the war'.[64] Binding individuals together as a political collective, essentially

---

[62] Compare B. Kingsbury et al., 'The emergence of global administrative law', Law and Contemporary Problems, 68 (2005), 15–61, 17 (identifying administrative action/governance on the international level as all 'decisions that are neither treaty-making nor simple dispute settlements between parties'); see also E. Benvenisti and A. Cohen, 'War is governance: explaining the logic of the laws of war from a principal–agent perspective', Michigan Law Review, 112 (2013), 1363–1415; E. Lieblich, 'Show us the films: transparency, national security and disclosure of information collected by advanced weapon systems under international law', Israel Law Review, 45 (2012), 459–91, 483.

[63] We set aside the idea that war itself is a form of 'punishment' – and, thus, of justice making – found in early just war thought. See D. Luban, 'War as punishment', Philosophy and Public Affairs, 39 (2012), 299–330.

[64] General Orders No. 100: Instructions for the Government of the Armies of the United States in the Field (Lieber Code), Article 21. It should be noted that this view was primarily dominant in Anglo-American thought. See L. Oppenheim, International Law, 2nd edn (London: Longman's, Green and Co., 1912), vol. II, para. 57.

holding them liable for state action, negates their individual agency and is hardly an example of justice or due process as the terms are regularly understood. Indeed, war was not about justice since it was generally perceived as 'a contention between States for the purpose of overpowering each other', in which each party was entitled to defend its own interests aggressively while weakening the adversary.[65] Even nowadays, the difference between justice making and war fighting is a key difference between understandings of the law enforcement paradigm versus that of hostilities.[66] Thus, absent significant theoretical expansion, IHL is not commonly understood as a 'system of justice', as implied by Asaro,[67] but, rather, a system aiming to minimize harm in a given, inherently unjust situation, where, in any event, military necessity remains the prime consideration.[68] Naturally, the divergence between war, justice and due process is most acute where conflicts are international or transnational, in which a 'social contract' between the warring parties cannot be assumed. Nonetheless, even in cases of civil wars, it could be argued that in some cases, the social contract is at least temporarily broken, thereby modifying the normal relations within the state in a manner that affects the regular application of the principles of due process.

The traditional view of war, thus, usually entailed at least some assumption of collectivity: war was a 'horizontal' confrontation between collectives, in which the 'enemy' comprised both the state apparatus and citizenry.[69] Accordingly, it was possible to dismiss offhand any special

---

[65] Oppenheim, *International Law*, para. 58: 'As war is a struggle for existence between States, no amount of individual suffering and misery can be regarded; the national existence and independence of the struggling State is a higher consideration than any individual well-being.'

[66] See E. Lieblich, 'Quasi-hostile acts: the limits on forcible disruption operations under international law', *Boston University International Law Journal*, 32 (2014), 101–55, 110–17.

[67] Asaro, 'On banning autonomous weapon systems', 701. The question whether there is a system of justice beyond the state is of course strongly contested among philosophers. See T. Nagel, 'The problem of global justice', *Philosophy and Public Affairs*, 33 (2005), 113–47; J. Cohen and C. Sabel, 'Extra rempublicam nulla justitia?', *Philosophy and Public Affairs*, 34 (2006), 147–75.

[68] As understood by the mainstream of writers, IHL is 'intended to minimize human suffering without undermining the effectiveness of military operations'. Y. Dinstein, *The Conduct of Hostilities under the Law of International Armed Conflicts* (Cambridge University Press, 2004), 17.

[69] See J. Dill, 'Should international law ensure the moral acceptability of war', *Leiden Journal of International Law*, 26 (2013), 253–70, 259. However, it should be noted that the collective view of war was already challenged by Rousseau. See J. Rousseau, *On the Social Contract* (1762; London: J. M. Dent, 1913), Book 1, ch. IV. Rousseau's view

obligations between a state and the enemy's citizens. Each state was responsible, beyond certain minimal obligations, only to safeguard the rights and interests of its own citizens against the belligerent actions of the other.[70] Thus, war envisioned a 'vertical' system of exclusive protection between sovereign and citizenry. These vertical obligations were only transferred from one sovereign (for example, the defender) to another (for example, the attacker) when the latter occupied its territory.[71] It is easy to see why, when holding this view of war, claims that AWS violate due process can be dismissed as being out of touch.

This perception of war was perhaps sustainable in an age dominated by conflicts between functioning states. Nowadays, conversely, most wars are fought between states and non-state actors, and armed violence is limited neither spatially nor temporally.[72] In many cases – and virtually in all instances where AWS are likely to be deployed – armed force will be used by advanced militaries against non-state actors in failing states or territories.

In such conflicts, the absence of functioning sovereigns where hostilities are conducted results in a gap in civilian protection. This gap is a product of three main characteristics of asymmetric conflicts. First, in many cases, such conflicts involve significant intermingling between militants and civilians, which naturally increases civilian harm. This intermingling is caused both by the deliberate failure of armed groups to distinguish themselves from the civilian population, and by the nature of guerrilla tactics, which almost always involve at least some concealment that puts civilians at risks.[73] Second, in many cases, armed groups are unaccountable, whether normatively because of shortcomings of the

---

about war became dominant in continental Europe during the nineteenth century but was not influential in British and American thought. In any case, as noted by Oppenheim – who unequivocally supported the collective view – this dispute did not have substantial legal consequences in international law. Oppenheim, *International Law*, para. 57.

[70] See, e.g., W. Hays Parks, 'Air war and the law of war', *Air Force Law Review*, 32 (1990), 1–225, 21 (noting that traditionally, 'collateral civilian casualties . . . were not regarded as the responsibility of an attacker, as the ability to limit such casualties lay more with the defender or, for that matter, with the civilian population itself').

[71] Hague Convention (IV): Respecting the Laws and Customs of War on Land (Hague Regulations), 18 October 1907, 187 CTS 227, Regulations, Articles 42–3.

[72] See *Uppsala Conflict Data Program, Armed Conflict Dataset*, vol. 4 (2014), available at www.pcr.uu.se/research/ucdp/datasets/ucdp_prio_armed_conflict_dataset/.

[73] See, e.g., the use of underground tunnels by Hamas in the 2014 Israel–Hamas conflict. Frequently, the tunnels' openings are inside civilian buildings. See H. Sherwood, 'Inside the tunnels Hamas built: Israel's struggle against new tactic in Gaza War', *The Guardian* (2 August 2014), available at www.theguardian.com/world/2014/aug/02/tunnels-hamas-israel-struggle-gaza-war.

legal regime;[74] whether in practice, due to lack of motivation to comply,[75] or because of the absence of pressure from constituencies, as such actors are not susceptible to political pressure as sovereigns in functioning states are. When armed groups are unaccountable, significant risk can be transferred to civilians under their control. Third, in asymmetric conflicts, the traditional concept of 'victory' is virtually non-existent.[76] In such scenarios, states might rephrase the notion of victory in ambiguous terms. One possibility is to discuss victory in terms of winning the sympathy of the local population and, therefore, seeking to reduce civilian harm.[77] However, the opposite process is just as plausible: states engaged in what they perceive as a zero-sum conflict might do just the opposite and adopt 'deterrence' as their main objective, making indirect use of incidental harm to civilians to further that purpose.[78] In sum, since in most situations of non-international armed conflicts individuals lack any substantial effective institutional protection, a protection gap emerges. If humanitarian considerations are to be taken seriously, this gap must result in some 'diagonal' responsibilities of protection between the potentially affected individuals and the attacker who is in a position to decide their fate.[79]

[74] See generally L. Zegveld, *Accountability of Armed Opposition Groups in International Law* (Cambridge University Press, 2002).

[75] See, e.g., D. Richemond-Barak, 'Nonstate actors in armed conflicts: issues of distinction and reciprocity', in W. C. Banks (ed.), *New Battlefields, Old Laws: Critical Debates on Asymmetric Warfare* (Columbia University Press, 2011), 106–29, 107.

[76] As successful confrontations with non-state actors usually require 'long-term change' rather than tactical advantages. See G. Blum, 'The fog of victory', *European Journal of International Law*, 24 (2013), 391–421, 391–4.

[77] *Ibid.*, 408; US Department of the Army, *The US Army/Marine Corps Counterinsurgency Field Manual* (University of Chicago Press, 2007), 294.

[78] Compare G. Eiland, 'The Third Lebanon War: Target Lebanon', *INSS Strategic Assessment*, 11 (2) (2008), 9–17. Of course, deterrence is a vague and speculative advantage. In essence, it can serve to justify almost any harm and thus cannot comport with legitimate military goals both under *jus ad bellum* and *jus in bello*. The law on the use of force, as generally understood, restricts self-defence to what is necessary to counter a specific threat. See T. Ruys, *'Armed Attack' and Article 51 of the UN Charter: Evolutions in Customary Law and Practice* (Cambridge University Press, 2010), 94; IHL defines military necessity narrowly, as comprising only as the need to 'weaken the military forces of the enemy'. Declaration Renouncing the Use, in Time of War, of Explosive Projectiles under 400 Grammes Weight, St Petersburg, 1868. In the same vein, military advantage that can be measured in relation to incidental civilian harm must be 'concrete and direct'. Protocol Additional to the Geneva Conventions of 12 August 1949, and Relating to the Protection of Victims of International Armed Conflicts (Additional Protocol I) 1977, 1125 UNTS 3.

[79] See generally E. Benvenisti, 'Rethinking the divide between *jus ad bellum* and *jus in bello* in warfare against nonstate actors', *Yale Journal of International Law*, 34 (2009), 541–8. When discussing AWS in terms of executive action, it becomes clear that questions

This analysis suggests that we must view modern warfare as a form of exercise of state power vis-à-vis individuals rather than a horizontal engagement between sovereigns. It therefore becomes possible to understand it as being closer to the exercise of administrative, executive action than to traditional war.[80] Once it is perceived this way, warfare should be subjected to widely accepted notions of accountability and responsiveness that are reflected in domestic administrative law that governs executive decision making. Of course, administrative power (and its scrutiny) is responsive to circumstances. When we suggest that battlefield decisions can be analysed as executive actions, we do not imply that the full spectrum of administrative law applies to each targeting decision. What we refer to are basic principles.[81]

Granted, administrative duties during warfare were triggered traditionally only once a territory was occupied.[82] However, it is important to stress that, ultimately, the 'active agent' generating such obligations is control rather than this or that legal status. Indeed, in recent years, the concept of control has been significantly broadened to include numerous situations in which state agents affect individuals even when control over territory is not complete.[83] States have been expected to act as benevolent

relating to computerized decision making extend well beyond the issue of targeting. For instance, during occupation, but also at the 'invasion' stage, autonomous weapons can be utilized for all kinds of measures of control, some bordering on law enforcement activities. Theoretically, they can be used for curfew enforcement, for dispersing demonstrations, population control or to destroy property. These possibilities are worthy of further exploration but are beyond the scope of this chapter. For AWS in law enforcement, see C. Heyns, 'Human rights and the use of increasingly autonomous weapons systems during law enforcement' (forthcoming).

[80] Compare Kingsbury et al., 'The emergence of global administrative law', 17 (asserting and explaining that nowadays 'much of global governance can be understood and analyzed as administrative action').

[81] We are aware of the claim that discussing contemporary warfare in administrative terms might have the adverse by-effect of normalizing a never-ending state of war (and thank Itamar Mann for pointing out this problem). However, problems of this order are a consistent risk when engaging in any form of transnational regulation, and thus we cannot resolve them here. For a discussion of these dynamics in another context, see I. Mann, 'Dialectic of transnationalism: unauthorized migration and human rights, 1993–2013', Harvard Journal of International Law, 54 (2013), 315–91. Specifically with regard to 'new' wars, compare P. W. Kahn, 'Imagining warfare', European Journal of International Law, 24 (2013), 199–226; with S. Moyn, 'Drones and imagination: a response to Paul Kahn', European Journal of International Law, 24 (2013), 227–33.

[82] See Hague Regulations, Arts. 42–3.

[83] ECtHR, Al Skeini v. UK, Appl. no. 55721/07, Judgment of 7 July 2011, paras. 131–40; Human Rights Committee, General Comment 31, 'Nature of the general legal obligation on states parties to the covenant', UN Doc. CCPR/C/21/Rev.1/Add.13 (2004), para. 10.

administrators even without boots on the ground, at least in relation to the functions they control vis-à-vis the civilian population.[84] In our context, when making a targeting decision, a state agent is making a life-and-death decision regarding an individual. As such, the process of targeting represents a form of control *par excellence*, even if not always accepted as such in positive international law concerning the accumulation of jurisdiction.[85]

However, we do not have to adopt a radical perception of control in order to ground the existence of administrative-like duties during warfare. This is because complementing the expanding notion of control is an evolving perception of sovereignty itself. As we suggest, this transformation is from the view of sovereignty as a 'trusteeship' of a certain body politic to a trusteeship of humanity at large. The concept of sovereignty as trusteeship of humanity, its justifications, as well as its possible critiques, were expounded elsewhere.[86] In this chapter, we shall only outline its basic (and relevant) aspects.

The gist of this approach is that states should bear a residual obligation to take other-regarding considerations in their decision-making processes – an idea that is increasingly reflected in international law.[87] The appeal of this approach lies in ever-growing interdependence. This interdependence means that sovereigns' decisions concerning development, natural resources or, in fact, any type of regulation, no longer affect only the polity of the territorial state but also the lives of individuals in other states – power and its effects are no longer aligned.[88] Put simply, the perception of sovereignty as a global trust rests upon the notion that those who exercise power bear responsibility, even if the results affect those found beyond borders. It is, in its essence, not only a corollary of

---

[84] This has been notably the case regarding the relationship between Israel and Gaza. See, e.g., Gisha – Legal Center for Freedom of Movement, 'Scale of control: Israel's continued responsibility in the Gaza Strip', 14 November 2011; O. Ben-Naftali *et al.*, 'Legal opinion concerning supply of electricity and water to the Gaza Strip', 20 July 2014, available at http://gisha.org/UserFiles/File/publications/letters/letter-en-20-7-14.pdf. In other contexts, see *Al-Skeini* v. *UK* (concurring opinion of Judge Bonello), paras. 11–12.

[85] See ECtHR, *Bankovic* v. *Belgium*. Appl. no. 52207/99, judgment of 12 December 2001, paras. 62–82.

[86] E. Benvenisti, 'Sovereigns as trustees of humanity: on the accountability of states to foreign stakeholders', *American Journal of International Law*, 107 (2013), 295–333; see also 'AJIL Symposium: sovereigns as trustees of humanity', *Opinio Juris* (23 July 2013), available at http://opiniojuris.org/2013/07/24/ajil-symposium-sovereigns-as-trustees-of-humanity/.

[87] Benvenisti, 'Sovereigns as trustees', 297.   [88] *Ibid.*, 298.

the idea of the equal moral worth of all but also of perceptions of global welfare and justice.[89]

However, from both normative and practical considerations, global trusteeship does not call for the eradication of the state in favour of a cosmopolitan utopia of a world federation, nor does it require that states relinquish their self-interest altogether. It merely recognizes a pragmatic administrative–legal notion, according to which a sovereign's decision-making process must take effect on others seriously.[90] Importantly, since this responsibility is inherent in the concept of sovereignty, it applies to every exercise of sovereign power, independent of specific treaty obligations.[91] Thus, global trusteeship spawns several minimal obligations that are firmly rooted in traditional notions of administrative law. Relevant to our context are the obligation to take others' interests into account (including human dignity), which implies a duty to exercise discretion when sovereign actions bear cross-border effects.[92]

Thus, the mere fact that a certain armed conflict crosses national borders does not, in itself, negate diagonal, administrative responsibilities, even when traditional effective control is absent. How could this understanding affect the debate on AWS? The answer lies in applying the principle of equal moral worth. In this context, Avishai Margalit and Michael Walzer offer a helpful argument. Using an illuminating thought exercise, they argue that when armed forces operate, they must assume the same level of risk – when choosing means and methods of warfare – whether operating in the vicinity of the enemy's civilians or among their own.[93] We do not claim that states cannot prefer their own civilians across the board. As David Luban convincingly notes, the issue is not whether states can require soldiers to take 'heroic risks' in order to save their 'own' civilians (they can) but, rather, that a state cannot treat 'enemy' civilians beneath minimum acceptable standards, in a manner that it would never treat its own.[94]

---

[89] *Ibid.*, 301–13.   [90] *Ibid.*, 300–1.   [91] *Ibid.*, 300.

[92] Benvenisti, 'Sovereigns as trustees', 313–25.

[93] A. Margalit and M. Walzer, 'Israel: civilians and combatants', *New York Review of Books* (14 May 2009). In their example, a state's village is taken by the enemy. Will the state be morally justified in acting differently, in terms of the risk undertaken by its forces and the resulting collateral damage to civilians, according to the citizenship of the persons within that village? Their conclusion is a firm no. Compare A. Kasher and A. Yadlin, 'Military ethics of fighting terror: an Israeli perspective', *Journal of Military Ethics*, 3 (2005), 3–32.

[94] See D. Luban, 'Risk taking and force protection', Georgetown Public Law and Legal Theory Research Paper no. 11–72 (2011), 12, 46.

The delineation of these minimum standards cannot be exhausted in this chapter. A possible cut-off point, suggested by Luban, refers to the identity of the risk creator. States have to treat 'enemy' civilians as their own, in terms of alleviating risk, at least when the risk is created by the state's own violence – for instance, when a targeting decision is made. In other words, as Luban stresses, while it is possible to defend the claim that a state is only obliged to defend its own citizens – but not others – against threats by an external enemy, the state must give the lives of the endangered civilians on the other side the same weight that it would give its own when the risk is created by its own actions (and to the extent that this is the case, we should add).[95] If we apply Margalit, Walzer and Luban's logic to the question of AWS, we may ask states that consider deploying such weapons, whether they would be willing to use them in situations where their *own* citizenry could be affected by the 'decisions' made by such systems.

It seems that some states have already answered this question negatively, albeit in an implied manner, by imposing limitations on the computerization of executive decision making. For instance, Article 15 of Council Directive (EC) 95/46 enshrines the right of every person 'not to be subject to a decision which produces legal effects concerning him ... which is based solely on automated processing of data'.[96] The article's key rationale is to limit predetermined decision making, which, as we shall see, is a key problem emanating from AWS.[97] Granted, Article 15 allows automated processes if they are 'authorized by law which also lays down measures to safeguard the data subject's legitimate interests'.[98] However, in order not to render the article meaningless, this would imply at least some form of appeal, to ensure that the final decision is not computerized.[99] In the jargon of AWS, this would require

---

[95] *Ibid.*, 32–3: 'Of course the soldier's job exists to protect co-civilians, not foreign civilians, against their enemies ... But it would completely beg the question to assert that the soldier's obligation to protect civilians against the soldier's own violence runs only to fellow citizens'; but see I. Porat and Z. Bohrer, 'Preferring one's own civilians: may soldiers endanger enemy civilians more than they would endanger their state's civilians?', *George Washington International Law Review*, 47 (2014), 99–158. We set aside the discussion whether it could be said, in any context, that the 'risk' is created, in the true sense, by the attacking party.

[96] Council Directive (EU) 95/46 on the protection of individuals with regard to the processing of personal data and on the free movement of such data, OJ L 281, 1995 Article 15(1).

[97] *Ibid.*, Articles 3–6.   [98] *Ibid.*, Article 15(2)(b).

[99] Keats Citron, 'Technological due process', 1265 (exemplifying automatic administrative systems that allow for appeals).

maintaining a 'human in the loop' before making irreversible decisions. Admittedly, in recent years, 'automated decision-making systems' have gained some ground in the United States, but these are used to apply rules rather than standards and, in any case, are not involved in life-and-death decisions.[100] Indeed, if states limit computerized decisions with regard to their own citizens – and in matters far less acute than life and death in the battlefield – it is questionable whether it would be legitimate to subject others to such decisions. The potential effect of an administrative perception of warfare over the question of AWS is thus clear: it means that AWS would be subject to additional, residual constraints, even if such weapons would perform reasonably, in terms of immediate results, under IHL.

It should be noted, that in actuality – and although not phrased as such – basic notions of administrative law are not entirely foreign to modern, positive IHL. For instance, the requirement to take 'constant care' in the conduct of military operations[101] is reminiscent of the traditional administrative law notion of the duty to exercise discretion when making decisions, upon which we will elaborate shortly. The duty to give effective warning 'unless circumstances do not permit'[102] or the obligation to direct an attack against the least dangerous target, in terms of civilian harm, when the attack of several military objectives would spawn the same military advantage, also requires active, administrative-like discretion.[103] The rights of internees to elect representatives to treat with the detaining power are not unlike well-recognized administrative obligations of due process and fair hearing.[104] The gradual elimination of belligerent reprisals against persons *hors de combat*[105] also demonstrates a shift from a perception of warfare as a series of reciprocal blows between black-boxed sovereigns into a more complex phenomenon, in which some diagonal responsibility is established between sovereigns and the adversary's civilians.

The same administrative law approach can be derived from IHRL, which is also considered applicable during armed conflict and, in some

---

[100] *Ibid.*, 1252, 1263 (providing examples for such decision-making systems in the United States).

[101] Additional Protocol I, Article 57(1).   [102] *Ibid.*, Article 57(2)(c).

[103] *Ibid.*, Article 57(3).

[104] Geneva Convention (IV) Relative to the Protection of Civilian Persons in Time of War 1949, 75 UNTS 287, Article 102.

[105] See R. Kolb, 'The main epochs of modern international humanitarian law since 1864 and their related dominant legal constructions' in K. Mujezinovi Larsen *et al.* (eds.), *Searching for a 'Principle of Humanity' in International Humanitarian Law* (Cambridge University Press, 2012), 23–71, 52–3.

cases, extraterritorially.[106] IHRL requires that the limitation or deprivation of rights, including the right to life, be subject to due process in the
course of limiting those rights.[107] As the European Court of Human
Rights (ECtHR) has asserted, 'the decision-making process leading to
measures of interference must be fair and such as to afford due respect to
the interests of the individual'.[108] And the British House of Lords, in an
interpretation of the requirement under the European Convention on
Human Rights that limitations on rights be 'in accordance with the law',
equated 'arbitrariness' with non-compliance with the rule of law by
public officials.[109] Whereas in *McCann* v. *UK*,[110] the ECtHR emphasized
the *ex-post* duty to conduct an effective investigation when individuals
had been killed as a result of the use of force by state agents, as derived
from the duty to protect the right to life,[111] there is little doubt that the *ex-
ante* duty to exercise discretion diligently and thoroughly also flows from
the same obligation. The administrative law perception of warfare can
thus provide the additional conceptual framework for understanding
what constitutes 'arbitrary' deprivation of life during armed conflict.
At large, the administrative law point of view can reveal that exercise of
proper administrative discretion is indeed a precondition for the application of human rights standards, considering that the latter are almost
always vague and balanced against other rights and interests.[112]

[106] For an overview, see N. Lubell, 'Human rights obligations during military occupation',
International Review of the Red Cross, 94 (2012), 317–37, 317–23.

[107] See E. Benvenisti, *The Law of Global Governance* (Hague Academy of International Law,
2014) ch. 3.

[108] ECtHR, *Taşkin* v. *Turk.*, Appl. no. 46117/99, judgment of 30 March 2005, paras. 124–5.

[109] *R. (on the application of Gillan (FC) and another (FC)) v. Commissioner of Police for the
Metropolis and another*, [2006] UKHL 12, para. 34. See also ECtHR, *Gillan and Quinton*
v. *UK*, Appl. no. 4158/05, judgment of 28 June 2010, paras. 76–7: '[W]ell established
case-law [indicates that] the words "in accordance with the law" require the impugned
measure both to have some basis in domestic law and to be compatible with the rule of
law.' This means that 'legal discretion granted to the executive [cannot] be expressed in
terms of an unfettered power. Consequently, the law must indicate with sufficient clarity
the scope of any such discretion conferred on the competent authorities and the manner
of its exercise.'

[110] ECtHR, *McCann* v. *UK*, Appl. no. 18984/91, judgment of 27 September 1995.

[111] *Ibid.*, para. 161. The right to life under international human rights law (IHRL) is
enshrined, e.g., in Article 6(1) of the International Covenant on Civil and Political
Rights 1966, 999 UNTS 171.

[112] For a related argument, see M. Koskenniemi, 'The future of statehood', *Harvard
International Law Journal*, 32 (1991), 397–410, 399. Indeed, the claim that discretion is
a precondition for the fulfilment of human rights could pre-empt, for instance, the
validity of a treaty that would formulate mandatory algorithms for autonomous
weapons.

The Martens Clause can also be invoked in order to introduce the administrative law approach into IHL. The Martens Clause, as introduced in the 1899 and 1907 Hague Conventions, and reiterated in Additional Protocol I, famously recognizes the 'laws of humanity' and the dictates of public conscience as residual gap fillers when positive IHL seems silent.[113] Indeed, relying on this clause, some deontological arguments claim that AWS inherently contradict the principle of humanity and therefore must be banned.[114] While the Martens Clause is undoubtedly significant, basing an objection to AWS strictly on principles of humanity or public conscience is problematic because it begs the question of what is the nature of the relations between those deploying AWS and individuals on the 'other side'. In other words, simply invoking the Martens Clause without further elaboration seems to overstretch it.[115] But informed by the trusteeship approach, this gap can be bridged to add support and content to the reliance on the Martens Clause as an additional ground for the administrative perception.[116]

Autonomous weapons and the problem of pre-bound discretion

As noted earlier, positive IHL requires belligerents to take 'constant care' to spare civilians.[117] 'Constant care' is an admittedly vague standard and, as such, is open to various interpretations, which are lenient as well as constraining. To be precise, the administrative law perception can guide us, as it allows us to understand properly this notion as a requirement of exercising continuous discretion when conducting hostilities.[118]

---

[113] Geneva Convention (II) with Respect to the Laws and Customs of War on Land, 29 July 1899, 187 CTS 227; Hague (IV); Additional Protocol I, Article 1(2); see generally T. Meron, 'The Martens Clause, principles of humanity, and dictates of public conscience', American Journal of International Law, 94 (2000), 78–89.

[114] Human Rights Watch, Losing Humanity, 35–6.

[115] See Meron, 'The Martens Clause': 'the Martens clause does not allow one to build castles of sand. Except in extreme cases, its references to principles of humanity and dictates of public conscience cannot, alone, delegitimize weapons and methods of war, especially in contested cases'; see also Schmitt and Thurnher, '"Out of the loop"', 275–6; for a discussion see also T. D. Evans, 'Note: at war with robots: autonomous weapons systems and the Martens clause', Hofstra Law Review, 41 (2013), 697–733.

[116] E.g., by arguing that the concept of 'humanity' per se requires the exercise of discretion.

[117] Additional Protocol I, Article 57(1).

[118] Compare Schmitt and Thurnher, '"Out of the loop"', 259–60.

The obligation to exercise discretion imposes upon the administrative authority the duty to consider, within the confines of its legal authority, each decision to exercise power in light of the specific goals of the norm that the executive is bound to promote, including the relevant rights and interests affected in the case at hand. This obligation calls for a duty to constantly exercise discretion. Of course, this duty implies a prohibition – and, indeed, the invalidity – of fettering one's discretion. The authorizing agency must be willing to listen to 'anyone with something new to say' and to alter or waive its policies in appropriate cases.[119] The very idea of delegating decision-making authority to actors is to have them exercise their discretion in individual cases, given the specific circumstances of each case. If there was no need to pay attention to the specific circumstances and to allow for fresh thinking, the superior organ could have made the decision itself. While some pre-commitment by administrative agencies is indeed a legitimate tool to promote transparency and equal treatment, it seeks to stipulate the boundaries of discretion, not to negate it altogether. Moreover, pre-commitment must be of such a nature that it can be altered in real time if circumstances require.[120]

Indeed, the fundamental requirement that discretion cannot be fettered is also reflected in general doctrines of international law, through the concept of 'reasonableness' (or, in IHL language, of 'feasibility').[121] The mere idea of reasonableness must require leaving open the possibility of making adjustments to one's policies, through the exercise of discretion. For instance, the international law of non-navigational use of watercourses requires upstream states to make 'equitable and reasonable' use of transboundary water sources.[122] It seems obvious that a state's attempt to predetermine what would be 'reasonable' use in all circumstances, and to act upon such criteria without reviewing them according to the changing circumstances, would be a clear violation of the reasonableness principle.[123] If there could be a clear *a priori*

---

[119] See, e.g., *British Oxygen v. Minister of Technology*, [1971] AC 610, HL (UK). See generally J. Jowell *et al.*, *De Smith's Judicial Review* (London: Sweet and Maxwell, 2014).

[120] See E. Magill, 'Agency self-regulation', *George Washington Law Review*, 77 (2009), 101–44, 104, 117.

[121] See, e.g., O. Corten, 'The notion of "reasonable" in international law: legal discourse, reason and contradictions', *International and Comparative Law Quarterly*, 48 (1999), 613–25.

[122] Convention on the Law of the Non-Navigational Uses of International Watercourses, 36 ILM 700 (1997), Article 5(1).

[123] *Ibid.*, Article 6 (requiring to take into account 'all relevant factors and circumstances' when utilizing international watercourses).

definition of what is to be considered 'reasonable', the parties would have agreed on it in advance.

There are two key rationales for the obligation not to fetter one's discretion. The first emanates from the rights of the affected individual. The executive is bound to give 'due respect' to individuals by considering the effects of a specific act on individuals, in light of the prevailing circumstances.[124] This is an essential characteristic of the trust relations that form the basis of administrative power, one that is especially significant in the context of hazardous activities, such as warfare.[125]

The second justification for the duty to exercise discretion has to do with decision-making quality. We assume that in the long run, 'good' executive decisions cannot be taken in a complex world without making constant adjustments.[126] These adjustments, which require constant discretion, are necessary due to epistemological human limitations, which H. L. A. Hart identified as comprising 'relative ignorance of fact' and 'relative indeterminancy of aim'.[127] These 'handicaps' limit any attempt to regulate decision making in advance.[128]

During hostilities, the duty to exercise discretion requires the active, ongoing intention not to inflict harm on civilians.[129] The components of this duty require the military commander to exercise discretion both when planning the attack[130] and, importantly, during the attack, up to the last moment before pulling the trigger.[131] Naturally, the last requirement applies primarily to 'those executing' the attack.[132] In our context, in an out-of-the-loop scenario, the duty to exercise discretion 'in the last moment' would have to be performed by the AWS.

This outcome is problematic when taking into account proper administrative discretion. AWS, as mentioned earlier, are only capable of exercising technical autonomy; they cannot engage in the metacognition required in order to exercise 'true' discretion in real time. Therefore, their use reflects a case where executive discretion is stringently bound in advance – through the pre-programmed algorithms that govern their

---

[124] Benvenisti, 'Sovereigns as trustees', 314.   [125] Compare *ibid.*, 316.

[126] See, e.g., Barth and Arnold, 'Artificial intelligence and administrative discretion', 338, 348–9.

[127] H. L. A. Hart, 'Discretion', *Harvard Law Review*, 127 (2013), 652–65, 661–4.

[128] *Ibid.*

[129] See M. Walzer, 'Coda: can the good guys win', *European Journal of International Law*, 24 (2013), 433–44, 437.

[130] Additional Protocol I, Article 57(2)(a)(i).   [131] *Ibid.*, Article 57(2)(b).

[132] C. Pilloud *et al.* (eds.), *Commentary on the Additional Protocols of 8 June 1977 to the Geneva Conventions of 12 August 1949* (The Hague: Martinus Nijhoff, 1987), 686.

'behaviour'. The deployment of AWS thus runs counter to the two rationales justifying the prohibition on fettering one's administrative discretion: respect for the individual and decision-making quality. First, pre-binding targeting decisions, for instance, clearly contradict the notion of 'due respect' for the individual since the potentially harmed individual is not considered at all in real time but, rather, is 'factored' into the predetermined processes. Second, AWS cannot be reconciled with the inherent need to make constant adjustments in a complex world, considering the epistemological limitations mentioned earlier. Indeed, if the legislator could not have promulgated an order to shoot in advance or if states parties could not have agreed in advance whether a certain military act was lawful or not, how could a military commander, at any level, fetter his/her discretion or anyone else under his/her command?[133]

In this context, it is important to reiterate that the duty to exercise discretion is concerned with long-term decision-making quality. Accordingly, it should not be judged in light of isolated results – while this or that predetermined decision can bring about good results, any administrative system based on rigid rules, taken as a whole, is likely to diminish the overall quality of the decision making or, worse, potentially bring about catastrophic results. The latter problem can be easily demonstrated in the context of autonomous targeting. For instance, while a human administrator (or commander) is prone to making an occasional 'wrong' decision, his/her decision is unique and affects the specific case at hand. Even if he/she is in the higher organizational (or command) echelons, his/her decision can still (at least in theory) be corrected by judgment exercised by subordinates. Arguably, the diversity of human

---

[133] A question related to the limitation on fettering discretion concerns delegation of authority. In general, administrative legal doctrines differentiate between 'lean' delegation of technical powers, on the one hand, and delegation of discretionary power, on the other. The latter, naturally, is placed under stricter scrutiny. See, e.g., J. Freeman, 'Private parties, public functions and the new administrative law', *Administrative Law Review*, 52 (2000), 813–58, 823 (noting the difference between delegation of 'management' and delegation of 'rule-making' authority). The use of semi-AWS – e.g., those that 'lock' on targets and track them – could reflect the former type of delegation. Fully autonomous ones, conversely, are reminiscent of the latter. The use of such weapons is, perhaps, a form of 'double' delegation: first, by delegating to programmers the power to design the weapon's 'discretion', it reflects a delegation of rule-making power; and then, by delegating the power to make battlefield decisions to a non-human, it reflects a delegation of powers to make individual decisions. Compare Keats Citron, 'Technological due process', 1253 (noting that computer programs 'seamlessly combine rulemaking and individual adjudications without the critical procedural protections owed [in] either of them').

discretion is mutually correcting, ultimately leading to reasonable overall results.[134] Conversely, decisions based on 'wrong' algorithms or, for that matter, on any predetermined rigid rule will be repeated by all systems in which they are embedded, to potential catastrophic effects.[135] While it is relevant to ask whether the life-saving potential of 'good' AWS is not sufficient to outweigh such concerns, one should not lose sight of the catastrophic potentials of a systemic mistake.

In a sense, computerized pre-commitment constitutes a significant shift in the 'vertical landscape' of discretion. If IHL requires common sense throughout the command chain – from the general all the way down to the private – the so-called 'discretion' embedded in AWS would probably represent mainly the pre-programmed perceptions of higher echelons. As such, it will negate field decision making, which is not only a legal requirement under IHL but can also be carried out better.[136] Naturally, the importance of on-the-field decision making (sometimes referred to as 'street-level' decision making) increases in intensively 'discretionary' environments, which involve complex decision making under uncertainty.[137] Most modern armed conflicts clearly constitute such environments.

A major pitfall in the instrumentalist arguments that defend AWS can be found precisely regarding the problem of discretion. In order to reassure us that a human still remains 'in the loop' – meaning that discretion is indeed being exercised – some instrumentalists claim that the only salience of AWS is that human discretion takes place on a different temporal level. As they argue, human discretion is embedded into the system through the human discretion of the programmers. As phrased by Schmitt and Thurnher, 'in an attack involving autonomous weapon systems ... targeting decisions remain subjective and continue to be made by humans. What may differ *is the phase in the*

---

[134] See, in another context, C. R. Sunstein, *Infotopia: How Many Minds Produce Knowledge* (Oxford University Press, 2006).

[135] See, e.g., J. Frémont, 'Computerized administrative decision making and fundamental rights', *Osgoode Hall Law Journal*, 32 (1994), 818–31, 826–7; the failures of automated administrative systems in the United States exemplify this problem. See Keats Citron, 'Technological due process', 1256, 1267–71. The same effect can emanate from programmers' bias. *Ibid.*, 1262.

[136] *Ibid.*, 1262–3.

[137] E. Z. Brodkin, 'Street-level research: policy at the front lines', in M. C. Lennon and T. Corbett (eds.), *Policy into Action: Implementation Research and Welfare Reform* (Washington, DC: Urban Institute Press, 2003), 145–64, 145, 151 (arguing that policy, in discretionary environments, should be analysed 'at the point of delivery').

targeting process when the subjective determinations occur.'[138] As Noel
Sharkey critically describes this process, it is 'like writing a knitting
pattern or recipe'.[139] To put it in our terms, what Schmitt and
Thurnher suggest (and Sharkey criticizes) is the binding of discretion
ex ante. However, this is precisely what makes AWS problematic, when
analysed through the lens of proper administrative action.

Granted, Schmitt and Thurnher reassure us that the 'decisive juncture'
of human discretion is found at the point where the decision is made to
deploy the weapon in specific circumstances.[140] However, this reassur-
ance is not entirely convincing for two reasons. First, it relies on the
contestable assumption that commanders would be able to foresee how
weapons would 'act', at least in a manner sufficient to amount to the
taking of 'constant care' to spare civilians. Here lies a paradox: for the
weapon's action to be predictable, it must be built to follow simple, rigid
rules, which seems to mean that it would not be capable of performing
IHL's complex standards to begin with. However, if it is unpredictable –
meaning, that it attempts to apply complex standards in a changing
environment – then deploying it per se violates the duty to take constant
care. Moreover, since humans tend to attribute to computers 'far more
intelligence than they actually possess', and are therefore unlikely to
'override' their decisions,[141] it is possible to envision a phenomenon of
'reliance-creep', where the duty to take constant care will be 'delegated'
more and more to the computer's pre-programmed discretion. In this
context, it is also unclear to what extent allowing autonomous systems to
select and 'recommend' human targets would alleviate the problem of
discretion, considering the 'automation bias' that may occur when
human beings assess computerized recommendations.[142]

Second, even under Schmitt and Thurnher's approach, the fact
remains that the last decision to use force will be made by the weapon,
upon pre-bound discretion. Indeed, Schmitt and Thurnher suggest that
systems would include methods of 'adjustment', allowing commanders to
'dial up and down' values in order to accommodate specific
circumstances.[143] If these adjustments can be made during all stages of
the attacks, including up to the last minute – this might indeed solve the

---

[138] Schmitt and Thurnher, "'Out of the loop'", 266 (emphasis added).
[139] Sharkey, 'Evitability of autonomous robot warfare', 789.
[140] Schmitt and Thurnher, "'Out of the loop'", 267.
[141] Barth and Arnold, 'Artificial intelligence and administrative discretion', 348; Keats
Citron, 'Technological due process', 1254.
[142] See *ibid.*, 1272.   [143] Schmitt and Thurnher, "'Out of the loop'", 267.

problem of pre-bound discretion. But then it would be fair to ask whether such weapons can be considered autonomous to begin with. In sum, the reading of relevant legal norms in the light of administrative law notions, and, specifically, the duty to take constant care and thereby exercise discretion, results in the conclusion that, technically, autonomous systems cannot be allowed to make final targeting decisions.

Subjecting warfare to administrative law standards and the problem of pre-bound discretion: possible challenges

Indeed, the administrative law approach at large, as well as our emphasis on the problem of pre-bound discretion, can raise some challenges or objections. However, as we briefly demonstrate, they are not sufficient to negate either of these ideas. One objection to the idea of residual 'administrative' constraints could be that during armed conflict IHL constitutes the *lex specialis*, replacing, as such, 'peacetime' notions of administrative law. This argument, essentially, mirrors the same debate regarding the application of IHRL during armed conflict.[144] In this context, we subscribe to the widely accepted view that even if specific IHL norms can serve as *lex specialis* in certain circumstances and, thus, override obligations from other areas of law, IHL as such does not replace other normative systems as a whole. Rather, there is significant space for complementarity between norms belonging to different systems or for interpreting IHL to include basic notions of administrative law concerning the proper exercise of discretion.[145] Thus, IHL and administrative law constraints can exist side by side. In this sense, it is interesting to note that administrative law is actually a more 'convenient' partner for dual application with IHL than IHRL, at least in light of a conservative understanding of the former. This is because much of administrative law is

---

[144] For the treatment of this question by the International Court of Justice (ICJ), see *Legality of the Threat or Use of Nuclear Weapons*, Advisory Opinion, ICJ Reports (1996) 226, para. 25; *Legal Consequences of a Wall in the Occupied Palestinian Territory*, Advisory Opinion, ICJ Reports (2004) 136, para. 106; *Case Concerning Armed Activities on the Territory of the Congo (DRC v. Uganda)*, ICJ Report (2008) 215.

[145] For a discussion see, e.g., M. Milanović, 'Norm conflicts, international humanitarian law, and human rights law' in O. Ben-Naftali (ed.), *International Humanitarian Law and International Human Rights Law* (Oxford University Press, 2011), 95–128; N. R. Quénivet, 'Introduction: the history of the relationship between international humanitarian law and human rights law', in R. Arnold and N. Quénivet (eds.), *International Humanitarian Law and Human Rights Law: Towards a New Merger in International Law* (Leiden: Brill, 2008), 1–14, 9–11.

concerned with secondary norms of process; it chiefly aims to regulate the manner in which decisions are made[146] rather than to replace the legal system's primary norms.[147] Indeed, precisely because of its focus on process, the administrative approach allows us to discuss AWS critically beyond the usual instrumental–deontological circle. It departs from the act of utilitarianism espoused by some proponents of AWS since it can serve to constrain specific actions even if their immediate results seem just (or legal), but it is also not deontological since it is minded towards achieving long-term results in terms of the quality of decision making.[148]

Challenges can also be presented to our claim that AWS give rise to a special problem of pre-bound discretion. One possible objection could be that regular, 'dumb' weapons, such as artillery rounds or rockets, also reflect pre-bound discretion – indeed, once fired, upon the discretion of the shooter, there is no turning back. However, we reject this *ad absurdum* argument on two counts. First, the time gap between the exercise of human discretion and the weapons' impact, in the case of regular kinetic weapons, is usually negligible. Any change of circumstances between the last human decision and impact, which would require re-engaging discretion, is unlikely (although not entirely impossible). This is not the case when deploying AWS, which by nature are expected to act in a relatively prolonged manner.[149] Second, a 'dumb' weapon does not presume to execute complex legal standards itself but, rather, follows simple physical

---

[146] See Kingsbury *et al.*, 'The emergence of global administrative law', 15 (defining global administrative law as 'as comprising the mechanisms, principles, practices, and supporting social understandings that promote or otherwise affect the accountability of global administrative bodies, in particular by ensuring they meet adequate standards of transparency, participation, reasoned decision, and legality, and by providing effective review of the rules and decisions they make'); see also *ibid.*, 29.

[147] Perhaps this is why the Supreme Court of Israel found no special problem in ruling that principles of Israeli administrative law apply extraterritorially to military action in the West Bank, while being far more reluctant to concede that IHRL applies to such operations. For the historical reluctance to apply IHRL in the occupied territories, see O. Ben-Naftali and Y. Shany, 'Living in denial: the application of human rights in the occupied territories', *Israel Law Review*, 37 (2004), 17–118. For application of administrative standards of proportionality in targeting by the Israeli Supreme Court, see, e.g., Case HCJ 769/02, *The Public Committee against Torture in Israel* v. *The Government of Israel* (*Public Committee* v. *Israel*), 62(1) PD 507, para. 40 [2006] (Isr.)

[148] It could be argued that our approach is one of rule consequentialism: it looks at the consequences promoted by a decision-making process guided by certain rules. See B. Hooker, 'Rule consequentialism' in Zalta, *Stanford Encyclopedia of Philosophy*.

[149] Similar problems are raised by anti-personnel landmines. See generally M. A. Lawson *et al.* (eds.), *To Walk Without Fear: The Global Movement to Ban Landmines* (Oxford University Press, 1998).

rules. To begin with, these weapons do not attempt to make distinction or proportionality decisions. The dumbness of the artillery shell must be taken into account by its launcher, who is also responsible for the potentially unlawful outcomes. In contrast, the sophistication of the AWS nullifies its launcher's opportunity to exercise discretion.

Nonetheless, it could be argued that the use of some 'dumb' weapons – most notably, landmines – does, in fact, create a significant time gap between deployment and impact, which entails the same binding of discretion that AWS presumably require. There are two (equally plausible) ways to engage this critique. One is to uncover the fact that, rather than vindicating AWS, this critique actually exposes the true problems arising from landmines and similar weapons: they are indiscriminate precisely because they involve the binding of discretion.[150] A landmine will blindly kill active combatants along with those *hors de combat*; it will destroy a combat-armed personnel carrier just as it will rip apart a military ambulance.[151] The other answer resonates with our claim in the previous paragraph, regarding the 'dumbness of the artillery shell' as a constraining element in the launcher's discretion. When using 'dumb' weapons, the 'dumbness' is likely to be taken into account as a relevant factor. For instance, the reasonable commander will (probably) not deploy landmines where civilians might be harmed excessively.[152] The commander will take more precautions exactly because he/she is aware of the weapon's crudeness. Indeed, this awareness has led to the adoption of specific rules to address the crudeness of the landmines and to ensure the ability to exercise constant care with respect to their use, including the requirements of self-deactivation or self-neutralization when constant care cannot be ensured.[153] However, when using, for instance, a sophisticated robot landmine, which 'intelligently' selects and engages its targets (not only according to weight, as some landmines nowadays do) and carries out a proportionality calculus, the commander will now operate under the assumption that the weapon does in fact exercise discretion and, moreover, considering the 'automation bias' discussed earlier, he/she will regard this 'discretion' as sufficient from the perspective of the law. The commander will thus be more inclined to absolve him/herself from exercising discretion by relying on the weapon's discretion instead.

---

[150] Compare G. S. Corn's contribution, 'Autonomous weapons systems: managing the inevitability of "taking the man out of the loop"', Chapter 10 in this volume.

[151] *Ibid.*   [152] *Ibid.*

[153] See Protocol on the Prohibitions or Restrictions on the Use of Mines, Booby-Traps and Other Devices 1983, 1342 UNTS 168. See also DoD, *Law of War Manual* (Washington, DC: DoD, June 2015), 356–79.

A related claim could be that we are overemphasizing discretion since in reality the essence of military discipline is that human soldiers also do not exercise discretion but, rather, follow orders. As the argument goes, even today, warfare assumes that the discretion of soldiers is fettered through their subjection to superiors. However, military thinkers have long been aware that, in practice, soldiers do exercise discretion, for better or for worse, even when receiving clear orders.[154] As Geoffrey Corn argues in a chapter in this volume, 'no amount of training or supervision can eliminate a very basic reality of human operatives: they are and have always been "autonomous" weapons systems, because all soldiers must exercise cognitive reasoning in the execution of their battlefield tasks'.[155] Normatively, it is clear that international law requires such discretion even from the lowest-ranked soldier, *inter alia*, through the negation of the 'superior orders' defence in certain circumstances.[156]

Diagonal obligations towards combatants, pre-bound discretion and the shrinking window of surrender

As we have demonstrated, the administrative law perception of warfare spawns diagonal obligations towards the adversary's civilians. Do comparable obligations exist in relation to enemy combatants? In this context, traditional laws of war set forth a bright-line rule: combatants, as well as civilians, that directly participate in hostilities could be attacked and killed, with no need to assess their individual threat. The 'necessity' of their targeting was presumed, unless they were *hors de combat*, meaning that they have surrendered, been captured or been injured.[157] In accordance with the bright-line rule, the laws of war, as traditionally understood, do not require attackers to grant enemy

---

[154] See, e.g., K. Kagan, *The Eye of Command* (University of Michigan Press, 2006), 176 (discussing Clausewitz).

[155] Note, however, that Corn makes this claim in support of AWS, by arguing that even human soldiers, in essence, are types of autonomous weapons systems. Corn, 'Autonomous weapons systems: managing the inevitability of "taking the man out of the loop"', Chapter 10 in this volume.

[156] For an overview, see E. van Sliedregt, *Individual Criminal Responsibility in International Law* (Oxford University Press, 2012), 287–306. Z. Bohrer, 'The superior orders defense: a principal-agent analysis', *Georgia Journal of International and Comparative Law*, 41 (2012), 1–74.

[157] Lieber Code, Article 15: 'Military necessity admits of all direct destruction of life or limb of armed enemies'; G. Blum, 'The dispensable lives of soldiers', *Journal of Legal Analysis*, 2 (2010), 115–70, 123–6.

combatants the chance to surrender prior to staging the attack. As opposed to law enforcement actions, under the hostilities paradigm, the assumption is that enemy troops represent a threat, and, thus, it is presumed that they have not surrendered, absent a clear expression to that effect.[158] Indeed, this remains the prevailing view.

However, recent years have seen an increasingly vibrant debate, challenging the enduring validity of this bright-line rule. Generally, the debate has 'migrated' from the question of targeted killings and, specifically, the duty to arrest, if possible, civilians directly participating in hostilities[159] to encompass also the rights of soldiers in international armed conflicts – whether through a reinterpretation of the concept of military necessity[160] or by an expansive understanding of the notion of *hors de combat*.[161] Whatever the basis for putative obligations to prefer capture of enemy combatants, under some circumstances, it seems that their underlying assumption is that there are diagonal obligations between a state and enemy combatants *qua* individuals and that such obligations might extend to scenarios beyond traditional scenarios of *hors de combat* (such as incapacitation or capture). Although these obligations have not yet crystallized as widely accepted *lex lata* – and, additionally, it is clear that even if only for practical reasons, they are much weaker than the obligations a state might owe to the enemy's civilians[162] – the discourse that requires that states parties consider the individuality of enemy combatants opens the door also for administrative law reasoning in this context, at least as *lex ferenda*.

This would mean that the problem of AWS and pre-bound discretion can also arise when civilians are not at all endangered by their

---

[158] See J. M. Henckaerts and L. Doswald-Beck, *Customary International Humanitarian Law*, vol. 1 (Cambridge University Press, 2005), Rule 47, 164.

[159] See Melzer, *Interpretive Guidance*, part IX; *Public Committee* v. *Israel*, para. 40; but see W. Hays Parks, 'Part IX of the ICRC "Direct participation in hostilities" study: no mandate, no expertise, and legally incorrect', *NYU Journal of International Law and Politics*, 42 (2010), 769–830, 783–5.

[160] See, e.g., Blum, 'Dispensable lives of soldiers'.

[161] R. Goodman, 'The power to kill or capture enemy combatants', *European Journal of International Law*, 24 (2013), 819–53; but see M. N. Schmitt, 'Wound, capture or kill: a reply to Ryan Goodman's "The power to kill or capture enemy combatants"', *European Journal of International Law*, 24 (2013), 855–61; J. D. Ohlin, 'The duty to capture', *Minnesota Law Review*, 97 (2013), 1268–1342.

[162] See, e.g., J. McMahan, 'Gaza: is Israel fighting a just war in Gaza', *Prospect* (5 August 2014), available at www.prospectmagazine.co.uk/philosophy/gaza-is-israel-and-hamass-conflict-a-just-war (arguing that at large, obligations towards civilians are more demanding than obligations towards soldiers).

deployment. This realization allows us to assess the compelling argument presented by Schmitt and Thurnher, that even if AWS should not be deployed where civilians are put at risk, this in itself should not result in their total ban. As they argue, this is because, just like any other weapon, the valid question, when considering the legal banning of AWS, is whether their deployment would be illegal in all circumstances. As Schmitt and Thurnher point out, deploying AWS in battlefield scenarios where only combatants are present, cannot be per se unlawful.[163] However, as the debate on kill or capture demonstrates, it seems that targeting combatants also might require some discretion.

Diagonal state–combatant obligations might have implications in other contexts beyond the problem of discretion. For instance, they can urge us to reconsider the seemingly well-established notion of 'surrender' as consisting not only of a duty to afford quarter once a combatant has clearly surrendered but also, perhaps, of an obligation to leave open, or at least not to actively narrow down, the option to surrender. An illuminating analogy through which we can better understand this obligation is through the idea that those affected by administrative decisions must be given the opportunity to be heard.[164] Of course, translating the right to be heard to the battlefield is not straightforward – it cannot be understood in the exact manner as the same obligation during peace. However, some parallels can still be made. For instance, the well-established prohibition on ordering that no quarter will be given[165] is essentially a duty to leave open – at least passively – the option of surrender, when clearly expressed. The option of surrender is thus akin to an open window for a primitive type of hearing: the surrendering combatant is letting the other side know that he/she has chosen the right to life over the right to participate in hostilities,[166] and, therefore, there are no longer grounds to exercise executive power against him/her.

Taking into account the objectives of IHL, it is safe to assume that increasing opportunities to surrender is a desired social good. This is so not only due to the individual human rights of troops but also because maximizing the option to surrender minimizes the adversary's motivation to 'fight to the last drop'. The question thus arises whether AWS widen or narrow the window in which surrender is feasible. Importantly,

---

[163] Schmitt and Thurnher, "'Out of the loop'", 249–50.

[164] Benvenisti, 'Sovereigns as trustees', 318.

[165] Henckaerts and Doswald-Beck, *Customary International Humanitarian Law*, Rule 46, 161–3 (detailing the development of the principle).

[166] See Additional Protocol I, Article 43(2).

this dilemma arises not only when AWS are deployed in the vicinity of civilians but also in scenarios where civilians are not present at all.

It goes without saying that surrender is not always viable; it requires some physical proximity and awareness of the enemy's presence.[167] Thus, the obligation to allow surrender can by no means be an absolute positive duty under IHL – as such a demand will virtually replace the doctrine of targeting under the hostilities paradigm, with the use of force continuum entrenched in IHRL. However, bearing in mind the human rights of combatants, it is still worthwhile to consider the effect of technological advancements on the feasibility of the option to surrender. These have not been entirely linear. Interestingly, for centuries, the battlefield scenarios in which surrender has remained a viable possibility have decreased in line with the development of technology. For instance, it was nearly always possible to surrender in a swordfight; it became harder to do so when fire-power was introduced and it has become virtually impossible in the era of ballistic weapons and air warfare, at least in most circumstances.[168] However, at least in some situations, the advent of smart technology can potentially reverse this trend, since weapons (and delivery platforms) can be controlled almost until final impact.[169]

Assuming that AWS would be deployed as a replacement for ground forces, the question arises whether they will increase or decrease surrender opportunities. Indeed, when a human is in control of the final decision to pull the trigger, there is a minimal time gap between discharging the weapon and impact; during this gap, of course, surrender is impossible. However, in the time gap between such decisions, there is (in theory) ample opportunity to surrender – even during the assault stage. Conversely, AWS – at least as currently envisioned – might narrow the 'surrender window' available to the adversary.[170] 'Swarm technology' is

---

[167] See Henckaerts and Doswald-Beck, *Customary International Humanitarian Law*, Rule 47, 168.

[168] Compare D. Leigh, 'Iraq war logs: Apache crew killed insurgents who tried to surrender', *The Guardian* (22 October 2010), available at www.theguardian.com/world/2010/oct/22/iraq-war-logs-apache-insurgents-surrender.

[169] A famous example is a 1991 incident where Iraqi soldiers surrendered to an American drone. See P. W. Singer, 'Military robots and the laws of war', *The New Atlantis* (Winter 2009), 25–45, 28.

[170] Of course, it is theoretically possible that technology will be developed that does not narrow the window of surrender. However, we find this unlikely, since one of the key interests behind states' development of such weapons has to do with their quickness. In other words, narrowing the enemy's options on the temporal level is one of the key rationales for their development to begin with. See Krishnan, *Killer Robots*, 40–1.

a prime example. In swarm attacks, large numbers of small, autonomous systems will engage the enemy, rapidly overwhelming it.[171] For example, as recently revealed by Lieutenant General Benny Gantz, Israel's former chief of general staff, the Israeli Defence Force aims to deploy, in the future, 'swarms of autonomous vehicles, robots and drones, at sea and maybe even land, interconnected, relying on micro and nano-technology'.[172] Thus, if more and more manoeuvres are be conducted through swarm attacks, it seems that the surrender window will be narrowed.

Indeed, as mentioned earlier, the shrinking sphere of surrender is a constant corollary of technological developments. Nonetheless, the novelty of AWS, in this context, lies in a combination of three considerations: first, in contrast, say, to ballistic missiles (and perhaps a bit like landmines), AWS create a wider temporal gap between deployment and the use of lethal force – the same gap in which surrender is theoretically possible. Thus, they might further reduce the temporal window for surrender. Second, the lightning quickness of such weapons, when engaging, will not only challenge human supervision but will also all but incapacitate the adversary's possibility to submit. Third, AWS represent a technological leap. An administrative law perception of warfare implies that increased power spawns increased obligations. For instance, a state that possesses such advanced systems can be expected, by virtue of its power, not to further reduce the sphere of possible surrender, when technology (such as the availability of semi-autonomous weapons) allows otherwise.

Conclusion

The debate on AWS will surely intensify in the near future in line with the advancement in technology. This chapter has sought to demonstrate that given the legal requirement to exercise discretion in targeting decisions, an analysis of the deployment of such weapons through the prism of administrative law might advance our understanding of the main challenges posed by such weapons. When looking at modern warfare as an executive action, notions of administrative law require that it would

Furthermore, even if autonomous weapons are somehow designed so as to not narrow the window of surrender, we will still run into the problem of pre-bound discretion.

[171]   Schmitt and Thurnher, "'Out of the loop'", 240.

[172]   Address at BESA Center, 9 October 2013, available at http://besacenter.org/new-at-the-besa-center/idf-chief-staff-benny-gantz-speaks-besa-center/.

be conducted while exercising constant discretion. As we have demonstrated, AWS, at least when understood as being technically autonomous, cannot exercise such discretion in the 'true' sense.

While the former is definitely true in cases where civilians might be at risk from such weapons, we have also advanced a preliminary argument regarding the deployment of AWS against combatants. As we claim, in line with the increasing calls to reconsider the traditional understanding of military necessity in relation to targeting combatants, the problem of discretion can also arise in this context. Furthermore, AWS might also narrow the window of surrender, which we identify as a problematic outcome, at least in terms of *de lege ferenda*.

12

Autonomy and uncertainty: increasingly autonomous weapons systems and the international legal regulation of risk

NEHAL BHUTA AND STAVROS-EVDOKIMOS PANTAZOPOULOS

Uncertainty and its problems

The debate concerning the law, ethics and policy of autonomous weapons systems (AWS) remains at an early stage, but one of the consistent emergent themes is that of uncertainty. Uncertainty presents itself as a problem in several different registers: first, there is the conceptual uncertainty surrounding how to define and debate the nature of autonomy in AWS. Contributions to this volume from roboticists,[1] sociologists of science[2] and philosophers of science[3] demonstrate that within and

---

[1] See, e.g., the chapters by Noel Sharkey and by Giovanni Sartor and Andrea Omicini in this volume. In each case, a concept of autonomy cannot be asserted stipulatively as reflecting some kind of self-evident technical consensus but must be specified and argued for as the preferred way to conceive of autonomy. N. Sharkey, 'Staying in the loop: human supervisory control of weapons', Chapter 2 in this volume. G. Sartor and A. Omicini, 'The autonomy of technological systems and responsibilities for their use', Chapter 3 in this volume.

[2] See, e.g., the chapter by Lucy Suchman and Jutta Weber in this volume, where the authors document the way in which the concept of autonomy has changed within robotics and computer science, generally as a function of the theoretical framework (cybernetics, symbol processing, behaviour-based robotics) dominant within a given decade. Strikingly, the concept of autonomy is shown to be internal to the theoretical self-definition of the discipline and its goals. L. Suchman and J. Weber, 'Human–machine autonomies', Chapter 4 in this volume.

[3] See Guglielmo Tamburrini's chapter in this volume, in which he asserts that autonomy in robotics can only be understood as task autonomy (t-autonomy) and that task autonomy is the property of a system, which is autonomous to the extent that it can complete a task independently of the intervention or control of some other system. On this definition, the distinction between automation and autonomy is simply one of degree as between the extent of the independence of a system from another system in the performance of tasks (t_n). G. Tamburrini, 'On banning autonomous weapons systems: from deontological to wide consequentialist reasons', Chapter 6 in this volume.

without the field of computer science, no stable consensus exists concerning the meaning of autonomy or of autonomy in weapons systems.
Indeed, a review of definitions invoked during a recent expert meeting
convened by states parties to the Convention on Certain Conventional
Weapons[4] shows substantially different definitions in use among military
experts, computer scientists and international humanitarian lawyers.

At stake in the debate over definitions are regulatory preoccupations
and negotiating postures over a potential pre-emptive ban. A weapons
system capable of identifying, tracking and firing on a target without
human intervention, and in a manner consistent with the humanitarian
law obligations of precaution, proportionality and distinction, is a fantastic
ideal type. Defining AWS in such a way truncates the regulatory issues to
a simple question of whether such a system is somehow inconsistent with
human dignity – a question about which states, ethicists and lawyers can be
expected to reasonably disagree. However, the definition formulated in this
manner also begs important legal questions in respect of the design,
development and deployment of AWS. Defining autonomous weapons
in terms of this pure type reduces almost all questions of legality to
questions of technological capacity, to which a humanitarian lawyer's
response can only be: 'If what the programmers and engineers claim is
true, then ... '[5] The temporally prior question of whether international law
generally, and international humanitarian law (IHL) in particular, prescribes any standards or processes that should be applied to the design,
testing, verification and authorization of the use of AWS is not addressed.
Yet these *ex ante* considerations are urgently in need of legal analysis and
may prove to generate deeper legal problems.

This brings us to the second register of uncertainty that characterizes
the current debate about AWS – a temporal uncertainty concerning the

[4] Meeting of Experts on Lethal Autonomous Weapons Systems, 13–17 April 2015, meeting
record available at www.unog.ch/80256EE600585943/(httpPages)/6CE049BE22EC
75A2C1257C8D00513E26?OpenDocument. Convention on Prohibitions or Restrictions on
the Use of Certain Conventional Weapons Which May Be Deemed to Be Excessively Injurious
or to Have Indiscriminate Effects 1990, 19 UNTS 1823.

[5] Indeed, this has largely been the response of humanitarian law experts, who while under-
standably insisting on the continued application and completeness of the existing framework of international humanitarian law, have essentially relegated themselves to the role of
handmaidens of technology. Yet, as Johnson observes, 'there is a lot more than technological feasibility involved in shaping future technologies ... [and] ... the development of
artificial agent technologies will be affected by a variety of human actors and actor groups
with varying interests, values, and capacities to influence development'. D. G. Johnson,
'Technology with no human responsibility?', *Journal of Business Ethics*, 127 (2015),
707, 712.

timeline for the expected development of these systems and the pathways over which 'autonomization' of weapons systems' functioning may be expected to take place. It is accepted that while nothing resembling a 'pure type' of AWS exists or is likely to exist in the near future, the progressive delegation of functions and tasks to computer systems, even as a human operator remains in overall control of the weapons system, is a present-day objective of advanced weapons research.[6] Under these conditions, and in the absence of a dramatic revolution in technology, it seems likely that we will witness the increasing autonomization of weapons systems over the medium-term horizon.[7] Thus, we can expect that old and new technological capacities will be deployed side by side, as the latter are developed and approved for use, and that the point at which we reach a 'tipping point', when certain critical functions and tasks are delegated to computer systems, is fundamentally uncertain from the vantage point of the present. This temporal uncertainty dovetails with our present perplexity about how to define autonomy in weapons systems. As functions and tasks are delegated piecemeal, exactly what constitutes 'human control' over an existing technology integrated into a new technological system may be very difficult to know *ex ante*. It is only as such complex human–machine systems are assembled, tested and used that we may fully and concretely appreciate whether, and to what extent, human judgment and human decision making remain significant variables in the functioning of the system.[8]

---

[6] See, e.g., the call for tenders by the US Department of Defense's Advanced Research Projects Agency, Doc. BAA-14-33, 25 April 2014, available at www.fbo.gov/index?s=opportunity&mode=form&id=2f2733be59230cf2ddaa46498fe5765a&tab=core&_cview=1. The call seeks proposals from private sector technology developers that would design and develop a platform enabling one human operator to operate four or more armed drones at the same time, with the drones performing the following functions autonomously: fuse data from multiple sources and multiple data types; develop a common decision-making and world-modelling framework that is robust to poor communications and random attrition among the team members; dynamically compose teams or sub-teams to achieve mission objectives; improve team performance in range, endurance, navigation, communication and all steps of a strike mission (find, fix, track, target, engage and assess); enable mission execution independently of space or other non-organic assets; accommodate large uncertainty and dynamic changes.

[7] See the astute working paper issued by the United Nations Institute for Disarmament Research, 'Framing discussions on the weaponization of increasingly autonomous technologies', working paper (2014), available at www.unidir.org/files/publications/pdfs/framing-discussions-on-the-weaponization-of-increasingly-autonomous-technologies-en-606.pdf.

[8] M. L. Cummings, 'The human role in autonomous weapon design and deployment', undated paper, available at www.law.upenn.edu/live/files/3884-cummings-the-human-role-in-autonomous-weapons.

The final register of uncertainty that appears in the debate is that of the unpredictability and uncertainty of how robotic and computer systems, charged with performing multiple, increasingly complex, and potentially lethal tasks, will behave in unstructured and rapidly changing environments.[9] This behavioural uncertainty is highlighted by the contribution of Guglielmo Tamburrini to this volume, in which he observes that under current technological constraints, robot behaviour is predictable only under strong closed-world presumptions and careful control of the external environment in which the robot is to be deployed. Neither of these conditions will hold in a conflict scenario, and the result is likely to be severe epistemic uncertainty about the boundary conditions under which the robotic system could be capable of satisfying the IHL obligations of distinction, proportionality and precaution.

Assuming even significant improvements in computer learning and in ensuring predictable responses to unpredictable environments, the fundamental problem raised by behavioural uncertainty is one of regulatory standard setting rather than technical progress: what level of unpredictability and risk of non-IHL-compliant behaviour is appropriate and lawful? How are such risks to be evaluated and measured? By what processes should benchmarks be set and considered internationally acceptable? How can compliance be verified and monitored? Risk and unpredictability cannot per se be eliminated, especially in operating environments that are by their nature very uncertain. However, the *management* of risk rather than its elimination is the basic problem of regulation in our contemporary risk society and depends on human action not technological determination:

> Artificial agents can be designed so that no human can understand or control what they do, or they can be designed so that they are transparent and well within human control or they can be designed so that certain aspects or levels of the machine behaviour are in human control and others are not. Which way they are designed depends on the humans involved in their development and acceptance.

[9] On the one hand, the effect of a given command cannot be predicted with definite certainty since the interactions between parts of large programs may lead to unforeseen results. On the other hand, this type of uncertainty may prove beneficial as AWS may learn from their own experience and thus respond positively to newly confronted situations, which could have not been predicted by the designer. But even in the latter scenario, uncertainty holds its distinguishing role, as it is difficult to prognosticate with reasonable certainty what an AWS will learn on its own. G. E. Marchant *et al.*, 'International governance of autonomous military robots', *Columbia Science and Technology Law Review*, 12 (2011), 272, 284.

In the past people have chosen technologies that have some degree of risk though we have also set up mechanisms to pressure those who make and use these technologies to operate them safely and to take responsibility when something goes wrong and the fault can be traced back to them.[10]

Getting risk regulation right

In light of these dimensions of uncertainty that characterize the problem of AWS, it is necessary to approach the problem from a regulatory perspective that aims, ultimately, to establish the right incentives for states to avoid setting the wrong benchmarks for risk management in the development, design and deployment of increasingly autonomous technology in weapons systems. To the extent that states acting within security dilemmas[11] face competitive pressures to develop such technology, the hazard is that each state will unilaterally determine when a given system is 'safe enough' in light of their own domestic regulatory frameworks and under the pressure of their own perception of the security threats they must meet and in respect of which the autonomous technology is deemed necessary.

The result will not only be wide divergences in acceptable levels of risk of non-IHL-compliant behaviour but also, potentially, even downward pressure on the processes of testing and verification. Of course, one might expect that states' military forces would be strongly disincentivized to authorize and field a weapons system that, through malfunction or unpredicted behaviours, may pose a risk of harm to its own soldiers or a reputational risk to the perception of its compliance with humanitarian law.[12] However, these expectations would not necessarily hold if – as countenanced by Pablo Kalmanovitz in his chapter and by Eliav Lieblich and Eyal Benvenisti in theirs – the weapons systems were used far from the states' own soldiers and citizens in asymmetric warfare

---

[10] Johnson, 'Technology with no human responsibility?', 714. In a similar vein, it has been argued that '[t]he difference between the type of risks created by high technology and those created by nature – such as plagues or natural disasters – lies in the human *decision* to accept or not to accept the risk'. J. Barboza, *The Environment, Risk and Liability in International Law* (The Hague: Martinus Nijhoff, 2010), 9 (emphasis in original).

[11] See R. Jervis, 'Cooperation under the security dilemma', *World Politics*, 30 (1978), 167.

[12] In his contribution to this volume, Geoffrey S. Corn argues that commanders would be loath to field a weapons system the behaviour of which is not sufficiently predictable. At the same time, he notes that commanders may well come under pressure to field the system nonetheless. See G. S. Corn, 'Autonomous weapons systems: managing the inevitability of "taking the man out of the loop"', Chapter 10 in this volume.

environments.[13] Indeed, we might expect extensive use of AWS precisely in such environments, where the relatively few advanced states that have the technology wish to achieve strategic security objectives without the political risk of deploying soldiers and while maximizing human resource efficiencies. In these environments, the risks of malfunction or non-IHL-compliant behaviour are shifted to foreign civilians, while deploying states could adopt a 'test as we go' approach in order to meet resource constraints and enable faster deployment of the technology.[14] States by no means have the right incentives to be risk averse concerning the hazards posed by AWS to foreign civilians in weaker, poorer states.

Behavioural uncertainty also makes individual accountability harder. If a commander reasonably relies upon the technical advice provided by the weapon's manufacturer, and by the relevant military officials who have reviewed that information and authorized the deployment of the weapon, it is difficult to imagine how the commander could bear individual criminal responsibility should the weapons system ultimately malfunction or function in a non-IHL-compliant manner (and assuming that the commander did not depart from the instructions for the proper use of the system provided by the manufacturer and military officials). It seems equally difficult to imagine that procuring officials, who reasonably rely upon assurances and technical advice given by the weapons developer, could be held liable either in tort or under criminal law for negligence. As Neha Jain points out in her chapter in this volume, individual criminal liability for recklessness or negligence requires subjective awareness of the kind or degree of risk of criminal behaviour by the weapons system, or at least awareness of a substantial and unjustifiable risk of harm from the weapons system's conduct and a failure to consider this risk when deploying the weapons system.[15]

To avoid this problem of a responsibility gap through the diffusion of specialized technical knowledge across different actors standing behind the development and deployment of the AWS (in which each actor pleads reliance upon the specialized knowledge of the actor further up in the process), relevant regulatory standards need to be information-forcing – requiring both the disclosure of information about the levels and nature

---

[13] P. Kalmanovitz, 'Judgment, liability and the risks of riskless warfare', Chapter 7 in this volume. E. Lieblich and E. Benvenisti, 'The obligation to exercise discretion in warfare: why autonomous weapons systems are unlawful', Chapter 11 in this volume.

[14] See Kalmanovitz, 'Judgment, liability and the risks of riskless warfare'.

[15] N. Jain, 'Autonomous weapons systems: new frameworks for individual responsibility', Chapter 13 in this volume.

of risks of non-compliant behaviour and the proactive identification and seeking out of information about such risks. This information must also be sufficiently internalized and comprehended by relevant actors, such that no actor can plausibly claim that she or he did not know, or could not have known, about such risks as are discernible through access to the information.

From international environmental law to Article 36 and beyond

In this chapter, we argue that a plausible and relevant set of international legal principles for addressing these problems of uncertainty derive from international environmental law. This is not surprising because the risks of environmental harm due to technological development generate a structurally similar problematic to the risks of IHL violations due to the unpredictable behaviour of AWS. In each case, *ex ante* scientific uncertainty makes it difficult to know whether the harm that a given activity or technology may cause necessarily violates an existing legal norm or whether the scale of the potential harm necessarily outweighs the potential benefits of the technology.[16] International environmental law (IEL) has developed a body of learning whereby special obligations of care – and stricter burdens of liability – are placed on states engaged in activities that may have highly uncertain and potentially damaging consequences to humans and the environment. The relevant IEL rules and principles are drawn from the International Law Commission's (ILC) Draft Articles on Prevention of Transboundary Harm from Hazardous Activities (Draft Articles)[17] and from the ILC's Draft Principles on the Allocation of Loss in the Case of Transboundary Harm Arising out of Hazardous Activities.[18] The underlying rationale that justifies the focus on these two instruments is that there is sufficient similarity between the activities of AWS and the activities within the scope of the ILC

[16] G. Hafner and I. Buffard, 'Obligations of prevention and the precautionary principle' in J. Crawford, A. Pellet and S. Olleson (eds.), *The Law of International Responsibility* (Oxford University Press, 2010), 521–37, 521–5.
[17] See International Law Commission (ILC), Draft Articles on Prevention of Transboundary Harm from Hazardous Activities, with Commentaries (ILC Draft Articles), Doc. A/CN.4/SER.A/2001/Add.1 (part 2), reprinted in 'Report of the Commission to the General Assembly on the work of its fifty-third session', *Yearbook of the International Law Commission*, 2 (2001) 146.
[18] ILC, Draft Principles on the Allocation of Loss in the Case of Transboundary Harm Arising Out of Hazardous Activities, with Commentaries, Doc. A/CN.4/SER.A/2006/Add.1 (Part 2), reprinted in 'Report of the Commission to the General Assembly on the work of its fifty-eighth session', *Yearbook of the International Law Commission*, 2 (2006), 106.

instruments for two reasons: (i) both kinds of activities are not prohibited under international law (for our purposes, we have assumed that the use of AWS are not *a priori* unlawful), even though they entail risk of harm through their physical consequences, and (ii) the occurrence of harm is deemed significant.

We must acknowledge at the outset that this is an analogy, not a claim that international environmental law applies to weapons development as a matter of *lex lata* or even *de lege ferenda*. Rather, we argue that the critical problems of uncertainty that characterize the development and deployment of AWS can be productively addressed through principles that are already well recognized in international law in relation to the problem of transboundary harm from hazardous activities – that is, we ought to think about AWS development in a manner analogous to the way we think in international law about the regulation of the risk of environmental harm due to hazardous industrial-technological change. Developing and deploying an AWS, it seems to us, can be reasonably understood as being closely analogous to an 'ultra-hazardous' or hazardous activity that has the potential to generate considerable harm outside the borders of the developing state.

Under the international environmental law framework, states engaged in an activity the consequences of which entail a risk of causing significant transboundary harm may be responsible even if the activity is not in itself unlawful.[19] The responsibility arises from the notion that states are under an obligation to effectively manage risks that can cause significant harm to other states and that the duty to effectively manage risks amounts to an obligation of due diligence in the identification, comprehension and minimization of the risk of harm. The obligation of due diligence is not an absolute obligation to prevent the harm (an obligation of result)[20]

---

[19] *Ibid.*

[20] 'A true obligation of prevention is not breached unless the apprehended event occurs, whereas an obligation of due diligence would be breached by a failure to exercise due diligence, even if the apprehended result did not (or not yet) occur. Thus obligations of due diligence are relative, not absolute ... States can assume obligations to prevent damage to particular persons or to the territory of other states, and it may be that on the proper interpretation of the particular obligation it is the occurrence of the damage which triggers responsibility, rather than the failure to take steps to prevent it. If responsibility is engaged by the failure to act in and of itself, regardless of the outcome, then the obligation is better categorized as an obligation of due diligence. But not all obligations directed towards preventing an event from occurring are of this kind.' J. Crawford, *State Responsibility: The General Part* (Cambridge University Press, 2013), 227–30.

but, rather, a continuing obligation of conduct under which a state engaged in the hazardous activity must – in proportion to the nature and magnitude of the risk posed by the activity – adopt and implement domestic measures that prevent the harm or at least minimize the risk thereof.[21] Critically, the international environmental law framework is premised on a kind of 'active vigilance' about the nature of the risk and implies a duty to constantly stay abreast of scientific developments and technological change in order to properly understand the risk and continuously minimize it.[22] Parochial domestic standards to this end may well be insufficient, depending on the scientific state of the art and the information that is shared between states with the objective of managing such risks. The ILC's commentary to its Draft Articles[23] observes that:

> (10) due diligence is manifested in reasonable efforts by a State to inform itself of factual and legal components that relate foreseeably to a contemplated procedure and to take appropriate measures, in timely fashion, to address them. Thus, States are under an obligation to take unilateral measures ... [including] ... formulating policies designed to prevent [the harm] or to minimize the risk thereof and, secondly, implementing those policies. Such policies are expressed in legislation and administrative regulations and implemented through various enforcement mechanisms.
>
> (11) The standard of due diligence against which the conduct of the State of origin should be examined is that which is generally considered to be appropriate and proportional to the degree of risk of transboundary harm in the particular instance. For example, activities which may be considered ultrahazardous require a much higher standard of care in designing policies and a much higher degree of vigour on the part of the State to enforce them. Issues such as the size of the operation; its location, special climate conditions, materials used in the activity, and whether the conclusions drawn from the application of these factors in a specific case are reasonable, are among the factors to be considered in determining the due diligence requirement in each instance. What would be considered a reasonable standard of care or due diligence may change with time; what might be considered an appropriate and reasonable procedure, standard or rule at one point in time may not be considered as such at some point in

---

[21] ILC Draft Articles, 154 (commentary).   [22] *Ibid.*

[23] The Draft Articles are widely considered codification of customary international law rather than progressive development. Birnie, Boyle and Redgwell observe: 'The 2001 Articles on Transboundary Harm essentially codify existing obligations of environmental impact assessment, notification, consultation, monitoring, prevention, and diligent control of activities likely to cause transboundary harm. These articles are securely based in existing precedents.' P. Birnie, A. Boyle and C. Redgwell, *International Law and the Environment*, 3rd edn (Oxford University Press, 2009), 141.

the future. Hence, due diligence in ensuring safety requires a State to keep abreast of technological changes and scientific developments.[24]

Other obligations of conduct related to the due diligence obligation include an obligation to undertake a risk assessment, an obligation to notify potentially affected states of the risks generated by the activity and an obligation to undertake consultations and information sharing about how to manage the risk with potentially affected states. Where the information concerning the risk includes information vital to the national security of a state or industrial secrets, such data and information may be withheld provided the state undertaking the risky activity continues to share as much information as it is able concerning the nature of the risk and in good faith.[25]

Needless to say, there can be no direct transposition of these principles into the realm of AWS development. Nonetheless, our contention is that principles of this type – obligations of due diligence, risk assessment, information sharing, monitoring and, ultimately, technical standard setting for the processes of verification, testing and evaluation – ought to be developed through a multilateral, multi-stakeholder process that aims at risk control and the harmonization of standards and processes for risk management. Existing technical standards for industrial robots, developed by the International Organization for Standardization (ISO), emphasize principles akin to those of due diligence in international environmental law: risk assessment to identify dangers and estimate risk; safe design to reduce risk; protective measures to manage risks that cannot be eliminated and user information to enable safe use.[26] However, as Tamburrini[27] and others note, industrial robotics is premised on highly controlled environments in which uncertainty is minimized or eliminated entirely. The added challenge posed by 'next generation' robotics, including autonomous weapons, is the creation and maintenance of an effective framework for the management of 'open-textured risk':

> For industrial robots, safety and reliability engineering decisions are guided by a combination of pre-safety (with a heavy emphasis on risk assessment) and post-safety regulations (focused on responsibility

---

[24] ILC Draft Articles, 154 (commentary).

[25] *Ibid.*, Articles 7, 8, 9, 12 and 14 and commentaries.

[26] International Standard ISO 10218-1, *Robots and Robotic Devices: Safety Requirements for Industrial Robots*, 2nd edn, 1 July 2011.

[27] Tamburrini, 'On banning autonomous weapons systems'.

distribution). Pre-safety rules include safeguards regarding the use and maintenance of robot systems from the design stage (e.g., hazard identification, risk assessment) to the training of robot controllers. In addition to describing basic hazards associated with robots, ISO rules are aimed at eliminating or adequately reducing risks associated with identified hazards . . .

Designed and constructed according to very specific standards, industrial robots are limited to performing tasks that can be reduced to their corresponding mechanisms – in other words, they cannot alter their mechanisms to meet the needs of changing environments. Therefore, the primary purpose for performing industrial robot risk assessments is to design mechanisms that match pre-approved safety levels. Complex Next Generation Robots, motions, multiobject interactions, and responses to shifts in environments resulting from complex interactions with humans cannot be reduced to simple performance parameters. Next Generation Robots and future Human-Based Intelligence designers and manufacturers must instead deal with unpredictable hazards associated with the legal concepts of core meaning and open texture risk.

The inherent unpredictability of unstructured environments makes it virtually impossible that we will ever see a fail-safe mechanism that allows autonomous robots to solve all open-texture problems. Consequently, Next Generation Robots safety regulations will require a mix of pre-safety and post-safety mechanisms.[28]

Technical standards for robotic safety formulated by the ISO in respect of personal care robots[29] reflect in part this shift from industrial robotics' concern for defining and controlling risk through control of the robot's operating environment to one in which the relevant risks to be assessed include 'uncertainty of autonomous decisions made by the robot and possible hazards from wrong decisions', 'unexpected movements' from either the robot or from humans and animals in the robot's environment, 'unexpected travel surfaces and environmental conditions' and risks arising from 'human anatomy and its variability' (where the robot is physically assisting a disabled human).[30] The regulatory approach mandated by the ISO towards such risks requires, first, an assessment of the risks generated through possible wrong decisions and incorrect actions by the robot and, second, a differentiation between acceptable and unacceptable risks. For example, a mobile servant robot may make an

---

[28] Y.-H. Weng, C.-H. Chen and C.-T. Sun, 'Toward the human-robot co-existence society: on safety intelligence for next generation robots', *International Journal of Social Robotics*, 1 (2009), 267, 276–7.

[29] International Standard ISO 13482, *Robots and Robotic Devices: Safety Requirements for Personal Care Robots*, 1st edn, 1 February 2014.

[30] *Ibid.*, 9.

incorrect decision and serve coffee rather than water in a cup – this may be an acceptable risk (provided the robot warns the consumer that the drink is hot!). On the other hand, an incorrect decision may lead the robot to serve water in a broken glass. This decision creates an unacceptable risk of serious harm. Both kinds of risks are generated by the behavioural uncertainty derived from the autonomous decisions and actions of the robot.

In an industrial environment, the solution would be to rigidly constrain the environment by eliminating choices and or requiring human intervention in the face of uncertainty. In the case of robots that are intended to respond to uncertain environments, the ISO standards propose an approach that tries to quantify the certainty of a correct decision,[31] followed by measures to reduce 'high uncertainty outcomes'. Where the outcomes of a decision remain acceptably uncertain, even after alternative approaches and additional information are integrated, then the ISO standard requires that 'external assistance shall be sought [by the robot]' and or 'a protective stop shall be initiated'.[32] The ISO standard also requires that users be provided with information in which instructions are given on how to prevent harm due to wrong actions or decisions and in which the limits of use exclude 'situations in which decisions cause an unacceptable risk of any harm, taking into account foreseeable misuse'.[33]

Obviously, an AWS is designed to harm and kill, not to care for an elderly or disabled person.[34] However, the design principles developed for personal care robots – and which we suggest are also consistent with the kinds of due diligence obligation one might expect from the application of international environmental law principles governing hazardous and ultra-hazardous activity – seem applicable *mutatis mutandis* insofar as they require: a differentiation between acceptable and unacceptable risks; a probabilistic assessment of the chances of incorrect decisions leading to unacceptable risks and measures to either reduce the chances of incorrect decisions to acceptable levels or to introduce fail-safes or timely human input where uncertainty concerning incorrect decisions cannot be adequately constrained. What should be noted is that for each of these principles, substantive content must be given to each of the key

---

[31] 'Identification algorithms shall be designed in a way that the probability of a certain decision being correct . . . is calculated and can be monitored.' *Ibid.*, 33, para. 5.12.3(b).

[32] *Ibid.* [33] *Ibid.*, para. 5.12.4.

[34] Indeed, the ISO standards state clearly that they are not intended to apply to 'military or public force application robots'. *Ibid.*, 1.

value terms as they might apply to AWS functioning: what qualifies as an incorrect decision; what is an unacceptable risk; what is an unacceptable probability of an incorrect decision and what measures are appropriate to constrain uncertain outcomes and incorrect decisions leading to unacceptable risks?[35]

In the case of personal care robots, the ISO process presumes that an expert technical consensus is in principle possible at the national and international levels, leading to regulatory harmonization concerning mechanisms, processes and standards that satisfy the ISO-mandated design requirements. And, indeed, in the case of such robots, with extensive civilian commercial uses and export markets, incentives for regulatory harmonization and compliance with transparent design standards may be significant. But as noted earlier, we consider that in the circumstances of autonomous weapons development, there may be considerable divergence on how such standards and design values are defined and implemented across states and that such differences engender a distinctive hazard in the case of autonomous machines with the capacity to apply lethal force. One of the critical challenges is to establish mechanisms through which common design standards for risk assessment, risk control and management, testing and verification, and safe-use information can be developed for AWS.

The existing legal framework under which these kinds of parameters could be considered on a state-by-state basis is Article 36 of Additional Protocol I to the Geneva Conventions (Additional Protocol I).[36] Article 36 requires that, 'in the study, development, acquisition or adoption of a new weapon, means or method of warfare', the high contracting parties to Additional Protocol I 'determine whether its employment would, in some or all circumstances, be prohibited by this Protocol or by any other rule of international law applicable to the High Contracting Party'. The obligation imposed by Article 36 is generally considered to imply an obligation of conduct, under which a high contracting party must 'establish internal procedures for the purpose of elucidating the issue of

---

[35] A personal care robot that shuts down awaiting further instructions every time it encounters uncertainty in its decision making that could lead to an incorrect decision may well still be a very functional and useful robot. But an AWS that aborts its mission or switches to 'safety mode' in every such situation may be a largely ineffective weapon, and it is doubtful that a state would make significant resource investments in designing a system that is so risk averse.

[36] Protocol Additional to the Geneva Conventions of 12 August 1949, and Relating to the Protection of Victims of International Armed Conflicts (Additional Protocol I) 1977, 1125 UNTS 3, Article 36.

legality, and the other Contracting Parties can ask to be informed on this point [viz. on the nature of the procedures]'.[37]

The procedure must evaluate whether the normal expected use of the weapon would violate the norms of discrimination and proportionality or any other applicable legal rules, and it is temporally 'very broad' in scope. It covers 'all stages of the weapons procurement process, in particular the initial stages of the research phase (i.e. conception, study), the development phase (i.e. development and testing of proto- types) and the acquisition phase (including "off-the-shelf" procurement)'.[38] Article 36 does not mandate any particular kind of procedure nor any particular methodology of review, and there is no obligation to disclose the results of the review.[39] The agency responsible for the review is at the discretion of states, although the International Committee of the Red Cross (ICRC) urges independent administrative mechanisms that can be made accountable to the Ministry of Defence or its equivalent and that can involve experts from all necessary disciplines.[40] A handful of states have disclosed their weapons review procedures.[41] The terms of Article 36 cannot be said to reflect customary international law, but, arguably, the requirement to evaluate *ex ante* whether a new weapon or means and method of warfare is illegal flows logically from 'the truism that States are prohibited from using illegal weapons, means and methods of warfare'.[42]

Article 36 is thus sparse in its express content and, indeed, even in its implied content. Nonetheless, it provides an existing, binding, legal *chapeau* under which all high contracting parties are obliged to develop some kind of procedure through which to meaningfully and effectively review new weapons in development. At the time of writing, it remains too early to determine the fate of the demand from some states and international non-governmental organizations for a pre-emptive ban on AWS. In our view, even if the necessary political will crystallized, both the conceptual and temporal dimensions of uncertainty outlined earlier make the complete efficacy of a ban doubtful. One might succeed in

---

[37] J. de Preux, 'Article 36: new weapons' in Y. Sandoz, C. Swinarski and B. Zimmermann (eds.), *Commentary on the Additional Protocols of 8 June 1977 to the Geneva Conventions of 12 August 1949* (Geneva: ICRC, 1987), 424, 428, paras. 1470, 1482.

[38] International Committee of the Red Cross (ICRC), *A Guide to the Legal Review of New Weapons, Means and Methods of Warfare: Measures to Implement Article 36 of Additional Protocol I of 1977*, January 2006, 23.

[39] de Preux, 'Article 36', 424, para. 1470. W. Hays Parks, 'Conventional weapons and weapons reviews', *Yearbook of International Humanitarian Law*, 8 (2005), 55, 135.

[40] ICRC, *A Guide to the Legal Review of New Weapons*, 21. [41] *Ibid.*, 20. [42] *Ibid.*, 4.

prohibiting weapons systems that meet a certain 'ideal-type' of autonomy, but it is not clear whether this will in fact capture the kinds of risks that may emerge with the progressive autonomization of tasks and functions over time as well as those risks (including a responsibility gap) associated with the diminution, rather than elimination, of the human role. Thus, while in no way precluding a ban on weapons systems meeting a certain definition of autonomy, complementary processes for coordination and harmonization of standards for risk assessment, management and control and information disclosure remain necessary.

Amendments to existing humanitarian law and weapons control treaties are possible, but a promising route towards harmonized standard setting could also be more informal administrative mechanisms established within the framework of a meeting of the high contracting parties to Additional Protocol I,[43] which could create a group of governmental experts to develop best practices and models of Article 36 review procedures and standards appropriate to ensuring that AWS can be effectively and meaningfully evaluated and that the necessary precautionary standards are incorporated at all stages of the system's design, development and deployment. The experience of the Nuclear Suppliers Group (NSG) may be instructive in this respect. Arising from an informal meeting of the member states of the Nuclear Non-Proliferation Treaty (NPT) that have the capacity or potential capacity to export dual use nuclear materials, the group over time adopted 'understandings' concerning the meaning of the NPT's vague export control provisions.[44]

These understandings were not formulated as explicit treaty interpretations but, rather, as means of promoting effective export control policies through harmonization and standard setting within the framework of the NPT's prohibition on the export of equipment or material designed or prepared for the processing, use or production of fissionable material. The understandings developed by the NSG relatively quickly became a template for guidelines adopted by a meeting of the NPT member states in the aftermath of India's May 1974 nuclear test, but because the NSG was open to even non-NPT member states (such as France), the understandings had wider normative effects. Daniel Joyner notes that the normative effects of the NSG's standard setting are highly imperfect and depend on the willingness of member states to implement

---

[43] Additional Protocol I, Article 7.

[44] D. H. Joyner, 'The Nuclear Suppliers Group: history and functioning', *International Trade Law and Regulation*, 11 (2005), 33. Treaty on the Non-Proliferation of Nuclear Weapons 1968, 729 UNTS 161.

these standards through domestic regulatory law and policy.[45] It remains very far from a completely effective regime of treaty interpretation and regulatory harmonization. Nonetheless, it has achieved an important function of facilitating cooperation and coordination in the formulation of national law and policy and in the development of multilateral minimum standards. It has also become a facilitator of information sharing among states wishing to contribute to non-proliferation efforts,[46] even where this information pertains to sensitive security-related matters.

Conclusion

The number of states and private corporations with the military research and development capacities and financial resources needed to develop AWS remains limited, perhaps no more than a handful at present. At this early stage of discussion, it is unclear whether these states could reach a common understanding of a shared interest in the appropriate regulation of the design, development and deployment of AWS. However, we have argued that existing principles of international environmental law concerning hazardous and ultra-hazardous activity provide a relevant heuristic framework for such regulation. The risks posed by AWS are diverse, and they demand an approach that adequately identifies and controls the risks arising from behavioural uncertainty and generates information that can be used to better evaluate, manage and prevent the risk of unlawful behaviour. The impetus for scrutiny and reflection that has been generated by anxieties about AWS creates an opportune moment for developing an appropriate mechanism through which fundamental questions concerning acceptable and unacceptable risks, safe design standards and necessary transparency measures could be addressed.

In our view, within the broad framework established for weapons review under Article 36 of Additional Protocol I, a formal or informal international group of experts and states could be established with a mandate to develop a framework to create effective technical standards and procedures for verification and evaluation as well as model protocols for risk assessment, end-user information and training, and fail-safe measures. The expert group should be open to both parties and non-parties to Additional Protocol I and also incorporate participation by

[45] D. H. Joyner, 'The Nuclear Suppliers Group: present challenges and future prospects', *International Trade Law and Regulation*, 11 (2005), 84.
[46] *Ibid.*, 86.

relevant private actors and non-governmental technical experts. The work of the group could entail both 'closed' and 'open' deliberations and should ultimately generate standards and principles that can be made public and that can be further scrutinized and discussed at the national level by governmental agencies and civil society actors.

Grappling with the multiple dimensions of uncertainty and 'open-textured risk' posed by the advent of AWS is not (only) a matter of technological solutions and better algorithms. Rather, as Deborah Johnson, a sociologist of science, points out:

> [i]n the process of development [of such autonomous agents], *decisions by humans* could lead to an arrangement in which humans accept robots knowing that no humans understand how they arrive at their decisions and how they will behave in certain circumstances. However, if things go this way, it will not be a natural evolution of technological development. Rather it will be because in the negotiations about the technology, certain actors pushed in that direction, were able to enroll others in their way of thinking, and together they won the day in terms of design *and* responsibility practices.[47]

The role we envisage for principles of due diligence derived from international environmental law, and for a standing body such as a group of governmental experts, is precisely to enable human agency and human responsibility from the outset as we move towards this new, and unsettling, technological horizon.

---

[47] Johnson, 'Technology with no human responsibility?', 714 (emphasis added).

PART VI

New frameworks for individual responsibility

Autonomous weapons systems: new frameworks for individual responsibility

NEHA JAIN

Introduction

The development of autonomous weapons systems (AWS) poses unique challenges for the attribution of individual responsibility. Criminal responsibility generally takes the individual human person as the central unit of action and the appropriate object of blame when things go terribly wrong. This assumption comes under strain, however, in numerous circumstances: when the unit of action is a collective (such as a group of persons, a corporation or a state), when the object of blame is a non-human entity (a dangerous animal or a corporation/ state) or when the object of blame is not the sort of entity that can be subject to responsibility (these are typically cases of exemptions from criminal responsibility, such as in the case of minors or the insane). Responsibility for the actions of AWS implicates issues common to these situations.

The actions of an AWS, being partly of the character of a weapon and partly the character of the combatant,[1] will be enmeshed to a great extent within the actions of human agents acting together, leading to overlapping claims of responsibility. Attribution of responsibility to the AWS itself will be difficult not only because it has 'no soul to be damned and no body to be kicked', but, arguably, also because it lacks capacity to act in a manner deserving of criminal liability. At the same time, because of the unique features of an AWS, several human agents might be potential candidates for legal responsibility for its conduct. As UN Special Rapporteur Christof Heyns notes, these could include 'the software programmers, those who

Many thanks to Oren Gross for his invaluable advice and guidance on the legal framework relating to AWS.
[1] H.-Y. Liu, 'Categorization and legality of autonomous and remote weapons systems', *International Review of the Red Cross*, 94 (2012), 627, 629.

build or sell hardware, military commanders, subordinates who deploy these systems and political leaders [who authorize them]'.[2]

By its very nature, the AWS will engage in conduct that is inherently unpredictable and dangerous. The question then is if an AWS engages in conduct that violates the laws of war, or if it commits an international crime due to malfunctioning, faulty programming or incorrect deployment, who can or should be held responsible for this violation? There is no single account of responsibility under which the various individuals performing diverse functions in relation to the AWS may be held liable. It may be possible, however, to conceive of their actions as creating a web of overlapping chains of responsibility, both criminal and civil in nature. This chapter provides a preliminary sketch of theories of responsibility that might be developed to capture the conduct of these individuals and the ways in which they will need to be modified to suit the special mode of functioning of an AWS.

Autonomy and responsibility

Attribution of responsibility for the actions of an AWS will need to grapple with a number of distinct questions: what exactly does it mean to say that the weapons system is acting 'autonomously'; what is the range of actors that might be responsible for the actions of the autonomously acting system and how could responsibility be distributed among them and, relatedly, is criminal responsibility the best way to conceive of accountability for the unlawful conduct?

The autonomy of the AWS has been described in various ways in the literature. A strong sense of 'autonomy' is found in Robert Sparrow's account of an artificially intelligent system that is capable of making its own decisions on the basis of reasons that are internal to it and in light of its own experience.[3] The system is autonomous in a manner that warrants moral responsibility because it possesses the capacity to reason and to choose its own ends. Sparrow argues that due to this autonomous functioning of the system, no human agents, including commanders or program developers, can be responsible for its actions.[4] Similarly, John Sullins advances the theory that an autonomous robot may be considered a moral agent if it satisfies three criteria: significant autonomy – that is,

---

[2] Christof Heyns, report of the Special Rapporteur on extrajudicial, summary or arbitrary executions, Doc. A/HRC/23/47 (2013), para. 77.

[3] R. Sparrow, 'Killer robots', *Journal of Applied Philosophy*, 24 (2007), 62, 65.

[4] *Ibid.*, 65–6.

the robot is not directly controlled by another agent and is effective at accomplishing its goals and tasks; intentional behaviour, where the complex interaction between the robot and its environment suggests deliberate and calculated behaviour; and responsibility, where the only way to make sense of the robot's behaviour is to assume it is responsible to some moral agent.[5] However, Sparrow and Sullins do not fully commit themselves to the proposition that such a full-blown autonomous system, which qualifies as a moral agent, currently exists or even if it will ever exist.[6]

On the other end of the spectrum, experts such as Noel Sharkey vigorously challenge these strong conceptions of autonomy and are deeply critical of the assumption that autonomous systems possess the cognition and agency to make moral decisions.[7] Sharkey describes an autonomous robot as one that 'operates in open or unstructured environments'. The decision-making process in an autonomous robot is still controlled by its program or set of programs, which can be highly complex in character.[8] Automated and autonomous systems both follow algorithmic or rule-based instructions that are largely deterministic, though their operation will be dependent to some extent on sensor data (which can be unpredictable) and on stochastic (probability-based) reasoning that is used for learning and error corrections.[9] Since the 'autonomous system' acts in a dynamic and unstructured environment based on feedback information from a number of sensors in its environment,[10] this inherently introduces uncertainty in its conduct.[11] Sharkey cautions that the term 'autonomy' in robotics 'should not be confused with how the term is used in philosophy, politics, individual freedom or in common parlance'.[12] Relying on the US Navy's classification, he categorizes

---

[5] J. P. Sullins, 'When is a robot a moral agent?', *International Review of Information Ethics*, 6 (2006), 23, 28–9.

[6] Sparrow, 'Killer robots', 65–6; Sullins, 'When is a robot a moral agent?', 29.

[7] N. E. Sharkey, 'The evitability of autonomous robot warfare', *International Review of the Red Cross*, 94 (2012), 787, 793–4.

[8] N. Sharkey, 'Saying "no!" to lethal autonomous targeting', *Journal of Military Ethics*, 9 (2010), 369, 376–7.

[9] P. Asaro, 'On banning autonomous weapon systems: human rights, automation, and the dehumanization of lethal decision-making', *International Review of the Red Cross*, 94 (2012), 687, 689, n 5.

[10] *Ibid.*, 689, n 5.

[11] International Committee of the Red Cross, report of the ICRC Expert Meeting on Autonomous Weapon Systems: Technical, Military, Legal, and Humanitarian Aspects, 9 May 2014, 8.

[12] Sharkey, 'Saying "no!"' 376.

autonomous robots as (i) scripted, where the robots carry out a pre-planned script; (ii) supervised, in which robots perform planning, sensing and monitoring functions with the help of human operators; and (iii) intelligent, which are described rather ambiguously as those in which 'attributes of human intelligence' are used in software for decision making, problem solving, and perception and interpretation of information.[13]

Some scholars who are sympathetic to this version of autonomy argue that there is no bright-line distinction between autonomous and automated systems. System autonomy exists on a continuum defined by a number of characteristics, including the extent to which the system requires operator interaction, its ability to operate in an uncertain environment and the system's level of 'assertiveness' – that is, its capacity to independently change its operating plan in order to achieve human-designed ends.[14]

On this account of robot autonomy, the analogy between human decision making and machine 'autonomy' is, at best, inexact and, at worst, misleading. Legal accountability for the conduct of a human is premised on his or her capacity to act as a moral agent who possesses the volition and intent to form and pursue his or her own desires and goals. The law assumes that every human being is a 'wild card' who can freely choose and accomplish his or her ends; it is for this reason that the traditional doctrine of legal responsibility treats the human as the final agent in a chain of causation through whom the causal link cannot pass any further.[15] If we take seriously the weaker sense of robot autonomy advanced by Sharkey, it seems unlikely that the AWS is autonomous in the relevant legal sense for attribution of responsibility, which will make it possible to trace the chain of causation through it and to the final human agent.

Indeed, the desire to avoid the confusion engendered by the different senses of human and robot autonomy has led some scholars to prefer to use the term 'emergent' instead of 'autonomous' to describe AWS behaviour. Emergence refers to the ability of the system to engage in

---

[13] *Ibid.*, 377; see also N. Sharkey, 'Cassandra or false prophet of doom: AI robots and war', *Intelligent Systems*, 23 (2008), 14, 16.

[14] W. C. Marra and S. K. McNeil, 'Understanding "the loop": regulating the next generation of war machines', *Harvard Journal of Law and Public Policy*, 36 (2012) 1139, 1151, 1154.

[15] H. L. A. Hart and A. M. Honoré, *Causation in the Law* (Oxford: Clarendon Press, 1959), 48–54; S. H. Kadish, 'Complicity, cause and blame: a study in the interpretation of doctrine', *California Law Review*, 73 (1985), 323, 360.

unpredictable useful behaviour.[16] Emergent intelligence arises due to the interaction of thousands of parallel processes, where small program fragments examine and extract data from a range of inputs depending on the context.[17] Which inputs are considered relevant is contingent on pre-existing analytical structures and assumptions, which, in turn, are modified by new inputs as the system exhibits 'learning'.[18] Thus, the context used to extract and relate data may itself undergo changes under the influence of this new input. In this scenario, the basic statistics do not change, but the system will on occasion follow pathways that are unpredictable due to the constant slippage between the data and the context.[19]

In contrast with the Sparrow and Sullins accounts, these weaker conceptions of robot autonomy or 'emergence' do not consider the AWS to be particularly different from a simple tool or machine, except in one respect that is salient for responsibility – the epistemic uncertainty that is built into the system design and that is in fact crucial to its successful functioning. If the conduct of an AWS is unpredictable by design, on what basis can a human agent be held responsible for this unintended and unanticipated action if it results in tremendous harm?

Doctrines of criminal responsibility

While the majority of the commentary on AWS functioning considers uncertainty and unpredictability in AWS behaviour to constitute the primary challenge for responsibility attribution, it is worth considering whether the stronger account of autonomy would pose any greater problems for a potential 'accountability gap'. If one takes the Sparrow and Sullins account of autonomy seriously (even if this merely represents the future potential of AWS development), the additional proposition that responsibility for the acts of this autonomous agent cannot be attributed to another entity requires further argument.[20] Indeed, the criminal law recognizes various instances where the immediate agent

[16] R. Calo, 'Robotics and the lessons of cyberlaw', *California Law Review*, 103 (2015) 101, 119.

[17] C. E. A. Carnow, 'Liability for distributed artificial intelligences', *Berkeley Technology Law Journal*, 11 (1996), 147, 159.

[18] *Ibid.*, 160.

[19] *Ibid.*, 160–1. See also H.-Y. Liu, 'Refining responsibility: defining two types of responsibility issues raised by autonomous weapons systems', Chapter 14 in this volume.

[20] For a sophisticated analysis that takes Sparrow's version of autonomy at face value but challenges the consequences for responsibility attribution, see M. Schulzke, 'Autonomous weapons and distributed responsibility', *Philosophy and Technology*, 26 (2013), 203–19.

who most directly realizes the elements of the offence is 'autonomous' in the material sense, but for whose conduct another (human) agent can still be held responsible. The modes of responsibility that capture this scenario best are indirect perpetration and command responsibility.

Perpetration

Most common law and civil law systems recognize various categories of perpetration or principal responsibility for an offence. In general, a person is considered a principal through personal fulfilment of the *actus reus* and *mens rea* elements of the offence – the principal is, in this case, the direct perpetrator.[21] However, several criminal legal systems recognize principal responsibility even when the accused acts 'through' another individual. The common law systems capture this scenario through the concept of an 'innocent agent', who is a person whose actions are not deemed free, informed and voluntary due to some personal factors such as insanity, ignorance or minority, and, for this reason, can be regarded as having been 'caused' by the words or conduct of another person (for instance, through coercion or deception).[22]

There is also some support for extending this concept to 'semi-innocent' agency, which applies when the perpetrator P satisfies the fault element of a less serious offence but is innocent because he or she lacks the fault element for the more serious offence intended by the 'secondary party' D, who shares the same *actus reus*.[23] P's actions are considered less than fully voluntary, but not to such an extent as to fully absolve him of any criminal responsibility.[24] They can be characterized as having been 'caused' to the extent that he did not possess complete knowledge with respect to the nature or circumstances of his conduct.[25] As Glanville Williams puts it, if D can act through a completely innocent agent P1, there is no reason why he cannot do so

---

[21] See, e.g., K. J. M. Smith, *A Modern Treatise on the Law of Criminal Complicity* (Oxford University Press, 1991), 27–8 (on English law); M. Bohlander, *Principles of German Criminal Law* (Oxford: Hart, 2009), 153 (on German criminal law).

[22] G. Williams, 'Innocent agency and causation', *Criminal Law Forum*, 3 (1992), 289, 294. In the United States, the Model Penal Code as well as several state statutes recognize the doctrine of innocent agency. See J. F. Decker, 'The mental state requirement for accomplice liability in American criminal law', *South Carolina Law Review*, 60 (2008), 237, 255–6.

[23] Law Commission, *Participating in Crime*, Law Com. no. 305, Cm 7084 (2007) paras. 4.14, 4.15; Smith, *A Modern Treatise*, 130.

[24] Kadish, 'Complicity, cause and blame', 388.   [25] Smith, *A Modern Treatise*, 130.

through a semi-innocent agent P2. It would be unreasonable for the partial guilt of P2 to operate as a defence against D.[26] P2 would be treated as an innocent agent in respect of 'part of the responsibility' of D.[27]

Civil law systems such as Germany similarly recognize the concept of an indirect perpetrator. Section 25 of the *Strafgesetzbuch* (StGB)[28] states that a person who commits a crime through another is an indirect perpetrator. The word 'through' signifies that the indirect perpetrator (*Hintermann*) controls the direct perpetrator (*Vordermann*) of the act in such a manner that he uses him as an instrument. Due to this 'tool' function, the *Vordermann* normally possesses some deficit (for instance, he lacks the requisite intent for the offence), which the *Hintermann* exploits in order to dominate him.[29] While the *Vordermann* still possesses *Handlungsherrschaft* (act hegemony), this is overlaid by the *Willensherrschaft* or domination over the will of the *Vordermann* by the *Hintermann*.[30] German scholar Claus Roxin formulates three main categories of indirect perpetration: (i) coercion; (ii) utilization of a mistake on the part of the *Vordermann* or on the basis of the *Hintermann*'s superior knowledge (which is a corollary of the mistake); and (iii) hegemony through control over an organizational apparatus (*Organisationsherrschaft*).[31]

The proposition that one may be held criminally responsible by virtue of acting 'through' another person is now acknowledged at the international level in the Rome Statute of the International Criminal Court, where Article 25(3)(a) provides responsibility for a person who commits a crime within the court's jurisdiction, 'whether as an individual, jointly with another or through another person, regardless of whether that other person is criminally responsible'.[32] Even though the words of the Statute refer to a 'person', the International Criminal Court (ICC) has held that the provision includes an accused who acts through an organizational apparatus (*Organisationsherrschaft*), thus recognizing the possibility of

---

[26] G. Williams, *Textbook of Criminal Law* (Andover, Hants: Stevens and Sons, 1983), 374.

[27] G. Williams, *Criminal Law: The General Part* (Andover, Hants: Stevens and Sons, 1961), 391.

[28] German Criminal Code in the version promulgated on 13 November 1998, *Federal Law Gazette* [*Bundesgesetzblatt*] I, p. 3322, last amended by Article 1 of the Law of 24 September 2013, *Federal Law Gazette* I, p. 3671 and with the text of Article 6(18) of the Law of 10 October 2013, *Federal Law Gazette* I, p. 3799.

[29] J. Wessels and W. Beulke, *Strafrecht, allgemeiner Teil: Die Straftat und ihr Aufbau (Schwerpunkte)* (Heidelberg: C. F. Müller, 2008), 190.

[30] C. Roxin, *Täterschaft und Tatherrschaft* (Berlin: Walter de Gruyter, 2006), 127.

[31] *Ibid.*, 242.

[32] Rome Statute of the International Criminal Court, UN Doc A/CONF.183/9, 1 July 2002.

attribution when a person exercises control over human agents (who may, in addition, be responsible themselves) but only through a non-human mechanism or apparatus.[33]

The *mens rea* of the direct perpetrator cannot be attributed to the perpetrator even in the case of a semi-innocent or innocent agent but must be judged in terms of the indirect perpetrator's own mental state. This will usually require intent or knowledge (with respect to the offence elements) on the part of the latter. Article 30 of the Rome Statute uses 'intent' to refer to situations where the perpetrator means to engage in the conduct and means to cause, or is aware that the consequence will occur in, the ordinary course of events. 'Knowledge' requires awareness that a circumstance exists or a consequence will occur in the ordinary course of events.

Command responsibility

The doctrine of command or superior responsibility holds civilian and military superiors responsible for the unlawful conduct committed by their subordinates. Command responsibility is a curious hybrid of direct and indirect responsibility: the superior or commander is held directly responsible for his or her own failure to supervise or intervene and indirectly responsible for the criminal acts of the subordinate.[34] While the doctrine has undergone various permutations in domestic and international law, its variations share certain common characteristics: (i) the existence of a superior–subordinate relationship where the superior has effective control over the subordinate; (ii) the requisite mental element, generally requiring that the superior knew or had reason to know (or should have known) of the subordinates' crimes; and (iii) the failure to control, prevent or punish the commission of the offences.[35]

---

[33] *Prosecutor v. Germain Katanga and Mathieu Ngudjolo Chui*, case no. ICC-01/04-01/07, Decision on the confirmation of charges (30 September 2008), paras. 495–9; *Prosecutor v. Muthaura, Kenyatta and Ali*, case no. ICC-01/09-02/11, Decision on the confirmation of charges pursuant to Article 61(7)(a) and (b) of the Rome Statute (ICC Pre-Trial Chamber II, 23 January 2012), paras. 407–10; *Prosecutor v. Ruto, Kosgey and Sang*, case no. ICC-01/09-01/11, Decision on the confirmation of charges pursuant to Article 61(7)(a) and (b) of the Rome Statute (ICC Pre-Trial Chamber II, 23 January 2012), paras. 313–32.

[34] K. Ambos, 'Joint criminal enterprise and command responsibility', *Journal of International Criminal Justice*, 5 (2007), 159, 176.

[35] A. M. Danner and J. S. Martinez, 'Guilty associations: joint criminal enterprise, command responsibility, and the development of international criminal law', *California Law Review*, 93 (2005), 75, 122.

The superior–subordinate relationship includes both *de jure* and *de facto* command situations. The commander should have 'effective control' over the subordinate at the time of commission of the act – that is, he or she should have the material ability to prevent and punish the offences.[36] The ICC has recently emphasized the importance of the time frame over which this control must be exercised – there must be a temporal coincidence between the control and the criminal conduct.[37] In the earlier case law, instances of partial control have been recognized as satisfying this requirement when the superior has failed to exercise his or her potential for full control in order to avoid personal responsibility.[38]

As far as the mental element is concerned, Article 28 of the Rome Statute distinguishes between military commanders and civilian superiors. While 'knowledge' is common to both kinds of superiors, in the case of the former, a 'should have known' or negligence standard suffices, whereas the higher standard of 'consciously disregarded' information about the crimes is mandated for civilian superiors. Further, the recent jurisprudence affirms the military commander's duty to keep informed and enquire about the conduct of his subordinates, regardless of the information having been available at the time the crimes are committed.[39] In contrast, civilian superiors must have consciously disregarded this information, indicating a *mens rea* level closer to recklessness.[40]

Additionally, Article 28(1) requires a causal connection between the crimes committed by the subordinates and the superior's dereliction of the duty to exercise adequate control over them. The commander's culpability thus stems from the fact that due to his/her omission, he/she facilitated or encouraged the crimes or, at the very least, increased the risk of their commission.[41] This omission is tied to the commander's duty

---

[36] *Ibid.*, 130.

[37] *Prosecutor v. Jean-Pierre Bemba Gombo (Bemba)*, case no. ICC-01/05-01/08, Decision pursuant to Article 61(7)(a) and (b) of the Rome Statute on the charges of the prosecutor against Jean-Pierre Bemba Gombo (Pre-Trial Chamber II, 15 June 2009), para. 418.

[38] See I. Bantekas, 'The contemporary law of superior responsibility', *American Journal of International Law*, 93 (1999) 573, 580 (citing the *Yamashita* and *High Command* cases).

[39] *Bemba*, para. 433.

[40] Ambos, 'Joint criminal enterprise and command responsibility', 179.

[41] D. Robinson, 'How command responsibility got so complicated: a culpability contradiction, its obfuscation, and a simple solution', *Melbourne Journal of International Law*, 13 (2012), 1, 45, 54–5 (citing the ICC's interpretation of risk aggravation as a basis for the commander's culpability in the *Bemba* decision).

to control, prevent or punish crimes committed by his/her subordinates. The duty to prevent exists at the time when the offences are going to, or are about to, be committed but may also materialize due to the commander's failure to account for factors such as the age or training of the subordinates, which give rise to the likelihood of the crimes being committed.[42] The duty to punish, which arises in the aftermath of the commission of the crimes, is directed towards establishing accountability for past crimes but is also meant to serve as a deterrent and prevent the recurrence of these crimes (and, only to that extent, indicates a causation requirement).[43]

Criminal responsibility for the unlawful conduct of AWS

Even if one takes the AWS to possess autonomy in the strong sense, there is still no conceptual barrier to holding another agent responsible for the unlawful result caused by its actions. Under the doctrine of indirect perpetration, one can consider the AWS akin to a *Vordermann* who possesses some defect or deficit, such as the lack of the capacity to act 'intentionally', which makes the AWS an innocent or semi-innocent agent whose will and actions can be controlled and/or caused by a human agent. The fact that an individual does not act through a human being but, rather, through a non-human agent such as an AWS will not automatically exclude the applicability of Article 25(3)(a).

Similarly, command responsibility for the actions of the AWS could be used to establish liability in one of two ways: (i) by treating the deploying soldier as a 'commander' who is responsible for the actions of his/her 'subordinate' and autonomous AWS or (ii) holding liable individuals such as civilian and military superiors who authorize the deployment of an AWS and retain overall control over the military operation in which it is engaged. Unless one truly believes that the AWS possesses some kind of independent agency (even if it is an incomplete one), the first option would appear to stretch the concept of command to the point of redundancy, effectively resulting in soldiers being adjudged commanders almost anytime sophisticated weaponry is used to carry out their orders. The second, more promising, responsibility proposal is developed by Marcus Schulzke, who argues that decision making in the military

---

[42] Bantekas, 'The contemporary law of superior responsibility', 591 (citing the *Abbaye Ardenne* case).
[43] *Ibid.*, 592.

context is based on the division of responsibility between different actors. The autonomy of the soldiers who take part in the conflict is typically severely constrained by the decisions of other actors, particularly the civilian and military commanders involved in the operation.[44] Given this division of responsibility, it does not seem unjust or unfair to hold civilian and military personnel responsible for the actions of the AWS due to their role in setting the operating conditions that result in the unlawful conduct of the AWS or because of their failure to place appropriate limits on the extent to which the AWS is authorized to act autonomously.[45]

Thus, the real challenge with establishing criminal accountability for AWS conduct would seem to follow not from its seemingly autonomous nature (autonomy in the strong sense), but due to the inherent unpredictability of its actions (autonomy in the weaker sense/emergence). This problem arises with both indirect perpetration and command responsibility.

Control

Indirect perpetration and command responsibility are premised on the ability of the indirect perpetrator/commander to control the actions of the direct perpetrator/subordinate. Regardless of which version of AWS autonomy one endorses, identifying a single human agent who controls the actions of the AWS may prove challenging. On the face of it, the programmer or software developer is too remote from the scene of the crime to control the AWS's conduct at the time of the commission of the offence. This is especially true given that the AWS is designed to apply non-deterministic decision making in an open and unstructured environment. Thus, not only will pre-set rules designed by the programmer not be capable of capturing the complete range of scenarios that the AWS will encounter, but the AWS will also be able to adapt the means and methods it uses to achieve programmer-designed ends. This will inevitably lead to uncertainty and error, which cannot be fully predicted or controlled by the programmer.[46]

---

[44] Schulzke, 'Autonomous weapons and distributed responsibility', 209–12.

[45] Ibid., 213.

[46] On the unpredictable functioning of the AWS, see Oren Gross, 'When machines kill: criminal responsibility for international crimes committed by lethal autonomous robots', unpublished manuscript, 2014, 9–10 (on file with author).

Similarly, the field commander who deploys the AWS may cause or control the AWS's conduct only to the extent that he/she may be in a position to call a stop to the immediate action and prevent future actions. The crucial feature of AWS functioning is its ability to individualize target selection and the means of carrying out an attack on the basis of changing circumstances.[47] Thus, the field commander will not necessarily be well equipped to direct, predict or second-guess the decision-making operation carried out by the AWS in real time. This would also be true of the civilian or military superior who is doubly distanced from the real-time operation of the AWS. While he/she may have the decision-making authority over whether the AWS is deployed in the first place and the operations with which it is tasked, the actual working of the AWS on the field is effectively supervised by the field soldier who is unlikely to fully understand the complex working of the AWS or to have the final word on whether or not the action should be carried out.

One possible solution to this dilemma is to shift the focus of control or causation from the time that the AWS is deployed to carry out the conduct that results in the crime to the point of time when the process of developing the AWS to act within the bounds of specific program features and the decision to deploy it in certain field operations is taken.[48] This will undoubtedly represent a departure from the temporal coincidence of the commander's control and the criminal conduct of the human subordinate normally required by the doctrine. However, the rationale behind this temporal requirement is that the field or operational commander is expected to exercise both *de facto* and *de jure* control over the human agent who he/she trains and deems fit for deployment and over whom he/she exercises disciplinary authority. In the case of the AWS, the analogous *de facto* and *de jure* control will be exercised by the commander who reviews the ability of the AWS to be able to perform the tasks assigned to it within the limits of the law and gives the authorization to deploy it for a certain operation. The commander may

---

[47] M. Wagner, 'The dehumanization of international humanitarian law: legal, ethical, and political implications of autonomous weapon systems', draft paper, 1, 13, available at www.law.upenn.edu/live/files/4003-20141120-wagner-markus-dehumanizationpdf.

[48] See, e.g., the suggestion by Schulzke, 'Autonomous weapons and distributed responsibility', 213–15. See also P. Kalmanovitz, 'Judgment, liability and the risks of riskless warfare', Chapter 7 in this volume. Indeed, Corn argues that decision making in the development and procurement phase might be the most vital site for considering compliance (with the laws of war). This, in turn, has implications for the locus of control. See G. S. Corn, 'Autonomous weapons systems: managing the inevitability of "taking the man out of the loop"', Chapter 10 in this volume.

still be considered to 'control' its actions due to his/her role in setting (or failing to set) the conditions under which the AWS operates.[49]

Mens rea

Even if the control or causation element is satisfied, the greater difficulty pertains to the establishment of the requisite *mens rea* element. If we want to hold the commander or field officer responsible as an indirect perpetrator, or the soldier responsible as a direct perpetrator, this will usually require intent or knowledge (with respect to the offence elements). Under Article 30 of the Rome Statute, in order to act with 'intent', the perpetrator must mean to engage in the conduct and mean to cause or be aware that the consequence will occur in the ordinary course of events. 'Knowledge' requires awareness that a circumstance exists or a consequence will occur in the ordinary course of events. Given the inherently unpredictable nature of AWS conduct, the harm caused by its actions is unlikely to fit either of these mental standards.

Command responsibility lowers this *mens rea* requirement considerably. Thus, under Article 28 of the Rome Statute, a civilian superior must have either known or 'consciously disregarded information which clearly indicated, that the subordinates were committing or about to commit such crimes'. The parallel standard of 'owing to the circumstances, should have known' for military commanders is still lower and amounts to negligence. The relaxing of the *mens rea* standard for command responsibility when compared to that required for perpetration or even complicity in international criminal law (where, generally, knowledge, or at least advertent recklessness, is necessary) has proven to be controversial in the academic literature, but it has sought to be justified in light of the serious nature of the commander's duties in situations of conflict and the severe consequences that can result from the dereliction of this duty.[50]

In the context of responsibility for the conduct of the AWS, two questions arise from these diminished *mens rea* standards: first, even if

---

[49] However, several factors may yet limit this control, including the epistemic uncertainty associated with AWS conduct and the commander's ability to actually prevent or punish the conduct. For a thoughtful discussion of these constraints, see Liu, 'Refining responsibility'.

[50] Robinson, 'How command responsibility got so complicated: a culpability contradiction, its obfuscation, and a simple solution', 9.

we accept the lower level of recklessness or negligence, will this enable us to assign responsibility for inherently unpredictable AWS conduct to the commanders/civilian superiors; and if the answer to this is in the affirmative, should the *mens rea* standard be lowered equally for all cases of perpetration responsibility in the case of deploying soldiers or field officers?

There is no unified understanding of what recklessness or negligence entails in international criminal law, but domestic law definitions of these mental states might be helpful in fleshing out the standards. For instance, under section 2.02(2)(c) of the United States Model Penal Code (MPC), a person acts recklessly with respect to a material element of an offence:

> when he consciously disregards a substantial and unjustifiable risk that the material element exists or will result from his conduct. The risk must be of such a nature and degree that, considering the nature and purpose of the actor's conduct and the circumstances known to him, its disregard involves a gross deviation from the standard of conduct that a law-abiding person would observe in the actor's situation.[51]

In addition, section 2.02(2)(d) considers a person to act negligently:

> when he should be aware of a substantial and unjustifiable risk that the material element exists or will result from his conduct. The risk must be of such a nature and degree that the actor's failure to perceive it, considering the nature and purpose of his conduct and the circumstances known to him, involves a gross deviation from the standard of care that a reasonable person would observe in the actor's situation.[52]

As the MPC makes clear, what distinguishes a reckless defendant from one who is merely negligent is the consciousness of the risk: while a reckless defendant is aware of the risk, the negligent defendant is not, but should have been aware of it.[53] However, what exactly the defendant must be aware of, or believe in relation to the risk, is highly disputed.

---

[51] United States Model Penal Code (MPC) (Official Draft and Explanatory Notes: Complete Text of Model Penal Code as Adopted at the Annual Meeting of the American Law Institute at Washington, DC, 24 May 1962 (American Law Institute, 1985)).

[52] For this interpretation of the 'should have known' standard, see K. Ambos, 'Superior responsibility' in Antonio Cassese *et al.* (eds), *The Rome Statute of the International Criminal Court: A Commentary* (Oxford University Press, 2002), 805, 849.

[53] D. Husak, 'Negligence, belief, blame and criminal liability: the special case of forgetting', *Criminal Law and Philosophy*, 5 (2011), 199, 200. Some commentators propose a different demarcating line between recklessness and negligence, and label advertent risk creation, which is unreasonable but relatively minor, as negligence. See M. S. Moore and H. M. Hurd, 'Punishing the awkward, the stupid, the weak, and the selfish: the culpability of negligence', *Criminal Law and Philosophy*, 5 (2011), 147, 149. See also K. W. Simons,

Should the defendant only be aware of the risk, with the question of whether it is substantial and unjustifiable being determined by the adjudicator? Alternatively, should he or she be subjectively aware that the risk is both substantial and unjustifiable? There is no consensus on these issues either in the academic community[54] or in the positive law.[55] Relatedly, how concrete or exacting the defendant's conception of the risk needs to be is also unclear. Should the defendant foresee the exact harm that occurs, roughly the same type or category of harm,[56] or simply be aware that there is a substantial and unjustifiable risk of a 'dangerous' occurrence?

Kimberly Ferzan proposes the category of 'opaque recklessness' to describe the last of these categories, where the defendant knows his or her conduct is risky but either fails to realize or consciously disregards the specific reasons for the riskiness.[57] She laments the current exclusion of this category of conduct from the MPC's definition of recklessness, though she identifies several instances where it has been recognized by courts in the United States and in the common law.[58] Ferzan argues that a person who is opaquely reckless is equally liable as one who adverts to the concrete risk that results in the harm, as long as he preconsciously recognizes why his behaviour is risky and this preconscious aspect informs his decision making.[59] Thus, when the defendant makes a choice to engage in 'risky' behaviour, he effectively chooses to commit some act that he deems 'risky'. Since his conception of the risky activity is part of his practical reasoning, he can legitimately be held liable for it.[60] In contrast, if his definition of risky behaviour

---

'Should the model penal code's *mens rea* provisions be amended?', *Ohio State Journal of Criminal Law*, 1 (2003), 179, 191.

[54] See K. W. Simons, 'When is negligent advertence culpable', *Criminal Law and Philosophy*, 5 (2011), 97, 112 (excluding the requirement of awareness of unjustifiability of the risk). In a similar vein, see D. M. Treiman, 'Recklessness and the model penal code', *American Journal of Criminal Law*, 9 (1981), 281, 365. In contrast, Larry Alexander suggests that unjustifiability, and not substantiality, is crucial to the recklessness evaluation. See L. Alexander, 'Insufficient concern: a unified conception of criminal culpability', *California Law Review*, 88 (2000), 931, 934–5.

[55] Husak, 'Negligence, belief, blame and criminal liability', 208.

[56] Moore and Hurd argue that the defendant should be aware that 'there is some risk of roughly the type that was realized'. See Moore and Hurd, 'Punishing the awkward, the stupid, the weak, and the selfish', 156.

[57] K. K. Ferzan, 'Opaque recklessness', *Journal of Criminal Law and Criminology*, 91 (2001), 597, 599.

[58] *Ibid.*, 603–4. See also Simons, 'Model penal code', 192–3.

[59] Ferzan, 'Opaque recklessness', 631–2.   [60] *Ibid.*, 634.

does not include the harm that ultimately occurred, he will not be reckless but only negligent.[61]

If we accept this broader notion of recklessness where the defendant is responsible even when he/she is not conscious of the exact risk his/her conduct creates, this could prove promising for the attribution of liability for the harm caused by an AWS. Thus, even if the actions of the AWS are uncertain and unpredictable and even if the defendant was unaware of the exact nature of the risk of harm posed by the AWS's conduct, he/she could still be deemed reckless and, hence, liable for the harm. However, liability for recklessness will still require showing some level of subjective awareness of some kind and degree of risk, and depending on the extent of epistemic uncertainty associated with AWS conduct, this might be difficult to prove in individual cases.

Negligence liability for AWS conduct would alleviate this problem to some extent. Negligence as a culpable mental state expands the responsibility regime since the defendant's inadvertent risk creation suffices for liability. The negligence standard under the MPC is higher than ordinary or simple negligence in tort. Thus, the defendant must deviate from the standard of care required of the reasonable person in a manner that is extreme or gross enough to warrant criminal liability.[62] In the context of harmful AWS conduct, the adjudicator will have to determine whether the commander/field officer/deploying soldier should have been aware of a substantial and unjustifiable risk of harm resulting from AWS conduct and if, given their circumstances and knowledge, their failure to advert to this risk constituted a gross deviation from the standard of care expected of a reasonable person in their situation. This version of negligence incorporates an 'individualizing standard' for the reasonable person, such that the negligence judgment depends to some extent on the individual capacities of the defendant.[63] The extent of the individualization is debated among commentators.[64] Some argue that the standard of the hypothetical reasonable person is incoherent and that there is no non-arbitrary way of specifying it in advance; others, like Peter Westen,

---

[61] *Ibid.*, 634.   [62] Husak, 'Negligence, belief, blame and criminal liability', 202.

[63] As the commentary to the Model Penal Code notes, there is some ambiguity as to which factors are to be considered part of the defendant's situation. If he suffers a blow or a heart attack, these would be relevant, but his temperament or intelligence level may not be material in evaluating negligence. Model Penal Code, 242, para. 2.02, cmt. 4.

[64] See the discussion at Husak, 'Negligence, belief, blame and criminal liability', 206; P. Westen, 'Individualizing the reasonable person in criminal law', *Criminal Law and Philosophy*, 2 (2002), 137.

offer an account where the reasonable person has all of the attributes and characteristics of the defendant, except that he/she also has the requisite 'respect for the values of the people of the state'.[65]

Depending on the extent to which this individualization might be carried out in the case of the commander/field officer/deploying soldier, there could be a potential exoneration from liability if the AWS behaves in an entirely unprecedented fashion that no reasonable individual who did not have some knowledge of the technical details of its operation could have foreseen. This is more likely to be the case the further one moves down the chain of command, especially to the deploying soldier who is unlikely to be aware of the exact mode of functioning of the AWS, the nature of the safety and security precautions that have been built into the system and when the machine may deviate from its standard operating procedure and behave in unexpected ways that cause unforeseen harm.

As the earlier analysis should make clear, lowering the *mens rea* levels to recklessness and/or negligence will not capture all of the instances of AWS functioning gone awry, but it will certainly broaden the potential scope of liability to cover individual cases. Further, a more flexible *mens rea* requirement might serve *ex ante* as a more effective deterrent where commanders and military officers are put on notice and encouraged to actively acquire information and knowledge about the consequences of using an AWS to conduct certain operations and the potential harm that could result from its ability to operate autonomously (in the weak sense). If negligence is sufficient for establishing criminal responsibility, commanders and decision makers in the military hierarchy are also more likely to use caution in deploying them only in circumstances where they are capable of complying with the laws of war and where the risks of harm are minimal.

Nevertheless, there are important policy questions that will have to be addressed as to whether the costs of lowering the *mens rea* requirement to recklessness and/or negligence are too great, even if doing so makes it easier to establish accountability for AWS conduct. There are acute concerns with embracing these standards even in the context of command responsibility (which has expressly adopted some variation of them), which only get heightened when one starts thinking of other modes of responsibility, including perpetration and accomplice liability, which might be more readily applicable in the case of the field

[65] Westen, 'Individualizing the reasonable person in criminal law'.

commander or deploying soldier. Any steps to embrace the negligence standard more widely must be attentive to the scepticism towards negligence liability in most domestic criminal legal systems. This caution usually takes one of the following forms. The culpability of the negligent defendant is difficult to isolate: the negligent defendant, unlike the purposeful, aware or reckless defendant, typically does not choose to risk harm and does not necessarily suffer from a 'character defect'; he/she may only be guilty of a lapse in his/her duty towards others in one particular instance.[66] Criminal law theorists also argue that the rules of criminal law must be capable of guiding conduct, and this guidance function is absent in the case of the negligent defendant since he/she is by definition unaware of the prohibited risk.[67] Such a defendant cannot, in addition, be deterred.[68]

On the other side of the spectrum, it is argued that the culpability of the defendant consists in his/her wrongful failure to exercise his/her capacity to not commit the wrongful act. This omission is just as significant as the choice to undertake the risk of harm.[69] Other scholars have proposed similar justifications for the recognition of liability where the defendant is unaware of the risk he/she creates. For instance, for Antony Duff, recklessness includes an attitude of 'practical indifference' where the defendant's conduct reflects that he 'cares too little about the risk that he is creating'.[70] This practical indifference can exist both when the defendant adverts to the risk and also when he/she fails to notice the risk.[71] Under the positive law, the latter category is akin to negligence, rather than recklessness.[72] The responsibility of the defendant in each case stems from his/her failure to exhibit sufficient concern for the welfare of others.[73]

---

[66] Husak, 'Negligence, belief, blame and criminal liability', 203; see also the discussion and references at Moore and Hurd, 'Punishing the awkward, the stupid, the weak, and the selfish', 150.

[67] Husak, 'Negligence, belief, blame and criminal liability', 203.

[68] Moore and Hurd, 'Punishing the awkward, the stupid, the weak, and the selfish', 150, outlining but not endorsing this objection.

[69] *Ibid.*, 151 discussing variations of this reasoning in the scholarship of Hart, Horder and Duff.

[70] R. A. Duff, *Intention, Agency, and Criminal Liability* (Oxford: Blackwell, 1990), 162–3.

[71] *Ibid.*, 163.

[72] Simons discusses the possibility that the line between negligence and recklessness may be blurry and that the difference between these forms of liability may be one of degree rather than kind. See Simons, 'When is negligent advertence culpable', 112.

[73] Ferzan, 'Opaque recklessness', 615.

It is possible to argue that an attitude of insufficient concern is enough to warrant criminal liability for unpredictable AWS conduct. This is especially true given the high costs associated with the creation of uncertain risks in situations of war and conflict.[74] While the AWS might exhibit machine learning in its decision to target a certain person or object or in the means it uses to conduct an operation, this decision will be linked inextricably to the prior human decision to deploy the particular AWS, with its program settings, into a particular circumstance and to carry out a defined task. The failure to exercise sufficient concern or judgment at this prior stage about the likelihood or risk of harm and the AWS's capabilities and limitations will doubtless have an impact on the nature and extent of harm caused by AWS conduct.[75] Nonetheless, more work will need to be done to identify precisely where the line between appropriate risk mitigation and respect for personal culpability should be drawn for criminal liability.

The liability of manufacturers and developers

The potential avenues for criminal liability sketched earlier mostly relate to the responsibility of civilian and military superiors, field officers and the persons in charge of deploying the AWS. Given the remoteness of software developers, programmers and manufacturers from the scene of the crime, and their general lack of control over the final instructions and deployment of the AWS, it will be difficult to hold them (criminally) responsible for personally perpetrating the crime that is caused by the unlawful conduct of the AWS. They might instead be liable as accessories who perform so-called 'neutral actions' that aid the commission of the unlawful conduct by the military or civilian superiors/soldiers. In this sense, they would be similar to arms suppliers or poison gas manufacturers for concentration camps who could be brought within the net of liability provided they meet the *actus reus* and *mens rea* requirements for accessorial liability. This will not be an easy task given that liability for neutral actions usually requires

---

[74] King distinguishes between negligence and inadvertence on the basis that though both mental states constitute a failure to pay appropriate attention, negligence involves cases where the expected negative value of the risk of harm exceeds some threshold. See M. King, 'The problem with negligence', *Social Theory and Practice*, 35 (2009), 577, 594. This condition might be fulfilled in the case of the risk of harm caused by AWS conduct.

[75] See K. Anderson *et al.*, 'Adapting the law of armed conflict to autonomous weapon systems', *International Law Studies*, 90 (2014), 386, 405–6.

a higher *mens rea* level of purpose, or at least of knowledge, rather than recklessness with respect to the aiding action.[76]

Here, one will again need to engage with serious policy considerations as to whether the *mens rea* should be lowered to recklessness or negligence for criminal liability for developers and manufacturers. These individuals are much more likely to be aware of the nature of the risks posed by AWS self-learning and the potential ways in which it might interact with complex environments to deviate from its original set of instructions. On the other hand, they will be fairly distanced from the actual deployment and operation of the AWS in terms of space as well as time. Indeed, several years may elapse between the time the AWS is developed or programmed and the time when the conduct that gives rise to the harm takes place. A criminal responsibility proposal based on recklessness/negligence will need to meet the very serious challenges raised by this temporal and spatial remoteness of the programmer/manufacturer/developer from the crime scene.

A potentially more promising route is to assess their responsibility under civil law principles of product liability for harm that results from malfunctions or from poor or error-prone software or hardware design features of the AWS.[77] In this exercise, it may be helpful to refer to the debates currently underway on the regulation of, and liability for, harms or accidents caused by autonomous vehicles or driverless/self-driving cars, as they are better known.[78] In the United States, for instance, the discussion has mostly revolved around the possibility of holding manufacturers liable under a negligence standard for unreasonable failure to prevent risk (of harm).[79] There have been arguments for going even further and imposing strict liability on the seller for the harm caused by the product when it is sold in a 'defective condition unreasonably dangerous to the

---

[76] For the English law position on the *mens rea* requirements for actions that are undertaken in the ordinary course of business, see, e.g., G. R. Sullivan, 'Intent, purpose and complicity', *Criminal Law Review* (1988), 641; Smith, *A Modern Treatise*, 150–3. On German law and the mental element for neutral actions, see Wessels and Beulke, *Strafrecht, allgemeiner Teil*, 222–3; Roxin, *Täterschaft und Tatherrschaft*, 207–15.

[77] Schulzke, 'Autonomous weapons and distributed responsibility', 214; P. Asaro, 'Robots and responsibility from a legal perspective', paper presented at the IEEE International Conference on Robotics and Automation (2007), 1, 2.

[78] See, e.g., the collection of papers in the 2012 special issue of the *Santa Clara Law Review* on driving the future, available at http://digitalcommons.law.scu.edu/lawreview/vol52/iss4/.

[79] See, e.g., the discussion in J. M. Anderson *et al.*, *Autonomous Vehicle Technology: A Guide for Policy Makers* (Santa Monica, CA: Rand Corporation, 2014), 119–20.

user'.[80] The strict liability standard for product liability, however, generally only applies to 'manufacturing defects', whereas 'design defects' and failures to warn of risks are subject to a balancing approach that relies on negligence and risk utility.[81] Nonetheless, these ongoing efforts to regulate the liability of manufacturers and developers for the harms caused by the actions of autonomous vehicles may prove helpful in thinking about the possibility of product liability for the manufacturers and developers of AWS based on a standard of negligence and/or strict liability given the unusually dangerous nature of the product.

The civil liability paradigm will also face some difficulties given the need to establish foreseeability of the harm in light of unintended and unanticipated AWS conduct.[82] In domestic legal systems such as the United States, and in most common law jurisdictions, negligence liability has traditionally been based on the concept of reasonable foreseeability. Thus, under the classic elements of negligence liability, if the injury that is caused by the defendant was not reasonably foreseeable, he/she will not be responsible for the injury.[83] The centrality of foreseeability in negligence liability has been emphasized for evaluating both whether the defendant breached his/her duty of care and to establish proximate cause.[84] Foreseeability remains important even when one abandons negligence and moves to most instances of 'strict liability', where courts often require proof of the foreseeability of one or more of three elements: the kind or type of risk of harm, the person likely to be harmed and the manner of harm.[85]

[80] American Law Institute, *Restatement of the Law, Second: Torts* (1977) para. 402A. The product is considered defective if it 'left the supplier's control lacking any element necessary to make it safe for its intended use or possessing any feature that renders it unsafe for the intended use'. Anderson *et al., Autonomous Vehicle Technology*, 120–2.

[81] Anderson *et al., Autonomous Vehicle Technology*, 122–3, citing para. 2 of the American Law Institute, *Restatement of the Law, Third: Torts – Product Liability* (1998).

[82] See Calo, 'Robotics and the lessons of cyberlaw', 141.

[83] See the discussion at B. C. Zipursky, 'Foreseeability in breach, duty, and proximate cause', *Wake Forest Law Review*, 44 (2009), 1247, 1256. As he notes, the Restatement (Third) of Torts proposes a modified standard of foreseeability than that endorsed in the classical doctrine.

[84] W. J. Cardi, 'Reconstructing foreseeability', *Boston College Law Review*, 46 (2005), 921, 925–7.

[85] C. E. A. Carnow, 'The application of traditional tort theory to embodied machine intelligence', The Robotics and the Law Conference, Center for Internet and Society, Stanford (April 2013), 13 citing D. A. Fischer, 'Products liability-proximate cause, intervening cause, and duty', *Modern Law Review*, 52 (1987), 547, 553. See also Calo, 'Robotics and the lessons of cyberlaw', 141.

The importance placed on foreseeability for tortious liability[86] might constitute a barrier for attributing negligence liability and/or strict liability to the programmer/manufacturer/developer for precisely the kinds of reasons that were identified in the case of criminal responsibility. An AWS is designed to observe, decide and act in a manner that responds to the pressures of evolving and complex environments. Rather than a design defect, the ability to function in an unpredictable fashion is built into the nature of the system and gives it value.

Conclusion

Central to most concerns relating to criminal responsibility for the unlawful conduct of the AWS is the challenge of understanding what exactly it means for the AWS to act 'autonomously' and how this compares to the way in which autonomy is conceptualized for the purposes of moral agency in human affairs. Robotics experts describe machine autonomy on a spectrum, ranging from entities that mimic higher human cognitive abilities to systems that rely on non-deterministic reasoning to operate in unstructured and dynamic environments. In either case, the primary barrier for establishing accountability for the harm caused by an AWS is the epistemic uncertainty associated with its conduct, which is a deliberate part of its design features.

The unpredictable nature of AWS conduct raises some serious questions for traditional responsibility doctrines in criminal law as well as civil law. Criminal law typically favours purpose, knowledge or at least some form of recklessness as the minimum standard for culpability; negligence liability is used only sparingly. If the harm caused by the AWS is inherently unpredictable and cannot be detected or anticipated by any of the individuals associated with its operations, the *mens rea* requirements for criminal liability may need to be modified in the ways suggested in this chapter to avoid an accountability gap. This will also be true of civil responsibility for manufacturers and developers where foreseeability usually plays a key role in determining the scope of liability. Any proposal to adapt these constituents of responsibility will have to address complicated issues of allocating risks inevitably associated with the new technology and how heavy or strict this burden should be for the individuals associated with developing, using and benefiting from it.

---

[86] On the importance of foreseeability for tort liability, see D. Owens, 'Figuring foreseeability', *Wake Forest Law Review*, 44 (2009), 1277, 1281–90.

Refining responsibility: differentiating two types of responsibility issues raised by autonomous weapons systems

HIN-YAN LIU

Introduction

The prospect of autonomous weapons systems (AWS) has raised persistent questions of responsibility and accountability, the contours and content of which remain ill defined. This chapter seeks to clarify these questions by differentiating between two distinct, yet converging, categories of responsibility issues. The first category of responsibility issues is created by the autonomy of the weapons systems itself and arises from the circumstances in which they are used (a 'circumstantial responsibility problem'). The second set of issues is only exposed by AWS because it is conceptual in nature, arising from the relationships between different conceptions of responsibility (a 'conceptual responsibility problem'). Drawing this basic differentiation is critical because it suggests the existence of two independent problems that both require a solution, whereas only the former has been addressed in the literature to date.

As identified, the core of the problem is that the would-be direct perpetrators, who would ordinarily be individually responsible for unlawful behaviour, will be replaced by autonomous entities that are incapable of bearing direct responsibility for such consequences at the outset.[1] There are two basic avenues to solve this circumstantial

I would like to thank Professors Nehal Bhuta and Claus Kreß for their valuable comments on previous drafts. I am grateful to the Max Weber Programme and the Academy of European Law at the European University Institute for supporting this work and for leading the broader AWS project that culminated in this volume. I would also like to express my gratitude to the Max Planck Institute for Foreign and International Criminal Law in Freiburg for the support and hospitality it provided to this research project.

[1] This distinguishes autonomous weapons systems (AWS) from other actors in armed conflict who may be absolved from (retrospective) accountability on grounds of capacity.

responsibility problem: either meaningfully ascribe responsibility to the autonomous entities themselves or impute responsibility to proximate human beings.[2] Neither avenue, however, is entirely satisfactory. On the one hand, assigning responsibility to artificial agents is unsatisfying and seems to entail impunity. On the other hand, imputing responsibility to proximate individuals raises a risk of scapegoating the individuals associated with these operations. These inadequacies suggest that alterations in legal doctrine are necessary to accommodate the prospect of AWS.[3]

I also argue, however that resolving the circumstantial responsibility problem issues surrounding autonomous weapons usage is necessary, but insufficient, because a distinct set of conceptual responsibility issues would still remain. This set of responsibility issues is inherent within the disparate, but interrelated, ideas that together inform the concept of responsibility and that occur where causal forms of responsibility are conflated or substituted with types of role responsibility. Unlike circumstantial responsibility issues, which are created by the autonomy of the weapons system breaking the chain of causality, I suggest that conceptual responsibility issues are merely revealed by the challenges of artificial autonomy and remain unchanged with alterations in practice. As such, conceptual responsibility issues may provide separate grounds upon which to challenge the prudence of deploying AWS without first developing governance mechanisms that are capable of structuring responsibility.

Taking these two sets of responsibility issues together suggests that there is a real risk of impunity for the consequences of AWS behaviour under contemporary legal doctrine. This conclusion, however, points to an overlooked hazard in zealous attempts to overcome impunity: the over-ascription of individual responsibility.[4] Proximate human beings

---

But see the contributions in this volume by N. Jain, 'Autonomous weapons systems: new frameworks for individual responsibility', Chapter 13, G. S. Corn, 'Autonomous weapons systems: managing the inevitability of "taking the man out of the loop"', Chapter 10 and P. Kalmanovitz, 'Judgment, liability and the risks of riskless warfare', Chapter 7.

[2] R. Sparrow, 'Killer robots', *Journal of Applied Philosophy*, 24 (2007), 62, 69–73. See generally A. Matthias, 'The responsibility gap: ascribing responsibility for the actions of learning automata', *Ethics and Information Technology*, 6 (2004), 175.

[3] See, however, Noel Sharkey's warning that the robustness of legal interpretation may be diluted by the availability of new technologies of violence. N. Sharkey, 'Staying in the loop: human supervisory control of weapons', Chapter 2 in this volume. The proposition advanced in this chapter is not intended to enable greater permissiveness in the use of force where AWS are concerned.

[4] There is little concern expressed in the literature to guard against the hazards of combating impunity.

may become scapegoats in the zealous quest to plug the responsibility gap.[5] Thus, any proposed resolution must be mindful of this imbalance, and it may become necessary to establish safeguards to mitigate this risk.

What autonomy? Implications raised for individual responsibility

A practical question that needs to be addressed is why these responsibility issues are raised by AWS at all. The characteristics that distinguish such systems from other weapons systems must be identified to answer this question. While the boundaries are themselves indistinct, the rising levels of automation in weapons systems are predicted to shift into autonomy in the near future. With the prospect of autonomous 'weapon systems that, once activated, can select and engage targets without further intervention by a human operator',[6] the existing legal categories between combatants and weapons become blurred.[7]

The AWS discussed in this chapter need to be differentiated at the outset from merely automated weapons.[8] AWS, as presently imagined and debated, possess discretionary autonomy insofar as these systems are said to be capable of selecting and engaging targets, or refraining from using force, without additional human intervention. This discretional autonomy substitutes the human decision-making processes involved in the use of lethal force and is thus the root of the responsibility conundrum. Conversely, automated weapons that are claimed to operate autonomously are characterized by a more limited form of functional autonomy. Thus, while automated weapons may be capable of undertaking independent action, this range of action is either predetermined or

---

[5] This over-ascription of responsibility may occur in the circumstantial sense where individuals are imputed with more control or foreseeability than they actually possess or in the conceptual sense where responsibility is expanded to cover consequences beyond their causal impact instead of being limited to fulfilling the obligations attaching to their roles.

[6] C. Heyns, report of the Special Rapporteur on extrajudicial, summary or arbitrary executions, Doc. A/HRC/23/47 (2013), para. 38. As Heyns notes, this definition has been widely endorsed. US Department of Defense (DoD) Directive 3000.09, 'Autonomy in weapon systems', 21 November 2012, Glossary part II: 'Definitions', 13; UK Ministry of Defence, 'The UK approach to unmanned aircraft systems', Joint Doctrine Note 2/11 (2011), paras. 202–3; Human Rights Watch, *Losing Humanity: The Case Against Killer Robots* (New York: Human Rights Watch and International Human Rights Clinic, 2012), 2.

[7] H.-Y. Liu, 'Categorization and legality of autonomous and remote weapons systems', *International Review of the Red Cross*, 94 (2012), 627, 634–7.

[8] But see G. Sartor's and A. Omicini's contribution, 'The autonomy of technological systems and responsibilities for their use', Chapter 3 in this volume.

strictly limited.[9] As proximate human beings direct and control automated weapons systems, they retain responsibility for causing the outcomes. Thus, the unique questions of responsibility are raised only where
weapons systems possess discretionary autonomy over the use of force.

Human beings proximate to weapons systems occupy a range of
functions, including programming, manufacturing, maintenance, operating and commanding.[10] Weapons systems that possess discretionary
autonomy destabilize this taxonomy, however, because the decision to
release the weapon is not taken by a human in the final instance.[11] It is
interesting to note that this development has gone unnoticed by some
proponents of AWS who continue to insist that an operator will be
responsible.[12] Other commentators, however, have implicitly recognized

---

[9] Similarly, the US Department of Defense differentiates between conceptions of autonomy: 'The future of autonomous systems is characterized as a movement beyond autonomous mission *execution* to autonomous mission *performance*. The difference between
execution and performance is that the former simply executes a preprogrammed plan
whereas performance is associated with mission outcomes that can vary even during
a mission and require deviation from preprogrammed tasks'. US Department of Defense,
Unmanned Systems Integrated Roadmap FY 2013–2038, Doc. 14-S-0553 (2013), 66–67,
available at www.defense.gov/Portals/1/Documents/pubs/DOD-USRM-2013.pdf
(emphasis in the original).

[10] This chapter treats these categories of individuals in the abstract as singular persons.
Further issues of responsibility arise where a collective dimension of responsibility is
introduced. Especially where the programmer is concerned, responsibility issues are
further diffused by increasing complexity of the programs. This may require teamwork
to produce the programming to the point whereby no one individual has a complete
understanding of the intricacies of the program. Alternatively, aspects of the program
may be incorporated from different sources such that their overall interaction is unknown
and may be exacerbated by subsequent updates. Taken together, these issues further
diffuse the potential responsibility of the programmer. According to Pablo Kalmanovitz's
contribution to this volume (Chapter 7: 'Judgment, liability and the risks of riskless
warfare'), this development implicates the entire complex command structure and fore-
grounds liability distribution through role responsibility.

[11] The operator of a weapons system is taken here to be the individual who ultimately
decides on weapons release. The replacement of the human operator deciding on
weapons release by an autonomous weapons system is the core source of the individual
responsibility issues raised in this chapter. The point here is that there would no longer be
any human being determining the behaviours of an AWS. Peter Asaro makes a different
claim when he notes the disappearance of the human operator, because he defines
a human operator as the individual who would be held responsible for the actions of an
autonomous weapons system in a given situation. P. Asaro, 'On banning autonomous
weapon systems: human rights, automation, and the dehumanization of lethal
decision-making', *International Review of the Red Cross*, 94 (2012), 687, 693.

[12] K. Anderson and M. Waxman, '*Law and ethics for autonomous weapon systems: why
a ban won't work and how the laws of war can*', Jean Perkins Task Force on National
Security and Law Essay Series (Hoover Institution, Stanford University, 2013), 16,

the demise of the human operator in this context by excluding the operator from considerations of individual responsibility.[13]

What is less clear are the responsibilities of the programmer and the commander and how these might be appropriately divided. The individual responsibility of a programmer who programmed, or a commander who ordered, an AWS to behave unlawfully is uncontentious.[14] In both instances, the behaviour of the weapons system has been determined in advance by the individuals concerned such that they are causally connected to the consequences. What is more controversial is the appropriate limitation and division of individual responsibilities between the programmer and the commander under other circumstances. Attached to both of these roles are obligations to constrain and restrain AWS behaviour prior to its actual deployment. The responsibility of the programmer and commander is both limited by their lack of control and foresight (circumstantial issues) and characterized by the need to fulfil the obligations that attach to, and define, their role (conceptual issues). Together, these issues erect obstacles to ascribing the responsibility for the outcomes to either the programmer or the commander, who have recourse to these two different types of defence. They can either argue that the outcomes were not foreseeable, or, alternatively, they can assert that they had discharged their role responsibilities. There could be no direct responsibility but only responsibility for negligence, recklessness or incompetence.[15]

Weapons systems possessing high levels of functional autonomy that permit less-than-direct and individuated control by the operator begin to subvert existing notions of individual responsibility.[16] The lack of direct

---

available at www.hoover.org/sites/default/files/uploads/documents/Anderson-Waxman_LawAndEthics_r2_FINAL.pdf; M. Schmitt, 'Autonomous weapons systems and international humanitarian law: a reply to the critics', *Harvard National Security Journal Features* [2013], 34 respectively. It is interesting that they word the responsibility issues in terms that would more closely fit the role of a commander.

[13] Sparrow, 'Killer robots', 69–73; A. Krishnan, *Killer Robots: Legality and Ethicality of Autonomous Weapons* (Aldershot: Ashgate, 2009), 103–5.

[14] Schmitt, 'Autonomous weapons systems and international humanitarian law', 33–4.

[15] But see Sartor and Omicini, 'The autonomy of technological systems and responsibilities for their use', in which they argue that the lack of direct responsibility in itself should not be a barrier to introducing the technology provided that a larger set of possible accidents are mitigated or obviated. The question hinges upon whether direct responsibility is merely a means of deterrence or whether it captures other interests or is intrinsically valuable.

[16] See further N. Jain, 'Autonomous weapons systems: new frameworks for individual responsibility', Chapter 13 in this volume.

control and foreseeability of the outcome introduce circumstantial responsibility issues. This is complemented by conceptual responsibility issues that are revealed by high levels of automation transforming direct control into supervisory control. Such an analysis suggests that both the circumstantial and conceptual issues of individual responsibility need to be revisited with the current existence of automated weapons systems, even if weapons systems possessing discretional autonomy are never developed.

Circumstantial responsibility issues: control, predictability and foresight

A responsibility gap was identified by Andreas Matthias for autonomous learning machines more generally because the manufacturer or operator of such a machine cannot, in principle, predict its future behaviour.[17] He highlights the diminishing influence of the programmer for machines that are capable of altering their behaviour from experience and in reaction to the environment: 'In a steady progression the programmer role changes from *coder* to *creator* of software organisms. In the same degree as the influence of the creator over the machine decreases, the influence of the operating environment increases.'[18] It is likely, however, that the control and predictability obstacles introduced by discretionary autonomy in weapons systems are understated because of the potential for emergent behaviour to affect the outcome.[19]

Such behaviour may arise from interactions between the component parts of AWS, between different systems, and between the systems and their operational environment. First, considering the complexity and range of programming involved in technologically advanced systems, it is unlikely that the consequences of the interaction between different programs can be understood, let alone foreseen.[20] This suggests that the behaviour of even a single AWS may be difficult to predict, even where the effect of each constituent part of its programming can be predicted independently. Second, some AWS have been envisaged to operate in

---

[17] Matthias, 'The responsibility gap', 175.

[18] *Ibid.*, 182 (emphasis in the original). Sparrow raises similar concerns with regard to AWS as discussed above. Sparrow, 'Killer robots', 70–1.

[19] On the unpredictability of emergent outcomes, see generally J. Gleick, *Chaos: Making a New Science* (New York: Vintage, 1997).

[20] This is analogous to the psychological concept of 'gestalt' where the whole is greater than the sum of its parts.

'swarms', opening the possibility for complex behaviours to emerge from adherence to simple rules.[21] In such situations, even if the behaviour of a single AWS is entirely controllable and predictable, the aggregate behaviour of such systems interacting with each other cannot be. Third, there is the influence of the environment in which the AWS operate. As each environment will be different, the behaviour of an AWS will vary even if its programming remains unchanged. Ultimately, the behaviour of an AWS is likely to be influenced by the cumulative effects of all of these factors combined, together creating circumstantial responsibility issues by erecting significant obstacles for control, predictability and foresight.

The programmer will constrain the range of AWS behaviour at the research and development stage, such that these constraints are likely to be broad and abstract.[22] Clearly, the programmer can displace blame to the commander by acknowledging the limitations of the system.[23] However, AWS behaviour also depends upon the commander who, in deploying that system, will be expected to apply more specific and contextual constraints.[24] This facilitates the displacement of responsibility by the programmer to the commander because it would be feasible for the programmer to argue that he/she had discharged his/her obligations by implementing general parameters. Thus, the programmer may argue that unlawful system behaviour is the responsibility of the commander, who failed to complement these general parameters with more specific and contextual constraints in the system's deployment.

While the commander may make the obverse argument to displace responsibility on to the programmer, the analysis of commander responsibility is more complicated. The commander necessarily acts at a later

---

[21] P. Scharre, *Robotics on the Battlefield*, part II: *The Coming Swarm* (Washington, DC: Center for a New American Security, 2014). See also P. W. Singer, *Wired for War: The Robotics Revolution and Conflict in the Twenty-First Century* (London: Penguin, 2009), 229–36.

[22] The prospect for dual- or multi-use technologies suggests that the programmer might not even envisage that his/her work will be incorporated into an AWS.

[23] Sparrow, 'Killer robots', 69.

[24] This treatment overlooks an additional complexity by treating the commander as one person. Not only does the military hierarchy consist of a chain of command that potentially implicates a succession of individuals, but command roles might be divided between the procurement officer and the field commander who bear quite different responsibilities in relation to constraining the behaviour of an AWS. On the latter point, see G. S. Corn, 'Autonomous weapons systems: managing the inevitability of "taking the man out of the loop"', Chapter 10 in this volume.

stage than the programmer.[25] Thus, the commander's ability to set constraints will be contingent upon the prior constraints established by the programmer.[26] This narrows the commander's control over the AWS and limits his/her predictability over the system's behaviour, which together justify that his/her individual responsibility over the consequences is curtailed.[27] Additional boundaries are erected to the flow of responsibility to the commander by the circumstances within which AWS are envisaged to be used. As a purely legal matter under the Rome Statute of the International Criminal Court (Rome Statute), the replacement of the direct human operator of a weapons system by an artificial counterpart may frustrate the prerequisite superior–subordinate relationship,[28] because this has been held to date as an interpersonal relationship.[29] Even were AWS to be accorded legal personhood, Article 25(1) only allows the International Criminal Court (ICC) jurisdiction

[25] The closer temporal, and most likely physical, proximity between the commander and the consequences of AWS behaviour may predispose the commander to assuming the greater share of responsibility for establishing the parameters within which an AWS may operate. This may be unjustified, given that his or her potential range of influence on the system will be restricted by the constraints imposed earlier by the programmer.

[26] Approaching this issue from a different perspective, Alexander Bolt notes that 'the legal advisor will be concerned with how the weapon is expected to operate on this particular mission, including . . . how the specific mission algorithms fit with weapon architecture'. A. Bolt, 'The use of autonomous weapons and the role of the legal advisor' in D. Saxon (ed.), *International Humanitarian Law and the Changing Technology of War* (The Hague: Martinus Nijhoff, 2013), 132.

[27] This is not, of course, to deny that the commander retains the role responsibilities attached to fulfilling the functions of a commander and can be held responsible for any failures to discharge his/her duties. The point is instead that the responsibility of the commander is not merely limited to his/her role but additionally falls within the strictures imposed by the programmer.

[28] This condition was established by the Trial Chamber of the International Criminal Tribunal in the Former Yugoslavia. ICTY, *Prosecutor* v. *Delalic* (IT-96-21-T) Trials Chamber, 16 November 1998, para. 346; subsequently reaffirmed in ICTY, *Prosecutor* v. *Halilovi* (IT-01-48-A), Appeals Chamber, 16 October 2007, para. 59; ICTY, *Prosecutor* v. *Perisic* (IT-04-81-A), Appeals Chamber, 28 February 2013, para. 86. Rome Statute of the International Criminal Court (Rome Statute), 1 July 2002, UN Doc. A/CONF.183/9.

[29] 'It is the Trial Chamber's conclusion . . . *that persons* effectively in command of such more informal structures, with power to prevent and punish the crimes *of persons* who are in fact under their control, may under certain circumstances be held responsible for their failure to do so'. *Prosecutor* v. *Delalic*, para. 354 (emphasis added). Similarly, commentators have opined that 'a relationship of superior authority for the purpose of that doctrine is one between two individuals: a superior on the one hand and another individual who is said to have committed a crime'. G. Mettraux, *The Law of Command Responsibility* (Oxford University Press, 2009), 139; see generally 138–56. Rome Statute, Article 25(1) stipulates that '[t]he Court shall have jurisdiction over *natural persons* pursuant to this Statute' (emphasis added).

over natural persons. This suggests, at least from a legalistic perspective, that it would be impossible to invoke the doctrine of command responsibility over an AWS for lack of a superior–subordinate relationship.

There may be further difficulties in establishing that the commander had 'effective control' over the AWS because this requires that he/she possess 'the power and ability to take effective steps to prevent and punish crimes which others have committed or are about to commit'.[30] From the inexhaustive list of indicators for effective control,[31] particular problems will arise with the existence of effective disciplinary and investigatory powers and the power to stop AWS crimes. The powers possessed by a commander to influence, let alone suppress or prevent, certain behaviours of an AWS may (i) be severely limited because of the technical parameters of the system's architecture; (ii) be contingent upon the technical prowess of the commander; and (iii) be impracticable because of the inability to meaningfully punish machines. Together, these considerations create daunting obstacles to establishing that a commander could be in command of an AWS and that he/she has the requisite capabilities to subjugate such systems assigned to him/her.[32] These circumstantial issues may be overcome by heightening the expectations made of the commander, obliging him/her to abort the mission or otherwise prevent unlawful consequences from occurring.[33]

Furthermore, because AWS may significantly increase the volume of available information from the battle space, their use may affect the

---

[30] Mettraux, *The Law of Command Responsibility*, 157; see generally 156–90.

[31] *Ibid.*, 164–7.

[32] Consider also Corn, 'Autonomous weapons systems', in which he argues that the commander is also responsible for establishing a command culture respectful of the laws of war. This requirement may become highly technical where autonomous weapons systems are concerned, however, and be beyond the practical means of military commanders as Corn has recognized.

[33] Looking ahead to the following section, however, this responsibility will remain characterized by omission. Thus, the responsibility borne by the commander will be limited to whether he/she had duly discharged the functions attached to his/her role as a commander and not as if he/she committed the crime him/herself. Furthermore, if the obligations attached to command are raised, this might be balanced by a more lenient approach when evaluating whether these have been fulfilled. It may, however, be that the weapons systems with final abort or self-destruct capabilities remaining in the hands of the commander are not truly AWS because they may not be able to 'select or engage targets without further human intervention'. It should also be noted that the severance of constant and reliable contact between the commander and the AWS is one of the key drivers for the development of the technology. Independent and self-contained operation would insulate the system from external influences (such as hacking) and make the system less detectable.

criteria governing the mental element of any crime. This is because advances in communication technologies potentially drown the commander in a deluge of information, such that the amount of information that can objectively be imputed to the commander potentially becomes overwhelming.[34] In the face of this prospect, Charles Garraway proposes that the 'should-have-known' standard should be transmuted instead to whether 'there was a degree of personal dereliction by the commander' in order to keep the doctrine manageable.[35] While this suggestion maintains the harmony between the actual abilities of the commander and the obligations that he/she bears, it is clear that this proposal shrinks both the content and the boundaries of his/her legal obligations considerably. The strength of the command responsibility doctrine is thus hollowed out, thereby increasing the mismatch between the reliance placed on it to overcome impunity for AWS and its actual ability to impose responsibility for their deployment.[36]

Whether the commander is capable of understanding and relying on the constraints imposed by the programmer of the AWS constitutes another facet of the mental element issue. This will affect the knowledge that can be imputed to the commander with regard to the AWS that is about to commit the crimes because the future behaviour of such systems depends on the cumulative influences of both the programmer and the commander.[37] This reduces further the residual scope of command responsibility where AWS are involved.

Yet, the programmer may be implicated with superior responsibility because it is the combined influences of the programmer and

---

[34] C. Garraway, 'The application of superior responsibility in an era of unlimited information' in D. Saxon (ed.), *International Humanitarian Law and the Changing Technology of War*, 203.

[35] *Ibid.*

[36] This discrepancy is thrown into stark relief considering the argument, made by Christof Heyns' contribution, that the deployment of autonomous weapons systems should be accompanied by higher and stricter standards because these systems are purportedly more capable. C. Heyns, 'Autonomous weapons systems: living a dignified life and dying a dignified death', Chapter 1 in this volume.

[37] Yet, International Criminal Court (ICC) jurisprudence suggests that it is sufficient to prove actual knowledge if the commander is enmeshed within an organized structure with established systems of monitoring and reporting. ICC, *Prosecutor* v. *Bemba* (ICC-01/05-01/08), Pre-Trial Chamber II, 15 June 2009, para. 431, quoting approvingly ICTY, *Prosecutor* v. *Hadzihasanovic* (IT-01-47-T), Trial Chamber, judgment of 15 March 2006, para. 94. This jurisprudence appears to be calibrated towards over-attributing responsibility to the commander, but see Corn's contribution to this volume arguing that this standard creates a powerful disincentive for commanders to fail in their role. Corn, 'Autonomous weapons systems'.

commander together that must constrain AWS behaviour. This is because the Rome Statute provides for the criminal responsibility of non-military superiors contingent upon 'effective authority and control, and as a result of his or her failure to exercise control properly over such subordinates'.[38] While similar barriers are likely to prevent the ascription of superior responsibility to the programmer, it may be that this form of responsibility can justifiably be extended to compensate for the constriction of command responsibility precisely because the constraining function hitherto reserved to the commander will become shared with the programmer.

The obstacles to responsibility attribution raised by discretional autonomy in weapons systems to issues of control, predictability and foreseeability are factual objections concerning the manner in which such systems are developed and deployed. The point here is that the responsibility gap is identified with the loss of control possessed by the individual over the behaviour of such a weapons system.[39] This discretional autonomy may prevent weapons systems from behaving in a manner intended by the programmer or directed by a commander. It may even prevent the programmer or commander from being able to reliably predict the system's behaviour or foresee the consequences of the system's behaviour, which, in indicating the failure to take necessary precautions, could be the grounds to claim that such systems are *ex ante* unlawful.

These, however, are circumstantial issues of responsibility that are ultimately grounded upon practical technological capabilities and how these are deployed. Thus, according to this view, the precise nature of the circumstances surrounding AWS usage will determine the distribution of responsibility among proximate human beings according to the criteria of control, predictability and foreseeability. If, however, technological advances enable accurate predictions of AWS behaviour, then the objections to ascribing responsibility for these consequences to the programmer and commander will lose force.[40] This would narrow the responsibility gap associated with AWS usage. Yet these changing

---

[38] Rome Statute, Article 28(2).

[39] In a very loose sense, this corresponds to H. L. A. Hart's concept of 'capacity responsibility'. While Hart's concept is broader, it encompasses the understanding of what conduct the relevant rules require, the ability to deliberate and decide on these requirements, and to conform to these decisions. But a core element is that of control of behaviour. H. L. A. Hart, *Punishment and Responsibility: Essays in the Philosophy of Law*, 2nd edn (Oxford University Press, 2008), 227–30.

[40] The point here is that improved praxis would mitigate this type of responsibility concern.

circumstances would have little effect on the responsibility gap subsisting between the very concepts of responsibility themselves.

Conceptual responsibility issues: between 'role responsibility' and 'causal responsibility'

A different type of issue arises from the very concepts of responsibility and their interaction, which cannot be resolved by increasing human control over an AWS or otherwise improving the operation of the system.[41] Hart recognized that the term 'responsibility' actually expresses a constellation of distinct, albeit connected, ideas.[42] This can be seen especially well in the distinction that he made between the 'role' and 'causal' forms of responsibility.[43] Role responsibility describes a sense of responsibility that attaches to an individual by virtue of the position he/she occupies or the function that he/she is expected to fulfil.[44] Thus, role responsibility is defined by the performance of obligations connected to an individual's role. It is clear from this account that role responsibility is strictly circumscribed, requiring only the fulfilment of existing obligations but, importantly, nothing more – an individual has discharged his/her role responsibility when he/she has acted in accordance with obligations and has accomplished whatever might be expected from his/her function.[45]

Unlike role responsibility, which has the effect of predefining the obligations for which one is responsible, however, the causal form of

[41] It is important to note that the notion of responsibility has not fragmented but, rather, that its constituent concepts have and continue to be independent. S. Veitch, *Law and Irresponsibility: On the Legitimation of Human Suffering* (London: Routledge-Cavendish, 2007), 38.

[42] See in particular, Hart, *Punishment and Responsibility*, 211–15.

[43] As Hart introduces, '[a] wide range of different, though connected, ideas is covered by the expressions "responsibility", "responsible", and "responsible for"'. *Ibid.*, 212–15. Scott Veitch observes that 'Hart's taxonomy therefore, perhaps unintentionally, provides us with an index of the roles that different versions of "responsibility" play, and are required to play, in contemporary life.' Veitch, *Law and Irresponsibility*, 38.

[44] There is considerable overlap here with Sartor and Omicini's notion of 'functional responsibility' in their contribution, Chapter 3 in this volume. Interestingly, their conception of blameworthiness, which implies a species of causal responsibility, is similarly constrained within the boundaries of role responsibility.

[45] Note that the actual performance of his/her obligations is not always necessary to discharge his/her role responsibility because the scope of his/her obligations may in fact be narrower. An example of this is where an objective or practical standard is applied, such that his/her obligation is to do only what is reasonable or feasible in relation to his/her position.

responsibility is both unbounded and unpredictable. Causal responsibility can be considered to be synonymous with the factual connection between cause and effect. As such, this species of responsibility is not limited to natural persons but can extend to inanimate objects, natural processes and other effects because causal responsibility simply forges a connection between sources and consequences.[46] AWS may be the factual cause of unlawful outcomes, but it may be meaningless to translate this causal responsibility into forms of liability under contemporary legal doctrine because the law is predominantly concerned with the actions and omissions of natural persons.[47]

To illustrate the disconnection between role and causal forms of responsibility, consider an individual fulfilling the role of a programmer, manufacturer or commander of an AWS. The individual is clearly responsible for fulfilling the expectations and obligations that attach to his/her function in relation to the AWS, but this equally becomes the full extent of his/her responsibility.[48] When he/she has fulfilled these obligations, he/she is deemed to have acted responsibly. For example, a programmer has discharged his/her role responsibility if he/she has taken sufficient care to ensure that his/her algorithms function according to the requirements. A manufacturer has fulfilled his/her duties where the AWS has been built according to the design specifications. A commander who has taken the necessary steps in deploying the system has satisfied the obligations of his/her position. Where an AWS nevertheless goes wrong, the individual in each instance would have discharged his/her role obligation.[49] The fact that a programmer,

[46] Hart, *Punishment and Responsibility*, 214–15.
[47] As Sparrow puts it, '[w]e can easily imagine a robot, or for that matter, any machine, being *causally* responsible for some death(s) ... However, we typically baulk at the idea that they could be *morally* responsible'. Sparrow, 'Killer robots', 71 (emphasis in the original). As the law is generally not concerned with describing the causal chains behind events unless these involve persons, this translation will only become meaningful when autonomous weapons systems are recognized as legal persons.
[48] Veitch, *Law and Irresponsibility*, 48. Indeed, the concept of role responsibility may insulate an individual from being ascribed causal responsibility. Even in situations where the individual's failure to perform his/her duties led to the outcome, she can only be punished for his/her failure to execute his/her tasks, and not for causing the impugned outcomes.
[49] The existence of a responsibility gap may hinge upon the attribution of agency to the AWS. The devastation caused by a typhoon, for example, does not generally raise the question of responsibility, let alone allegations of impunity. This would imply that autonomous weapons systems are treated differently from natural disasters as far as responsibility is concerned, but still differently from natural persons who the law commends or condemns accordingly.

manufacturer or commander did a bad job (that is, failed to do what was expected or required in his/her role) is not the crux of the responsibility question, however, because the core concern focuses on causal responsibility for the consequences.

The types of concerns over responsibility for AWS that are expressed in attempts to ascribe individual responsibility fall largely within the concept of causal responsibility. The core concern is to assert individual responsibility for the unlawful consequences that are caused by the AWS. Considerations that revolve around the proper performance of due diligence obligations are often secondary and parasitic to such causal responsibility because they are usually considered only when the consequences are negative, and rarely otherwise. The core of the problem is this discrepancy between the fixed role responsibility possessed by an individual and the unbridled outcomes of autonomous system behaviour that are imported through causal responsibility. Thus, a gap is created between the very concepts of responsibility, at least in situations where individuals have discharged their role responsibility obligations, but unlawful outcomes are nevertheless caused by the AWS.[50]

To discuss the limits of role responsibility, and its independence from causal responsibility, we revisit the doctrine of command responsibility as a paragon example. We had previously examined the diffused control and limited predictability experienced by the commander as an example of circumstantial responsibility issues. Now, we turn to how the concept of command responsibility focuses the question of responsibility upon the obligations attached to a role and whether these have been discharged. Nowhere in the contemporary doctrine has this been more clearly articulated than in the foundational judgment of the US Military Commission in *Yamashita*: 'Clearly, assignment to command military troops is accompanied by broad authority and heavy responsibility ... *It is absurd, however, to consider a commander a murderer or rapist because one of his soldiers*

---

[50] An alteration in the circumstantial aspects of responsibility may affect the scope of role responsibility but does not affect the conceptual limitations imposed by role responsibility and its segregation from causal responsibility. Adopting the scenario above where an advanced algorithm would be able to predict all possible behaviours of an autonomous weapons system, the role responsibility possessed by the programmer and the commander may be expanded accordingly, and the due diligence standard is likely to become more expansive. Yet, this does not translate into the programmer or the commander becoming causally responsible for the outcomes arising from the behaviour of that AWS. A conceptual distance in the nature of responsibility remains between proximate human beings and an AWS, regardless of the circumstantial issues related to control and foreseeability.

commits a murder or rape.[51] This concept of command responsibility has been unambiguously reaffirmed by both the Trial Chamber of the International Criminal Tribunal for the former Yugoslavia and the Pre-Trial Chamber of the ICC.[52] From this line of jurisprudence, it is clear that the commander is not to be held accountable in a causal sense for the consequences of his/her underlings' behaviour. While the position is less clear for programmers, it would be similarly absurd to attribute unlawful consequences of AWS behaviour as though these unlawful acts were directly committed by the programmers themselves.

Thus, while Kenneth Anderson and Matthew Waxman recognize that 'there will still be human decision-makers who can be held individually accountable for *grossly improper* design or deployment decisions',[53] they make a basic error in relying upon role responsibility to cover the gap that inheres within causal responsibility. In their example, individual accountability arises from the failure of those individuals to fulfil the obligations attaching to their role, rather than from the outcomes caused by the AWS.[54] This solution raises two very different problems. First, while the fulfilment of role responsibilities may restrict the range of possible outcomes, this does not equate with establishing direct causal responsibility for those outcomes. Rather, it is because a responsibility gap will remain for results that occur beyond the limits of role responsibility. Second, even where these individuals are held accountable, their accountability will be limited only to their failure within their

---

[51] *United States of America v. Tomoyuki Yamashita* [1945] United States Military Commission, Manila Case no. 21, IV Law Rep Trials War Crim 1, 35 (emphasis added). The judgment continues: 'Should a commander issue orders which lead directly to lawless acts, the criminal responsibility is definite and has always been so understood.' In the latter situation, the commander bears additional 'causal' responsibility for those consequences through his/her orders.

[52] '[T]he superior cannot be considered as if he had committed the crime himself, but merely for his neglect of duty with regard to crimes committed by subordinates.' ICTY, *Prosecutor v. Oric* (IT-03-68-T) Trials Chamber, judgment of 30 June 2006, para. 293. Similarly, the Pre-Trial Chamber of the ICC has explicitly noted 'that article 28 of the Statute reflects a different form of criminal responsibility than that found under article 25(3) (a) of the Statute in the sense that a superior may be held responsible for the prohibited conduct of his subordinates for failing to fulfil his duty to prevent or repress their unlawful conduct or submit the matter to the competent authorities'. *Prosecutor v. Bemba*, para. 405.

[53] Anderson and Waxman, 'Law and ethics for autonomous weapon systems', 17 (emphasis added). Note here that they stress the role form of responsibility in couching responsibility as an omission but do not grapple with the gap in causal responsibility.

[54] This does not include the situations, canvassed earlier, where individuals direct or order an autonomous weapons system towards unlawful ends.

roles, which is a very different proposition than being held accountable for the outcomes caused by this failure.[55] Thus, accountability for the outcomes remains elusive because individuals are only accountable for their failures within their roles, rather than for directly bringing about the consequences.[56] Anderson and Waxman's assertion that the 'provisions in [US Department of Defense Directive 3000.09] point to practical ways to strengthen human accountability'[57] perilously masks these critical differences.[58]

In this context, Scott Veitch observes that 'the perpetuation of harm and suffering may come about *not* through so many broken promises, but rather through something far more disturbing, its opposite – promises fulfilled and *jobs well done*'.[59] While this observation was made in the context of the social division of labour, its implications are magnified where weapons systems possess discretional autonomy over the use of force. Irresponsibility will pervade the outcomes caused by the behaviour of AWS because the concepts of causal and role responsibilities remain distinct and largely independent. Furthermore, this type of irresponsibility is likely to languish within the development and deployment of AWS into the future because of the policy shift evidenced in US Department of Defense Directive 3000.09.[60] This document, *inter alia*, 'assigns responsibility for the development and use of autonomous

[55] Not least because the former is a form of omission, rather than of commission, and that its scope is clearly bounded.
[56] I argue that this is the case even where role responsibilities include the obligation to avoid or minimize the risk of certain outcomes. In this case, accountability concerns whether or not the risk was mitigated or avoided but does not connect the individual with the outcome directly. There may also be a lack of accountability for the actor who directly caused the outcome. A different perspective may be found in punishment: it is likely that those who failed in their functions will be punished for omission, and will receive lighter sentences than those held accountable for actions directly connected to the consequences.
[57] Anderson and Waxman, 'Law and ethics for autonomous weapon systems', 17. US Department of Defense (DoD) Directive 3000.09, 'Autonomy in weapons systems', 21 November 2012, available at www.dtic.mil/whs/directives/corres/pdf/300009p.pdf. The Directive, and its focus on role responsibility, is discussed in the following paragraph.
[58] Dan Saxon, in his contribution, asserts that Directive 3000.09 does not affect the criminal responsibility of commanders involved with the operation of autonomous weapons systems. This reinforces the suggestion that command responsibility will remain as a species of role responsibility under the Directive. D. Saxon, 'A human touch: autonomous weapons, DoD Directive 3000.09 and the interpretation of "appropriate levels of human judgment over the use of force"', Chapter 9 in this volume.
[59] Veitch, *Law and Irresponsibility*, 50 (emphasis in the original).
[60] See DoD, 'Autonomy in weapon systems', Glossary part II: 'Definitions', Enclosure 4. See Saxon, 'A human touch', for detailed discussion of the contours of this Directive.

REFINING RESPONSIBILITY 341

and semi-autonomous functions in weapon systems' but crucially is couched in the language of oversight, review, policy, evaluation, monitoring, design, certification and assessment.[61] Thus, this Directive assigns only role responsibilities – it is silent on the question of causal responsibility for the adverse results of using AWS. The overall effect of this policy is twofold. On the one hand, it clarifies the type of obligation borne by individuals involved with the development and deployment of AWS. On the other hand, however, clarifying only role responsibilities may have the subtle effect of immunizing these individuals from bearing causal responsibility for any adverse consequences arising from AWS use. Since the policy stipulates the obligations that individuals in various positions have to fulfil, it funnels any questions of accountability towards issues of role responsibility. The policy leaves untouched the issue of causal responsibility where AWS are concerned.

Thus, there are two possible, but unsatisfactory, outcomes to the development and deployment of AWS under the current conceptions of responsibility. The first is quite simply the persistence of impunity for the outcomes caused by AWS, which cannot be held to meaningful account. The second option is to scapegoat proximate human beings by blurring two distinct forms of responsibility: over-extending beyond the limits of individual role responsibilities to cover the gap in accountability for consequences. As these are both intractable problems arising from the very conceptions of responsibility and their interaction, they cannot be solved by merely altering the circumstances in which AWS are developed and deployed. Instead, any solution must come from redefining these concepts and in clearly establishing their interrelationship. Attention must therefore be paid to addressing the conceptual responsibility issues in parallel with efforts to ameliorate the conditions under which AWS are to be used.

Between impunity and scapegoating: drawing analogies with child soldiers under international law

This chapter has demonstrated that two different categories of responsibility issues arise from the introduction of AWS, suggesting that an adequate resolution must address both the circumstances in which these systems are used and reconceptualize the very notion of

---

[61] DoD, 'Autonomy in weapon systems', Glossary part II: 'Definitions', 1, 9–12. Note that the terminologies used define obligations to be fulfilled.

342 NEW FRAMEWORKS FOR INDIVIDUAL RESPONSIBILITY

responsibility itself. As alluded to earlier, attempts to resolve these responsibility issues run the very real risk of scapegoating individuals because the simplest way to overcome allegations of impunity is to over-extend individual responsibility. Analogies to this approach are apparent in legal systems that ascribe responsibility for the activities of animals to their owners or of children to parents.[62] Within non-military settings, such ascription of responsibility may be justifiable in order to ameliorate harm through material compensation. Yet, within the context of armed conflict and other activities that potentially engage international criminal law, safeguards are necessary to prevent scapegoating.[63] Thus, the fight against impunity for the development and deployment of AWS must be tempered with limitations to prevent the law from perpetrating injustice.

A possible avenue might be to draw an analogy with the treatment of child soldiers under international law. While Robert Sparrow argues that there is sufficient similarity to treat child soldiers and AWS analogously, he does this to suggest that both occupy an awkward position on the auton-omy spectrum that makes the attribution of responsibility difficult.[64] While his observations may ground this analogy, I seek to draw out a very different implication of this comparison by way of conclusion.

The question of who is legally responsible for the harm and injury caused by child soldiers is short-circuited by the unambiguous treatment of those who recruit or use them under international law. Under inter-national humanitarian law, both Additional Protocols to the Geneva Conventions contain provisions that prevent parties from recruiting children under the age of fifteen into the armed forces or groups and from allowing them to take part in hostilities.[65] More pertinently for establishing individual responsibility, the Rome Statute expressly crim-inalizes individuals '[c]onscripting or enlisting children under the age of

---

[62] A different aspect of this type of ascribing responsibility can be seen in English tort law, where Cairns LC approvingly cited the decision from Blackburn J in the court below: 'We think that the true rule of law is, that the person who, for his own purposes, brings on his land and collects and keeps there anything likely to do mischief if it escapes, must keep it in at his peril; and if he does not do so, is *prima facie* answerable for all the damage which is the natural consequence of its escape.' *Rylands* v. *Fletcher* (1868) 1868 UKHL 1 (UK House of Lords).

[63] Safeguards are needed to maintain the consistency of international criminal law itself, in addition to protecting the innocence of individuals until proven guilty.

[64] Sparrow, 'Killer robots', 73–4.

[65] Article 77(2) of Additional Protocol I, and Article 4(3)(c) of Additional Protocol II, to the Geneva Conventions of 12 August 1949, and relating to the Protection of Victims of International Armed Conflicts, 8 June 1977, 1125 UNTS 3 for international and non-international armed conflicts respectively. These provisions are subsequently reiterated in Article 38 of the UN Convention of the Rights of the Child 1989, 1577 UNTS 3.

fifteen years into the national armed forces or using them to participate actively in hostilities'.[66] While there is significant weight to the argument that these provisions are aimed specifically at protecting children,[67] this way of structuring responsibility may offer insights for the development and deployment of AWS.

It is clear that children accused of perpetrating international crimes will not be held individually responsible by the ICC.[68] The UNICEF Paris Principles affirm this position by stating that '[c]hildren who are accused of crimes under international law ... *should be considered primarily as victims of offences against international law*'.[69] The point is that international criminal law absolves children of responsibility for their participation in, or perpetration of, international crimes. The potential void that this creates in terms of individual responsibility is avoided by the clear prohibition of child soldiers from armed conflict at an earlier stage. Hence, the Rome Statute criminalizes those individuals who militarize children, regardless of the actual conduct of the child soldiers and whether they comply with international humanitarian law.[70] Unlike the

[66] Rome Statute, Article 8 (2)(b)(xxvi) and (e)(vii), respectively for international and non-international armed conflicts.

[67] The difficulties surrounding how to frame child soldier-related offences can be seen in relation to the Statute of the Special Court for Sierra Leone [16 January 2002] 2178 UNTS 138. The original proposal couched the offence in the terminology of coercion, but this was rejected to maintain consistency with the Rome Statute. See N. Jørgensen, 'Child soldiers and the parameters of international criminal law', *Chinese Journal of International Law*, 11 (2012), 657, 660–5. There are a constellation of reasons including the relative lack of autonomy, the vulnerability and the limited moral agency possessed by child soldiers that undergird their special treatment under international law. G. A. Sinha, 'Child soldiers as super-privileged combatants', *International Journal of Human Rights*, 17 (2013), 584. This suggests that there may yet be undiscovered reasons to treat child soldiers in a special manner. Indeed, an argument has also been made that child soldiers fall within a class of combatant who are victims by virtue of being combatants.

[68] Rome Statute, Article 26 precludes the jurisdiction of the ICC to individuals under the age of eighteen years. Note, however, that international law more generally does permit the prosecution of child soldiers for acts of atrocity. Instead, recourse to these international legal mechanisms is declined because '[t]he international legal imagination does not much wish to confront the quandary of the child soldier as atrocity perpetrator'. M. A. Drumbl, *Reimagining Child Soldiers in International Law and Policy* (Oxford University Press, 2012), 103–16.

[69] UNICEF, Paris Principles: Principles and Guidelines on Children Associated with Armed Forces or Armed Groups, February 2007 para. 3.6 (emphasis added).

[70] This position is clearly borne out by the first judgment issued by the ICC, where the emphasis of the conviction was upon conscripting, recruiting and using children under the age of fifteen actively in armed hostilities and not for any alleged war crimes committed by those children. ICC, *Prosecutor* v. *Thomas Lubanga Dyilo* (ICC-01/04-01/06), Trial Chamber I, judgment of 14 March 2012, paras. 1351–8.

344   NEW FRAMEWORKS FOR INDIVIDUAL RESPONSIBILITY

modalities of causal responsibility canvassed earlier, the individual is not responsible for colluding or controlling the crimes committed by the child soldiers[71] but, rather, for introducing irresponsible entities into armed conflict.

A parallel can now be considered between the treatment of child soldiers and of AWS under international criminal law for the purposes of establishing individual responsibility. Like child soldiers, AWS are excluded from bearing individual responsibility under the Rome Statute.[72] To prevent situations of impunity associated with the use of AWS, a solution would be to criminalize the introduction of such irresponsible systems onto the battle space. This approach has the advantage of simultaneously precluding situations of impunity and preventing individuals from becoming scapegoats.

This approach may also ground an alternative basis for a moratorium on the deployment of AWS and offers three benefits over the current campaign for pre-emptive prohibition.[73] First, the emphasis is placed directly upon individuals, which skirts issues associated with signing and ratifying international conventions, of international enforcement and of establishing state responsibility. Second, the criminalization is based upon the adopted legal position. This highlights the fact that the situations of impunity arising from AWS are a function of legal, rather than technical, inadequacy and reflect in turn the dual nature of the responsibility problem. Third, where a pre-emptive prohibition may unduly stifle the development of autonomous technologies, which may have legitimate civilian applications, the criminalization approach may be readily rescinded if these issues are subsequently resolved. Indeed, the criminalization approach may provide strong incentives to develop robust legal responses to the problems posed by AWS. Thus, the responsibility approach to a moratorium on AWS confers several benefits by focusing remedial attention upon both the circumstances within which such systems are used and upon the concepts that govern the very notion of responsibility.

---

[71] This is not to say, of course, that child soldiers per se are able to frustrate the doctrines of joint criminal enterprise or of perpetration through an organization.

[72] Rome Statute, Article 26 excludes minors in the former case, and Article 25(1) restricts the ICC's jurisdiction to natural persons for the latter.

[73] Human Rights Watch, *Losing Humanity*.

PART VII

Conclusion

Present futures: concluding reflections and open questions on autonomous weapons systems

NEHAL BHUTA, SUSANNE BECK AND ROBIN GEISS

Introduction: surveying the arguments

The chapters collected in this volume address an as-yet unrealized future potentiality: something called an 'autonomous weapons system' (AWS), the definition of which remains open to vigorous contestation. To debate an uncertain future is necessarily to represent it, to sketch and engage with competing visions of it and, in a very practical sense, to try to shape it through our contemporary reflections.[1] As historian of science Jenny Andersson observes about the emergence of 'futurology' in the 1960s, predicting and contesting the contours of possible future realities (neologized as *'futuribles'* by French intellectual Bertrand de Jouvenel) was a kind of 'world-making . . . a veritable battlefield of competing images of the future of the world'.[2] In such an exercise, the lines between forecasting, prediction, speculation, envisioning, and even science fiction are blurred.[3] The point of such conjecturing – no matter how fanciful – is to influence action and thought in the present by making some future states of the world seem desirable or undesirable, inspiring or terrifying, comforting or anxiety producing:

> Speculation, predictions, and especially visions, have rhetorical power;
> they can be used as a form of persuasion, to enroll others into activities
> that help make a particular future a reality. They can also be used to lay the
> groundwork making us comfortable with a situation that might occur in
> the future. Visions can be dangerous as well, insofar as they draw attention

[1] J. Andersson, 'The great future debate and the struggle for the world', *American Historical Review*, 117 (2012), 1411–30.

[2] *Ibid.*, 1429.

[3] For a reflection that characterizes the current controversies concerning autonomous weapons systems (AWS) as a kind of science fiction, see O. Ben-Naftali and Z. Triger, 'The human conditioning: international law and science fiction', *Journal of Law, Culture and Humanities* (forthcoming).

away from other possibilities and other possible agendas for research and development.[4]

To contest the future is necessarily to contest the present. One might add a corollary relevant to AWS: to contest the future of machines is to always contest the future of the human and how we understand what – if anything – is necessarily and distinctively human about a given field of activity. In her *Reflections on Violence*, Hannah Arendt seeks to distinguish between violence and power in order to capture a dimension that she considers to be specifically human: violence is instrumental – a means to an end – and those means could well be enhanced by technological progress. However, violence in and of itself is in the service of something human: power, force and strength. Arendt speculates that:

> [o]nly the development of robot soldiers, which would eliminate the human factor completely and, conceivably, permit one man with a pushbutton at his disposal to destroy whomever he pleases could change this fundamental ascendancy of power over violence. Even the most despotic domination we know of, the rule of master over slaves, who always outnumbered him, did not rest upon superior means of coercion as such but upon a superior organization of power, that is, upon the organized solidarity of the masters.[5]

In her controversial distinction between power and violence,[6] Arendt reaches for the idea that the ends of violence – domination, order, aggression, defence – are essentially purposive human actions that cannot in themselves be reduced to (or reproduced by) technological instruments. In her example, 'robot soldiers' mark a limit case or fantastic scenario that might conceivably make power secondary to violence. However, for her, such a vision is decidedly dystopic – removing the human factor completely from organized violence does not necessarily render it more dispassionate or more efficient but, rather, cauterizes its organic connection with the human faculty of action. The faculty of action is that which 'enables [man] to get together with his peers, to act in concert, and to reach out for goals and enterprises which would never enter his mind, let alone the desires of his heart, had he not been given

[4] D. Johnson, 'Technology with no human responsibility?', *Journal of Business Ethics*, 127 (2015), 707, 708.
[5] H. Arendt, 'Reflections on violence', *New York Review of Books* (29 February 1969), available at www.nybooks.com/articles/archives/1969/feb/27/a-special-supplement-reflections-on-violence.
[6] For detailed consideration, see R. J. Bernstein, 'Hannah Arendt's reflections on violence and power', *Iris*, 3 (2011), 3–30.

this gift – to embark upon something new'.[7] Where human judgment and the faculty of action are displaced entirely from a field of activity, the activity itself is disarticulated from concrete, embodied, acting humans in a manner that makes the activity purely technical.

Something is lost in such pure technicity, although it is not entirely clear what: perhaps the recognizable humanness of armed conflict as an all-too-human institution, in which our darkest and most disturbing capacities are pressed into the service of political objectives (noble or ignoble) and tempered through an ethically and legally constrained persona – the professional soldier, the reasonable commander, the politically committed insurgent, all participating in one way or another in what Michael Walzer calls the moral reality of war as a human institution.[8] This moral reality, in Walzer's still unsurpassed account, is predicated on the intuition that war is:

> a human action, purposive and premeditated, for whose effects *someone* is responsible ... [The moral theorist] searches for human agents. Nor is he alone in this search. It is one of the most important features of war, distinguishing it from the other scourges of mankind, that the men and women caught up in it are not only victims, they are also participants. All of us are inclined to hold them responsible for what they do.[9]

We need not follow Arendt's theory of action to nevertheless perceive the sense of discomfort or disorientation that is generated by the idea that, due to technological capacities, the most proximate human agents to whom we would look to make sense of the consequences of devastating mortal violence may be software engineers. The moral and juridical categories that we have laboriously constructed as a fragile scaffolding to separate lawful from unlawful violence, and tolerable killing from radical evil, presuppose concrete human beings judging and acting in concrete circumstances: reasonable commanders, using proportionate means and methods, while taking feasible precautions and always distinguishing (reasonably) between combatants, civilians and persons taking part in hostilities.[10] These cautiously stylized terms and the minutiae of their juridical elaboration only underscore the dependence of our moral

[7] *Ibid.*
[8] M. Walzer, *Just and Unjust Wars: A Moral Argument with Historical Illustrations*, 3rd edn (New York: Basic Books, 2000), chs. 1–3.
[9] *Ibid.*, 15 (emphasis added).
[10] See, e.g., R. D. Sloane, 'Puzzles of proportion and the "reasonable military commander": reflections on the law, ethics, and geopolitics of proportionality', *Harvard National Security Law Journal*, 6 (2015), 300–42.

and legal conventions governing warfare upon a deep ecology of human action, conditioned by history, political and legal institutions (national and international) and, nowadays, interconnected cadres of professionals and legal experts forming transnational communities of judgment.[11]

None of the foregoing necessarily pre-empts the answer to the question: are autonomous weapons systems lawful and ethical? Rather, as the chapters collected in this volume demonstrate, it directs our attention to what is at stake in trying to ask and answer such a question. In retrospect, we can identify three thematic clusters of questions that subtend this principal question.

Human judgment and machine autonomy

What kinds of human cognitive judgment and decision making are the archetypes for what is variously understood as 'autonomy'? Can machines adequately replicate such judgment and decision making in the kinds of situations characteristic of armed conflict environments? Is 'autonomy' best understood as task autonomy, with increasing autonomization of judgments and decisions being the relevant index? Can autonomization be human-judgment enhancing, without also becoming human-judgment displacing? Can the risks posed by the behavioural uncertainty attendant upon increasing autonomization be adequately controlled in battlefield environments?

The answers to these questions offered in this volume remain tentative but certainly suggestive and conducive to further research and reflection. Geoffrey S. Corn points out that in our current military organization, we engender international humanitarian law (IHL) compliance and try to contain the risk of non-compliance through a particular dependence on human capacity to be socialized and embedded within institutional and personal relationships that form dispositions and propensities – the habitus of the reasonable commander and reasonable soldier is made, not born, and is a product of human relationships (including legal ones) that condition human judgment and reasoning. He argues that to the extent that an AWS cannot be shaped in the same way by the field level commander, much greater emphasis must be placed at the stages of design and procurement on ensuring the reliability and compliance of the system. Noel Sharkey expresses his scepticism that anything approaching sophisticated human judgments (for example, distinguishing between combatant and civilian in highly cluttered environments

[11] See, e.g., D. Kennedy, *Of War and Law* (Princeton University Press, 2006), ch. 1, 3.

with ambiguous markings) could be replicated by a machine, but he explains that the accuracy of human judgments could potentially be enhanced by technology that excels at calculation and routine following rather than managing ambiguity and deliberative reasoning. Guglielmo Tamburrini argues that autonomy is best understood as task autonomy and that as the number of tasks delegated to a machine grows and as environmental complexity increases, the behavioural uncertainty of how the machine will respond to novel circumstances also increases. Performing complex tasks in highly uncertain environments requires machines to have recourse to a pre-programmed rule architecture, while simultaneously learning to (very quickly) identify and appropriately respond to situations that have not previously been encountered. At the same time, we would expect that any such response conforms with expectations and design intentions about how the machine ought to respond – for example, we would expect that the novel response should not violate humanitarian law by reaching an incorrect conclusion about whether an object is military or civilian in nature.

Thus, the paradox of the autonomy that proponents of AWS wish to realize is that it demands both predictability and stable expectations of law-conforming behaviour with adaptation and responsiveness to new information and situations. We expect not only that the machines will learn and act according to what they learn, but that the outcomes of their learning and acting will also be consistently norm appropriate rather than norm violating when engaging in mortal violence. As Tamburrini concludes, this imaginary construction of autonomy is a long-term vision of what robotics aspires to achieve; it does not represent the expected outcome of an existing research programme.[12] Rather, it is a useful heuristic to inspire research. Failing to distinguish between an existing technological reality and its short- and medium-term frontiers, and an indefinite future time horizon in which regulative and inspiring visions of technological possibility could be realized, is a kind of:

> temporal framing mechanism of ignorance production. This mechanism induces false beliefs about the time scales of envisaged technological advancements from a failure to convey clearly the distinction between the long-term (and often admittedly visionary) goals of ambitious technological research programs, on the one hand, and their expected short-term outcomes, on the other hand.[13]

---

[12] G. Tamburrini, 'On banning autonomous weapons systems: from deontological to wide consequentialist reasons', Chapter 6 in this volume.
[13] *Ibid.*, 134.

Indeed, in the current debate about autonomous weapons, humanitarian lawyers seem especially susceptible to perpetuating such ignorance production, writing breezily that:

> [s]oftware for autonomous weapon systems that enables visual identification of individuals, thereby enhancing accuracy during autonomous 'personality strikes' against specified persons, is likely to be developed ...
>
> Being able to adjust values would provide much greater flexibility since autonomous weapon systems could be programmed prior to launch based on the current situation or even reprogrammed remotely while it is hunting for targets should the situation change. As the technology advances, algorithms that would permit the autonomous weapon system to itself adjust the base level threshold to account for specified variables it encountered on a mission will likely be developed ...
>
> It will still be necessary to set the doubt threshold at which an autonomous weapon system will refrain from attack. In a sense, doing so will resemble programming autonomous weapon systems to refrain from attack because of the risk of violating the proportionality rule. Although it is challenging, it is possible to envision how this might be done. For instance, the system could be programmed using the doubt values just discussed; it would not attack if a particular level of doubt were reached. The system could not be used in situations in which the pre-programmed threshold would be 'unreasonable'. For instance, more doubt can be countenanced on a 'hot' battlefield than in a relatively benign environment. In light of the pre-set doubt values, it might only be reasonable to employ the system in the former situation.
>
> An autonomous weapon system may also have adjustable doubt thresholds that can be set before launch to account for the circumstances in which it will be employed (for example, for use in an area where enemy forces have been highly active as distinct from one where they have not). Advanced autonomous weapon systems of the future will possibly be capable of being adjusted remotely while operations are underway to account for unexpected developments, such as intelligence reports of displaced civilians in the area. Systems may even be developed that can adapt *sua sponte* to pre-programmed variables, such as the movement of vehicles towards or away from friendly forces.[14]

Although this is a particularly imaginative exercise in science fiction, these passages represent a wider tendency among lawyers debating the legality of AWS under international humanitarian law to fail to distinguish between real frontiers of technological capacities and hypothesized scenarios that amount to future visions of robotics. The result is that

---

[14] M. Schmitt and J. Thurnher, '"Out of the loop": autonomous weapons systems and the law of armed conflict', *Harvard National Security Law Journal*, 4 (2013), 231, 247.

among lawyers the debate has a peculiarly chiliastic quality that merges prediction, speculation and aspiration about what 'autonomy' could mean. The discussion also assumes that relatively black-and-white answers can be given about how increasingly autonomous machines will behave, how their behaviour can be governed and rendered stable, and that the answers to such issues are essentially technological. Law arrives after the fact, ready to render sober judgment about whether the algorithms are up to scratch, and if the answer is no, the scientists go back to the drawing board.

However, of course, as Merel Noorman and Deborah G. Johnson point out, this is a fiction that ignores what we know about real technological development:

> [T]he field of Science and Technology Studies (STS) shows that the trajectory of technological development is contingent, multidirectional, and dependent on complex negotiations among relevant social groups. Technologies that are adopted and used ... cannot be predicted in advance with certainty. In the course of development, the design of a new technology may morph and change in response to many factors, including changes in funding ... wars, changes in the regulatory environment, accidents, market indicators etc.[15]

Noorman and Johnson contend that the very notion of autonomy has no technical meaning and is a matter for negotiation and contestation between different actors: '[T]he variety of conceptions of machine autonomy in the discourse of autonomous robots reflects the many ideas, ambitions and goals of the various social groups with a stake in the development of these technologies.'[16] As Lucy Suchman and Jutta Weber document in their chapter, a conceptualization of autonomy has always been partly constitutive of robotics self-definition as a discipline, with the concept's content shifting considerably as paradigms in robotics have changed.[17] This only seems to underscore the idea that by promoting different claims about what we can expect or aspire to in the future ('software for identification of individuals ... is likely to be developed'), we are in fact trying to enrol different actors and stakeholders into a vision that shapes the activities and expectations in the present. As Dan Saxon shows in his chapter on US Department of Defense (DoD) Directive 3000.09, the DoD adopted the concept of 'appropriate

---

[15] M. Noorman and D. G. Johnson, 'Negotiating autonomy and responsibility in military robots', *Ethics and Information Technology*, 16 (2014), 51–62, 51.
[16] *Ibid.*, 56.
[17] L. Suchman and J. Weber, 'Human–machine autonomies', Chapter 4 in this volume.

levels of human judgment' concerning the use of force in order to shape the normative terrain for the development of such weapons systems by assuaging anxieties about their possible uncontrolled development, while, at the same time, seeking to encourage research into such technologies by providing 'clarity so that researchers and developers could incorporate autonomous functions in weapons system within legal and ethical boundaries'.[18] Suchman and Weber conclude their chapter by suggesting that 'the question is less about automation versus autonomy than it is about what new forms of agency are enabled by contemporary configurations of war fighting and with what political, ethical, moral and legal consequences'.[19]

What is at stake in the debate about whether a projected autonomous weapon can or cannot do something, or whether it would be legal under such conditions, is whether we wish to enable such possibilities by reconfiguring our views about what is, or is not, essentially or desirably human in the conduct of hostilities. For this reason, the notion of 'human dignity' has become a central term in the discussion.

Dignity

As Dieter Birnbacher observes in his contribution to this volume,[20] 'dignity' has become an open-ended concept for which we reach to ground an evaluation of emergent technologies and new social practices. By virtue of its openness – which is not tethered to any single metaphysics, compatible with considerable human plurality in moral and ethical systems and consistently invoked in contemporary law as the *Grundbegriff* of human and constitutional rights – 'human dignity' is invoked to capture a variety of inchoate intuitions about AWS.[21] Some of these uses of dignity seem

---

[18] D. Saxon, 'A human touch: autonomous weapons, DoD Directive 3000.09 and the interpretation of "appropriate levels of human judgment over the use of force"', Chapter 9 in this volume, 197. DoD Directive 3000.09, 'Autonomy in weapon systems', 21 November 2012, available at www.dtic.mil/whs/directives/corres/pdf/300009p.pdf.

[19] Suchman and Weber, 'Human–machine autonomies', 112.

[20] D. Birnbacher, 'Are autonomous weapons systems a threat to human dignity?', Chapter 5 in this volume.

[21] As political theorist Anne Phillips observes, there has been an 'explosion' of interest in human dignity among theorists. Phillips points out that we disagree sharply on how to understand what we mean when we say something violates human dignity and that the theoretical accounts of the concept have strikingly different foundations: some take dignity as closely connected to human rights protection, while others claim that dignity necessitates a philosophical anthropology, and others yet maintain that dignity is a revalued form of status-thinking through which we have come to accord to all humans

'inflationary', as Birnbacher points out, threatening to strip dignity of specific argumentative force and, instead, rendering it coeval with morality, making it an ascriptive 'species' property or simply using it to express a 'yuk factor' unmediated by reasoned argument that balances both deontological and consequentialist considerations. In other sections of this conclusion, some of the arguments concerning human dignity and autonomous machines are addressed more specifically, but it seems clear that both the inflationary and more limited uses of the term in this debate aim to articulate an anxiety about the consequences of delegating certain kinds of human action and human judgment to machines.

What is it about AWS that evokes this sense of threat to human dignity? It seems to us that it is here where much work remains to be done in the spirit of Birnbacher's analytical reflections. It has been observed, from a consequentialist standpoint, that a lack of fear, sentimentality and emotion may well be a virtue on the battlefield. But the image of a bloodless machine deploying lethal force against targets that it selects based on pre-programmed information and its own capacities for machine learning, nonetheless, generates discomfort if not fear. Again, perhaps one reason for this reaction is the deeply ingrained idea that war is a human activity – humans killing humans, even if at a distance, is somehow more comprehensible, more locatable within everyday understandings of agency and responsibility, than a robot that takes or spares a life by algorithm (as Christof Heyns seems to imply in his chapter).[22] War and its terrible miseries are rendered tolerable not by efficiency and accuracy (even efficient and humane wars are terrible from the point of view of those who lose friends, relatives, compatriots) but, rather, because it is amenable to pathetic meaning making – myth and fable, stories of justice and injustice, righteousness and moral failing – stories about humans, not machines.

The point cannot be that human suffering and human killing are somehow dignified or even necessary to the dignity of humans. But where, for one side (the side with autonomous weapons), the risks and problems of war become largely technical and materiel constraints, while, for the other, they involve facing an inhuman adversary with neither fear nor sympathy, the asymmetry of existential threat and mortal fear does seem to portend a kind of differential status between states and populations – a differential that would be corrosive of the equal dignity of

the kind of status we previously ascribed to aristocrats – a nobility of personhood. A. Phillips, *The Politics of the Human* (Cambridge University Press, 2015), ch. 4.

[22] C. Heyns, 'Autonomous weapons systems: living a dignified life and dying a dignified death', Chapter 1 in this volume.

humans if it became a normal and regular characteristic of the incidence of armed conflict.[23] A related concern, expressed not only by Pablo Kalmanovitz[24] but also by Eliav Lieblich and Eyal Benvenisti,[25] is the asymmetry of risk of technical failure in the functioning of such weapons systems if AWS are deployed by rich and powerful states in conflicts with non-state actors located within states that lack effective governmental control over their territory and population. If one of the grave concerns about AWS is their behavioural uncertainty and the unknown nature of their risk of malfunctioning or inappropriate functioning,[26] the bearing of such a risk principally or exclusively by the populations of poor and conflict-ridden states also seems to generate a categorical distinction in who is more susceptible to the fatal consequences of such design failures.

Responsibility

Closely connected to the debate about whether AWS are incompatible with human dignity is the question of responsibility. As noted earlier,

---

[23] Grégoire Chamayou captures this anxiety rather dramatically in his recounting of a 1960s futurological debate in the *New Scientist* about 'telechiric machines', the term used by engineer John Clark in his proposal to develop machines that could be controlled at a distance in order to undertake activities in environments otherwise hostile to humans (deep underwater or above ground where atmospheric temperatures were extreme). One of the magazine's readers drew attention to the possible military applications of such technology and prognosticated that '[a]ll conventional wars might eventually be conducted telechirically, armies of military robots battling it out by remote control, victory being apportioned by neutral computers, while humans sit safely at home watching on TV . . . Far-flung imperial conquests which were ours because we had the Maxim gun and they had the knobkerry will be recalled by new bloodless triumphs coming our way because we have telechiric yeomanry and they, poor fuzzy-wuzzies, have only napalm and nerve-gas.' J. W. Clark, 'Remote control in hostile environments', *New Scientist*, 22 (389) (April 1964), 300; Anonymous, 'Last word on telechirics', *New Scientist*, 22 (391) (May 1964), 400, 405, quoted in G. Chamayou, *Drone Theory* (London: Penguin, 2014), 23–4.

[24] P. Kalmanovitz, 'Judgment, liability and the risks of riskless warfare', Chapter 7 in this volume.

[25] E. Lieblich and E. Benvenisti, 'The obligation to exercise discretion in warfare: why autonomous weapons systems are unlawful', Chapter 11 in this volume.

[26] An interesting contemporary example of inappropriate functioning which is not malfunctioning has been noted in the Google car, where the car's inability to interpret characteristically human behaviour (very bad parking, edging forward at a four-way intersection in order to signal an intention to other drivers) leads the car to behave in a way that endangers both the occupant and other human drivers. These inappropriate behaviours could not be predicted but only known and corrected *ex post*. See M. Richtel and C. Dougherty, 'Google's driverless cars run into problems: cars with drivers', *New York Times* (1 September 2015), A1, available at www.nytimes.com/2015/09/02/technology/personaltech/google-says-its-not-the-driverless-cars-fault-its-other-drivers.html.

a crucial dimension of war as a moral reality is arguably the possibility of attributing responsibility for conduct and its consequences to human agents and evaluating their conduct in terms of moral and legal standards. How else are we to make sense of war and, perhaps, exercise some kind of agency ourselves by criticizing it, supporting it or otherwise adopting a reflective stance in relation to it? The fear that no human may be judged meaningfully responsible for the actions of an AWS perhaps springs from an anxiety that we will lose our own sense of agency as moral and political beings in relation to this field of human action.[27]

Of course, as has been regularly observed in the chapters in this volume, humans are always responsible at some level for the design, programming, deployment and decision to activate an AWS: without humans acting and making decisions, the chain of causation from design to deployment to use of force could not be completed. However, as Neha Jain[28] and Hin-Yan Liu[29] show in their chapters, there is nonetheless a real risk that our existing legal norms concerning responsibility for the actions of an AWS may be inadequate to properly and effectively attribute criminal responsibility to a human being. Specific legal concerns about the attribution of responsibility are addressed later in this conclusion, but here we note that the kinds of concerns about responsibility raised by Jain and Liu reflect problems characteristic of complex technological change. Noorman and Johnson point out that:

> the complexity of autonomous robotic systems involves complex techno-
> logical components, many human 'hands', and human–machine inter-
> faces, and this means responsibility is distributed broadly. Thus it can be
> a daunting challenge to trace back who or what is at fault when something
> goes wrong.[30]

---

[27] Some 'post-human' theorists suggest that our need to know who is responsible is a kind of delusion, one that insists on singular agency where in fact there is contingency and distributed agency. As an account of causation, this may be more realistic, but it nonetheless begs the question *why* we cling to this desire to attribute responsibility and to make sense of what happens to us in this manner. There may be better ways of thinking about responsibility than our current individualist liability-oriented one, but it seems we cannot do without frameworks for responsibility whether forward or backward looking. See Phillips, *The Politics of the Human*, 128–9.

[28] N. Jain, 'Autonomous weapons systems: new frameworks for individual responsibility', Chapter 13 in this volume.

[29] H.-Y. Liu, 'Refining responsibility: differentiating two types of responsibility issues raised by autonomous weapons systems', Chapter 14 in this volume.

[30] Noorman and Johnson, 'Negotiating autonomy and responsibility in military robots', 61.

The challenge is exacerbated by the behavioural adaptiveness that, on the one hand, we hope autonomous machines will exhibit (the capacity to respond to novel situations) but that, on the other hand, raises the problem of the unforeseeability of behaviour and uncertainty about the likelihood of norm-violating behaviour. Both Jain and Liu conclude that this behavioural uncertainty and the segmented diffusion of specialized knowledge about the propensities of the system may stretch existing frameworks for individual responsibility to breaking point, requiring either an extension of our current rules concerning criminal and civil liability or even a ban on autonomous weapons.

However, it should be emphasized that the so-called responsibility gap is not a function of the technology itself. Rather, as Jain shows, it is a result of a certain mismatch between how we conceptualize what ought to be a basis for criminal or civil liability and the diffusion of knowledge, intention and agency that characterizes complex autonomous systems. It may well be that current rules may be poorly suited to grappling with 'distributed agency' of this kind, but it does not follow that we are unable to conceive of different models and different rules that could establish responsibility and accountability. Deborah Johnson observes that in the past, when confronted with new technologies that generate risks, 'we have also set up mechanisms to pressure those who make and use these technologies to operate them safely and to take responsibility when something goes wrong'.[31] If it is quite persuasively argued that current frameworks for responsibility under international or domestic criminal law, or IHL, will confront serious difficulty in meaningfully attributing responsibility for the unforeseen behaviour of increasingly autonomous weapons, then the contemporary challenge is not so much to lament a responsibility gap but, rather, to devise new 'responsibility practices' better suited to the technology, which could include a ban on the delegation of certain functions to a machine.

A 'responsibility practice' is a term coined by science and technology studies scholar Merel Noorman as a way of capturing 'the interplay between technological development and the ascription of responsibility. It refers to the [conventionally] established ways that people, within a particular environment or moral community, understand and ascribe responsibility, based on shared values and ideas about fairness and

---

[31] Johnson, 'Technology with no human responsibility?', 712.

utility.'[32] Responsibility practices are both formal and informal, comprising law and legal devices such as duties of care and reasonable foreseeability as well as organizational and professional norms. Since the 'delegation of tasks to unmanned technologies changes human activities and decision-making throughout the broader sociotechnical network',[33] new negotiations, contestations and questions about responsibility are triggered; new technologies make possible new arrangements/relationships between people and, thus, we must consciously rethink how responsibility is to be conceived and ascribed in such relationships. Noorman and Johnson helpfully summarize the kinds of questions that need to be asked in order to design and implement the right responsibility practices in respect of increasingly autonomous weapons systems – a process that can begin even now and need not await a technological 'breakthrough':

> Responsibility questions for these technologies have to do with the decisions and strategies employed in designing the system or in the operation of the system. Did the designers of the system construct accurate models of the problem domain? Did they provide an appropriate interface for human actors to interact with the system? Did they adequately test the system? Did those that deployed and used the system sufficiently take the known risks into account? ...
>
> [The responsibility practices generated by trying to answer such questions] are both backward- and forward-looking ... Forward-looking responsibility involves decisions about which tasks and duties are going to be assigned to which individuals or non-human components, that is, who will be responsible for what. Backward-looking responsibility involves tracing back where precisely an error or errors occurred after an untoward event has taken place. The fault may lie in how the software was programmed to behave, how human actors in various roles behaved, the comprehensibility (friendliness) of the interface between the human actors and hardware, and so on. Backward-looking responsibility generally relies on or at least presumes something about forward-looking responsibility. That is, when we understand how tasks and responsibilities were assigned in a system, it helps us to understand what went wrong. Also, when we trace back the cause of a failure we may discover that something else should have been, and in the future should be, delegated to a human or non-human component. For example, we may discover that another human should be put in a particular loop.[34]

---

[32] M. Noorman, 'Responsibility practices and unmanned military technologies', *Science and Engineering Ethics*, 20 (2014), 809, 810.

[33] *Ibid.*, 818.

[34] Noorman and Johnson, 'Negotiating autonomy and responsibility in military robots', 60.

In his contribution to this volume, Geoffrey S. Corn in effect argues for an enhanced set of responsibility practices that would strengthen due diligence norms governing the design and procurement of AWS by promoting a thicker set of obligations on military officials involved in the development, procurement and deployment authorization of AWS. These officials may have to be 'responsibilized' through new bureaucratic and legal norms in order to guarantee a certain level of 'compliance confidence' in an AWS before it can be cleared for deployment at the discretion of a field commander. Nehal Bhuta and Stavros-Evdokimos Pantazopoulos argue that international environmental law principles governing hazardous transboundary activity can be a model for responsibility practices such as due diligence, risk identification, risk control and information sharing. These responsibility practices can be applied to the context of weapons development and operationalized through the creation of a group of governmental experts charged with creating a framework for sharing information, harmonizing national review processes and building consensus around appropriate standards for risk regulation.

Transparency is also an important component of any effective responsibility framework and is necessary to facilitate reflection, debate and discussion about the kinds of risks that need to be addressed, how best to address them and who to hold responsible for managing (or failing to manage) those risks. In her chapter, Sarah Knuckey[35] argues that transparency is essential in our law- and policy-oriented discussions concerning AWS so that governmental and non-governmental actors with relevant expertise can meaningfully contribute to adequate responses and regulation. The fact that we must develop such responsibility practices in relation to a domain characterized by considerable secrecy (weapons development) need not lead us to give up on trying to facilitate transparency. As Knuckey points out:

> Key to a productive transparency dialogue is the unpacking and maintaining of distinctions between the categories of AWS information and the levels and direction of information flows, as well as clarity about information release justifications . . .

At the international level, this could include consideration of various models of new mechanisms for transparency, such as voluntary but structured sharing of information around core concerns (e.g., best

---

[35] S. Knuckey, 'Autonomous weapons systems and transparency: towards an international dialogue', Chapter 8 in this volume.

practices for Article 36 weapons reviews) or establishing reporting obligations up to an oversight body. The development of shared expectations for minimum information disclosure could also be beneficial, and might include, for example, whether or not a state is intending to advance autonomy in critical functions, and how a state intends to ensure human control and legal compliance as autonomy advances.[36]

The creation of appropriate and effective responsibility practices for AWS is a serious challenge to their viability. Unless we can be confident that we have set the right standards for their engineering, verification and validation and for holding persons responsible in the event of failure (including failures to comply with humanitarian law norms), we are generating a range of serious risks. These risks apply not only to human life and limb on or beyond the battlefield but also to our very status as moral, juridical and political agents with the capacity to hold each other and ourselves responsible for the consequences of the complex systems we have created. If we give up on trying to develop adequate responsibility practices, or allow these systems to develop in a way that we come to accept without knowing how they arrive at the decisions or how they will behave in certain circumstances, we will have created a responsibility gap and, in an important sense, permitted these technological changes to diminish our humanity.

Putting the debate about AWS in its place: autonomous machines in contemporary society

It is important to note that the discussion about AWS is not undertaken in a legal vacuum. Already, the participants in the debate about AWS have integrated arguments from a more general legal debate about autonomous machines in contemporary society. This is especially the case not only for the problem of the meaning of autonomy, of the responsibility gap and of the potential violation of human dignity but also for the problems of civil liability, of public laws ensuring safe (or safe as possible) usage of such machines and of possibilities to protect the data collected by AWS. The intersection and interweaving of these discussions is important and necessary: it clarifies that society is confronted with a general development and not a trend limited to isolated spheres or only certain industries. Especially with respect to the fundamental legal concepts such as action, ascription, liability and responsibility or the potential need to consider the identification of new legal actors/persons, it is

---

[36] *Ibid.*

important to not discuss these questions in isolation. Thus, in this section, we identify and reflect upon the ways in which the legal debate about AWS is not just part of the broader debate about how to deal with autonomous machines in law,[37] but also about how it can actually be regarded as a limit case that illustrates the underlying common problems. For both legal analysis and in order to develop adequate policies, it is crucial to connect these debates. This way, one cannot only transfer arguments and potential solutions but also understand the general development of robotics and the law and include its implications from relevant debates in civilian robotics, such as, for example, the changes of legal concepts brought about by new technology. The legal changes and their consequences can only be understood in the light of the changes in society as a whole.

Robotics has been discussed in legal contexts only recently.[38] Even today, the debate does not fully mirror the social importance of this technology now and in the near future. The main reason for this is that until now there have not been too many actual cases[39] in which legal practitioners would have had to decide about the applicability of existing laws in the context of robotics. However, this does not mean that there is no need for a legal debate – on the contrary, in many areas of life the researchers and developers of robots have asked for legal security before they are prepared to develop this technology further. Legal security for the parties involved in the process of developing, distributing and deploying autonomous machines means resolving the applicability of the existing laws beforehand. This analysis might then lead to discovering

---

[37] For an overview, see, e.g., the report of the project 'Robolaw'. E. Palmerini *et al.*, 'Guidelines on regulating robotics', 22 September 2014, available at www.robolaw.eu/ RoboLaw_files/documents/robolaw_d6.2_guidelinesregulatingrobotics_20140922.pdf or the 'Suggestions for a Green Paper on legal issues in robotics', 31 December 2012, available at www.eu-robotics.net/cms/upload/PDF/euRobotics_Deliverable_D.3.2.1_An nex_Suggestion_GreenPaper_ELS_IssuesInRobotics.pdf. See also the contributions in F. Battaglia, N. Mukerji and J. Nida-Rümelin (eds.), *Rethinking Responsibility in Science and Technology* (Pisa University Press, 2014); for the German debate, see S. Beck, 'Grundlegende Fragen zum rechtlichen Umgang mit der Robotik', *Juristische Rundschau*, 6 (2009), 225–30 and the contributions of the research centre RobotRecht, available at www.robotrecht.de.

[38] Inspired by debates in philosophy and ethics, see, e.g., A. Matthias, *Automaten als Träger von Rechten*, 1st edn (Berlin: Logos, 2008); N. Sharkey, 'Automating warfare: lessons learned from the drones', *Journal of Law, Information and Science*, 21 (2) (2012), 140–54; R. Sparrow, 'Killer robots', *Journal of Applied Philosophy*, 24 (1) (2007), 62–77.

[39] For decisions on robots used for surgical interventions (robodoc), see German Federal Supreme Court (BGH), Urteil vom, Az. VI ZR 323/04, 13 June 2006. These machines were in no way autonomous, though.

the necessity of changing the law or at least its adaptation. The debate is still mainly focused on the developments in robotics in general, discussing the possible change brought about to the legal concepts by this development (such as to the concepts of legal responsibility or negligence),[40] the potential introduction of machines as new legal actors,[41] the new liability regimes for robots in general[42] as well as insurance regulations, data protection laws, security laws or risk assessments.[43] Recently, the debate has become more detailed, though, meaning that some legal researchers are focusing on specific machines/ areas of usage and the legal questions connected, such as autonomous cars[44] and robots that can be used in health care,[45] and this inquiry will continue in other areas in the future.

'Autonomous machines': the concept and its problems

One debate that seems to be crucial for pinpointing the problems of the technological development in robotics, the adaptation of existing laws and the necessary changes of the legal system is the meaning of 'autonomous' in this context.[46] Sometimes it is stated that only by analysing this characteristic can it become clear why the law is confronted with problems that are new and unknown. And, surely, it is true that discussing autonomous (weapons) systems is only possible if one knows which systems one is talking about (although, as will be discussed shortly, it is questionable if it is plausible to call them autonomous or if one should define them differently).

[40] See, e.g., the contributions in Battaglia, Mukerji and Nida-Rümelin, *Rethinking Responsibility in Science and Technology.*
[41] S. Chopra and L. White, 'Artificial agents: personhood in law and philosophy' in *Proceedings of the European Conference on Artificial Intelligence* (Amsterdam: IOS Press, 2004), available at www.pdf.aminer.org/000/164/763/artificial_agents_person hood_in_law_and_philosophy.pdf; S. Chopra and L. White, *A Legal Theory of Autonomous Artificial Agents* (Michigan University Press, 2011); E. Schweighofer, T. Menzel and G. Kreuzbauer (eds.), *Auf dem Weg zur ePerson* (Vienna: Verlag Österreich, 2001); S. Wettig and E. Zehendner, 'The electronic agent: a legal personality under German law?', available at www.wettig.info/biometrie_uni_jena-s/el_agent-legal_personality_under_german_law20030624.pdf. See also 'Suggestions for a Green Paper on legal issues in Robotics', 58ff.
[42] Battaglia, Mukerji and Nida-Rümelin, *Rethinking Responsibility in Science and Technology,* 53ff. with further references.
[43] For some specific scenarios, see Palmerini et al., 'Guidelines on regulating robotics'; see also, *inter alia,* A. Bertolini, 'Robots as products: the case for a realistic analysis of robotic technologies and the law', *Law Innovation and Technology,* 5 (2) (2013), 214–47.
[44] Palmerini et al., 'Guidelines on regulating robotics', 36ff.   [45] *Ibid.,* 74ff.
[46] See, *inter alia,* the project, www.isi.fraunhofer.de/isi-de/v/projekte/wak-mti.php.

As discussed by Neha Jain, autonomy can be used in a strong and in a weak sense.[47] The strong interpretation, understanding an autonomous machine as 'capable of making its own decisions on the basis of reasons that are internal to it, and in light of its own experience',[48] is suggesting new players for the legal game. In the case of such machines' acting and deciding instead of, and for, humans in the future, one cannot just adapt the existing legal categories, but one would have to deal with them as new legal entities in some way. Thus, if machines with these capacities will exist and interact with humans in the near future, it would change legal concepts such as action, decision and responsibility in a way that some-how takes into account the machines as agents.[49] Even if these machines do not yet exist, one can focus on them as a thought experiment or as an anticipated development that we have to address beforehand.

However, even the already existing 'weak autonomy' that AWS have, in the sense that the machine 'acts in a dynamic and unstructured environ-ment based on feedback information from a number of sensors in its environment',[50] leads to new legal problems. Because of the 'epistemic uncertainty'[51] of these machines, ascribing responsibility after something goes wrong becomes difficult, as does making reasonable decisions about the areas in which such machines are acceptable *ex ante*. Which notion of autonomy is used often remains unclear, and it is possible that some disagreements are based on the usage of different notions. Of course, one can analyse the different contributions in terms of the notion they are based on, and, furthermore, one can discuss which notion one should use in the future. But it is questionable that one can unify the different disciplines and debates, especially since some of them are descriptive, some normative, some focus on the present and some on the future.

Thus, from a legal perspective, there is plausibility in not merely focusing on the notion of 'autonomy'. First of all, the characteristics that morality and the law generally ascribe to humans can be confused with the characteristics of machines, thus producing unnecessary com-parisons between humans and machines. Second, the use of purely technical language can be transferred into the normative disciplines, which leads to a high degree of speculation about the nature of the machine one is purportedly describing and results in many hypothetical scenarios but little concreteness in concept – as we have seen in the

---

[47] Jain, 'Autonomous weapons systems'.
[48] *Ibid.*, referring to Sparrow and to the similar argument of Sullins.
[49] Sparrow, 'Killer robots', 62–77, with further references.
[50] Jain, 'Autonomous weapons systems', referring to Sharkey.   [51] *Ibid.*

autonomous weapons discussions – thus, making it unclear what machines one is actually talking about. This tendency is intensified by the divergent use of 'autonomy' even in robotics. Therefore, for future laws at least, it could make sense to focus not on the abstract ideas of autonomy as the proper object of regulation but, rather, on the different kinds of tasks, functions and processes undertaken by the machine.

Relevant legal areas

In some areas of law, the debate about how to deal with machines making any kind of decision has accelerated over the last few years, either generally discussing autonomous machines or focusing on specific machines or specific areas of life. Some of the arguments involved in these debates can be found in the contributions here. In many ways, the connection between the debates should become even closer. In civil law, for example, it is discussed if and how electronic agents can conclude a contract and who then are the parties in the contract.[52] The traditional concepts, such as tool, messenger or representative, do not really fit the situation when a machine is making the final decision in the contract. However, the main question is how to address any damages caused by the machines,[53] and, connected to this question, if it is necessary to impute to these machines a form of legal personality in order to affix responsibility, creating a so-called 'electronic person'.[54] This new legal actor might be necessary because the traditional liability concepts (for example, negligence, product liability or strict liability) are difficult to apply in the context of autonomous machines.[55] As will be discussed shortly, this leads to a responsibility or liability gap that has to be bridged in all areas of law. One way of doing this could be through the introduction of the 'electronic person', an entity that is recognized by law as having the legal power to conclude contracts, is liable for misconduct and damages and can be addressed in front of a civil court.

In public law, one discusses, *inter alia*, whether administrative and regulatory laws in certain areas have to be adapted to the usage of

---

[52] J. Hanisch, *Haftung für Automation* (Göttingen: Cuvillier, 2010); R. John, *Haftung für künstliche Intelligenz: Rechtliche Beurteilung des Einsatzes intelligenter Softwareagenten im E-Commerce* (Hamburg: Kovač, 2007).

[53] Suggestions for a Green Paper on 'Legal issues in robotics', 53ff. with further references.

[54] *Ibid.*, 58ff.

[55] S. Beck, 'Dealing with the diffusion of legal responsibility: the case of robotics' in Battaglia, Mukerji and Nida-Rümelin, *Rethinking Responsibility in Science and Technology*, 167–82, with further references.

autonomous machines – be it the laws about medical devices, traffic laws, laws about the conduct of research in private or public areas, safety standards and so on.[56] Additionally, there are regulatory and safety standards developed by non-governmental institutions, such as the International Organization for Standardization (ISO). The interaction of state and social norms, of government and governance, is challenged by the development of robotics because no consensus exists on the social standards for adequate behaviour and one is challenged by having to develop such standards from scratch. While in other areas, standards such as ISO norms are generally well integrated into the legal system, this is sometimes questioned in the area of robotics. Thus, an important debate circles around how to develop socially acceptable security standards for such an important, dangerous and unpredictable new technology as the development of 'autonomous' machines. Additionally, there are some debates – depending on the area of usage – about data protection[57] since autonomous machines can only function if they collect enormous amounts of data, which then have to be managed in some way according to the appropriate legal norms.

In general, criminal law is based on the culpable conduct of the offender, on his or her intent, recklessness or negligence concerning the violation of the goods or person of a third party. All of this is challenged by the usage of 'autonomous' machines. Even if, as mentioned, we are talking merely (at least for the moment) about machines acting in a dynamic and unstructured environment based on the feedback derived from sensors,[58] it is almost impossible to pinpoint one individual who is criminally responsible if the machine has violated the person or goods of a third party.[59] In most cases, the humans involved will not have intent about the specific action of the machine, and recklessness or negligence cannot easily be affirmed because of the 'epistemic uncertainty' of the machine's decisions. None of the human parties may be able to foresee the actions of the machine in a way that could legitimate criminal accountability – even strict criminal liability, just for the usage of such a machine, would be more than questionable. As pointed out by Jain, one could ascribe some criminal responsibility to the involved human parties based on divided responsibility, but, still, this ascription does not fully mirror the situation if one leaves out the contribution of the machine.

---

[56] Suggestions for a Green Paper on 'Legal issues in robotics'. [57] *Ibid.*, 46ff.
[58] Jain, 'Autonomous weapons systems'. [59] For this debate, see *ibid.*

Responsibility

From this overview of the legal debate about robotics and autonomous machines, one can see that a major problem is the responsibility gap.[60] In some ways, this lack of responsibility might even be the point of these machines: the over-complexity of modern society, in which one has to make numerous decisions every day and knows that many of them bear the potential to harm others, leads to the construction of machines that help us to manage complexity – to decide how best to find our way in traffic or to get our car into a parking spot, to remind us about our medicine or buying food. The building of machines that could make the decision about the life and death of other human beings is arguably an extreme version of this same objective – the delegation of the processing and analysis of large amounts of complex information in order to make a human decision simpler or even transfer it altogether away from humans. The transfer of the decision only makes sense if the human parties involved are not fully responsible for the decisions. This development has to have consequences for the concept of responsibility as such.[61] From an inner perspective, it does not pose an overwhelming problem to the legal system to reduce individual responsibility in the case of robots making decisions to create new legal entities with specific legal responsibilities and to support these changes by strengthening institutional responsibility in the background, because institutions will decide about the direction of robotics – by financing research, giving out licences, insuring under-conditions and so forth.

However, one has to be aware that by constructing machines that make decisions for us, we are giving away a part of our (social) identity or, more importantly, perhaps reconstructing our identity in a way that includes machines because we have earlier decided to use them for a specific part of our autonomy space – conduct and decisions that hitherto we had presupposed only humans could undertake directly. Thus, the very notion of what qualifies as a necessary or essential human judgment is socially, historically and technologically embedded, and autonomous machines challenge our self-understanding of what qualifies as human action. It has to be discussed further if and how machines or human–machine hybrids can 'respond' to mistakes in a socially acceptable way.

---

[60] Beck, 'Dealing with the diffusion of legal responsibility: the case of robotics'.
[61] For the following, see also *ibid.*

Responsibility – moral or criminal – is one part of this problem. Another major concern of the involved parties – in different variations – is the question of (financial) liability for damages.[62] Although connected to responsibility, liability is not based as strongly on moral blame, on the personal ascription of the mistake, but, rather, focused on the risk ascription concerning the risks of the machine's decision. Thus, it is possible to deal with liability in terms of insurance or even, as mentioned earlier, by constructing an 'electronic person' without having to face the same problems as in the context of, for example, criminal responsibility.[63] The inner perspective of the legal system is more relevant here than in the case of responsibility and opens up different plausible possibilities to deal with 'autonomous' machines. However, the risk ascription of damages caused by machines still poses problems, such as the distribution of liability between the parties involved, the proof of mistakes, the relevance of profit by using the machine for being liable and so on. Of course, as soon as insurance for autonomous machines becomes standard, many of these questions will be answered, but even insurers do not yet have adequate categories for dealing with this new kind of machine.

Human dignity

Another crucial point of the debate is how the introduction of autonomous machines could change society in a negative way, even dehumanize it, and how the law can prevent this from happening (or not). One aspect of this discussion is the question of human dignity.[64] One could argue, for instance, that the confrontation with machines in certain contexts, without the possibility of escaping the situation, is a violation of human dignity – education, care and psychological therapy, for example. Or one could even regard the introduction of autonomous machines, because of the possible dehumanization of the society, to be a violation of the dignity of humanity as such. It is questionable, though, if these developments are really captured by the legal category of human dignity. The mere feeling of social changes being problematic, the 'slippery-slope' argument cannot by itself substantiate the violation of human dignity.

More plausible is the statement that some decisions violate human dignity of the person concerned if the decision is made by a machine, which is especially the case for life-and-death decisions[65] but could also

---

[62] Suggestions for a Green Paper on 'Legal issues in robotics', 53ff.   [63] *Ibid.*, 51ff.
[64] Birnbacher, 'Are autonomous weapons systems a threat to human dignity?'   [65] *Ibid.*

be plausible for decisions about marriage and relationship choices, jobs and career, child education and so on. Sometimes it is speculated that computers could make legal decisions at some point,[66] and these decisions could also be a case where the 'human in the loop' is legally necessary. Another aspect worth considering is the human dignity of the humans involved in the usage of autonomous machines, such as the soldiers fielding the AWS.[67] Their autonomy could be restricted significantly by the necessity of deploying such machines. Again, one can discuss whether the law can regulate these problems, but surely one has to be aware that morally and, to some extent, legally one also has to consider the role of the users.

The debate about human dignity in the context of autonomous machines is connected to the overall development from the human–machine dualism towards a social system in which the actions are attributed to hybrids – to the human–machine system (be it human–machine cooperation, a human-like machine or a machine-like human). This development has to be accompanied critically and one must be aware of the potential changes and challenges for society,[68] but this does not necessarily mean legal intervention – one has to differentiate cautiously between legal and social questions.

Technological and legal challenges to an autonomous machine's adherence to the rules of the law of armed conflict

It is beyond any controversy that AWS may only be deployed if they can safely adhere to the rules of the law of armed conflict (LOAC).[69] Yet in spite of over two years of increasingly intense international debate, the answer to the question whether, and at which point, AWS will be able to do so – especially if they are to be deployed on more complex combat missions – remains speculative and controversial.[70] What may be said with relative certainty is that the more limited the temporal, spatial and

---

[66] T. F. Gordon, 'Künstliche Intelligenz und Recht', *Jur-PC*, 5 (1990), 605ff.

[67] Tamburrini, 'On banning autonomous weapons systems: from deontological to wide consequentialist reasons'.

[68] Suchman and Weber, 'Human–machine autonomies'.

[69] See K. Anderson and M. C. Waxman, 'Law and ethics for autonomous weapon systems: why a ban won't work and how the laws of war can', Jean Perkins Task Force on National Security and Law Essay Series (Hoover Institution, Stanford University, 2013), 18, available at www.media.hoover.org/sites/default/files/documents/Anderson-Waxman_Law AndEthics_r2_FINAL.pdf.

[70] N. E. Sharkey, 'The evitability of autonomous robot warfare', *International Review of the Red Cross*, 94 (886) (2012), 787, 788.

strategic scope of a mission, the more likely it is that AWS will be able to adhere to the rules of LOAC.[71] As Kalmanovitz argues in this volume, 'IHL is flexible and conventional enough to allow for the development and deployment of AWS *in some suitably accountable form*.'[72] A close-in, point-defence system for defence against anti-vessel missiles with an operational radius of a few nautical miles is a case in point. And, of course, scenarios that from the outset do not involve any civilians or combatants – that is, no human beings whatsoever (such as two autonomous military submarines or satellites fighting each other in the deep sea or in outer space) – will neither challenge the principle of distinction nor invoke the principle of proportionality, the prohibition to cause unnecessary suffering or the obligation to take precautions.

However, there is also, of course, a plausible military-strategic incentive to deploy AWS in more complex scenarios in which they will be in direct contact with enemy fighters/combatants and civilians alike.[73] Indeed, it is in these unclear, high-risk situations, such as house and urban area searches, in which a military commander could mitigate risks for his or her soldiers by deploying AWS instead of human soldiers. It is these kinds of scenarios that are most problematic from a technological, as well as from an ethical–legal, perspective, and it is here where the fundamental LOAC principles that govern the conduct of hostilities, namely the principle of distinction, proportionality and precautions would be challenged.[74] Especially in asymmetric conflict scenarios where distinctions and conflict lines are inherently blurred,[75] many decisions will require the interpretation of human behaviour, which poses a significant and at least for the time being insurmountable technological challenge.[76] For example, in order to conclude whether a person is directly participating in hostilities, it may be necessary to

---

[71] Statement by W. Boothby, delivered at the CCW Expert Meeting on Lethal Autonomous Weapons Systems, Geneva, 13–17 April 2015, available at www.unog.ch/80256 EDD006 B8954/(httpAssets)/616D2401231649FDC1257E290047354D/$file/2015_LAWS _MX_B oothbyS+Corr.pdf.

[72] Kalmanovitz, 'Judgment, liability and the risks of riskless warfare', 145 (emphasis added).

[73] H. Münkler, 'Neue Kampfsysteme und die Ethik des Krieges', Heinrich Böll Foundation, 21 June 2013, available at www.boell.de/de/node/277436.

[74] Kalmanovitz, 'Judgment, liability and the risks of riskless warfare', 145. See also K. Anderson, D. Reisner and M. Waxman, 'Adapting the law of armed conflict to autonomous weapons systems', *International Law Studies*, 90 (2014), 386–411.

[75] R. Geiß, 'Asymmetric conflict structures', *International Review of the Red Cross*, 88, 864 (2006), 757–7.

[76] Sharkey, 'The evitability of autonomous robot warfare'.

interpret the person's conduct, gestures, facial as well as vocal expressions in order to distinguish behaviour that leads to a loss of protection from direct attack from other forms of behaviour that have no legal relevance under the rules of LOAC. For the time being, it remains an open question whether technological development will one day allow sensors and processors to adequately grasp and process the sheer amount of information and data that such a complex battlefield scenario presents.

In addition to the technological perspective, the question needs to be pursued whether there is something inherent in the decisions required by the core principles of LOAC that requires a human being to make them. This question is brought to the fore by the principle of proportionality.[77] As UN Special Rapporteur Christof Heyns wrote in his report in 2013, '[p]roportionality is widely understood to involve distinctively human judgement'.[78] The decision whether an attack 'may be expected to cause incidental loss of civilian life, injury to civilians, damage to civilian objects, or a combination thereof, which would be excessive in relation to the concrete and direct military advantage anticipated',[79] is complex, situational and value-based.[80] It requires a factual probability assessment whether civilians or civilian objects could be harmed in the course of an attack, a strategic decision as to which military advantage is pursued, the ascription of relative values to both of these parameters and a balancing decision as to which value prevails over the other.[81] To illustrate the complexity, consider the relative military value of an enemy tank, which may differ depending on whether it is just one tank among many, whether it is defending a strategic key position or whether it is attacked in order to distract the enemy and to ensure the success of a larger military operation.[82]

---

[77] N. E. Sharkey, 'Automated killers and the computing profession', *Computer*, 40 (2007), 122.

[78] C. Heyns, report of the Special Rapporteur on extrajudicial, summary or arbitral executions, Doc. A/HRC/23/47, 9 April 2013, para. 72, available at www.ohchr.org/Documents/HRBodies/HRCouncil/RegularSession/Session23/A-HRC-23-47_en.pdf.

[79] The humanitarian law principle of proportionality is firmly anchored in Articles 51(5)(b), 57(2)(a)(iii) of Additional Protocol I as well as customary international law. See J. M. Henckaerts and L. Doswald-Beck (eds.), *Customary International Humanitarian Law*, vol. I (Cambridge University Press and International Committee of the Red Cross, 2005), Rule 14.

[80] Y. Dinstein, *The Conduct of Hostilities under the Law of International Armed Conflict*, 2nd edn (Cambridge University Press, 2010), 140.

[81] R. Geiß, 'The principle of proportionality: force protection as a military advantage', *Israel Law Review*, 45 (2012), 71–89.

[82] Dinstein, *The Conduct of Hostilities under the Law of International Armed Conflict*.

In light of the sum total of the complexities involved in applying the proportionality principle in practice and the situational, value-based decisions that this assessment requires, one may indeed seriously doubt whether algorithms could ever master this task. At the same time, it cannot be wholly excluded either. The challenge is twofold. On the one hand, there is the technological challenge to design sufficiently inter-linked autonomous systems that could aggregate and process the vast amount of information required to deal with all of these complexities and eventualities. Thus, in order to assess the military advantage to be ascribed to a particular target, the system would need to know for example why that target is to be attacked and how the attack would relate to other military operations.

On the other hand, an even greater challenge would seem to result from the fact that the proportionality assessment does not lend itself to arithmetical precision and that we may simply lack the relevant data to program an autonomous system in the first place. There is, of course, widespread agreement that the relevant benchmark for the proportion-ality assessment is that of a reasonable military commander – that is, what a reasonable military commander would do under similar circum-stances and with the same amount of information prior to the attack. Thus, it is acceptable that different military commanders may arrive at different conclusions when carrying out the proportionality analysis for as long as their decision falls in the range of what a reasonable military commander would do under similar circumstances.[83] However, there is no fully clear or internationally agreed standard of what it is that a reasonable commander should do. In other words, we know what the relevant standard is (that is, that of a 'reasonable commander'), but there is significant ambiguity surrounding the standard's actual content. This is largely inevitable as it is owed to the myriad of (unforeseen) circum-stances in which the proportionality assessment may have to be applied under battlefield conditions and which seem impossible to anticipate in their totality. It is thus a general problem surrounding the LOAC pro-portionality analysis and not one that is specific to autonomous technol-ogy. However, it is brought to the fore in relation to this novel technology since the programming of autonomous systems would seem to require the existence of clear(er) standards.

---

[83] ICTY, *Prosecutor* v. *Stanislav Galic* (IT-989-29-T), Trial Chamber, 5 December 2003, para. 58: '[A] reasonably well-informed person'.

It is not clear, however, whether this technology indeed imposes an insurmountable obstacle to the deployment of autonomous systems in scenarios in which civilians are present and in which the principle of proportionality may have to be applied.[84] Obviously, as mentioned above, a robot whose mission from the outset, because of its geographical and temporal constraints, will not have any direct contact with, or repercussions on, the civilian population or a robot that, although in contact with civilians, is programmed to abort an attack if there is a risk that harm will be done to civilians does not raise any issues from the perspective of LOAC.

An alternative solution to this particular problem, however, could be to program autonomous systems to abide by much stricter standards than those applicable to human soldiers. In other words, the operational and interpretatory leeway that is granted to human soldiers could be significantly curtailed in the case of autonomous systems. Thus, instead of relying on the notion of a reasonable commander, autonomous systems could potentially be programmed to operate under the standard of the most cautious commander. Their (default) modus could be to not cause any civilian casualties, and, simultaneously, they could be programmed to always adhere to a relatively low, absolute maximum limit of acceptable civilian casualties even in cases that involve high-value military objectives. In other words, while it may be difficult, or even impossible, to translate the existing proportionality standard into a programmable code, this may not be the case with a stricter, more precise standard that is more protective than what is normally required under LOAC in order to ensure sufficient precision.

Nota bene, the argument here is not that states are under an obligation to design each and every robot in such a way, and these suggestions are not to be understood as policy recommendations. Rather, these are hypothetical options, which are meant to illustrate that there are different possibilities to attenuate uncertainties regarding a robot's capability to fully and safely adhere to, and implement, the rules of LOAC as they currently stand. As Corn argues in this volume, the decisive point in the process of ensuring that an AWS is used in accordance with IHL will thus shift from the tactical phase (as is usually the case with 'traditional'

[84] See also Kalmanovitz, 'Judgment, liability and the risks of riskless warfare', 152, who makes a similar argument by stating that 'IHL applies at least at the decision levels of programming, assigning parameters and deploying AWS. The law does set limits in each of these, but it need not proscribe AWS use.'

weapons) to the development and procurement phase.[85] And as Kalmanovitz has rightly pointed out, what ultimately counts is not whether a machine can act reasonably but, rather, whether *operators* could reasonably expect that a given AWS, which is programmed to estimate probabilities in certain ways, and given certain thresholds for attack, would duly protect civilians.[86] Indeed, with conservatively programmed robots, this could be the case.

More protective legal standards for robots?

Another question is whether states are indeed under an obligation – deriving directly from the rules of LOAC – to program AWS to operate more conservatively than human soldiers and to abide by more protective legal standards. If AWS are indeed so much superior to human soldiers as their proponents claim they are,[87] the question may be asked whether these systems should only operate under the comparably rudimentary protective legal standards that apply to their human counterparts. Thus, in addition to the question whether and how it can (best) be ensured that AWS abide by the rules of LOAC, as they stand – or, in the words of Corn, whether they can operate in 'a manner that replicates the level of legal compliance expected from the human actor – the soldier'[88] – more attention should arguably be devoted to the question whether the existing legal framework is still the right, or the optimal, legal framework if AWS are deployed on the battlefield instead of human soldiers. Thus, while it is certainly true that LOAC is sufficiently dynamic to apply to new military technologies,[89] when faced with a technological sea change such as fully autonomous weapons technology, it cannot be excluded that technological novelties such as fully autonomous weapons systems would alter the delicate balancing of military necessity and humanitarian considerations that underlie the existing humanitarian legal framework.[90]

---

[85] G. S. Corn, 'Autonomous weapons systems: managing the inevitability of "taking the man out of the loop"', Chapter 10 in this volume, 209.

[86] Kalmanovitz, 'Judgment, liability and the risks of riskless warfare', 152–8.

[87] R. C. Arkin, 'Governing lethal behavior: embedding ethics in a hybrid deliberative/reactive robot architecture', Technical Report GIT-GVU-07-11, 58, available at www.cc.gatech.edu/ai/robot-lab/online-publications/formalizationv35.pdf.

[88] Corn, 'Autonomous weapons systems', 211.

[89] Schmitt and Thurnher, 'Out of the loop', 280.

[90] R. Geiß, 'The law of weaponry from 1914 to 2014: is the law keeping pace with technological evolution in the military domain?' in J. Delbrück *et al.* (eds.), *Aus Kiel in die Welt: Kiel's Contribution to International Law* (Berlin: Duncker & Humblot, 2014), 237.

To be sure, the laws of armed conflict are not about fairness. Achieving technological supremacy over potential enemies is perfectly legitimate, and it is only natural that states develop technologies that will mitigate the risks for their soldiers in combat situations.[91] However, it should also not be considered heresy to ask whether the protective minimum baselines prescribed by the core rules on the conduct of hostilities are still adequate if autonomous machines are involved in combat. After all, these rules – namely the prohibition against causing unnecessary suffering and the principle of distinction (at least a rudimentary version thereof) had emerged already during the second half of the nineteenth century. While they certainly continue to set the absolute minimum baseline for any present and future military technology, it should simply not be taken for granted that they are the exclusive benchmark for the regulation of military technologies of the twenty-first century. And while in view of the current geopolitical climate, it is admittedly not the time to attempt a large-scale reconsideration of existing rules of LOAC, at least a progressive and dynamic interpretation of the existing rules, which takes into consideration the specificities of AWS, should not be excluded.

In this regard, it could potentially be argued that at least in certain types of missions there is simply no plausible necessity for robots to resort to lethal force and, therefore, that they are legally required to operate in non-lethal ways even when they are faced with enemy combatants, fighters and civilians who have temporarily lost protection from direct attack.[92] As the International Committee of the Red Cross (ICRC) argued in chapter IX of its Interpretive Guidance on the notion of direct participation in hostilities, 'the kind and degree of force which is permissible against persons not entitled to protection against direct attack must not exceed what is actually necessary to accomplish a legitimate military purpose in the prevailing circumstances'.[93] Whether or not this principle of least harmful means is binding as a matter of law or merely a (plausible) policy recommendation remains controversial.[94] If it is

---

[91] Corn, 'Autonomous weapons systems', 217–19.

[92] Here is not the place to delve into the debate whether there is such a thing as a non-lethal weapon, but see D. Fidler, 'The international legal implications of non-lethal weapons', *Michigan Journal of International Law*, 21 (1999), 51–100.

[93] N. Melzer, *Interpretive Guidance on the Notion of Direct Participation in Hostilities under International Humanitarian Law* (Geneva: ICRC, 2009), 77ff., available at www.icrc.org /eng/assets/files/other/icrc-002-0990.pdf.

[94] See, e.g., W. Hays Parks, 'Part IX of the ICRC direct participation in hostilities study: no mandate, no expertise, and legally incorrect', *New York University Journal of International Law and Politics*, 42 (2010), 769; N. Melzer, 'Keeping the balance between

accepted that it is binding as a matter of law and transposed to the
domain of AWS it could be argued that at least in situations in which
AWS directly engage human beings on the ground – for example, in
house and urban area searches – their resort to potentially lethal force
should strictly be limited to situations in which less harmful means for
rendering unprotected persons *hors de combat* are not available.

Indeed, it seems that in relation to AWS this suggestion has even
greater plausibility than it had in relation to human soldiers as envisaged
in chapter IX of the ICRC's Interpretive Guidance. After all, one of the
main points of critique regarding this chapter has always been that it
would unduly shift risks towards one's own soldiers who in high-risk
scenarios should not be burdened with the additional task of having to
evaluate the availability of less harmful means.[95] This concern, however,
is mitigated in scenarios in which (armoured) robots that do not face any
(existential) risk are deployed. And whereas one can easily imagine
numerous scenarios in which human soldiers engaged in high-risk
ground operations could not reasonably be expected to resort to less
harmful means, in the case of autonomous robots this would seem to be
the default scenario. Indeed, it is difficult to imagine why it should be
necessary for them to resort to lethal force. Of course, this particular
limitation, derived from the principle of necessity, would not play out
in situations where there are simply no alternative modes of less harmful
action. Thus, whereas it can reasonably be argued that in a ground
operation in which an autonomous robot directly engages with human
beings, the default mode of combat should be to act in a non-lethal
manner and to render enemy combatants and fighters *hors de combat*
by less harmful means, in the case of an autonomous drone that lacks
alternative options, such a line of argumentation would seem difficult to
sustain. However, given that it remains fiercely contested whether such
a situational military necessity constraint may be validly invoked at all –
that is, whether LOAC, which is already imbued with military necessity
considerations permits the situational invocation of this principle – the
chances that this particular line of reasoning will function, in practice, as
a valid constraint with regard to AWS are rather limited.

---

military necessity and humanity: a response to four critiques of the ICRC's interpretive
guidance on the notion of direct participation in hostilities', *New York University Journal
of International Law and Politics*, 42 (2010), 831. For a more recent analysis of the issue,
see R. Goodman, 'The power to kill or capture enemy combatants', *European Journal of
International Law*, 24 (3) (2013), 819–53.

[95] See Parks, 'Part IX of the ICRC direct participation in hostilities study incorrect'.

Human dignity: again

A more comprehensive constraint that could lead to a partial ban on full autonomy with respect to certain critical functions of a weapons system could be derived from the principle of human dignity. This principle is firmly rooted in human rights law and, arguably, also in the rules of LOAC.[96] Certainly, the so-called Martens Clause, in its traditional as well as in its modern occurrence in Article 1(2) of Additional Protocol I,[97] by referring to the principles of humanity and the dictates of public conscience, allows for the consideration of human dignity for the purposes of LOAC. In light of the inherent difficulties of positively defining a broad concept such as human dignity, the issue is often approached negatively – that is, from the perspective of acts that would violate human dignity.[98] In this regard, as Heyns has argued in this volume as well as at the recent CCW conference in April 2015, '[d]eath by algorithm means that people are treated simply as targets and not as complete and unique human beings, who may by virtue of this status deserve to meet a different fate'.[99]

Indeed, if objects were empowered and allowed to autonomously kill human beings – civilians and combatants alike – such mathematically

---

[96] See Heyns, 'Autonomous weapons systems', 10–12. See also B. Schlink, 'The concept of human dignity: current usages, future discourses' in C. McCrudden (ed.), *Understanding Human Dignity* (Oxford University Press, 2013), 632. See also P. Carozza, 'Human dignity and judicial interpretation of human rights: a reply', *European Journal of International Law*, 19 (5) (2008), 931–44; N. Petersen, 'Human dignity, international protection', *Max Planck Encyclopedia of Public International Law*, October 2012, available at www.opil.ouplaw.com/view/10.1093/law:epil/9780199231690/law-9780199231690-e8 09?print.

[97] According to Article 1(2) of Protocol Additional to the Geneva Conventions of 12 August 1949, and Relating to the Protection of Victims of International Armed Conflicts (Additional Protocol I) 1977, 1125 UNTS 3: 'In cases not covered by this Protocol or by other international agreements, civilians and combatants remain under the protection and authority of the principles of international law derived from established custom, from the principles of humanity and from the dictates of public conscience.'

[98] See German Constitutional Court, BVerfGE 30 (1971), 26; 87 (1992), 228; 96 (1997), 399: '*indem sie die Achtung des Wertes vermissen lässt, der jedem Menschen um seiner selbst willen, kraft seines Personseins, zukommt*'.

[99] See Heyns, 'Autonomous weapons systems', 11. At the conference to the Convention on Prohibitions or Restrictions on the Use of Certain Conventional Weapons Which May Be Deemed to Be Excessively Injurious or to Have Indiscriminate Effects (CCW), 1990, 19 UNTS 1823 in April 2015, Heyns argued: 'A human being in the sights of a fully autonomous machine is reduced to being an object – being merely a target. This is death by algorithm; it has also been called ethics by numbers', available at www.unog.ch/80256ED D006B8954/(httpAssets)/1869331AFF45728BC1257E2D0050EFE0/$file/2015_LAWS_M X_Heyns_Transcript.pdf.

calculated life or death decisions would compromise the fundamental idea of the infinite or incommensurable value of each individual as a subject of law and arguably place human beings on the same footing with objects.[100] What is more, robots operating on the basis of pre-programmed algorithms, once deployed, would seem to irrevocably execute their mission and thereby create an inescapable situation for their potential targets and eliminate any deliberative moment from the targeting process. Whether this latter consideration would also constitute a violation of human dignity seems somewhat less clear. Concerns in this regard could arguably be attenuated if robots were programmed to operate under additional legal constraints such as a default consideration of the availability of less harmful means. However, there is no such possibility as far as the former consideration is concerned. For as long as any possibility has remained that robots could autonomously kill or harm human beings, there has been a violation of the fundamental principle of human dignity. At the same time, of course, it also follows that it is not autonomy per se that is problematic but, rather, autonomy over decisions that may affect a person's right to life and bodily integrity. Hence, the challenge that now remains is to identify those decisions and steps in the targeting process over which human control must remain and to determine what human control should actually entail.

Quo vadis?

At the current juncture, it seems unlikely and indeed unrealistic that a more comprehensive ban on autonomous technology in military systems will see the light of day in the near future. A treaty concluded between only a few, like-minded states – thus far, only Bolivia, Cuba, Ecuador, Egypt, Ghana, the Holy See, Palestine and Pakistan have publicly endorsed a comprehensive ban – but without the participation of states with high-tech military, would be of little avail. The military-strategic promises and anticipated advantages of this technology appear to be such that high-tech states will only agree to certain limitations regarding further development if other competing high-tech states do the same. During the discussions in Geneva in 2014 and 2015 under the aegis of the CCW, two main areas have emerged that seem to warrant further deliberation and that could serve as constructive starting points for a future international regulation of autonomous weapons technology:

---

[100] Heyns, 'Autonomous weapons systems', 10.

enhanced weapons reviews and the notion of 'meaningful human control'.

Weapons review

During the recent experts' discussions under the framework of the CCW in Geneva in April 2015, the idea of enhancing weapons reviews in accordance with Article 36 of Additional Protocol I has gained ground among states. At the latest round of discussions, a number of delegations presented their national legal review procedures under Article 36 of Additional Protocol I.[101] In its final statement, Germany summed up what many delegations seemed to support: 'We see merit in elaborating further on the idea to share national regulations in this regard, to look for common standards and to discuss specific procedures for detecting transgression in the direction of LAWS.'[102] The ICRC likewise endorsed this approach.[103] Enhanced information exchange, increased transparency and the formulation of good (or, ideally, best) practices with regard to domestic weapons reviews are certainly desirable, and it seems that there would be a good chance of reaching consensus.[104] Precisely what a meaningful weapons review under Article 36 of Additional Protocol I entails has remained somewhat vague, and this provision would certainly benefit from further clarification.[105] What is more, given that fully

[101] For a useful summary of the 2015 Expert Meeting, see E. Minor, 'Prohibiting autonomous weapons systems', 23 April 2015, available at www.opendemocracy.net/opensecurity/elizabeth-minor/prohibiting-autonomous-weapons-systems.

[102] Germany's statement is available at www.unog.ch/80256EDD006B8954/(httpAssets)/07006B8A11B9E932C1257E2D002B6D00/$file/2015_LAWS_MX_Germany_W.A.pdf. The statement continues: 'Germany is of the opinion that given the actual state of the art of artificial intelligence and other important components of LAWS, a legal weapons review for the time being inevitably would lead to the result of LAWS being illegal, as they are not able to meet the requirements set out by Article 36 AP I.'

[103] The ICRC's statement is available at www.unog.ch/80256EDD006B8954/(httpAssets)/E2917CC32952137FC1257E2F004CED22/$file/CCW+Meeting+of+Experts+ICRC+closing+statement+17+Apr+2015+final.pdf. The statement continues: 'We encourage States to share their experience and outcomes of legal reviews of existing weapons with autonomy in their critical functions. In this respect, we also welcome proposals on sharing good practices for legal review mechanisms in order to improve implementation of the said legal obligations.'

[104] As Sarah Knuckey points out in this volume, so far Article 36 Additional Protocol I has done little to advance transparency. See Knuckey, 'Autonomous weapons systems and transparency', 176.

[105] ICRC, 'A guide to the legal review of new weapons, means and methods of warfare: measures to implement article 36 of Additional Protocol I of 1977', International Review of the Red Cross, 88 (864) (2006), 956.

autonomous weapons systems do not (yet) exist and that levels of autonomy are likely to increase gradually and rather subtly, better monitoring mechanisms that could prevent states from crossing the Rubicon would be helpful indeed.[106]

Enhancing existing weapons review mechanisms, however, should only be regarded as one among different steps towards the regulation of AWS. Weapons reviews, in spite of the rather broad and open wording of Article 36 of Additional Protocol I, which refers not only to Additional Protocol I but also to 'any other rule of international law applicable to the High Contracting Party', are typically more narrowly focused on LOAC rules pertaining to the conduct of hostilities. Indeed, as the ICRC commentary confirms, Article 36 of Additional Protocol I is linked to Article 35 of Additional Protocol I, which lays out 'basic rules' for the conduct of hostilities.[107] What is more, as the ICRC commentary explains, the reference to 'any other rule of international law applicable to the High Contracting Party' is to be understood to refer 'to any agreement on disarmament concluded by the Party concerned, or any other agreement related to the prohibition, limitation or restriction on the use of a weapon or a particular type of weapon, concluded by this Party, which would relate, for example, to a new generation of small calibre weapons or any other type of weapons'.[108] In other words, a weapons review under Article 36 of Additional Protocol I is primarily focused on the question whether a new weapon could be used in conformity with LOAC as it currently stands, whereas questions whether a new weapon would raise additional concerns could easily be omitted.

What is more, even though the enhanced standardization and harmonization of weapons reviews under Article 36 of Additional Protocol I are desirable, such reviews remain a domestic endeavour. And as the ICRC commentary clarifies, '[d]etermination by any State that the employment of a weapon is prohibited or permitted is not binding internationally, but it is hoped that the obligation to make such determinations will ensure that means or methods of warfare will not be adopted without the issue of

---

[106] See also Germany's statement.

[107] J. de Preux, 'Article 36: new weapons' in Y. Sandoz, C. Swinarski and B. Zimmermann (eds.), *Commentary on the Additional Protocols of 8 June 1977 to the Geneva Conventions of 12 August 1949* (Geneva: ICRC, 1987), paras. 1466, 1463: 'There was a need for a link between the principles laid down in Article 35 (Basic rules) and the concrete prohibitions or the effective restrictions on arms which cause superfluous injury or unnecessary suffering, or have indiscriminate effects.'

[108] *Ibid.*, para. 1472 (footnotes omitted). According to the commentary: 'Naturally, it also includes the rules which form part of international customary law.'

legality being explored with care'.[109] However, as far as autonomous weapons technology is concerned, the question whether, and under which conditions, AWS would be in violation of the existing rules of international law is currently very much under discussion. Leaving it up to individual states to decide in the context of a domestic weapons review whether or not an AWS would be in violation of the law will not do justice to the complex legal and ethical questions posed by AWS. It follows that, as the ICRC stated at the recent CCW conference, efforts to encourage implementation of national weapons reviews should be seen as complementary to other options at the international level to address the legal and ethical limits to autonomy.[110]

Meaningful human control

Against this backdrop, the question arises about what those other options could look like. In this respect, the notion of 'meaningful human control' has emerged as the most promising starting point for a more holistic approach towards regulating AWS during the discussions in Geneva in 2014 and 2015. It seems safe to say that this notion has become the buzzword of the contemporary debate. Of course, discussing 'meaningful human control' in the context of fully autonomous weapons systems seems paradoxical – for if there is meaningful human control, there cannot be full autonomy. Thus, the notion of 'meaningful human control' is just another word – but most likely more constructive and internationally agreeable – for a partial prohibition, namely a ban on full autonomy over certain (critical) functions of a weapons system.

The notion of meaningful human control arguably allows the consideration of issues such as human dignity, which many states would otherwise regard as human rights issues, that (in their view) have no relevance when it comes to assessing the legality of the means of warfare and that do not necessarily fall within the mandate of the CCW. As is well known based on experiences in the UN Human Rights Council and before the European Court of Human Rights, states such as the United States, the United Kingdom and Israel are adamantly opposed to the consideration of the means and methods of warfare in light of substantive human rights. It is no coincidence that both the United States and the United Kingdom during the recent CCW round of experts in Geneva

---

[109] *Ibid.*, para. 1469.   [110] The ICRC's statement.

CONCLUSION

pointed out explicitly that humanitarian law is the right (read: exclusive) framework to assess AWS and that this narrow focus corresponds to the mandate of the CCW regime.[111]

In terms of substance, the notion of human dignity may be criticized for its openness and ambiguity. However, at the present (early) juncture of the international debate, this openness is not (just) to be seen as a risk but also as a chance. The notion of 'meaningful human control' is sufficiently open to encapsulate the more restrictive human dignity concerns mentioned above while, at the same time, granting sufficient room for striking a balance between prohibition and permission of autonomy. The final statement issued by Germany at the last CCW conference in April 2015 reflects this potential for compromise. According to this position, 'Germany will not accept that the decision over life and death is taken *solely* by an autonomous system without any possibility for a human intervention.'[112] This statement leaves significant space for requiring different levels of control and for demarcating critical functions that would require high levels of human control from less critical functions that would require lower or no direct human control.

Against this backdrop, the main challenge now lies in the determination of relevant degrees and modes of control, on the one hand, and on the identification of those critical functions and segments in the targeting process, which must not be outsourced to algorithms and over which meaningful human control must remain, on the other hand. If it is accepted that the limiting notion of meaningful human control derives from the principle of human dignity, it follows that such control must be maintained whenever (severe) harm may be caused to a human being. With respect to the question of what meaningful levels of control entail, it

[111] The US delegation stated: 'We believe our discussion here in CCW, a forum focused on international humanitarian law, remains the relevant framework for this discussion', available at www.unog.ch/80256EDD006B8954/(httpAssets)/8B33A1CDBE80EC60 C1257E2800275E56/$file/2015_LAWS_MX_USA+bis.pdf. The United Kingdom argued: 'From our perspective, to discuss LAWS is to discuss means and methods of warfare. As such, international humanitarian law provides the appropriate paradigm for discussion', available at www.unog.ch/80256EDD006B8954/(httpAssets)/1CBF996AF7 AD10E2C1257E260060318A/$file/2015_LAWS_MX_United+Kingdom.pdf.
Conversely, UN Special Rapporteur Christof Heyns emphasized that in any case AWS may not only be of relevance in times of armed conflict but also in law enforcement contexts. Obviously, this line of reasoning paves the way to also take (stricter) human rights standards into consideration in the assessment of AWS.
[112] Germany's statement (emphasis added).

seems important to insist on realistic possibilities to exert control also in combat scenarios where in the future – in light of the speed of events and the sheer amount of data that needs to be processed in real-world combat scenarios – there will be an increasingly stronger pull to leave decisions to autonomous systems that – unlike human decision makers – can react within milliseconds.

INDEX

delegation of authority, pre-bound
  discretion and, 272n.133
de lege ferenda norm
  accountability for AWS and, 157n.40
  international environmental law and
    AWS development, 291–3
de lege lata norm, accountability for
  AWS and, 157n.40
deliberative processes
  Kahneman's theory
    concerning, 30–4
  proportionality judgments and, 152–4
  supervisory control of weapons
    and, 34–7
democratic decision making
  moral debate over AWS and, 132–7
  transparency of AWS and, 179–83
Dennett, Daniel, 47–8
deontological-dignitarian ethics
  debate on AWS and, 256–9
  gaps in responsibility and liability in
    AWS and, 71–2
  pre-emptive bans on AWS and,
    122–4, 137–41
Department of Defense (DoD) (US).
  See also Directive 3000.09,
  'Autonomy in weapon systems'
  (US DoD, 2012)
  autonomous weapons research
    and, 23–7
  definition of AWS by, 124–7
  levels of autonomy in studies by,
    78n.11
  moratorium on AWS development,
    245–8
design failure, blameworthiness
  and, 62–5
'design stance', cognition and
  anticipation and, 47–8
desires, values *vs*, 52–3
determinism philosophy, technical *vs*
  substantive autonomy and,
    248–51
deterrence, war as governance and,
    261–2
diagonal state-combatant obligations,
  pre-bound discretion and, 278–82

dignity, right to
  autonomous weapons systems and,
    10–12, 105–21, 377–8
  bans on AWS on basis of, 138n.30
  human dignity concepts and,
    105–7
  inflationary tendencies, danger of,
    108–13
  inflationary tendencies concerning
    human dignity and, 108–13
  integrative and open concept of,
    105–7
  intrinsic incompatibility of AWS
    with, policy implications of,
    119–21
  legal framework for concepts of,
    368–9
  meaningful human control paradigm
    and, 381–3
  morality and, 110–12, 131–2
  open-endedness of, 354–6
  protection from humiliation and,
    114–16
Directive 3000.09, 'Autonomy in
  weapon systems' (US DoD, 2012),
  58–61, 179–83, 185–208
  alternative concepts of autonomy in,
    200–8
  'appropriate levels of human
    judgment' standard and, 191–208,
    245n.3
  coactive design model and, 203–6
  command responsibility and,
    340n.58
  definitions and basic principles in,
    186–9
  historical and military context for,
    189–92
  legality of AWS and, 245–8
  LOAC compliance standards and,
    224–9
  machine autonomy *vs* human
    judgment and, 353–4
  policy and legal issues in drafting of,
    192–200
  role responsibility and, 339–40
  vagueness in wording of, 186n.3